Revolution and Counterrevolution

REVOLUTION AND COUNTERREVOLUTION

Class Struggle in a Moscow Metal Factory

Kevin Murphy

Haymarket
Books

CHICAGO, IL

First paperback edition published
in 2007 by Haymarket Books
P.O. Box 180165
Chicago, IL 60618
773-583-7884
info@haymarketbooks.org
www.haymarketbooks.org

First published in 2005 by Berghan Books
©2005 Kevin Murphy

Trade distribution:
In the U.S. through Consortium Book Sales, www.cbsd.com
In the UK, Turnaround Publisher Services, www.turnaround-psl.com
In Australia, Palgrave MacMillan, www.palgravemacmillan.com.au

This book was published with the generous support of the
Wallace Global Fund.

Cover design by Eric Ruder and Rachel Wilsey
Cover image of Hammer and Sickle Factory workers, Moscow 1922

ISBN-13: 978-1931859-50-9

Printed in Canada by union labor on recycled paper
containing 50 percent post-consumer waste in accordance with the guidelines
of the Green Press Initiative, www.greenpressinitiative.org

Library of Congress CIP Data is available

2 4 6 8 10 9 7 5 3 1

Contents

ARCHIVES

Gosudarstvennyi Arkhiv Rossiiskoi Federatsii (GARF)
State Archive of the Russian Federation

Rossiskii Gosudarstvennyi Arkhiv Ekonomiki (RGAE)
Russian State Archive of the Economy

Rossiiskii Gosudarstvennyi Arkhiv Sotsial'no-Politicheskoi Istorii (RGASPI)
Russian State Archive of Social-Political History

Tsentr Khraneniia Dokumentov Molodezhnykh Organizatsii (TsKhDMO)
Center for Preservation of Records of Youth Organizations

Rossiiskii Gosudarstvennyi Istoricheskii Arkhiv g. Moskvy (RGIAgM)
Russian State Historical Archive of Moscow

Tsentral'nyi Munitsipal'nyi Arkhiv Moskvy (TsMAM)
Central Municipal Archive of Moscow

Tsentral'nyi Arkhiv Obschestvennukh Dvizhenii Moskvy (TsAODM)
Central Archive of Social Movements of Moscow

Tsentral'nyi Gosudarstvennyi Arkhiv Moskovskoi Oblasti (TsGAMO)
Central State Archive of Moscow Oblast

GLOSSARY OF TERMS

brak	defective output
bedniak	poor peasant
khozraschet	commercial cost accounting
kolkhoz	collective farm
kulak	rich peasant
Left SR	Left Socialist Revolutionary Party
MK	Moscow Committee of the Communist Party
MKG	Moscow City Party Committee
MKK	Moscow Control Commission of the Communist Party
MOPR	International Aid Society for Revolution Fighters
Narkomtrud	People's Commissariat of Labor
NEP	New Economic Policy
NKVD	People's Commissariat for Internal Affairs
Okhrana	Tsarist secret police
OGPU	Unified State Political Administration; political police
otkhodnik	peasant engaged in seasonal labor
pud	approximately 36 pounds
raikom	District Committee of the Communist Party
subbotnik	Voluntary workday
RSDLP	Russian Social-Democratic Labor Party
Rabkrin	Workers' and Peasants' Inspectorate
RKK	Rates Conflict Commission
samokritika	self-criticism
seredniak	middle peasant

sovkhoz	state farm
smychka	link between town and country
SR	Socialist Revolutionary Party
Sovnarknom	Council of People's Commissars (Sovnarknom)
TNB	Norm Setting Bureau
Vesenkha	Supreme Council of the National Economy
VTsSPS	All-Union Central Trade Union Council
VKP(b)	All-Union Communist Party (Bolshevik)
VLKSM	All-Union Leninist Communist Youth League (the Komsomol)
VTsIK	All Union Central Executive Committee of Soviets
TsK	Central Committee of the Communist Party
TsKK	Central Control Commission of Communist Party
Zhenotdel	Women's Section of the Communist Party
ZRK	Closed Workers' Cooperative

ACKNOWLEDGEMENTS

Many people have aided me during the course of this project. I owe much of the strength of the study which follows to being in the right place at the right time, and surrounded by so much expertise, dedication to scholarship, and pure talent. I owe a special thanks to the peerless dissertation committee that supervised this project in the Comparative History Program at Brandeis University. I am grateful for their thoughtful comments and advice over a long and, at times, difficult process of research and writing. Gregory Freeze, the preeminent social historian of Russian and Soviet society, first suggested a systematic factory study and insisted that I pursue rigorously any and all archival materials, challenges which I have done my best to pursue. Donald Filtzer, the indisputable authority on the Soviet working class, made special arrangements to act as an outside reader and repeatedly inquired about the status of my "final" revisions of the manuscript. Without Don's friendship and belief in the importance of my project this book would never have seen the light of day. Antony Polonsky acted as committee chair and continued to offer encouragement long after his institutional relationship with the project had ended.

Among Antony's many words of wisdom, the most fortuitous was his suggestion that I contact Berghahn Books. Having heard a litany of horror stories from first-time authors who have published elsewhere, I have to say that I am absolutely elated with the professionalism and generosity with which my work has been handled by everyone at Berghahn Books and the Institute for Social History in Amsterdam. I thank Marion Berghahn for her advice and her patience during an extended delay after the birth of my son Peter. Catherine Kirby meticulously copy edited the entire manuscript and Christine Marciniak did a remarkable job typesetting the book. Vivian Berghahn and Michael Dempsey responded promptly to a seemingly endless string of inquiries I posed about the mysterious production process, which turns out to have been not quite as mysterious as I had imagined. Marcel van der Linden's enthusiastic comments reassured me that my work was important enough to reach a wider audience beyond Russian specialists, and Kristina Graaff developed a marketing strategy to make sure that this would happen. Two anonymous readers offered very constructive and detailed criticisms. I hope that I have done their suggestions justice.

I would also like to thank Julie Fain and Anthony Arnove from Haymarket Books for all their fantastic work in the production of this paperback edition.

The American Council of Teachers of Russian and the Comparative History Program at Brandeis University sponsored several of my trips to Russia. Numerous scholars offered thoughtful comments on parts of this manuscript. I owe a special thanks to Brian Kelly, whose scholarship in American labor history sets a high standard and whose close reading of this study improved it immeasurably, and to Jan Plamper, Frank Schauff, Michael David Fox, Sally Boniece, Wendy Goldman, and Jeffery Rossman for their many suggestions. My colleagues at the University of Massachusetts at Boston—Lester Bartson and Esther Kingston-Mann—generously offered their encouragement and advice.

This project involved five lengthy research trips to Moscow, none of which would have been possible—or productive—without the help and support offered by many historians, archivists, friends, and family. I offer special thanks to the Moscow archive expert, Leonid Wientraub, a dear friend without whom this project would have been impossible. I also want to thank Lena Drozdova, Marina Dobronovskaia, and all of the many archivists who generously assisted me during my visits. Andrei Sokolov kindly pointed me in the right direction during my first trip to Moscow. Alexei Gusev and Simon Pirani challenged many of my assumptions about the Russian Revolution and repeatedly reminded me about the importance of critical, non-dogmatic Marxism. Philip Gerstein reviewed literally hundreds of my Russian translations. I also want to thank Bob Dahlgren, Kaveh Afrasiabi, James and Jodi Murphy, and Cathy and George Woods for their friendship. James and Else Murphy gave me the freedom to pursue my dreams. Oksana and Peter gave me their love and tolerated the long hours it took to finally finish this book.

Last, but not least, I want to acknowledge the intellectual and personal contributions of the many international socialists I worked with over a period of fifteen years, from whom I have learned much. For revolutionary socialists, the problem of understanding the fate of Russian Revolution has always meant far more than it has for the small community of academics who have grappled with it intellectually. The "Russian Question" remains, even after the collapse of Stalinism, one of the central issues that those who seek to change the world must confront and answer. How was a movement based on egalitarianism and freedom transformed into a system based on exploitation and repression? In many ways this book is my answer to questions that I started to ask as a teenager sneaking into the stacks of Princeton's Firestone Library. I will not feign neutrality on the two topics that frame the Russian Revolution: October and Stalinism. There is no doubt in my mind that the Marxists got it right. Leon Trotsky and Tony Cliff provided the theoretical groundwork for much of my understanding of the Russian Revolution, while Victor Serge acted as the "conscience" of the Revolution by giving it such an inspirational and principled voice. I especially want to thank Brian Kelly, Ahmed Shawki, David Crouch, Mike Haynes, Alpana Mehta, John Charlton, Sebastian Budgen, and Bill Roberts for helping me keep things in perspective over the last ten years. If this book offers even just a few insights for those actively involved in fighting for a better world, then my efforts will have been worth it.

Kevin Murphy
kevinj.murphy@umb.edu

In Memory of
James Harold Murphy II

INTRODUCTION

The opening of the archives of the former Soviet Union has altered fundamentally the study of the most globally significant social upheaval of the twentieth century, presenting historians of the Russian Revolution with both exciting opportunities and awesome challenges. The "hidden transcript" of the sentiments and actions of ordinary people, which social historians in Western Europe and North America have labored so painstakingly to recover in recent years,[1] has until now been left almost entirely unexamined in Soviet historiography. Archival limitations compelled even the most diligent and objective historians to reconcile themselves to a predominantly top-down view of the Soviet state's attempt to realize changing goals and priorities. The availability of new sources means that it is now possible, for the first time, to measure the reliability of prevailing historiography against an empirically grounded reconstruction of working-class life in the revolutionary era.

The astounding variety and volume of newly accessible primary materials that focus on the working class is not accidental. Not just Soviet authorities, but all contemporary contestants recognized the combativeness and potential power of Russian workers in the early twentieth century. *Revolution and Counterrevolution* attempts to fill a long-vacant gap in the study of the Russian working class by providing the first systematic, archival-driven study to span the revolutionary era. It examines that period through the prism of a single strategically important factory, tracing the fluctuations in shop floor activism and bringing the voices of workers themselves to bear on the central questions about the character of the Russian Revolution and the origins of the Stalinist system.

For the better part of the last fifty years, the historiography of the Russian Revolution was inextricably bound up in the all-consuming confrontation known as the Cold War. The stakes in that debate were extremely high: its outcome would determine not merely the ascendancy of one or another school of scholarly thought, but also the ideological legitimacy of each of the two preeminent world powers. Western scholarship was dominated by what Stephen Cohen has aptly termed the "continuity thesis," which posited an

uncomplicated, natural evolution from early Bolshevik organizational practice to the Gulags. These accounts typically began by holding up Lenin's
What Is to Be Done? as an embryonic dictatorial blueprint, fully developed
well before the Revolution. From here it was but a short step to the assertion
that a conspiratorial minority had seized power in 1917 through a coup d'é-
tat, monopolized the state for its own purposes, and created the totalitarian
party-state. Through iron discipline and brutal terror, the Bolsheviks subsequently prevailed in the Civil War of 1918-1921, but the exhausted victors
were forced to retreat temporarily during the New Economic Policy (NEP,
1921-1928). Driven by ideological zealotry, the thesis concludes, the totalitarian machine then proceeded to pulverize society. State-imposed collectivization, forced rapid industrialization, and mass terror are thus viewed as
organic elements in an inevitable process driven by the Bolsheviks' inner
totalitarian logic.[2]

For its part, the Soviet academy took up the gauntlet thrown down by
critics of the USSR, mirroring Western efforts in the battle to construct a
usable past. Lewis Siegelbaum and Ronald Suny have characterized the Soviet
academy's glowing, uncomplicated rendering of the past as the "Immaculate
Conceptualization" of the Soviet working class.[3] The depiction of the steady
and heroic march of the Soviet people from 1917 toward Communism under
the leadership of the party was an inverted image of the "Original Sin" version put forward by Western academics. Soviet scholars advanced linear
accounts purged of contingency, in which alternative political strategies and
possibilities were trivialized or completely ignored, and which depicted ordinary Soviet citizens as passive followers of the dictates of an unerring party.

Few issues in Soviet historiography have been more contested than that of
working-class attitudes toward the evolution of the Stalinist system. "It
would be hard to imagine an interpretive controversy with the opposing
sides farther apart," Stephen Kotkin has argued, noting that historians depict
"either disgruntled workers who despised the regime or contented workers
who applauded it."[4] As the government claimed to rule in the name of the
proletariat, questions about the relationship between the state and the working class encompass issues crucial to an understanding of Soviet society. How
did a movement that promised thoroughgoing social equality transform into
its opposite—a system of exploitation and repression? Why did the most
unruly proletariat of the century come to tolerate the ascendancy of a political and economic system that, by every conceivable measure, proved antagonistic to working-class interests?

Scholarly responses to these problems have been framed by the ideological imperatives of the Cold War rather than by a thorough analysis of archival
sources. An integral component of the continuity thesis is the mass "Red Terror." While most of the historiography on terror focuses on the 1930s, even
studies of early Soviet labor have attempted to explain the demise of working-
class militancy by echoing continuity arguments with grossly inflated estimates about early state repression, concentration camps, and coercion.[5]

Rejecting Cold War-inspired paradigms, many "revisionist" scholars of
the 1980s leaned too far in the opposite direction, naively repeating argu-

ments by Soviet historians and inflating the level of support for Stalinism. While historians could draw on a mountain of empirical data to prove popular participation during the epochal events of 1917,[6] several historians rather clumsily tried to do the same for Stalin's "revolution." Attempts to demonstrate such popular support legitimized a revisionist version of the continuity thesis, positing that various Stalinist campaigns were indeed "radical," that they authentically had reflected popular aspirations.[7] This "revisionist" body of work—constructed, like the scholarship it targeted, on scant archival evidence of workers' sentiments—has left a lasting impression on the field, particularly among U.S. scholars.[8] Yet fifteen years after the doors to the archives swung wide open, not a single source-driven study has supported either of the contending speculative arguments—that workers were either terrorized by the early Soviet state or impressed with Stalinism.

More recently, the postmodern (or linguistic) trend has challenged both the meaning and utility of class as an analytical method for understanding the past. At its inception, as Alex Callinicos has shown, postmodernism reflected the failed aspirations of the French New Left and the rightward drift of many former Marxists who had rejected class as the fundamental division in society. The refusal to ground societal power relations within the class structures of capitalism not only led postmodernists to pessimistic conclusions about the future, but also made it harder to attribute any coherence to the past. While postmodernism cloaks itself in a veneer of sophistication, it offers no new tools for historians.[9] In a summary of recent trends in European labor history, Lex Heerma van Voss and Marcel van der Linden similarly situate the rise of postmodernism within the right shift in European and American politics in the 1980s and 1990s. While the optimism of the social movements of the 1960s and 1970s inspired a generation of historians to reconstruct "history from below" by exploring the actions and recovering the voices of working people, a sharp decline in labor's fortunes over the next two decades created the context for the pessimism that permeates much of the postmodern vision. While van Voss and van der Linden criticize the postmodern drift for its retreat from overarching interpretations and argue for a return to the "Grand Narrative" to explain the past, they applaud the call to integrate gender, religion, ethnicity, and non-workplace experience into the fabric of working-class history.[10] Indeed, the need for serious attention to the many-sided complexity of working-class experience is now almost universally accepted among labor historians, though this consensus cannot be attributed to the postmodernist mantra.

The postmodern turn came rather belatedly to Soviet labor studies, occurring almost simultaneously with the collapse of the former Soviet Union and the opening of its archives. At a conference in 1990, prominent labor historians asserted that the new methodology would offer qualitative advances over the previously dominant social history. Several scholars claimed that a more textured view of Russian and Soviet labor could be drawn if historians turned away from their concern with class formation and class conflict in the factories and instead shifted their focus to workers' lives outside the workplace. The linguistic influence inspired a call for close investigation of the "language of class" and to reduce class to merely one of many "contested" identities.[11]

Several works demonstrate that postmodernism provides neither the theoretical framework nor the methodical tools necessary to address the larger interpretive questions about the Soviet working class. In his *Magnetic Mountain*, Steven Kotkin has the confidence to address these issues, but his study of "power at the micro-level" is tainted by the postmodernist proclivity to view language as the source of power relations, with workers "speaking Bolshevik." In his conclusion Kotkin cites a 1931 visitor to Magnitogorsk who recalled the piled corpses of starved peasants who had frozen to death after being forced to live in tents during the winter, and later wrote, "The cemetery grew faster than the steel works." Hostile to a materialist explanation for the rise of Stalinism, however, Kotkin concludes with a bizarre and indefensible assertion on the same page that the regime's self-congratulatory claim that "the recognized evils of capitalism" had been overcome "was available to quell even the deepest doubts" among workers.[12] Like Kotkin, David Hoffman crudely associates Stalinism with socialism, asserting that the industrialization of the 1930s "represented a moment of truth for the Bolshevik Revolution—a Marxist revolution in an overwhelmingly peasant country." Yet Hoffman largely avoids theoretical questions about Stalinism, focusing instead on reconstructing the "social identity" of peasant in-migrants to Moscow, attempting to do so by incorporating a mere handful of archival workers' quotations.[13] Matthew Payne's more serious monograph on the construction of the Turksib railway includes a chronicle of brutal attacks perpetrated by ethnic Russians against Kazhakh workers. Payne takes the "equal opportunity" approach to identity fetishism to absurd levels, protesting that, "Race should not be privileged above other fundamental divisions in the Soviet working class, such as peasant worker versus urban worker or Stakhanovite versus the 'selfish workers.'" Yet Payne's own evidence shows that race *was* the most divisive issue—certainly more significant than tensions caused by the Stakhanov movement that only started seven years later. At a loss to explain the dynamic of the ethnic tensions that he describes, Payne offers only the tautological assertion that the racism surged on Turksib because of "a crisis of identity."[14]

Several pre-archival studies point the way toward an approach that moves beyond the simplistic Cold War stereotypes and the profound confusion of postmodernism. These works frame the evolution of Stalinism as a process aimed at whittling away the power workers had won in 1917. E.H. Carr and R.W. Davies detail the intensification of the labor process in their seminal—but frequently overlooked—study of Soviet society during NEP. Rather than state repression, strike actions were avoided by trade union intervention, as over eight million workers turned to arbitration in industrial disputes. Chris Ward's study of cotton workers shows that in 1923 the regime was "more than willing to accommodate itself to the workforce," but later, "as the 1920s drew to a close, there was a move away from compromises and toward something resembling mobilization on the part of the government." Michal Reiman posits that the change in state policy "cannot be understood without considering the profound social, political, and economic crisis that erupted at the very height of NEP." The state response entailed bringing together "forces that were to become the vehicles of extremist solutions" and required a ruling social stratum, "separated from the people and hostilely disposed toward it." Moreover, Reiman rejects the absurd identification of Stalinism with socialism: "These two systems of ideas are not only different; in many respects they are diametrically opposed." In the most compelling scholarly study to date, Donald Filtzer argues that Stalinism arose against the backdrop of an increasingly divided and apolitical working class. Preoccupied with personal survival, workers found the means to subvert and challenge the state, but they did so on less favorable and less overtly confrontational terms than previously.[15]

Revolution and Counterrevolution attempts to build on the strengths of the rich but limited pre-archival studies that have avoided the crude Cold War methodology. Rather than picking and choosing anecdotal data to reconstruct events, a systematic archival study of a strategically important metal factory restricts the selection of source materials and minimizes the issue of bias. The central role of the factory in Soviet society has encouraged several Western historians to follow the example set by Soviet scholars.[16] It was in their workplaces that Russian workers forged an unprecedented sense of class solidarity and power; here that socialists succeeded in infusing the labor movement with revolutionary politics; and here that both Tsarist and Soviet authorities focused their social engineering efforts. Moreover, the Soviet factory was much more than just a place of employment—it lay at the very heart of workers' civic life. As Kenneth Straus has argued, the Soviet factory acted as the community-organizing center for food and housing distribution, as well as workers' leisure activities.[17]

Because the party and the state devoted extraordinary effort, over a long period of time, to winning the hearts and minds of rank-and-file metalworkers, the Hammer and Sickle Factory[18] (Guzhon or Moscow Metalworks Company for the pre-Soviet period) provides a potentially unequalled source base for a case history of workers' attitudes toward the Revolution and their acquiescence in or support for the development of Stalinism. Central Committee members spoke regularly at the plant, the party produced one of the earliest factory newspapers, and metalworkers located in a high-priority industry in the political center enjoyed considerable material advantages compared to their counterparts in other industries and locales. If Soviet workers generally exhibited a sense of "terror" in their relations with the state in early Soviet society, or later volunteered their support for Stalinism, one would reasonably expect that evidence of such sentiments could be found in the largest metal factory in the capital.

A rich and diverse document base provides the foundation for the most extensive archival study of the Russian working class during the Revolutionary era. Three factory-specific collections in the Central Archive of Social Movements of Moscow (TsAODM), the Central Municipal Archive of Moscow (TsMAM), and the State Archive of the Russian Federation (GARF) offer an unparalleled source base for a view of worker-state relations. For the prerevolutionary period, Tsarist secret police (Okhrana), factory inspector, management, and owners' association reports and announcements are utilized, supplemented with pertinent material from workers' autobiographies. For 1917, management, press reports, factory committee, union, and party records illustrate the general trajectory of events, with workers' memoirs employed as supplementary material when their general accuracy can be verified in contemporary sources. Factory and shop-level union and party minutes offer a largely untapped view of workers' discussions, grievances, and activity for the early revolutionary period through NEP, along with factory announcements and anonymous notes to speakers. Soviet, party, and union summaries (*svodki*) are included but not emphasized in reconstructing events during the 1920s.[19] All historians who study the period after 1928 will encounter a source problem that mirrors the repressive descent of the regime. While open and vibrant discussion on various issues was the norm during the early revolutionary period, the state's most ardent loyalists at the factory level later attempted to curb public pronouncements against state policies, and were largely successful in doing so. *Svodki* and factory newspaper (*Martenovka*) articles offer invaluable insights on workers' dissent, the effects of intimidation campaigns, and party corruption at the grassroots level.

The book is chronological for the pre-revolutionary, revolutionary, and First Five-Year Plan, and thematic for the NEP period. The focus on NEP is intentional: this was the golden era for documentary evidence about Soviet society, precisely because lively and animated voices from below could still be heard. This was also the period in which Stalinism clashed head-on with the ideals of 1917. Extensive evidence shows that the late NEP rift between state and society extended beyond class conflict (Chapter 3) to developments in diverse areas of workers' day-to-day lives (Chapter 4), and formal opposition politics (Chapter 5).

Every historian must choose which questions to ask and what topics are most important, even when the arena of study is a single factory. Marxism provides the theoretical framework for understanding the contours of the Russian Revolution and Stalinism. The simple but pithy passage from the first page of the *Communist Manifesto* about class struggle is utilized because a grasp of the dynamics of "now hidden, now open fight" between exploiter and exploited is absolutely critical to understanding both Russian and Soviet society. The continual conflict between employers and workers over the surplus value produced by labor included disputes over work hours, wages, and the intensity of work, but also less overtly economic issues such as benefits to women, religious holidays, and workers' behavior inside and outside the workplace. At times labor grievances took on a political dimension—particularly during 1917 when class conflict escalated into class warfare. The multiple issues over which workers' desires and state priorities clashed are examined in the context of a constantly changing relationship between rank-and-file workers and the state. The explicit emphasis on workers' grievances and their willingness or unwillingness to challenge management and regime is viewed as integral to the development (and later demise) of the proletariat as a class "for itself." Class unity and the decline—later absence—of this solidarity are treated as the central historical problems of the Russian Revolution.

Stalinism is defined in this monograph as the long-term trend and interest of the state bureaucracy as it developed into an exploitative class in opposition to the proletariat.[20] While the Marxist analysis provides the most convincing framework for understanding the political economy of the Soviet Union, very little systematic archival work has been done from any perspective to explain the advent of Stalinism in the factories and the role of the working class during the transformation. *Revolution and Counterrevolution* aims, therefore, to plot a new course in the study of Soviet working-class history—one that avoids both the condescension of Cold War historiography and the incoherence offered by the linguistic turn.

Notes

1. The notion of the "hidden transcript" was pioneered by James C. Scott in his *Weapons of the Weak: Everyday Forms of Peasant Resistance* (New Haven, 1985) and has been applied with positive effect in the fields of American labor and African-American history. See, for example, Robin G. Kelley, *Hammer and Hoe: Alabama Communists During the Depression* (Chapel Hill, 1990).
2. Stephen Cohen, *Rethinking the Soviet Experience: Politics and History Since 1917* (New York, 1985), 1-74.
3. Lewis Siegelbaum and Ronald Suny, "Class Backwards? In Search of the Soviet Working Class" in *Making Workers Soviet: Power, Class, and Identity*, Siegelbaum and Suny eds. (Ithaca, NY, 1994), 13. I.I. Mints, *Istoriia velikogo oktiabria*, 3 vols. (Moscow, 1967-1973).
4. Stephen Kotkin, *Magnetic Mountain: Stalinism as Civilization* (Berkeley, 1995), 199-200.
5. For example, Jonathan Aves in *Workers against Lenin: Labor Protest and the Bolshevik Dictatorship* (New York, 1996) argues that workers' grievances during the Civil War were based on the state's coercive labor strategy, rather than on the material conditions attendant to near-total economic collapse. Similarly, Diane Koenker in "Labor Relations in Socialist Russia: Class Values and Production Values in the Printers' Union, 1917-1921," in *Making Workers Soviet: Power, Class, and Identity*, 192, contends that while workers "might engage in 'stoppages,'" by 1921 a 'strike' was a serious political act and punished accordingly," and asserts, that the socialism that emerged from the Civil War "relied on the power of the state agencies—the Cheka and the concentration camp—to ensure adherence to its centrally defined goals and policies." Andrew Pospielovsky, in "Strikes During the NEP," *Revolutionary Russia*, 10, 1 (June 1997), notes that after 1922 reports of worker arrests were rare but suggests that it is "likely that leading shop-floor organizers were arrested in the general roundups of 'anti-Soviet' elements, Socialist Revolutionaries, Mensheviks, and 'members' of other political parties."
6. David Mandel, *The Petrograd Workers and the Soviet Seizure of Power* (London, 1984); S.A. Smith, *Red Petrograd: Revolution in the Factories 1917-1918* (Cambridge, 1983); Alexander Rabinowitch, *The Bolsheviks Come to Power: The Revolution of 1917 in Petrograd* (New York, 1976); Diane Koenker, *Moscow Workers and the 1917 Revolution* (Princeton, 1981).
7. William Chase in *Workers, Society, and the Soviet State: Labor and Life in Moscow, 1918-1929* (Urbana, Ill., 1987) 299, claims that in 1928-1929 "the party and workers, especially

urban workers, reforged the old alliance of 1917-1918." Arch Getty in *Origins of the Great Purges: The Soviet Communist Party Reconsidered, 1933-1938* (Cambridge, 1985), 206, asserts popular support for the purges, which was a "radical, even hysterical, reaction to bureaucracy." Lynne Viola, in *The Best Fathers and Sons of the Fatherland: Workers in the Vanguard of Collectivization* (Oxford, 1987), 215, argues that in the countryside it was "the most active supporters of the revolution from among the working class" who "helped to implement the Stalin revolution." Sheila Fitzpatrick in "Cultural Revolution as Class War," *Cultural Revolution in Russia, 1928-1931* (Bloomington, 1978), 25, asserts a positive response to Stalinist rhetoric, particularly among Komsomol members whom she describes as "enthusiasts of Cultural Revolution."

8.   David Shearer, in *Industry, State, and Society in Stalin's Russia, 1926-1934* (Ithaca, NY, 1996), 14, claims that Stalin was able "to draw on significant working class support" for an alliance whose existence is now an "increasingly accepted view."

9.   Alex Callinicos, *Against Postmodernism: A Marxist Critique* (Cambridge, 1989).

10. Lex Heerma van Voss and Marcel van der Linden eds., Introduction to *Class and Other Identities: Gender, Religion and Ethnicity in the Writing of European Labour History* (New York, 2002).

11. Siegelbaum and Suny, "Class Backwards? In Search of the Soviet Working Class" in *Making Workers Soviet*.

12. Kotkin, *Magnetic Mountain*, 198-237, 359.

13. David Hoffman, *Peasant Metropolis: Social Identities in Moscow, 1929-1941* (Ithaca, 1994), 36-40, 61, 116, 124, 197, 198.

14. Matthew J. Payne, *Stalin's Railroad: Turksib and the Building of Socialism* (Pittsburgh, 2001), 126-155.

15. E.H. Carr and R.W. Davies, *Foundations of a Planned Economy* (London, 1969), 1:545; Chris Ward, Russia's Cotton Workers and the New Economic Policy (Cambridge, 1990), 261; Michal Reiman, *The Birth of Stalinism* (Bloomington, 1987), 115-122; Donald Filtzer, *Soviet Workers and Stalinist Industrialization* (New York, 1988).

16. S. Kostiuchenko et al. *Istoriia kirovskogo zavoda (1917-1945)*, (Moscow 1966). Kotkin, *Magnetic Mountain*; Clayton Black, "Manufacturing Communists: 'Krasnyi Putilovets' and the Politics of Soviet Industrialization, 1923-1932" (Ph.D. Dissertation, Indiana University, 1996).

17. Kenneth M. Straus, *Factory and Community in Stalin's Russia* (Pittsburgh, 1997).

18. The common English translation of "serp i molot" is used throughout the text but is reversed—the literal translation is "sickle and hammer."

19. On *svodki* as sources, see Sarah Davies, *Popular Opinion in Stalin's Russia* (Cambridge, 1997), 1-19.

20. Tony Cliff, *Russia: A Marxist Analysis* (London, 1955).

1

THE EMERGING WORKING CLASS MOVEMENT

> "Find the ones at the factory who are the worst scoundrels and who set the tone for others."
>
> —Mayor's office memorandum to Okhrana, June 1912

Iulii Petrovich Guzhon, the largest shareholder of the Moscow Metalworks and president of the Moscow Society of Factory and Mill Owners (MSFMO), addressed the society's annual convention in March 1913. The French-born industrial mogul congratulated his colleagues for their steadfast unity and for "creating for themselves a conception of the might of the industrial corporation that could not be ignored." The most important responsibility for the group's newest members, he reminded them, was guarding "the prestige of that might."[1]

Guzhon's confident posturing caught the attention of one of the factory owners' principal adversaries. Ten days later, in the pages of *Pravda*, the Bolshevik leader Vladimir Ilyich Lenin described the presentation as "full of arrogance" and "reminiscent of the speech of some army clerk." In their annual report, the owners had expressed concern over the "frequency of the demonstration strikes, which happen one after another, and the unusual variety and difference in the importance of motives for which workers considered it necessary to interrupt work." Significantly, the report detected "not only a considerable thickening of the political atmosphere, but also the decline of factory discipline." In response, industrialists resolved to adopt "severe measures," including the imposition of fines, the retraction of bonuses and—in extreme cases—lockouts. Increasing Russia's industrial output, they resolved, "urgently demands the raising of factory discipline to the high level at which it stands in the Western European countries." Although "the factory owners wish to raise 'discipline' to the 'Western' level," Lenin retorted, they showed no such proclivity for "raising the 'political atmosphere' to the same level."[2]

Notes for this section begin on page 37.

Despite the employers' acknowledgment that they faced renewed labor militancy, the 1912 statistics compiled by the owners showed that they had been slightly more successful at defeating economic strikes. Lenin countered that in comparison to the previous year, most of the 1912 stoppages were *offensive* actions in which workers had fought for improved conditions, and in which a new sense of determination was evident, with workers willing to stay out for longer periods of time. "You are wrong, you gentlemen who own the factories! Even in the economic sense, to say nothing of the political strikes, the workers' gains are terrifying."[3]

The intransigence evident in the perspectives of Guzhon and Russian capital on one side and Lenin and the newly reawakened workers' movement on the other is indicative of the deep social rift that had developed in the years before the war. Leopold Haimson has shown that, far from being diverted from the path of gradual and peaceful reform by the war, prerevolutionary Russian society was racked with widespread urban unrest and mounting class confrontation. Socialists intervened in these developments, playing "a significant catalytic role" in the revival of working-class militancy, particularly evident in the activity of the Bolsheviks in St. Petersburg.[4] This notion of chronic "social instability" exacerbated by the conscious intervention of revolutionaries can be extended to describe most of the first third of the twentieth century.

A survey of developments in Guzhon's metal factory prior to 1917 reveals a number of key aspects in the evolution of the workers' movement. First, how did the volatile shifts in the political climate change the confidence and mood of the workers and management? Second, a variety of workplace institutions (legal—including Tsarist and management, semi-legal, and illegal) competed for labor support. To what extent did these bodies gain workers' trust and participation? Third, the workers' movement eventually overcame many obstacles and imposed an ethos of solidarity upon a workforce divided by multiple and overlapping loyalties. What factors contributed to weakening these divisions and forging unity among employees against their employer and, conversely, what caused these sectional differences to be reinforced?

Background

Guzhon's huge metalworks epitomized the main features of Russian industrial development, embodying the striking contradictions that flowed from the autocracy's late, halfhearted conversion to modernization. By the time industrialization finally began to sink deep roots in Russian soil in the late nineteenth and early twentieth centuries, the country's political and economic backwardness meant that manufacturing developed, according to Leon Trotsky, in a "combined and uneven" manner, incorporating some of the most modern aspects of capitalism, such as huge industrial enterprises, side by side with the most backward elements.

Under military pressure from its wealthier European rivals, the Tsarist state had extracted a far greater relative portion of the people's wealth than its competitors in the West (a feature that would later characterize Soviet society as well), which extended the longevity of a stagnant and brutal feudal regime and imposed harsh impoverishment on its subjects. The absence of an indigenous nascent bourgeoisie meant that the state and foreign capital played unusually prominent roles. Russian society made up for its late conversion to industry with an astounding pace of growth, doubling between 1905 and 1914. Moreover, Russian industry diverged from the path of incremental development that had been evident earlier in Europe, where industry developed from small artisans' workshops to slightly larger enterprises and eventually large industrial factories. Russia largely skipped the intermediary stage: by the start of the war, nearly half of Russian enterprises employed more than a thousand workers. Significantly, however, Lenin's quip about the flagrant discrepancy between economic dynamism and political stagnation in prewar Russia exposed one of the critical features of Russia's industrial evolution. Political advances clearly did not match economic development: workers labored twelve hours a day and were regarded legally as peasants excluded from even token participation in Russian civil society. The exceptional concentration of industrial workers in colossal enterprises; the failure of political reforms; the intense character of government persecution; and the impulsiveness of an unruly proletariat all combined to produce an extraordinary level of political strikes with the potential to shake Russian society to its core.[5]

The importance of machine building, railways, and armaments placed metal production at the center of Russia's industrial revolution. By 1917, the metal industry employed more than 60 percent of St. Petersburg's four hundred thousand workers. Moscow industry was more diverse, yet even in "calico" Moscow (so-called because of the predominance of textiles) fifty-seven thousand metal workers outnumbered textile workers by seven thousand by 1917. Government war contracts drove the 40 percent expansion of Moscow's industry. By 1917 Moscow had two hundred thousand industrial workers, over half employed in enterprises of more than five hundred workers.[6]

The son of a French merchant who owned a silk factory in Moscow, Iulii Petrovich Guzhon had invested his family fortune in Russia's burgeoning metal market. Arriving in Moscow in 1871, Guzhon worked alongside his brother to construct and then manage a nail factory. In 1883 he opened the Moscow Metalworks, employing two hundred workers in a rolled metal shop. A voracious demand for metal and the ready availability of a large pool of cheap labor permitted Guzhon to expand his enterprise during the economic boom of the late nineteenth century. Employing two thousand workers by 1900, it was the largest metal factory in Moscow, and through its operation Guzhon reaped nearly a million rubles in profit a year.[7]

Guzhon's values personified both the paternalism and intransigence of Russian corporate liberalism. Among the Moscow industrial community, he was considered an enlightened industrialist—assisting workers in need, setting up a workers' cooperative, helping workers construct dachas, allowing regular church services in the plant, and offering his employees a three-year technical course.[8] In 1895 the factory opened a school for workers' children because, Guzhon asserted, "if workers know that education for their children is guaranteed then they will value their service to the factory."[9] Yet Guzhon also enjoyed a reputation as a tough and outspoken defender of his class. His refusal to yield to workers' demands of any kind helped propel Guzhon to a leading position in the Moscow Stock Exchange Committee.[10] Like Lenin, Guzhon studied his class enemies carefully. During the anti-German riots of May 1915, the Okhrana raided his apartment and found an impressive collection of political leaflets, lists of workers' demands, and social democratic literature.[11]

The massive Moscow Metalworks was located in the eastern Rogozhskii (later Rogozhsko-Simonovskii, then Proletarskii) district of the city.[12] Employing between 1,806 and 3,289 workers in the years 1901 to 1916—the largest fluctuations due to two major wartime drafts—the sprawling factory complex encompassed enormous shops in adjacent buildings. By 1914, half the workforce of three thousand was employed in the three larger "hot" departments involved in various stages of steel production. Five hundred workers in the steel foundry used four forty-ton and three smaller open-hearth furnaces to produce steel from pig iron and coke. In the form-casting department four hundred employees molded steel into wagon wheels, machine gears, and other large steel products, making use of eleven ovens and ten large casting machines. Over five hundred rolled metal department employees worked on six large mills and an assortment of presses. Three hundred bolt shop workers punched out bolts and screws on one hundred and thirty five machines while a hundred nail shop workers worked with similar machinery. One hundred and forty stretching department employees operated pressing mills to produce various grades of wire, with similar numbers in the mechanical, electrical, and repair shops.[13]

The partition of the factory grounds into separate production departments fostered shop-loyalty (*tsekhovshchina*) among employees. *Tsekhovshchina* transcended craft divisions because former peasants maintained strong ties between specific shops and particular villages. Nail makers, for example, were recruited from the Tver' region.[14] The mass exodus of peasants from nearby provinces supplied the labor-power for Moscow's rapid industrialization, but many of these workers retained their land holdings in their villages.[15] At the turn of the century only about a quarter of the workforce had been born in Moscow province, while nearly two-thirds of the workforce had migrated from the seven other provinces of the central industrial region, a migration pattern similar to those for other Moscow factories.[16]

Ideological, skill, and age differences also divided the workforce. Many workers were sympathetic to the autocracy, embracing an aggressive Russian nationalism, while others were either active revolutionaries or sympathetic to the demands of the left organizations. Twenty-five skill categories ranged from the most skilled metalworkers, lathe operators, smelters, and rolling mill operators to apprentices and unskilled laborers. A skilled worker earned more than twice the wage of an unskilled worker, a disparity that was usually tied to experience and therefore age. The workforce was young, with about half under the age of thirty, a third between thirty and forty years old, and a smaller group over forty.[17]

The handful of unskilled women workers earned low wages and suffered abuse in the traditionally male-dominated metal industry. Conditions in the shop were "particularly difficult for teenage girls" as heavy conditions "messed up hair, tore dresses, and forced many to leave the factory."[18] A 1905 Russian Social Democratic Workers' Party (RSDWP) leaflet claimed that the bolt shop timekeeper repeatedly "raped women and girls working in his shop."[19] Most had been driven to the factory by economic necessity, their entry made possible by family ties. For example, after E.I. Voronina's husband lost both legs in an accident in the steel foundry, Guzhon agreed to hire her to work in the bolt shop, where some fifty women were employed in the early years of the century.[20] All female workers earned either eighth or ninth category (of ten) rates—slightly less than half that of a skilled metal worker.[21] By 1909 women also started working in the rolled metal shop, where they had to undergo an initiation ritual that involved having male workers expose themselves while the entire shop laughed.[22] Clearly these women represented an exploited, marginalized, and particularly vulnerable minority of the workforce in the prewar period.

The Workers' Movement Before 1912

The first stirrings of worker discontent in the Moscow Metalworks arose out of disputes over work hours. Management had defeated the first known strike in February 1894 by firing thirty bolt shop workers who refused to work fifteen-hour days.[23] The factory was one of a dozen Moscow workplaces first organized by socialists in the Workers' Union in 1895. By 1896 the group had two thousand members in forty plants and agitated with some success around economic grievances and work hours. The Workers' Union most likely played a role in a second strike in Guzhon in 1896.[24] In November of that year, management agreed to shorten the workday from twelve to eleven and a half hours in cold shops,[25] and when other metal factories' owners shortened work hours in 1897, labor unrest in the industry dissipated. Though socialists played a modest role in the early workers' movement, their influence should not be exaggerated.[26] That labor advocates espousing autocratic politics succeeded in eclipsing the authority of the newly formed (1898) Russian Social Democratic Workers' Party says much about the weak influence of socialism among industrial workers in the formative period of industrialization.

In the first years of the new century a surprising competitor outflanked socialists for workers' allegiance in Moscow—the police-sponsored Zubatov unions. Between 1898 and 1903, deep social unrest affected all sections of Russian society, including the growing working class. Fearful of socialist influence among the city's workforce, the Chief of the Moscow Okhrana, Sergei Zubatov, created the Council of Workers of the City of Moscow, an organization that explicitly promoted loyalty to the Tsar. Zubatov believed that workers had many legitimate complaints, and that monarchial reformism had to address their grievances lest they turn to more radical solutions. The council's activities included lectures, general meetings that discussed the material needs of workers, mutual aid funds, and the filing of over a thousand collective complaints against employers. By 1902, the Zubatov unions had gained enormous influence in Moscow and throughout the Central Industrial Region. On 19 February, the anniversary of peasant emancipation, a peaceful Zubatovist demonstration of fifty thousand workers marched within the walls of the Kremlin in memory of Alexander II. The procession included a requiem mass and the patriotic hymn "God Save the Tsar," impressing elated government officials while horrifying socialists. The Socialist Revolutionary press acknowledged that Zubatov "succeeded in imparting the aspect of unity between workers and government" and even the Moscow Committee of the RSDWP admitted, "social democracy was powerless to deal with police socialism."[27]

The council's attempt to control labor discontent, however, also necessitated proving to skeptical workers that it was not a mere tool of management—a strategy that led Zubatov to a confrontation with factory owners. Zubatov's Society of Machine Workers gained a following in the Metalworks as employees repeatedly petitioned the government about unsanitary work conditions and other grievances.[28] One worker recalled that the Zubatovs were particularly strong in the steel foundry shop.[29]

The "Guzhon affair" with striking weavers and in his silk mill attracted national attention and catapulted the French industrialist into Moscow's industrial inner circle. Zubatov had asserted that the council was "compelled" to side with the workers "for the maintenance of its reputation," and went so far as to organize a strike fund. Even the Moscow governor-general, Grand Duke Sergei Alexandrov, supported the council, exerting his influence to wrest concessions from factory owners. The strike had wider implications because under the council's leadership, labor militancy spread in 1902, with workers expecting government support for "a rapid and great improvement in their position at the expense of the owners." A factory inspector noted that workers believed that the council had gained the prestige of a government organ, "created specifically for the defense of workers' class interest." Unyielding in the face of the weavers' demands, Guzhon blamed the conflict on Okhrana interference, refused to negotiate, and marshaled the industrial community to support him in a showdown with the workers. After a bitter battle involving leading government officials and industrialists, Zubatov was reassigned to St. Petersburg on 17 August. Police unionism would continue in Moscow for several more years, but Zubatov's departure marked the beginning of its decline.[30]

Although the RSDWP devoted much energy to denouncing the Zubatov, the demise of police unionism had more to do with its embrace of a new, more conservative strategy that prohibited confrontations with management—a tactical shift that inevitably led to a loss of workers' allegiance. The activities of the Moscow Okhrana again emphasized repression rather than appeasement. So powerful was the Okhrana in the city that experienced revolutionaries often refused to work in Moscow, while many workers feared contact with them. Repression, isolation, the internal schism over "economism" (agitation focused exclusively on workers' economic, rather than political, demands), and a brief period of working-class retreat at the start of the Russo-Japanese War in January 1904 all limited the activities of the Moscow RSDWP after 1902. The few party members working in the Moscow Metalworks managed to establish a factory cell only for a brief period during the 1905 rebellion.[31]

The organization that led the January 1905 workers' revolt in St. Petersburg, Father Gapon's Assembly of Russian Factory and Mill Workers, had much in common with the Zubatov movement. Originally funded by the police, the Assembly briefly eclipsed socialist influence among workers in the capital in 1904. The attempt to contain labor discontent by initiatives from above again entailed the risk of events moving beyond the boundaries acceptable to authorities. After some of its members were dismissed from the Putilov works, Gapon's Assembly helped initiate a strike of 120,000 workers, and then organized the huge Sunday 9 January procession to the Winter Palace. The peaceful demonstration of sixty thousand, replete with Orthodox crosses and icons, anticipated a sympathetic response from "father" Nicholas II to their humble supplication that included an appeal for an eight-hour day, higher wages, and free elections. Instead, government troops fired on the crowd—killing over one hundred and detonating the 1905 Revolution.[32]

The events of "Bloody Sunday" represented a fundamental turning point, severely undermining workers' faith in a benevolent Tsar and a sympathetic state that would voluntarily acquiesce to their concerns. Thereafter socialists dominated the leadership of the labor movement, contributing to an increased level of organization and confidence. More importantly, as Orlando Figes has argued, this new militancy was the result "of workers themselves becoming more class conscious and violent as their conflicts with employers and police became more bitter and intense." The rebellion also gave rise to the general strike and a new revolutionary institution: the workers' soviet (council). From St. Petersburg, soviets spread to other cities and provided the embryonic form of a workers' government—organizing militias, publishing newspapers, and distributing food supplies.[33]

The 1905 revolt in the Moscow Metalworks started at 1:30 on 12 January. *Tsekhovshchina* shaped the form of the strike as workers from the nail shop, then the repair and bolt shops stopped work, in turn gathering workers from other departments. Cognizant that the strike movement had started in Moscow two days earlier, the administration summoned cavalry and troops into the territory of the factory, though a confrontation was avoided as workers peacefully left the factory grounds and convened a meeting. The next day, elected senior workers issued management a written list of demands for an eight-hour day, a wage increase, better conditions in the shops, regular paydays, lowering of fines, and the dismissal of four abusive managers.[34] The government had established a system of "factory elders" in 1903 in an attempt to channel worker grievances through official channels,[35] but the strategy of containing labor discontent by forming workers' institutions from above again led to unexpected consequences as the elders issued the workers' demands. Management agreed to lower fines, issue pay regularly, and shorten work hours from eleven to ten hours in the cold shops, but refused the other demands, and the stoppage ended.[36]

Socialist groups competed for workers' loyalty during the 1905 Revolution. The RSDWP had split in 1903 between the Bolsheviks and Mensheviks over disagreements about the definition of party membership, but more profound theoretical differences emerged. The Mensheviks argued that because the prerequisite economic development under capitalism had yet to fully develop in Russia, the revolution would be bourgeois-democratic—a position that led them to attempt to pursue an alliance with the liberal bourgeoisie and to argue against socialists bidding for power, as this "would cause the bourgeois classes to recoil from the revolution and this would diminish its sweep."[37] Lenin and the Bolsheviks harbored no such illusions about the Russian bourgeoisie, whom they repeatedly condemned as thoroughly "reactionary." In what became the Bolshevik theoretical credo for the next twelve years, Lenin argued in *Two Tactics of Social Democracy in the Democratic Revolution* that the decisive role in the coming revolution had fallen on the proletariat and the peasantry, though he also chastised "the absurd and semi-anarchistic ideas of giving immediate effect to the maximum program for a socialist revolution." Socialists should call for a democratic republic, the confiscation of the landed estates, and the eight-hour day.[38] The Socialist Revolutionaries (SRs) also organized among Moscow workers. The SRs encompassed many political tendencies, including terrorists, and their rank and file was often far to the left of the formal party leadership.[39]

Both the SRs and Bolsheviks vied for the allegiance of workers in the Moscow Metalworks. One Bolshevik activist asserted that the bad blood between the organizations was based on the SRs' unscrupulous recruitment methods rather than larger political questions. "In order to attract Guzhon workers to them," he wrote, "they would resort to enticing them and began organizing not far from us, in Annengofskii Grove, and handing out a lot of sausages, cheese, and bread at mass meetings."[40]

During the first seven months of 1905, the workers' movement in Moscow followed closely the events unfolding in the politically charged atmosphere of the capital. Moscow strikes involved 42,700 workers and started in large factories, most of them metal plants with a history of Social Democratic (or Zubatov) influence. Economic issues triggered nearly all the strikes that lacked coordination between enterprises. Government officials responded to the labor unrest by creating commissions and by issuing a decree on 18 February, which conceded limited popular representation. After January and February, the number of Moscow strikes declined sharply, though the political ferment gave rise to unprecedented mass rallies, meetings, and a wide distribution of socialist literature.[41]

By the late summer, the regime reverted to a hard-line strategy that met with stiff popular resistance. On 6 August, Tsar Nicholas II rescinded earlier reforms regarding freedom of speech and assembly, and decreed that the Duma would act only as advisory body. Students and workers defied the authorities, however, and continued to organize. In Moscow, Sytin print workers went on strike in September for shorter work hours and a wage increase, and then were joined by other print workers, followed by workers in other industries. Police battled workers on the central boulevards and many employers attempted to counter the labor unrest with layoffs and lock-outs. After the strike wave abated somewhat, railway workers gave both new life and a more political dimension to the movement. Nearly fifty thousand Moscow workers participated in a general strike that spread quickly through-out the empire, advancing demands for legislative power based on universal suffrage, political amnesty, and the eight-hour day. The Tsar responded to public pressure with the "October Manifesto," promising a legislative body and civil liberties—a maneuver that effectively divided the opposition move-ment. Many workers continued to take political action, and by the end of November socialists helped organize the Moscow Soviet. Once again, authorities reverted to the hard-line approach, arresting leaders of the St. Petersburg Soviet. When police arrests spread to Moscow, the Soviet responded with a call to renew the political strike movement, and over eighty thousand workers participated. During the December uprising workers' mili-tias fought pitched battles with government forces. The state regained the upper hand only after it became clear that the uprising had failed to win active support among the troops. On 18 December the last stronghold of the revolt in the Presnia district was crushed.[42]

Moscow Metalworks workers' demand for the removal of abusive managers remained their main grievance. Although workers did not participate in the October strike wave, on 4 November they again demanded the removal of the four managers. Management responded with a threat to shut down the fac-tory on 21 November, but workers preempted this by striking on 12 Novem-ber, remaining out throughout the December rebellion and only returning to work nearly two months later. Factory-centered demands gave way to more general political issues as workers elected representatives to the Moscow Soviet and participated in the December uprising. A handful of workers died in the revolt; many others were jailed or exiled after the rebellion was crushed.[43]

Guzhon's aggressive intervention during the 1905 Revolution solidified his position as a champion of order. Before 1905, the Moscow owners' asso-ciation had supported liberal reforms, including equality before the law, free-dom of speech, and even the right to organize unions. But during the 1905 revolt, Guzhon headed a special owners' commission that branded the November strike by post and telegraph workers "a criminal undertaking" that "must be prosecuted by the law." By December, manufacturers had col-lected 165,000 rubles to aid the forces of order. In direct response to the resurgence of the workers' movement, Moscow capitalists formed the Cen-tral Society of Manufacturers (later the MSFMO). Its leader, S.I. Chet-verikov, expressed their concern that "as long as they do not meet the necessary resistance, the workers will find it hard to understand the possible limits to their demands."[44] In 1907 the owners' society elected Guzhon pres-ident, and by 1914 the MSFMO represented owners of over six hundred fac-tories that employed nearly three hundred thousand workers.[45]

The political repression introduced by Minister of Interior Petr Stolypin in the wake of the defeat of the 1905 revolt was harsh. From 1906 to 1908, sixty thousand political detainees were exiled, sentenced to penal servitude, or executed without trial.[46] Whereas the Moscow Bolsheviks' membership expanded to five thousand in 1905, it dropped to 150 members by 1909 and the next year, with Okhrana agent Kukushkin at its head, completely collapsed.[47] Every Bolshevik Central Committee member inside Russia was arrested at least once, and Lenin complained to Gorky about "the tremendous decline among the organizations everywhere."[48]

Despite state repression, a handful of Bolsheviks and SRs continued underground agitation in the Metalworks throughout this period. One worker later recalled, "for workers the years of reaction were particularly difficult" because "Guzhon had many methods to extract profits out of us." Management blacklisted militant workers: "Revolutionary workers in Guzhon were fired," wrote another worker, "and this was communicated to other factories."[49] One Bolshevik claimed that he had been arrested near the end of 1910 for participating in a strike and had been imprisoned for several months.[50] Other memoirs stress the sense of political isolation and fear that dominated factory life. "For the first three or four years of my work in Guzhon, from 1908 to 1911, all workers were suppressed," recalled one worker, "and it seemed that at that time no kind of revolutionary work was conducted."[51] An SR member recalled being unaware of any Bolshevik presence: "At this time the Socialist Revolutionaries were the only party in the factory," he asserted. "I did not hear or see anything about the Bolsheviks."[52]

In the face of such challenges, a small group of revolutionaries managed to maintain an underground network. Illegal May Day meetings in Izmailovskii Woods included several dozen Guzhon workers with workers from nearby factories.[53] One Bolshevik described how, "before 1912 we were driven deeply underground … we received *Krasnaia zvezda* that we passed around from hand to hand until it became impossible to read them because of mud and because we had concealed them in our pockets." Significantly, even among socialists shop loyalty prevailed: "I considered the nail shop the leader in political work because there we had a strong group of Bolsheviks."[54]

The nadir of Russian labor activism came in 1910, when just over 200 strikes took place involving less than fifty thousand workers. The perseverance of small groups of revolutionaries through this difficult period helped lay the groundwork for a palpable, but tenuous, upturn in strike activity that more than doubled in 1911.[55] Memoirs record two short-lived strikes in Guzhon during this period. An SR member described a strike in the form-casting shop at the end of 1911, in which workers "did not leave the shop, but did not work for the entire day." Eventually Guzhon acceded to their economic demands.[56] Another economic strike in January of 1912 lasted for three days.[57]

A wave of student activism and an economic revival likewise contributed to the modest upturn in labor confidence before the Lena Goldfields massacre. Students demonstrated in the autumn of 1910 in commemoration of the death of the former liberal Duma president Muromtsev; then in memory of Leo Tolstoy; and later against the treatment of political prisoners. The death of Tolstoy also spurred demonstration strikes in the RSDWP strongholds of Bromlei, Gustav List, Bari, and other factories.[58] In 1911, a student general strike against state repression spread throughout Russia, and the general ferment created an atmosphere in which newly radicalized students initiated contacts with workers.[59] A Bolshevik described how students had met with Metalworks workers in apartments, "discussed revolutionary themes with us and provided leaflets on the economic situation of workers." At the end of 1911, he recounted, "We began to get leaflets from students and distribute them in the shop."[60] Similarly, an SR member recalled participating in a study circle led by students who supplied workers with both SR and Social Democratic literature.[61] Renewed labor activism coincided with an unprecedented expansion of the Russian economy between 1910 and the beginning of the war, a crucial factor in giving the movement new life.[62]

The Lena Goldfields Massacre and Continued State Repression

While an economic revival and the student movement contributed to renewed proletarian confidence, the Lena Goldfields massacre signaled the rebirth of working-class militancy on a mass scale. On 4 April 1912, government troops opened fire upon striking Lena miners, leaving five hundred casualties. Minister of Internal Affairs Makarov's remarks offered a menacing warning to the workers' movement: "So it has been, and so it will be in the future," he declared.[63] Across the empire, workers responded with a show of force. During the post-Lena and May Day strikes several weeks later, police estimated that nearly three hundred thousand workers struck in St. Petersburg alone, a figure that exceeded the total number of all strike participants in the entire nation between 1909 and 1911.[64]

In the Moscow Metalworks, according to the Okhrana, "the form of the protest was not limited to the events of the Lena massacre but also displayed a negative attitude towards the government, the clergy, the death sentence, and the speech by the Minister of Internal Affairs." Bolsheviks participated in "a group that made it their goal to organize a strike at the factory ... against the best interest and wishes of the well-intentioned workers."[65] *Pravda* reported that workers met in the steel foundry department at eight o'clock on 23 April, passed a resolution for a one-day strike, and sent the resolution to Duma deputies.[66] Participants describe how two hundred mostly young workers struck and met in Vadlinsky Woods, listened to speeches about the massacre, sang the *Marseillaise*, and raised the red flag. The Bolsheviks collected between three and four hundred signatures for a petition against the massacre and forwarded it to Duma deputies.[67]

The turnout of several hundred was extraordinarily low, given that 140,000 struck in St. Petersburg and 70,000 in industrial plants elsewhere in Moscow.[68] Memoirs recall that the Bolsheviks and SRs did not enjoy significant support beyond their immediate circles, and that their first attempts to organize after the Lena massacre met with only limited success. The revolutionaries' inability to connect with a larger circle of workers and the ease with which government and plant officials managed to isolate and victimize them indicate that socialists in the Moscow Metalworks faced exceptional difficulties.

The small Moscow Bolshevik organization made the factory a political priority, with almost 10 percent of their membership working in the plant, but Okhrana infiltration, arrests, and firings thwarted these efforts. An August 1912 report noted that I.M. Lidvanskii had sat in Butyrskaia Jail because he was "unmasked as belonging to the Social Democratic organization" and was "a leader in the one-day strike in the Guzhon Factory after the Lena incidents."[69] State agents also jailed F.I. Riabtsov for his leadership in the one-day strike and Duma petition, and police reports listed four other "participants" who worked with Riabstov.[70] A few weeks later, Okhrana reports name two other factory Bolsheviks arrested.[71] In addition, agents detained V.F. Medvedev on 27 August 1912 who, like most others, claimed under interrogation that he did not belong to the RSDWP.[72] Significantly, "an agent belonging to RSDWP and factory party committee" provided the April and May 1912 reports.[73] One Bolshevik later claimed they had been betrayed by a provocateur in the construction shop and that the arrests resulted in "a collapse in the organization in the factory."[74] Other workers' memoirs attest to the arrest of between sixteen and eighteen members.[75]

The Moscow Okhrana apprehended socialists throughout 1912; with nineteen RSDWP members arrested on 15 April 1912, another eight in May, fifteen in August, seven in September, and six more in November.[76] The 15 August arrests included most of the Moscow Committee along with Dimitreev from the Guzhon factory.[77] Okhrana roundups of socialists were not limited to the Bolsheviks. In October 1912, the SRs apparently led strikes in the defense of court-martialed Sevastopol sailors and subsequently the Okhrana arrested seventeen of their members.[78]

The May Day test of revolutionary strength several weeks after the Lena strike shows that the Bolshevik organization in Guzhon's factory was no match for the Okhrana. St. Petersburg police estimated that 120,000 workers struck on May Day 1912, 110,000 the next year, and 125,000 in 1914.[79] Memoirs claim that Bolsheviks and SRs organized separate May Day 1912 gatherings, and five hundred workers walked out two years later on the revolutionary holiday.[80] Yet despite the participation of tens of thousands in Moscow, Okhrana and MSFMO reports conspicuously omit references to May Day strikes in the Metalworks. An attempt to revive the Bolshevik cell in 1913 failed when the secret police arrested five Bolsheviks in the days leading up to May Day. The preemptive arrests, rather than the usual raids after the event, illustrate the secret police strength in the factory. The Okhrana detained an eighteen-year-old Bolshevik, N.S. Boronin, for distributing several hundred leaflets and agitating for a May Day strike, and expelled him from Moscow for a year and a half. N.P. Komarov, who agitated for the May Day stoppage, supported Bolshevik deputies in the Duma, helped organize a "factory Social Democratic *kruzhka* [circle]," and was exiled because his activities were deemed "harmful for the peace and order of society."[81] A post-revolution list identifies just fifty-four prerevolutionary May Day demonstrators in the Metalworks, with almost half of them located in the steel foundry shop.[82] The May Day actions in the Moscow Metalworks were apparently led by the SRs, as even the Bolsheviks acknowledged the strong SR influence in this shop.[83]

The Moscow Okhrana organized more than thirty rounds of arrests after each of the political strikes between 1912 and 1916.[84] These arrests were greatly facilitated by fifty-five agent provocateurs in Moscow, including twenty working in the RSDWP and seventeen in the SRs.[85] When Central Committee member Alexander Shliapnikov traveled to Moscow in November 1914, he found the organization shattered. An attempt to unify party work in the summer of 1915 also met with arrests and led to a collapse of the center.[86] After the Moscow Committee convened a meeting in April 1916, its leaders were again apprehended.[87] Many Bolshevik leaders in the Moscow union movement were Okhrana agents.[88] A Bolshevik organizer who worked in many cities, Cecilia Bobrovskaia, claimed that Moscow "broke the record for provocateurs," and that efforts to restore the Moscow Committee "inevitably got entangled with one of these provocateurs." Plans to establish a Bolshevik press in Lefortovo collapsed in 1912 because the most active worker in the district turned out to be an Okhrana agent.[89]

The Okhrana had also infiltrated the St. Petersburg Bolsheviks but the organization managed to sustain its operations and continued to act as an effective catalyst for the labor movement. Despite three Okhrana agents on the St. Petersburg Central Committee and repeated roundups, the group was able to bounce back, rebuild a center, and agitate for strikes, and by 1916 had expanded to three thousand members.[90] The most reliable membership figures for Moscow are about two hundred members in the spring of 1913 and about six hundred three years later.[91] The heightened political atmosphere in St. Petersburg and the extraordinary ability of Bolshevik cells to articulate demands that connected with workers' frustrations meant that during the war, three quarters of all political strikes occurred in St. Petersburg, compared with only 9 percent in Moscow.[92] State repression had a more deleterious effect on the relatively weaker Moscow labor movement. Yet time and again, the Okhrana and factory owners mistakenly believed that arrests of key activists would be sufficient to repel the movement. An astounding transformation in the confidence of the Russian working class had occurred in the aftermath of the Lena massacre, a shift too powerful to be derailed by police operations.

The Rebirth of Militancy:
From the Lena Goldfields Massacre to the War

The Lena Goldfields massacre led to the revival of the workers' movement as six times as many workers in the Russian empire participated in strike action during 1912 as in the previous year. This sea change in labor's confidence after the Lena massacre drove the movement forward. An SR member wrote that after the Lena events "we saw that we had strength. For us," he wrote, "and for all the activists in the factory this had been a touchstone event."[93]

Soon after the Lena strike, employees petitioned Guzhon for an eight-hour workday and organized economic strikes in different shops. On 17 July, 334 workers in the form-casting department struck. "The strike is economic, asking for a raise in pay," an Okhrana telephone dispatch explained. "Previously work was done in two shifts, but at a certain point work began in three shifts, and workers want to know why there is a difference in pay." Five days earlier, workers in the department had demanded a raise, and even the Okhrana noted that management had not posted the rate for the three-shift work at fewer hours. Workers complained to the factory inspector that they wanted to receive the same total as they had when they had worked longer hours on two shifts.[94]

The strike became increasingly bitter when management brought in strikebreakers from southern Russia.[95] The Okhrana reported that all 334 workers in the steel foundry department were still out on 20 July and that if they did not return to work by the 23rd, they would be replaced. A factory announcement two days later stated that "former workers" could pick up their passports at the factory entrance, but that their pay would be transferred to the court.[96] The strike was strong within the department: the Okhrana figure of 344 participants represented the total number employed in the shop in July 1912.[97] New workers started at the factory on 26 July, one of whom told the Okhrana that strikers had followed him from the factory and had threatened that "they would deal with him," while another claimed that strikers threatened to "throw him off the bridge."[98] The next day, apparently having lost confidence that they could win, striking workers sought negotiations with management, but "the administration had no desire to have any negotiations with them."[99]

Management attempted to foment divisions between departments by threatening lockouts in sections affected by the strike. A 17 July factory announcement declared that the unauthorized stoppage had resulted in shortages of materials and that steel foundry workers "probably will not be working tomorrow or the day after" and would not be paid. A similar management announcement was addressed to rolled metal shop workers.[100]

Guzhon apparently exerted his political influence in the city in order to target strike leaders. The mayor's office sent an order to the Okhrana chief of the third precinct in Lefortovo on 21 July, asking him to "Find the ones at the factory who are the worst scoundrels and who set the tone for others."[101] In response, the Okhrana reported that eight workers had played important roles in the strike and that at least three were Bolshevik members or sympathizers, one of whom, according to an undercover Okhrana agent, had worked in the factory for eighteen years and "enjoyed a certain popularity among the workers in the aforesaid factory."[102]

Although the strike was solidly organized within one shop, it lacked solidarity from workers in other departments. The Okhrana categorized it as one of several seasonal stoppages related to speedups for summer rail construction that were purely economic and not coordinated by "the revolutionary underground." While it was true that revolutionaries were not the only instigators, the arrests show that they were part of a wider milieu of militants who collaborated to organize economic actions, though the weak level of intra-shop coordination is evident in that the workers in other departments did not participate. Agents reported a noticeable "disorganization of politically conscious and generally left elements among the workers."[103] One worker wrote that after the defeat "not everyone was taken back to work."[104] Many skilled workers participated in the strike movement, but women workers and teenagers were noticeably absent. Though they earned low wages and experienced financial hardship, "they remained outside the movement and did not participate in strikes."[105]

A distinguishing feature of the post-Lena movement was the lack of significant involvement by working women. If strikes were largely spontaneous events that lacked coordination, the women's tenuous connection to the developing political radicalization and their inclination against taking risks would help to explain their remaining aloof from the movement. But a plethora of Okhrana reports on strikes and subsequent arrests demonstrate that the stoppages were highly organized actions and suggest an alternative explanation. Organizers themselves apparently made little effort to involve women, focusing their efforts on traditional socialist strongholds in the metal and printing industries. A wave of strikes in early November in support of court martialed Sevastopol sailors was overwhelming male, yet women workers, including four hundred from the Bonaker Metalworks, did participate.[106] Thus, the reason women workers "remained outside the movement" had more to do with the priorities and mindset of the predominantly male organizers than any innate disdain for militancy among women workers.[107] As we shall see, when male militants in the Moscow Metalworks started to take women's concerns more seriously in 1916 and 1917, women workers joined the strike movement in large numbers.

The relative weakness of revolutionary influence, however, meant that even male workers in the factory refrained from strike activity for the rest of 1912. Sixty thousand St. Petersburg workers struck in support of the Sevastopol sailors involved in a mutiny, an action supported by fourteen thousand workers in eighty-two factories in Moscow, including nine factories in the Lefortovo district.[108] By the spring of 1913, the Okhrana was confident that it had again managed to obliterate the revolutionary underground in Moscow, anticipating a demonstration-free anniversary of the Lena massacre because, "To have any organized event, appropriate agitation is necessary, which assumes the presence of some kind of underground party organization." However, "thanks to the most recent arrests, everything has been extracted that was considered more or less capable of even creating a semblance of such activity ... the most conscious carriers of Social Democratic ideals, are terrified and avoid even appearing at meetings and lectures that are completely lawful and have been permitted by the administration." The Okhrana did not rule out "the possibility of certain individual attempts at temporary stoppages of work in several of the skilled workshops or the larger factories and mills."[109]

The Okhrana, like all contemporary protagonists in Russia's class conflict, acknowledged the leadership of revolutionaries in political strikes, and their prognosis was proven correct. On the anniversary itself, eighty-five thousand workers struck in St. Petersburg, but the Moscow response was weak, with less than three thousand workers from eleven different enterprises participating in the stoppage. The Moscow Metalworks was not among these, but in Bromlei, where the Bolsheviks continued to agitate, the Okhrana reported that 1,100 workers stopped work "wishing to honor the memory of the anniversary of the 'Lena events.'"[110]

The Okhrana's confidence was misplaced, however. On May Day 1913, four weeks after the secret police claimed that the revolutionary underground had been crushed, thirty-three thousand Moscow workers struck.[111] The revival of Moscow's political strikes continued in June with forty-eight of fifty-seven stoppages overtly political, but only a small minority of Moscow Metalworks employees participated because of the previous rounds of arrests. Moscow workers struck "in memory of the anniversary of executed Sevastopol sailors." Okhrana agents reported that the strikes were "of a peaceful character and nowhere were there attempts at demonstration actions," but noted the distribution of RSDWP newspapers. The largest strikes were in the Social Democratic strongholds of Sytin Printing, Dinamo and Bari. In contrast, workers in Guzhon's factory did not participate. On 24 June renewed strikes included six factories in the Lefortovo district but only 198 of 2,759 Moscow Metalworks employees participated three days later.[112]

By July 1913 Guzhon expressed concern to other factory owners that "the strike movement taking place at present in Moscow industrial organizations does not show a clear economic form and the essence of the demands and other characteristics are reminiscent of 1905-1906 with all the qualities of a political demonstration." Again the industrialists' response was to call for harsh measures. Guzhon reported that the Metal Group of the MSFMO had called for "listing the names of the most zealous strikers," and requested that members circulate information about the movement's leaders.[113] Although Guzhon was justifiably concerned about the reemergence of political strikes, the only other political action during 1913 in his Metalworks occurred during September, when a mere seventy-five employees stopped work to protest against the harassment of the labor press in Moscow.[114] This was at a time when not only industrialists but also government officials expressed deep concern about the mood of Moscow workers.[115]

A comparison with the Bromlei factory, a metalworking plant with a strong Bolshevik cell,[116] illustrates the degree to which workers responded to shop floor agitation. At Bromlei 900 (of 1,100) workers struck on the anniversary of Lena, while Moscow Metalworks employees continued to work. On May Day 1913, 800 Bromlei workers stopped work, but again there was no reported stoppage in Guzhon's factory. At the beginning of the strike in defense of Baltic sailors in June, 600 Bromlei employees went out, but less than 200 Moscow Metalworks employees participated on the last day of the action. Bromlei's 1,100 workers led the strike wave in November 1913 in support of arrested St. Petersburg workers; employees in Guzhon's enterprise did not participate.[117] Where Bolshevism exercised a powerful influence, many workers repeatedly went out at the start of the strike, pro-

viding inspiration for workers in other factories. But in the Moscow Metalworks, where the cell had been decimated by repression, workers hesitated
and either did not strike or else struck in small numbers several days after the
start of the protests.

The Bolshevik collapse meant that the SRs set the tone for political strike
action in the factory for the duration of the prerevolutionary period. SR
members wrote that they had attracted fifty young workers, had organized a
study circle and a drama group, and apparently led a successful economic
strike in the steel foundry shop in April 1913.[118] One of the few Bolsheviks
also admitted that the SRs had had more influence in organizing political
strike action.[119]

By the eve of the war the sectarian bad blood appears to have subsided as
socialists cooperated in an attempt to establish the metalworkers' union in
the plant as they did in other Moscow factories.[120] One SR member noted a
strengthening of ties among different factories, including a general strike
fund established through cooperation between the SRs and Bolsheviks, Mensheviks, and the metalworkers' union.[121] The metalworkers' union attempted
to agitate against management's increased imposition of fines.[122] Management had imposed 1,111 fines for "violation of order" in 1912, but that
number rose dramatically to 2,320 by 1914.[123] The "best way to fight against
increased fines for absenteeism and lateness," according to the Bolshevik
newspaper, was to "join the metalworkers' union." Renewed collaboration
probably encouraged several economic strikes, the first of their kind since the
spring of 1913. *Pravda* reported a work stoppage in the steel foundry shop
in March 1914.[124] Workers' memoirs also mention two short one-day strikes:
one in the cable shop, which was defeated, and a second in the bolt shop,
which resulted in a wage increase.[125]

Though factory owners claimed to support the right of unions to organize, they made it clear that they were against union intervention in strikes.
After the MSFMO complained about the Moscow metalworkers' activities in
August 1913, authorities conducted raids and carried out arrests, temporarily shutting down the union. The dilemma for union activists was that
although they had the legal right to recruit members and publish newspapers,
as soon they engaged in activities to defend their membership they were subject to state repression. Therefore legal unionism did not gain a strong
foothold in Moscow in the prewar years—the metalworkers counted less
than two thousand members.[126]

In early 1914 owners once again believed that they had routed the political strike movement. On 15 March 1914, Guzhon reported to the owners
"the latest workers' demonstration in St. Petersburg shows an extremely weak
reverberation" in Moscow with only seven hundred workers participating. A
few days later four thousand employees were on strike in Moscow but by then
the movement in St. Petersburg that had earlier included fifty thousand workers had collapsed.[127] On May Day 1914, Guzhon informed the MSFMO that
more than twenty thousand workers in seventy-three enterprises had struck in
Moscow but that the citywide total represented a downward trend from
thirty-eight thousand in 1912 and thirty-three thousand in 1913.[128]

The owners were again overconfident about the decline of the labor movement. Over one million workers struck in the first seven months of 1914, a level of strike activity comparable to that of the 1905 revolt. Moreover, 74 percent of the participants were involved in political stoppages. St. Petersburg continued to provide a lead, with 621,324 workers participating in political strikes.[129] In July of 1914, after government troops fired on Putilov workers, a general strike developed and workers erected barricades on the streets of St. Petersburg.[130]

Two SR-led political strikes in 1914 moved the Moscow Metalworks to the forefront of the Moscow political movement. On 26 April management informed the factory inspector that 1,120 Guzhon workers had struck "because of the expulsion of some members from the State Duma from several meetings." The strike included all employees in the nail, cable, and pattern shops, two-thirds of the workers in the steel foundry and repair shops, and half of the workers in the bolt and construction shops.[131] Employment statistics indicate that 187 workers struck in unison in three smaller shops and in a portion of the medium-size shops, but of the four large shops, only two-thirds of the workers in the steel foundry shop, an SR stronghold, participated.[132] Thus, a few organizers successfully carried the strike proposal in small departments, but insufficient organization on the shop floor in the larger shops resulted in either partial action or complete abstention from the strike.

The stoppage in response to the July 1914 general strike of 120,000 in St. Petersburg was larger and better organized. Management informed the factory inspector that 1,500 (of 3,000) Guzhon workers had struck on 7 July.[133] The weaker Moscow response began on the 5th and peaked two days later, with just under ten thousand workers out on strike.[134] Thus Metalworks strikers represented 15 percent of Moscow strikers in support of Putilov workers—an extraordinary show of class solidarity. Management letters to the factory inspector indicate that this was a well-organized action: workers left in unison at 8 a.m. on 7 July and the next day all workers returned "at the usual time and started work." Two days later the same workers "after lunch again stopped work in the form of a protest against the imposition of fines for the above-mentioned unauthorized work stoppage."[135] The SR-dominated steel foundry shop was, yet again, the only "hot" shop to participate and apparently few women struck, as no workers from the rolled metal shop went out and only from half the bolt shop.[136]

Before the war, the long-term trend throughout industrial Russia toward confrontation between capital and labor resonated in the factory, as workers struck over economic and political issues. While all contemporary protagonists recognized that the revolutionary underground played a catalytic role in recurrent political strikes, the Bolsheviks' presence was negligible, having been decimated by repeated arrests, while the SRs played a leading role in several large stoppages in the months prior to the war. A variety of obstacles had yet to be overcome in forging shop-floor unity, including divisions between different departments, between skilled and unskilled, young and old, and male and female workers. While political strikes had begun to transcend such divisions, *tsekhovshchina* continued to dominate economic strikes.

Wartime Patriotism and the Decline of Worker Activism

On 19 July 1914, Nicholas II declared war on Germany, a move that found an immediate resonance at the factory level. "On the day the war was declared," wrote one worker, "there was a demonstration from the factory to the city center to the governor-general's office with slogans of 'Down with Germany!' and 'Long live Russia, France, and England!'"[137] "When the war was announced," recalled another worker, "a large procession was organized and many of our workers took part in the demonstration."[138]

World War I brought working-class militancy to a virtual halt. The factory inspector reported that less than ten thousand workers in the whole of the empire had gone on strike in the last five months of 1914.[139] No strikes were recorded in the Moscow Metalworks for the first seven months of the war.[140] The Okhrana repeatedly reported that throughout the district, "the mood of workers was calm."[141] "At the start of the war," wrote an SR leader, "there was a complete stoppage of strikes and later, although they happened, they were small and short-lived."[142] The decline in strike activity did not correlate with the deterioration in workers' living standards as management utilized the patriotic mood to cut the average monthly wage from 48.3 to 34.1 rubles by March 1915.[143] Another memoir recalled that during the first year of the war "it was tense and you could not say a word against the war … after the capture of Przemysl, workers were taken to Red Square for a prayer service" and if one did not participate "you were considered an opponent of the war."[144] In the March 1915 pro-war demonstration after the capture of Przemysl several workers "grabbed a portrait of the Tsar from the main office and about five hundred workers left the factory."[145]

The first wartime strike on 15 April 1915 shows how far solidarity had slipped. The Okhrana reported that eighty workers in the rolled metal shop nightshift had turned down management's offer of a 10 to 30 percent raise and then struck, demanding a piece-rate increase of 50 to 100 percent. The factory administration claimed the strike occurred because of "some secret agitation" connected with work stoppages at other factories.[146] In the entire district, however, this small, short-lived strike was the only stoppage in April 1915.[147] Guzhon's strategy for defeating this strike involved a combination of compromise and intimidation. On the same day, management informed the factory director, "because of the rise in prices of goods, all workers in the factory would receive an increase of ten kopecks an hour."[148] The average monthly wage jumped from 34.1 to 52.5 rubles—the largest wartime wage increase in the factory.[149] The MSFMO reported that management fired thirty-four strikers.[150] Additionally, management apparently victimized the remaining rolling mill operators as their real wages fell to half their 1913 level.[151] An activist admitted that "things went badly" during the strike because "other shops would not support it." Significantly, the sectional divisions between older skilled workers and younger workers were strengthened at the start of the war: "We had many young workers and at that time it was impossible to raise the issue of equality in the shop."[152] As workers retreated from unified action, latent divisions within the workforce resurfaced, allowing management to regain the upper hand and force through concessions.

Hundreds of skilled workers were conscripted during the war. During the first mobilization in July 1914, the male workforce declined by 594, to 2,402, in just a month. Although management gradually replaced these workers, another call-up of the same magnitude took place in the spring of 1916. A disproportionate number of skilled workers from "hot" shops were recruited, including 159 foundry workers in July 1915 and 316 rolled metal workers in the spring of 1916.[153]

Management used the threat of military conscription to discipline employees. One worker recalled that, "the factory regime became more severe than earlier. For the slightest offense one could be sent to the front."[154] The extent to which management and the Okhrana used conscription to punish worker activists is not clear, but the loss of skilled workers generally had an adverse effect on war profits. In October 1916 management appealed to government officials, complaining that, "eight hundred workers have been called to war, the majority of whom are skilled workers" while "all requests and efforts" to recall employees from the front had failed. The letter suggested that calling back workers from the front "gives us the possibility of fulfilling urgent defense orders on time and almost twice as fast." Management's entreaties eventually bore fruit. "In agreement with the resolution of the factory meeting for the Moscow region," wrote a Lieutenant General, 206 workers "shall be returned from the army to the stated factory."[155]

The shortage of skilled labor led Guzhon to use his position of authority with the War Department to import skilled workers from Riga, paradoxically a Bolshevik stronghold. Riga in 1914 had eclipsed Moscow in strikes commemorating Bloody Sunday (9 January 1905) with almost forty thousand workers participating compared with just seven thousand in Moscow.[156] One Riga metalworker wrote that an official from the War Department and an engineer from Guzhon arrived at his factory in the fall of 1915 and ordered seventy army reserves to work at the Moscow Metalworks. "We decided we would go only under the condition that they gave us a written agreement to guarantee that our real pay and other conditions in Moscow would be no worse than in Riga." Such a demand was not enough to scare Guzhon management, though Riga workers, according to this metalworker, would be the main instigators of the December 1916 strike in the factory.[157]

Guzhon also deployed prisoner-of-war labor to deal with the shortage. In August 1916 management reported to the factory inspector that 275 Austrian prisoners of war had arrived and were living in barracks in the factory yard.[158] Workers' memoirs also note Ruthenian, Czech, and Slovak prisoners working in the factory.[159] One worker wrote that prisoners had been "kept under brutal continuous supervision" in the wooden barracks, but that he had become "good friends with a few of the prisoners" and often went to their barracks with his balalaika to play music with them.[160] In contrast, the future Bolshevik factory secretary expressed frustration in dealing with those who did not understand Russian.[161] Another account noted that Austrian prisoners working in the rolled metal shop had been kept at a distance by native employees, "but later when they started to speak Russian, workers became very friendly with them and treated them well."[162]

An outpouring of nationalist sentiment at the start of the war helped set the stage for anti-German riots in May 1915. The political context for the unrest was the Russian withdrawal from Przemysl. "Instead of giving way to despondency, as after previous defeats, public opinion is protesting, quivering with indignation, demanding penalties and remedies, and affirming its determination to win," the French ambassador recorded just two days before the outbreak of riots.[163] Rumors of German wrecking activities in munitions factories were rampant, and city officials inflamed the xenophobia by issuing orders that no foreign language was to be used in telephone conversations and that all German signs were to be removed.[164] Mayor General A.A. Adrianov's report on the causes of the riot stated that six workers at the Trekhgornaia mill had died of intestinal sickness and another 140 became sick. As rumors quickly spread that German spies had poisoned the water, exaggerated casualty counts climbed to sixty deaths and three hundred sick workers. At the Giubner mill, workers struck on 26 May and demanded the firing of several Alsatian employees, then Tsindel' mill workers also struck and demanded the firing of German personnel, arguing that while the German military used asphyxiating gas at the front, within Russia the Kaiser's spies were using poison.[165]

On the night of 27 May, according to *Russkoe slovo*, workers at the Tsindel' and Shrader mills attacked German office workers in their apartments. The next morning, a small crowd gathered near Borovitskii Gates with Russian flags and portraits of the Tsar. They sang "God Save the Tsar," and shouted, "Long Live the Emperor, Our Ruler, and Russian Army." As they headed for Red Square, new groups joined them. At the outset, leaders herded small numbers of rioters from store to store; where proprietors could prove that they were neither German nor Austrian, their stores were left alone. But after the crowd grew to a "colossal size" of thousands, including many who were intoxicated, riot leaders lost their authority.[166] A Guzhon participant in the riots also noted that at first, "among the pogromists there were those who indicated which stores to tear apart."[167]

The anti-German riots grew in size and ferocity, eventually spreading throughout Moscow. City Duma speakers addressing an emergency session on 28 May 1915 warned of the "threatening character" because rioters started to loot Russian as well as German firms and forty fires raged throughout the city.[168] The riots illustrate the volatile shift in popular opinion during the war. The French ambassador noted that press reports did not accurately capture the crowds' political sentiments. Whereas the capture of Przemysl two months earlier had led to prayer services with portraits of the Tsar in Red Square, the May riots expressed strong indignation against the autocracy. The crowd in Red Square "insulted the royal family, demanded that the Empress should be incarcerated in a convent, the Emperor deposed and the crown transferred to the Grand Duke Nicholas, Rasputin hung, etc."[169] Despite the presence of troops on the streets of Moscow, the disturbances continued for two more days. Moscow Duma member M.M. Novikov wrote that troops had fired on a crowd near Pokrovskii Bridge in Lefortovo, killing twelve and wounding thirty.[170]

City authorities were horrified by the scope of the riots and preferred to have workers at their benches. In an emergency session of the Moscow City Duma, Constitutional Democrat (Kadet) N. Astrov compared the events to 1905 and asked, "When will it end?" *Russkoe slovo* printed an appeal from 150 Kerting Brothers workers who demanded the sequestering of German firms for the Russian people and protested against their ruin and destruction. The appeal included a donation "to our brothers in the front positions who are holding back the most evil enemy."[171] *Utro Rossii* weighed the military sacrifices at the front with those required by industry, saying that enterprises needed "every worker standing by his bench."[172]

Moscow Metalworks employees participated in the riots. Management disingenuously stated to the factory inspector six weeks later "none of the Moscow Metalworks Company office staff or workers left the factory."[173] The Okhrana, however, reported that on 29 May, "after the pogrom incidents in Moscow, none of the factories returned to operation" for fear that employees would leave work to participate in the riots.[174] One memoir claimed, "Many Guzhon workers participated in the procession," including one worker who announced: "We just smashed the Keller Factory and now we are going to burn the Vogay Warehouse."[175] One riot participant wrote that, "a rumor spread that the tea-weighing factory 'Caravan,' a German firm, was on fire." Workers stopped work and ran to Caravan: "I saw many people grabbing tea and sugar ... I also decided to take tea."[176] Another Guzhon worker recalled seeing "workers from the Guzhon factory had loaded up a whole sack of goods." After the riots had ended, "the police entered apartments and arrested those who had participated in the looting. In a short time many people were arrested, as participants of the pogrom started to inform on each other."[177]

Many of the riot participants were working-class men, but the press and authorities were especially appalled that even women and youth looted businesses. *Utro Rossii* exclaimed that "women and suspicious-looking youths" had pillaged stores.[178] The vicious actions of a small number of thugs apparently contrasted with the festive atmosphere among the majority of participants. A Duma member claimed to have seen "many very young people" participating with happy faces "like it was Easter night." Another Duma member saw a crowd near Red Square that was "mainly youths and women."[179] *Russkoe slovo* also claimed "women and juveniles started grabbing piles of goods from the pogrom places." Nor were all those who stole goods proletarian: "Soon after darkness," the same account noted, "you began to see even well-dressed people with looted goods on the streets."[180]

More scandalous than the crowd's composition was the role of the police. In the emergency Duma session Mayor Guchkov accused the police of negligence. "Police officers stood peacefully in their places smoking their cigarettes, talking, joking and doing nothing to return Moscow to peace," he charged.[181] "At first," wrote the French ambassador, "police let the rioters do as they liked" but later "the agitation assumed such a scale that it has become necessary to suppress it by force."[182] A British citizen visiting Moscow claimed that he had seen "the Governor-General of Moscow himself seated on his horse, quietly watching the pogrom of large German firms. Neither he nor the group of police officials around him were making any attempt to stop the rioters."[183] Moscow Duma deputy M.M. Novikov confirmed police involvement in the riots. Among the wounded was a policeman from the Lefortovo precinct who had been in the front row of the demonstration. Moreover, "in the preceding days the same policeman participated in the street demonstrations and pogroms and even led some of them."[184]

Memoirs similarly attest to official and police involvement in the riots. One worker wrote that socialist literature that circulated among workers after the riots had devoted "much attention to the State Duma and anti-German pogrom in Moscow," while another worker posited that the police had organized the riot in an attempt to create a "lift" because the war was dragging on. "Workers understood the police had organized it–this was clear."[185] Labor historian and socialist Margaret Dewar wrote that when she lived in Moscow in 1915, rumors spread that government agents and Black Hundreds had led the riots.[186]

The war and the anti-German riots demonstrate the volatility of workers' attitudes and actions. After a strike in solidarity with St. Petersburg workers in July 1914, the war broke the momentum of the labor movement, and management easily crushed the single isolated economic strike. Nationalist sentiment permeated the factory as workers participated in patriotic demonstrations, prayer services for the troops, and chauvinistic anti-German riots. Yet continued war losses, workers' deteriorating economic position, and their perception that gendarmes had led the riots and then arrested other participants all undermined the patriotic mood that had seemed so impregnable.

Renewed Worker Activism

Workers' memoirs indicate that after the riots the political mood began to change. "Soon after the pogroms in May 1915 were over," one activist recalled, "workers began to express their dissatisfaction with the war."[187] A Bolshevik activist wrote that "comrades again renewed work that had been interrupted" after the upheavals.[188] Another Guzhon worker described the deteriorating living standards and growing political anger against the regime: "Our skilled workers began discussions about political events ... that the Tsar was a fool incapable of governing and that Rasputin ruled Russia." The revolutionary underground became bolder, putting up political leaflets in the general lavatory near the sheet metal shop calling for "the overthrow of the Tsar, for arming workers. Frequently these included quotes from the speeches from the meetings of the State Duma by the Bolshevik deputies, because the newspapers did not publish the full text of these meetings."[189]

By the summer's end, the patriotic fervor had dissipated, giving way to a new round of militancy. Six hundred and fifty workers in the rolled metal shop struck for seven days in August 1915 and prevailed in the first substantial wartime economic stoppage, securing a small wage increase.[190] In a meeting of the Russian Council of Ministers on 2 September 1915, Minister of Internal Affairs N.B. Shcherbatov warned that, "The testimony of all agents is unanimous ... the labor movement will develop to an extent which will threaten the safety of the state." In Moscow the sentiment was "violently anti-government" and "workers and the population as a whole are gripped by some sort of madness and are like gunpowder." He complained that "authorities in Moscow have virtually no forces," and that those at their disposal were "far from reliable." Moreover, Moscow had a "wild band" of thirty thousand convalescent soldiers who clashed with police and freed prisoners. In the event of disorders, Shcherbatov feared, "this whole horde will be on the side of the crowd."[191]

On the following day Tsar Nicholas prorogued the Duma and triggered the largest wartime political strike wave in Moscow. Alexander Shliapnikov wrote that in Moscow during the late summer of 1915, rising prices and the dismissing of the State Duma led to "meetings and rallies everywhere."[192] Guzhon reported to the MSFMO that on 4 September 31,166 workers in sixty-one enterprises struck.[193] SR agitation again placed the Moscow Metalworks at the head of the movement as the entire factory struck in unison. On 5 September 1915, "workers in all departments appeared at work at the prescribed time, but then did not start work and without permission left the factory without issuing any kind of demands."[194] The Okhrana reported that three thousand Guzhon workers had "stopped work for two days in the form of a protest about the incident of interrupting the activity of the State Duma."[195]

This brief SR militancy during the war was exceptional, as their members in Moscow tended to be more conservative than in (now renamed) Petrograd. On 19 August 1914, SRs from Guzhon and other factories resolved that, because of "the liberationist character of the war," no attempt should be made to hinder it. Nevertheless, responding to the growth of antigovernment sentiment following the dismissal of the Duma, Moscow SRs shifted to the left, playing an important role in the September 1915 strike wave. On 3 September, the Moscow SRs issued an antigovernment proclamation calling for the creation of factory committees, but retreated again after another round of arrests. Moscow SRs convened to pass resolutions that de-emphasized strikes and demonstrations in favor of building their party organization.[196]

The Bolsheviks, on the other hand, were so weak in the district that in September 1916 their Moscow Committee decided to combine the Lefortovo and Rogozhskii districts that had a combined membership of only thirty-three: ten in Dinamo and smaller cells in Bari, Guzhon, Tsindel', and Postavshchik. Dinamo was the only cell that survived an Okhrana sweep in October, and went on to spark three political strikes in 1916.[197] The SRs' strategy of refraining from political strike action, together with the decimation of the Bolsheviks' organization helps explain the absence of overtly political stoppages for the duration of the prerevolutionary period.

Factory SRs also advocated participation in the War Industries Committees. The government and industrialists established the Committees in an attempt to co-opt workers into championing wartime production.[198] In Petrograd, the Bolsheviks managed to turn the War Industries Committees against the government by winning positions on an antiwar platform that openly denounced cooperation in the war. In Moscow, however, authorities prohibited preelection meetings.[199] One SR recalled, "the Bolsheviks were against workers participating in the War Industries Committees, but we had Socialist Revolutionaries who proved that it was necessary." Either apathy or possibly Bolshevik agitation caused an extremely weak initial response to the Committees as only 102 of 3,048 employees participated in their elections.[200]

SRs and other activists attempted to render the Committee an effective weapon in their confrontation with Guzhon. In May 1916, during the largest wartime economic strike, workers petitioned the War Industries Committee, complaining, "In the current conditions it is impossible to continue working." They also attempted to wield Guzhon's preeminent position among Moscow industrialists against him, asking the Committee "to take into account that the head of the factory, Iu. P. Guzhon, is also a member of the Moscow War Industries Committee." The petition also contained a patriotic aspect, requesting the workers' release and transfer to work at other defense enterprises.[201]

Seven economic strikes in the year and a half before 1917 demonstrate renewed labor confidence and improved organization in the face of Okhrana and management threats of reprisals. Two strikes in August 1915 involved 400 and 650 workers, extended beyond a single shop, and lasted nine and seven days respectively. A two-day strike in December 1915 involved nearly 500 workers. Strikes in 1916 were even stronger: 3,000 workers participated in a May stoppage, 760 struck in June, and more than 1,000 participated in an eight-day strike in September, with another 489 going out for six days in December.[202]

The May 1916 stoppage was the best organized of the wartime strikes. Plant managers, possibly sensing trouble, issued a factory announcement on 30 April that increased insurance benefits for workers and their dependents.[203] On 2 May three thousand employees stopped work and demanded a raise in the minimum rate from 2.5 to 4 rubles.[204] On the following day, according to management, some departments began work, but under threats from strikers in other shops the strike soon engulfed the entire factory. At 9:30 a.m., workers from all departments gathered at the main office and handed the factory administration a list of demands. These included: doubling sick pay; minimum wages of fifteen kopecks for apprentices and women, twenty-five kopecks for male workers, and thirty kopecks for skilled workers; ending work at 2:30 on Saturdays and the day before holidays; and issuing wages and bonus pay on Saturday.[205]

The new grievances reflected a demographic shift to a younger and more female workforce that had occurred during the war. Whereas on the eve of the war, teenage workers made up 15.7 percent of the workforce, two years later they constituted 26.6 percent. Similarly, the number of women had steadily increased from 193 in July 1914 to 363 in December 1916, an increase from 5.8 to 13.1 percent of the workforce, with women working in six shops instead of just two as they had earlier.[206] Thus, the project of forging unity against management necessitated the drawing up of more inclusive demands that addressed the concerns of an increasingly significant minority.

The strike apparently ended in at least a partial victory for the workers. The Okhrana reported on 3 May that after lunch, all workers with the exception of seven hundred workers in the rolled metal and repair shops returned to work.[207] Some workers expressed dissatisfaction with the results, and a subsequent 22-day strike by 760 workers in June was the longest of the pre-revolutionary period. One memoir describes the difficulties of maintaining such a long action because in "the third week of the strike, the morale of many workers suffered. Many were forced to sell their things to somehow survive." By the fifth week, many workers secretly returned to work, and by the sixth week "almost all" workers returned. Management managed to break the strike with "some comrades" not returning to work as they were "subject to repression."[208]

In the context of the rising working-class movement, such management tactics only encouraged more effective labor organization. The eight-day strike of more than a thousand workers in September and October 1916 shows the increased level of workers' solidarity, organization, and confidence. The Okhrana reported that this was the only strike in the district for the month.[209] To avoid victimization, shops elected delegates to meet with Guzhon and workers did not leave the plant. "We were Italian strikers," wrote one participant.[210] The strike started in the form casting and steel foundry shops on 26 September and spread to the bolt and cable shops the next day. Employment figures show that the strike included all employees in the four shops, including 123 women in three shops and 33 teenage laborers. This was also a well-timed strike, as management complained it caused delays in "orders for various items needed for state defense." Management was compelled to ask the inspector to certify that the strike had caused the holdup, reporting that on 5 October the strike had been "liquidated," but provided no details of the result.[211]

Form casting workers struck again a few weeks later. The six-day strike by almost five hundred workers in December was the last action of the prerevolutionary period, and again showed a high level of organization with solid participation of the entire shop and elected delegates to avoid victimization.[212] Workers demanded pay for days when it was impossible to work because the machines were frozen, and despite the threat of sending military reservists to the front, almost all workers in several shops struck.[213] The strike ended in a partial victory for the workers, as management conceded to some of the demands.[214]

Workers' activism in the Moscow Metalworks closely mirrored the contours of the Russian labor movement that went through three waves of militancy after the turn of the century. Aside from the repressive interlude following the 1905 Revolution and the more transitory retreats during the first months of the Russo-Japanese War and World War I, the normative posture of the Russian working class was combative. The first upsurge culminated in the 1905 Revolution in which almost two million workers struck. Few workers participated in strikes after 1907 but the Lena Goldfields massacre in April 1912 triggered the rebirth of labor activism. More than 700,000 workers participated in strikes in 1912; nearly 900,000 the following year; and over 1.3 million during the first seven months of 1914. The rise in patriotic sentiment at the start of the war brought a temporary decline in industrial unrest, but the third phase brought a resurgence of militancy, with over a half million workers engaged in strikes in 1915 and almost 900,000 in 1916.[215]

The class polarization evident throughout Russia society during this period reverberated powerfully in the Moscow Metalworks. From the Lena massacre in 1912 to the end of 1916, workers struck nineteen times, with nearly fifteen thousand employees participating. Eight of the strikes were overtly political and included over seven thousand workers.[216] The temporal delimiters to these volatile shifts in Moscow Metalworks workers' confidence can be discerned almost to the day. The defeat of the December 1905 rebellion and the start of World War I ushered in temporary periods of retreat. Bloody Sunday 9 January 1905, the Lena massacre, and the arrests after the May 1915 anti-German riots were turning points in which workers took the offensive.

Many workplace organizations—including those loyal to the Tsarist state—vied for employees' loyalty. The Zubatov movement, the factory elders system, and War Industry Committees illustrate the risks for employers of building labor associations from above. Workers' pressure from below gave each a dynamic more militant than originally intended by authorities. Yet the hardline strategy adopted by Guzhon and other captains of industry was hardly a viable alternative. Their policy of economic and political intransigence, combined with their failure to build and sustain loyal employee institutions, meant that they conceded participatory politics to the revolutionaries.

Worker involvement in political strikes began modestly, but showed a clear trajectory toward increasing radicalization and more effective organization. All the contemporary protagonists—nonparty workers, revolutionaries, management, the MSFMO, and the secret police—recognized that socialists played a leadership role in the thirty political strikes that took place between the Lena massacre and 1917. Believing that political and economic power resided at the point of production, members of the various Marxist parties concentrated their efforts in the factories, and strike activity was often determined by shop-level agitation for action. Only several hundred Moscow Metalworks employees participated in the political strikes that followed the April 1912 Lena massacre, the May Day 1912 strike, the June 1913 action in support of Baltic sailors, and the September 1913 repression of labor press in Moscow. The three political strikes in early 1914 included 500, 1,120, and 1,500 workers respectively and the entire workforce struck after the Tsar prorogued the Duma in September 1915. Employees refrained from the five political strike waves in 1916 because the SRs adopted a more conservative, patriotic stance and focused their efforts on economic issues. If caution and pragmatism marked SR policy, audacity and tenacity defined Bolshevism, but repeated Okhrana sweeps meant they paid a heavy price for their boldness.

Workers, however, were not passive recipients to socialist agitation. Prior to 1917, most workers did not show loyalty to any particular party. The salient question is, why were Russian workers so receptive to revolutionaries' call to action? The "us against them" mentalité increasingly evident among groups of workers was rooted in the commonality of their workplace experiences and the failure of political and economic reforms. Moreover, the unyielding and repressive management strategy paradoxically encouraged subversion and fostered strong solidarity. With the threat of arrests and conscription, the choice was either to acquiesce or improve their organization to deter victimization. Fluctuations in workforce divisions coincided with the waves of retreat and advance in labor movement power. When workers went on the offensive in 1905, after the Lena massacre, and again in the summer of 1915, the tendency was for various divisions between shops, between older and younger workers, and between male and female workers to weaken and for workers to develop bold strategies to counter management and the Okhrana. Conversely, when workers were pushed onto the defensive, sectional interests were reinforced, repression became more effective, and fear and suspicion dominated the workplace. By 1916 workers' demands had become noticeably more inclusive, supporting grievances of women and younger workers, moving beyond the confines of single shops, and electing representatives to strengthen interdepartmental cooperation.

Though the Moscow Metalworks was swept up in the rising tide of workers' militancy in the Russian empire, in his own enterprise Iulii Petrovich Guzhon maintained an advantage in the conflict between capital and labor during the prerevolutionary years. The war years were the best of times for Guzhon as company profits doubled in the first fiscal year of the war and again in the second year.[217] But it was workers who paid for this profit, their wages falling in an almost inverse ratio to their owner's increasing prosperity. By March 1917 real wages were half of what they had been four years earlier,[218] and as one worker memoir notes, employees seemed increasingly aware that Guzhon's earnings during the war had come at their expense.[219] Ultimately, the hard-line strategy of war profiteering came at a price that could not be measured in rubles. It fueled workers' fierce hatred toward their bosses and contributed to the widening chasm between rulers and ruled in a society increasingly divided along class lines.

Notes

1. *Pravda*, 30 May 1913, cited in Lenin, *Collected Work* (Moscow, 1977), 19: 125.
2. *Pravda*, 30 May, 2, 5, 9 June 1913, cited in Lenin, *Collected Works*, 19: 125-131.
3. *Pravda*, 30 May, 2, 5, 9 June 1913, cited in Lenin, *Collected Works*, 19: 125-131.
4. Leopold Haimson, "The Problem of Social Stability in Urban Russia, 1905-1917" (part 1) *Slavic Review* 23 (December 1964): 619-42; (part 2) 24 (March 1965): 1-22.
5. Leon Trotsky, *The History of the Russian Revolution*, 3 vols. (New York, 1998), 1: 3-15.
6. Koenker, *Moscow Workers*, 25-26. Chase, *Workers, Society, and the Soviet State*, 106.
7. I.L. Kornakovskii, *Zavod 'Serp i Molot' 1883-1932: Opyt Istoriko-Sotsiologicheskogo Issledovanniia* (Moscow, 1979), 36-41.
8. Jeremiah Schneiderman, *Sergei Zubatov and Revolutionary Marxism* (Ithaca NY, 1976), 150. GARF, f. 7952, op. 3, d. 273, l. 91. F.I Karpukhin memoir.
9. Kornakovskii, *Zavod 'Serp i Molot' 1883-1932*, 46.
10. Schneiderman, *Serge Zubatov and Revolutionary Marxism*, 150.
11. GARF, f. 63, op. 35, d. 444. ll. 45-6. Okhrana report, 29 May 1915.
12. The Lefortovo Okhrana reported on the factory.
13. TsGAMO, f. 186, op. 3, d. 3, ll. 1-17. Employment statistics by shop, Moscow Metalworks; RGIAgM, f. 498, op. 1, d. 229, ll. 5-6. 1914 factory management report to factory inspector on departments, n.d. 1914.
14. GARF, f. 7952, op. 3, d. 274, l. 34. P. V. Leshkovtsev memoir.
15. GARF, f 7952, op. 3, d. 275, l. 10. P. V. Lavrenov memoir.
16. GARF, f. 7952, op. 3, d. 209, l. 25. Workers' passports from 1898. Koenker, *Moscow Workers*, 47-48.
17. GARF, f. 7952, op. 3, d. 209, ll. 24-25. Wage and age (as of 1905) statistics collected after revolution.
18. GARF, f. 7952, op. 3, d. 276, l. 45 P. I. Tarasov memoir.
19. GARF, f. 7952, op. 3, d. 209, l. 70. Rogozhskii district Moscow Committee of the RSDWP leaflet, n.d. 1905
20. GARF, f 7952, op. 3, d. 271, l. 234. E.I. Voronina memoir; TsGAMO, f. 186, op. 3, d. 3, ll. 1-12. Employment statistics by shop.
21. TsGAMO, f. 2122, op. 1, d. 248, ll. 4-8. Wage categories in the Moscow Metalworks.
22. GARF, f. 7952, op. 3, d. 272, l. 60. N.I. Igorov memoir. Igorov claims that women already working in the department participated in the laughter.
23. GARF, f. 7952, op. 3, d. 209, l. 30. Prerevolutionary document collection.
24. Laura Engelstein, *Moscow 1905* (Stanford, 1982), 56-57.
25. Kornakovskii, *Zavod 'Serp i Molot' 1883-1932*, 43.
26. Engelstein, *Moscow 1905*, 56-57.
27. Schneiderman, *Sergei Zubatov and Revolutionary Marxism*, 99-134.
28. Schneiderman, *Sergei Zubatov and Revolutionary Marxism*, 151.
29. GARF, f. 7952, op. 3, d. 275, l. 10. P.V. Lavrentov memoir.
30. Schneiderman, *Sergei Zubatov and Revolutionary Marxism*, 141-172, 350; GARF, f. 7952, op. 3, d. 275, l. 10. P.V. Larvrenov memoir.
31. Schneiderman, *Sergei Zubatov and Revolutionary Marxism*, 173-192.
32. Orlando Figes, *A Peoples Tragedy* (New York, 1996), 174-178.
33. Figes, *A Peoples Tragedy*, 179-187.
34. *Martenovka*, 19 December 1925. GARF, f. 7952, op. 3, d. 209, l. 61.
35. Engelstein, *Moscow 1905*, 61.
36. *Martenovka*, 19 December 1925. GARF, f. 7952, op. 3, d. 209, l. 61.
37. Lenin, *Collected Works*, 9: 23-57.
38. Theodore Dan, *The Origins of Bolshevism* (New York, 1964), 332.
39. Michael Melancon, *The Socialist Revolutionaries and the Russian Anti-War Movement, 1914-17* (Columbus, 1990).
40. GARF, f. 7952, op. 3, d. 271, l. 7. M.M. Avdeev memoir.
41. Engelstein, *Moscow 1905*, 64-73.
42. Engelstein, *Moscow 1905*, 73-229.

43. GARF, f. 7952, op. 3, d. 209, l. 70. 1905 RSDWP leaflet, n.d. *Martenovka*, 19 December 1925.

44. Thomas Owen, *Capitalism and Politics in Russia* (Cambridge, 1981), 186, 199-202.

45. RGIAgM, f. 526, op. 1, d. 24, l. 79. Guzhon letter to MSFMO, 15 March 1914.

46. Figes, *A People's Tragedy*, 224.

47. David Lane, *The Roots of Russian Communism* (Assen, 1969), 104, Leon Trotsky, *Stalin* (New York, 1941), 95.

48. Lenin, *Collected Works*, 17: 581; 34: 411.

49. GARF, f. 7952, op. 3, d. 275, l. 17. P.V. Lazrenov memoir.

50. GARF, f. 7952, op. 3, d. 271, l. 35. V.N. Arapov memoir.

51. GARF, f. 7952, op. 3, d. 276, l. 12. I.F. Toptov memoir.

52. GARF, f. 7952, op. 3, d. 273, 1. 97. Kochergin memoir.

53. GARF, f. 7952, op. 3, d. 271, l. 34. V.N. Arapov memoir.

54. GARF, f. 7952, op. 3, d. 275, ll. 48-49. S.S. Leshkovtsev memoir.

55. Leopold Haimson and Eric Brian, "Labor Unrest in Imperial Russia," in *Strikes, Social Conflict and the First World War*, Leopold Haimson and Giulio Sapelli, eds. (Milan, 1992), 444.

56. GARF, f. 7952, op. 3, d. 273, l. 94. Kochergin memoir.

57. GARF, f. 7952, op. 3, d. 274, ll. 39-40. P.L. Lavrent'ev memoir.

58. *Ocherki istorii Moskovskoi organizatsii KPSS, 1883-1945*, 2 vols. (Moscow, 1966), 1:257.

59. Tony Cliff, *Lenin: Building the Party* (London, 1975), 318.

60. GARF, f. 7952, op. 3, d. 276, l. 12. I. F. Toptov memoir.

61. GARF, f. 7952, op. 3, d. 271, l. 39; V. N. Arapov memoir.

62. Leon Trotsky, "Report on the World Economic Crisis and the New Tasks of the Communist International," in *First Five Years of the Communist International*, 2 vols. (New York, 1972), 1: 210.

63. Michael Melancon, "The Ninth Circle: The Lena Goldfield Workers and the Massacre of 4 April 1912," *Slavic Review* 53:3 (fall 1994): 786-795.

64. Robert McKean, *St. Petersburg Between the Revolutions: Workers and Revolutionaries, June 1907-February 1917* (New Haven, 1990), 495; Haimson and Brian, "Labor Unrest," 444.

65. GARF, f. 63, op. 32, d. 1497, l. 22. Okhrana report, 12 June 1912.

66. *Pravda*, 26 April 1912.

67. GARF, f. 7952, op. 3, d. 265, l. 17. Seruev recollection; d. 271, l. 306. S.S. Gerasimov memoir; d. 274, ll. 40, 103. P.L. Lavrent'ev, I. Lidvanskii memoirs; d. 275, ll. 17, 49. P.V. Lazrenov, S. S. Leshkovtsev memoirs; RGASPI f. 70, op. 3, d. 150, l. 88, F.I. Karpukhin recollections of RSDWP in Rogozhskaia district, 1906-1917. "Recollection" denotes a speech or summary that is *not* part of the Hammer and Sickle Factory memoir collection. The SRs organized a separate protest, in which, according to one member, "we brought out workers from all the shops." GARF, f. 7952, op. 3, d. 273, l. 96, Kochergin memoir.

68. *Kommunisticheskoi partii Sovietskogo Soiuza*, 5 vols. (Moscow 1966), 2:381.

69. TsMAM f. 176, op. 2, d. 7, ll. 2-5. Okhrana reports released in 1917.

70. GARF, f. 63, op. 32, d. 1497, ll. 10- 23. Okhrana reports, 12 June 1912, 13 March 1913.

71. GARF, f. 63, op. 32, d. 1488, ll. 1-9. Okhrana report, 25 May 1912; d. 1489, ll. 1-10. Okhrana report, 22 May 1912.

72. GARF, f. 63, op. 33, d. 1206, ll. 1-17. Okhrana reports, 27, 28 August 1912.

73. GARF, f. 63, op. 32, d. 448. Okhrana reports, April, May 1912.

74. GARF, f. 7952, op. 3, d. 275, l. 49. S. S. Leshkovtsev memoir.

75. GARF, f. 7952, op. 3, d. 257, l. 72. I.M. Lidvanskii recollection; d. 271, l. 306, S.S. Gerasimov memoir; d. 273, l. 5; P.N. Klimanov memoir; d. 274, l. 40, P.L Lavrent'ev memoir; d. 275, l. 5. P.V. Lazrenov memoir.

76. GARF, f. 63, op. 32, d. 934, ll. 1, 7, 8, 13, 16; d. 1019 l. 3, d. 1422, l.1; d. 1573, l.1, 1578, l. 5. Okhrana reports 1912.

77. GARF, f. 7952, op. 3, d. 256, l. 33. Kochergin recollection.

78. GARF, f. 63, op. 32, d. 1645, ll. 1-8. Okhrana reports, November 1912.

79. McKean, *St. Petersburg between the Revolutions*, 495-496.

80. GARF, f. 7952, op. 3, d. 276, l. 13. I.F. Toptov memoir; d. 256, l. 89, Kochergin recollection.
81. GARF, f. 63, op. 33, d. 458, ll. 1-34. Okhrana reports, 13 May 1913, 4 October 1914.
82. TsAODM, f. 429, op. 1, d. 1, l. 1. List of factory May Day participants.
83. GARF, f. 7952, op. 3, d. 263, l. 182. P. N. Klimanov recollection.
84. See GARF, f. 63, op. 32-36 (1912-1916).
85. Victor Serge, *What Everyone Should Know About State Repression* (London, 1979), 8.
86. Alexander Shliapnikov, *On the Eve of 1917, Recollections from the Revolutionary Underground* (London, 1982) 100; Shliapnikov, *Kanun samnadsatogo goda*, 2 vols. (Moscow-Petrograd 1923) 1:10-11.
87. *Ocherki istorii Moskovskoi organizatsii KPSS, 1883-1945*, 1:334.
88. Victoria Bonnell, *Roots of Rebellion: Workers' Politics and Organizations in Petersburg and Moscow, 1900-1914* (Berkeley, 1983), 417-427.
89. Celilia Bobrovskaya, *Twenty Years in Underground Russia* (Chicago, 1978), 222-223.
90. Shliapnikov, *Kanun semnadtsatogo goda*, 1: 292.
91. G.A. Arutiunov, *Rabochie dvizhenie v Rossii v periode novogo revoliutsionnogo pod'ema 1910-1914 godov* (Moscow, 1975), 214.
92. Tony Cliff, *Lenin: All Power to the Soviets* (London, 1975), 28.
93. GARF, f. 7952, op. 3, d. 273, l. 98. Kochergin memoir.
94. GARF, f. 63, op. 32, d. 1142, ll. 1-2, 9. Okhrana telephone dispatches, 12, 17, 21 July 1912.
95. GARF, f. 7952, op. 3, d. 255, l. 83. Ermolaev recollection.
96. GARF, f. 63, op. 32, d. 1142, ll. 8, 16. Okhrana telephone dispatch, 20 July 1912; Moscow Metalworks Company announcement, 25 July 1912.
97. TsGAMO, f. 186, op. 3, d. 3, l. 12. Monthly employment figures.
98. GARF, f. 63, op. 32, d. 1148, ll. 12, 22. Okhrana telephone dispatch, 26 July 1912; Okhrana report, 1 August 1912. Under questioning, the two accused leaders denied intimidating strikebreakers.
99. GARF, f. 63, op. 32, 1722, l. 18. Okhrana report, 27 July 1912.
100. GARF, f. 63, op, 32, d. 1148, ll. 6-7. Moscow Metalworks announcements, 17 July 1912.
101. GARF, f. 63, op. 32, d. 1148, l. 11. Okhrana report, 21 July 1912.
102. GARF, f. 63, op. 32, d. 1148, ll. 18-19; d. 1206, ll. 11, 19-32. Okhrana reports, August and September 1912.
103. GARF, f. 63, op. 32, d. 1148, l. 18. Okhrana report, 3 August 1912.
104. GARF, f. 7952, op. 3, d. 255, l. 83. Ermolaev recollection.
105. GARF, f. 7952, op. 3, d. 276, l. 13. I. F. Toptov memoir.
106. GARF, f. 63, op. 32 (1912), d. 1645, ll. 74-217.
107. Nadezhda Krupskaya, in her preface to V.I. Lenin's *The Emancipation of Women* (New York, 1972), 5-6, explained how the perception of women as "backward" influenced Social Democratic practice during the 1890s: "The leaflets were usually addressed to the workmen. At that time the class-consciousness of the mass of the workers was still little developed, the most backward among them being workingwomen. They received very low wages and their rights were flagrantly violated. So the leaflets were usually addressed to the men..."
108. McKean, *St. Petersburg between the Revolutions*, 495. GARF, f. 63, op. 32, d. 1645, ll. 7, 8, 74-76, 97, 150-152. Okhrana reports, November 1912.
109. GARF, f. 63, op. 33, d. 1399, l. 38. Okhrana report, 3 April 1913.
110. GARF, f. 63, op. 33, d. 1399, ll. 44-45. Okhrana report, 4 April 1913.
111. RGIAgM, f. 1076, op. 1, d. 17. l. 31; TsMAM f. 526, op. 1, d. 24, l. 24. Guzhon letter to MSFMO, 1 May 1914.
112. GARF, f. 63, op. 33, d. 1399, ll. 113-115, 171, 209. Okhrana reports, June 1913.
113. RGIAgM, f. 1076, op. 1, d. 17, l. 15. Guzhon letter, 12 July 1913.
114. GARF, f. 63, op. 32, d. 191 T2, l. 494. Okhrana report, 2 October 1913.
115. Robert Thurston, *Liberal City, Conservative State, Moscow and Russia's Urban Crisis, 1906-1914* (New York, 1987), 115.
116. Arutiunov, *Rabochee dvizhenie v Rossii*, 374.

117. GARF, f. 63, op. 33, d. 338, ll. 43-4; d. 1399, l. 141; d. 1400, ll. 210-211. Okhrana reports, 1913.
118. GARF, f. 7952, op. 3, d. 275, l. 79. M.G. Ob"edkov memoir. GARF, f. 7952, op. 3, d. 256, ll. 47-60, d. 273, l. 97. F.I. Karpukhin recollection and memoir.
119. GARF, f. 7952, op. 3, d. 265, l. 23. Klimanov recollection.
120. Bonnell, *Roots of Rebellion*, 415.
121. GARF, f. 7952, op. 3, d. 256, ll. 47-60; d. 273, l. 97. F. I. Karpukhin recollection and memoir.
122. RGIAgM, f. 498, op. 1, d. 241, l. 14. Factory announcement, 12 August 1911.
123. RGIAgM, f. 2322, op. 1, d. 3, ll. 52-60. Annual factory summaries.
124. *Pravda*, 18 March 1914.
125. GARF, f. 7952, op. 3, d. 256, l. 54, d. 275, l. 91, d. 76, l. 59. F. I. Karpukhin recollection; M. G. Ob"edkov, and E. D. Tumanov memoirs.
126. Bonnell, *Roots of Rebellion*, 358, 386-389.
127. RGIAgM, f. 526, op. 1, d. 24, ll. 79, 81. Guzhon reports to MSFMO, 14, 19 March 1914.
128. RGIAgM, f. 1076, op. 1, d. 17. l. 31. Guzhon letter to MSFMO, 1 May 1914.
129. Haimson and Brian, "Labor Unrest," 444-448.
130. McKean, *St. Petersburg Between the Revolutions*, 297-317.
131. RGIAgM, f. 498, op. 1, d. 211, l. 5. Management letter to factory inspector, 26 April 1914.
132. TsGAMO, f. 186, op. 3, d. 3, l. 14. Shop employees per month.
133. RGIAgM, f. 498, op. 1, d. 211, l. 10. Management letter to factory inspector, 8 July 1915.
134. RGIAgM, f. 1076, op. 1, d. 17, l. 45. Vice president letter to MSFMO, 12 July 1914.
135. RGIAgM, f. 498, op. 1, d. 195, ll. 251-253; d. 211, ll. 10-12. Factory management letters to factory inspector 8, 9, 10 July 1914.
136. TsGAMO, f. 186, op. 3, d. 3, l. 14. Monthly employment statistics.
137. GARF, f. 7952, op. 3, d. 273, l. 91. F.I Karpukhin memoir.
138. GARF, f. 7952, op. 3, d. 275, l. 91. M.G. Ob"edkov memoir.
139. Haimson and Brian, "Labor Unrest," 446.
140. GARF, f. 7952, op. 3, d. 209, l. 24. Factory list of wartime strikes.
141. GARF, f. 63, op. 32, d. 191 T4 ll. 249, 278, 344, 380; T5 ll. 50, 103, 130, 182. Monthly Okhrana reports 1914-1915.
142. GARF, f. 7952, op. 3, d. 271, l. 38. V.N. Arapov memoir.
143. RGIAgM, f. 2322, op. 1, d. 3, l. 246. Report of monthly wages, 8 May 1916.
144. GARF, f. 7952, op. 3, d. 276, l. 117. E.D. Tumanov memoir.
145. GARF, f. 7952, op. 3, d. 256, l. 86. Kochergin recollection.
146. GARF, f. 63, op. 35, d. 25 T1, l. 88. Okhrana report 15 April 1915.
147. GARF, f. 63, op. 35, d. 191 T5, l. 263. Okhrana report, 4 May 1915.
148. RGIAgM, f. 498, op. 1, d. 229, l. 20. Management letter to factory inspector, 15 April 1915.
149. RGIAgM, f. 2322, op. 1, d. 3, l. 246. Monthly wages reported on 8 May 1916.
150. RGIAgM, f. 1076, op. 1, d. 17, l. 62. MSFMO vice president letter to MSFMO, 20 April 1915.
151. GARF, f. 7952, op. 3, d. 209, l. 24. Factory statistics collected after Revolution.
152. GARF, f. 7952, op. 3, d. 265, l. 81. Kochergin recollection.
153. TsGAMO, f. 186, op. 3, d. 3, ll. 14-16. Factory monthly employment statistics.
154. GARF, f. 7952, op. 3, d. 276, l. 14. I.F. Toptov memoir.
155. RGIAgM, f. 848, op. 1 d. 38, ll. 64-65. Letters dated 27 October, 1 November 1916.
156. GARF, f. 102, ch. 4, op. 122, d. 144, l. 114. Department of Police report, February 1914.
157. GARF, f. 7952, op. 3, d. 271, ll. 221-222. I.Ia. Bredis memoir.
158. RGIAgM, f. 498, op. 1, d. 249, l. 14. Management letter to the factory inspector, 13 August 1916.
159. GARF, f. 7952, op. 3, d. 271, l. 41. V.N. Arapov memoir; d. 274, l. 41. S.S. Leshkovets memoir; d. 276, l. 60. E.D. Tumanov memoir.
160. GARF, f. 7952, op. 3, d. 271, l. 41. V.N. Arapov memoir.
161. GARF, f. 7952, op. 3, d. 276, l. 60. I.D. Tumanov memoir.

162. GARF, f. 7952, op. 3, d. 275, l. 92. M.G. Ob"edkov memoir.
163. Maurice Paléologue, *An Ambassador's Memoirs* (New York, 1925), 10-11.
164. Allan Monkhouse, *Moscow 1911-1933* (Boston, 1934), 48.
165. *Russkoe slovo*, 2 December 1915.
166. *Russkoe slovo*, 31 May 1915.
167. GARF, f. 7952, op. 3, d. 275, ll. 18-19. P. V. Lazrenov memoir.
168. RGIAgM, f. 179, op. 22, d. 3384, ll. 252-266. Moscow Duma meeting minutes, 28 May 1915.
169. Paléologue, *An Ambassador's Memoirs*, 11-12.
170. RGIAgM, f. 179, op. 3, d. 62a, l. 13. M. Novikov letter, 3 June 1915.
171. *Russkoe slovo*, 30 May 1915.
172. *Utro Rossii*, 30 May 1915.
173. RGIAgM, f. 498, op. 1, d. 229, l. 24. Management letter to factory inspector, 27 June 1915.
174. GARF, f. 63, op. 32, d. 191 T5, l. 277. Okhrana report, 4 June 1915.
175. GARF, f. 7952, op. 3, d. 271, l. 39. V.N. Arapov memoir.
176. GARF, f. 7952, op. 3, d. 275, ll. 18-19. P.V. Lazrenov memoir.
177. GARF, f. 7952, op. 3, d. 274, l. 54. A.F. Kuznetsov memoir.
178. *Utro Rossii*, 29 May 1915.
179. RGIAgM, f. 179, op. 22, d. 3384, ll. 258, 269, Moscow City Duma meeting, 28 May 1915.
180. *Russkoe slovo*, 31 May 1915.
181. RGIAgM, f. 179, op. 22, d. 3384, l. 264, Moscow City Duma meeting, 28 May 1915.
182. Paléologue, *An Ambassador's Memoirs*, 11. A similar description of the police as "completely passive" at the start of the riot is in Serge Sergeevich Oldenburg's *Tsartvovaia Imperator Nokolaya II* (Belgrade, 1939), 2: 168.
183. Allan Monkhouse, *Moscow 1911-1933* (Boston, 1934), 48.
184. RGIAgM, f. 179, op. 3, d. 62a, l. 13. M. Novikov letter to mayor, 3 June 1915.
185. GARF, f. 7952, op. 3, d. 271, l. 39, d. 274, l. 41. V.N. Arapov, P.L. Lavrent'ev memoirs.
186. Margaret Dewar, *The Quiet Revolutionary* (London, 1989), 56.
187. GARF, f. 7952, op. 3, d. 275, l. 19. P.V. Lazrenov memoir.
188. GARF, f. 7952, op. 3, d. 276, l. 14. I.F. Toptov memoir.
189. GARF, f. 7952, op. 3, d. 273, l. 39. F.I. Karpukhin memoir.
190. RGEA f. 9597 op. 1, d. 16, l. 42; M.I. Gil'berg history of Guzhon factory.
191. Michael Cherniavsky, ed., *Prologue to Revolution* (Englewood Cliffs, New Jersey, 1967), 234-237.
192. Alexander Shliapnikov, *On the Eve of 1917*, 101.
193. RGIAgM, f. 179, op. 21, d. 3391, l. 153; Guzhon letter to MSFMO, n.d. September 1915.
194. RGIAgM, f. 498, op. 1, d. 241, l. 4. Management letter to factory inspector, 5 September 1915.
195. GARF, f. 63, op. 32, d. 191 T5, l. 263. Okhrana report, 2 October 1915.
196. Melancon, *The Socialist Revolutionaries and the Russian Anti-War Movement*, 67- 81.
197. L. A. Karlova, *Istoriia zavoda "Dinamo"* (Moscow, 1961), 135-137.
198. Lewis Siegelbaum, *The Politics of Industrial Mobilization in Russia, 1914-1917. A Study of the War-Industries Committees* (London, 1983).
199. Tony Cliff, *Lenin: All Power to the Soviets*, 42.
200. GARF, f. 7952, op. 3, d. 255, ll. 84-5. Ermolaev recollection.
201. *Russkoe slovo*, 6 May 1916.
202. GARF, f. 7952, op. 3, d. 209, l. 24. List of factory economic strikes during the war that omits the May stoppage. GARF, f. 63, op. 33, d. 1403, l. 32, Okhrana report, 2 May 1916.
203. RGIAgM, f. 498, op. 1, d. 249, l. 9. Factory announcement, 30 April 1916.
204. GARF, f. 63, op. 33, d. 1403, l. 32. Okhrana report 2 May 1916.
205. GARF, f. 7952, op. 3, d. 210, l. 93. RGIAgM, f. 498, op. 1, d. 249, l. 7. Management report to factory inspector, 3 May 1916.
206. TsGAMO, f. 186, op. 3, d. 3, ll. 14-17. Factory employment statistics.

207. GARF, f. 63, op. 33, d. 1403, l. 34. Okhrana report, 3 May 1916.

208. GARF, f. 7952, op. 3, d. 275, ll. 19-20. P.V. Lazrenov memoir.

209. GARF, f. 63, op. 12, d. 191 T5, l. 578. Okhrana report for September 1916.

210. GARF, f. 7952, op. 3, d. 275, ll. 92-93. M.G. Ob"edkov memoir.

211. TsGAMO, f. 186, op. 3, d, 3, l. 16. Monthly employment statistics; RGIAgM, f. 498, op. 1, d. 272, l. 1. Management report to factory inspector, 11 October 1916.

212. GARF, f. 7952, op. 3, d. 209, l. 24.

213. GARF, f. 7952, op. 3, d. 257, ll. 1-2. P.N. Klimanov recollection.

214. GARF, f. 7952, op. 3, d. 274, l. 20. P.V. Lazrenov memoir.

215. Haimson and Brian, "Labor Unrest," 444-448.

216. Exact number of participants is problematic because of the discrepancy in sources. One shop-specific economic strike before the war is based on *Pravda* and two economic and May Day strikes are based on worker memoirs.

217. GARF, f. 7952, op. 3, d. 186, l. 23. Annual fiscal year profits (in rubles without inflation which approximately doubled between the beginning of 1913 to the end of 1916) were: 1910-1911: 316,700; 1911-1912: 497,000; 1912-1913: 551,100; 1913-1914: 755,800; 1914-1915: 1,399,000; 1915-1916: 2,980,800; 1916-1917: 1,687,000. GARF, f. 7952, op. 3, d. 185, l. 5 shows that factory output dropped each fiscal year. With 1913-1914 as a baseline (100 percent) the factory produced 15.383 million *puds* (one *pud* equals about 36 pounds) of steel products; in 1914-1915: 75.86 percent; in 1915-1916: 53.49 percent; in 1916-1917: 42.45 percent.

218. The average monthly worker wage was 43.5 rubles in June 1914, dropped to a low of 34.1 rubles in March 1915, increased to 59 rubles by September 1915, then starting falling again to 42.7 rubles in February 1916 (RGIAgM, f. 2322, op. 1, d. 3, l. 246). Total paid wages dropped from 2,238,092 in 1914-1915 to 1,865,017 the next year, even though the number of employees increased from 2,666 to 2,907 (RGIAgM, f. 176, op. 2, d. 2, l. 9) These wage figures do not include inflation, which had more than doubled (207.5 percent) from the beginning of 1913 to the end of 1916 (Iu. P. Bokarev, "*Rubl' v epokhu voinu i revoliiutsii*" in: *Russkii Rubl', Dva veka istorii XIX-XX v.v.* (Moscow, 1994), 178). Using March 1913 as a baseline of 100 percent, real wages dropped by March 1915, to 72.0 percent, increased slightly to 79.5 percent by March 1916, then fell to 53.3 percent by Mach 1917 (GARF, f. 7952, op. 3, d. 209, l. 24. Factory real wages for the prerevolutionary years).

219. GARF, f. 7952, op. 3, d. 271, l. 46. V.N. Arapov memoir.

2

REVOLUTION AND COLLECTIVE ACTION, CIVIL WAR AND PERSONAL SURVIVAL

"The workers made new threats of violence in the peacekeeping chamber."
— Management letter to the Provisional Government, 9 June 1917

At the beginning of 1917 the vast Russian empire was still ruled by the Romanov monarchy. Eight months later the Bolsheviks stood at the helm of the world's first workers' government. "You will not find another such sharp turn in history—especially if you remember that it involves a nation of 150 million people," wrote Leon Trotsky in the introduction to his classic work on the Russian Revolution. It was not merely the magnitude of the political upheaval or the rapidity of events, but the active intervention of ordinary people that made the revolt the most far-reaching social upheaval of the twentieth century.[1]

Class conflict defined the events of 1917, and those who labored in the factories were at the center of the rebellion. Unrest in the Moscow Metalworks exhibited all of the characteristics common to the Russian Revolution as a whole: the spontaneous flowering of a public political discourse, the rise of popular democracy, direct action and the threat of force, and the complete collapse of a possibility of compromise in a decisive confrontation between contending classes. While scholars have produced countless hundreds of books from a range of perspectives on the events of 1917, few present-day scholars would dispute the findings of social historians in the 1970s and 1980s that demonstrated that there was indeed a profound social transformation at the heart of the revolutionary process.[2] The compelling interpretive problem no longer concerns whether or not an authentic revolution occurred, but which social forces drove it forward?[3]

While the upheaval from 1917 to the end of the Civil War can be properly understood as a single, continuous running battle whose outcome determined who would rule Russian society, within the Moscow Metalworks three distinct periods marked the revolutionary era. First, between February and late June, employees battled with management over control of the factory. Second, during the summer, fundamental political questions came to the fore and in the Moscow Metalworks—as in the Russian working class as a whole—revolutionary politics rather than reform strategies dominated. Third, if the workers' movement of 1917 approximated the Marxist ideal of a united class, conscious of its power to collectively transform society, then the Civil War witnessed the opposite—the disintegration of proletarian unity and a regression to the politics of personal survival. This chapter, then, traces both the rise of the workers' powerful collective élan and its precipitous deterioration under conditions of intensifying deprivation.

February to June: The Workers' Movement versus Guzhon

The revolutionary year in Moscow started when thirty-one thousand workers went on strike to commemorate the twelfth anniversary of Bloody Sunday; including those in the Bolshevik stronghold of Dinamo.[4] Only 272 workers in the Moscow Metalworks participated in the stoppage, however, as neither the few Bolsheviks nor the SRs (because of their reluctance to strike) provided such a lead.[5] No one could have predicted that within a few weeks a spontaneous revolt would render the presence or absence of revolutionary agitation somewhat irrelevant.

The fall of Tsarism came swiftly in Petrograd. On International Women's Day (23 February), working-class women demonstrated outside the municipal Duma demanding bread. The next day, half the workforce of the city went on strike and government troops clashed with protesters. By 26 February, police had conceded the Vyborg side to the rebels, who then marched across the ice to the city center. Police fired on the demonstrators, killing forty, but large numbers of soldiers began to break ranks and side with the revolt. The liberal president of the Duma, Rodzianko, demanded that reliable troops be sent from the front to crush the rebellion, but by 27 February the entire garrison of 150,000 had already collapsed. The insurgents then freed political prisoners, arrested Tsarist ministers, and sacked the central headquarters of the Okhrana. On 2 March, Nicholas II abdicated his throne.[6]

The Petrograd rebellion triggered spontaneous strikes throughout Moscow. On 28 February 3,500 Metalworks employees left after lunch and "did not present any kind of demands. Order has been violated," reported the Okhrana.[7] One worker later took credit for spreading the news. "Under full steam, I ran from shop to shop and shouted, 'Down with the Tsar.' They asked me, 'Are you crazy?' I told them the whole story." After a hastily organized meeting, "everyone, like an avalanche, advanced through the main gate towards the city center." The festive atmosphere was shared even by the administration, which made no attempt to curtail the actions and "even congratulated us for the holiday." Shop loyalty (*tsekhovshchina*) predominated in the procession. "Workers from the form-casting and steel foundry shops were in the first two rows," wrote another worker. "I was in the third row with workers from our shop." [8]

Shortly after leaving the factory, the workers' contingent engaged the police in a violent confrontation on the bridge over the Iauza River. After noon, according to the Okhrana, the three thousand-strong contingent surged over the bridge "without incident" and headed toward the city center. Marching in an orderly procession, they returned from Taganskaia Square at six o'clock to the bridge over the Iauza. The "noisy, growing crowd" was too large for the police even to attempt to disperse as the throng shouted "Hooray!"[9] Conspicuously, the police report failed to explain why the crowd returned to the bridge that evening. After leaving the factory, the workers had been blocked by the police as they attempted to cross the bridge and in the first violent incident of the revolution in Moscow, the police shot Illarion Astakhov. Another Guzhon worker then "threw the police officer into the Iauza River" and the crowd proceeded "quietly to the Kremlin."[10] Another account also describes how workers disarmed the police and "threw the head of the gendarmes and his assistant from the bridge into the Iauza. The remaining police, who saw that they were powerless, fled."[11] One of the first acts of the newly created factory committee was to send a collection to Astakhov's parents.[12]

The February Revolution established a regime of "dual power" with two institutions vying for political supremacy. Believing that the revolution was "bourgeois," moderate Menshevik, SR, and even Bolshevik leaders of the Petrograd Soviet of Workers' and Soldiers' Deputies insisted that Duma representatives should form a Provisional Government. Because the Duma electoral laws heavily favored those with property, political parties of the bourgeoisie and the landowners (Kadets and Octobrists) dominated the new government. Throughout Russia, workers and soldiers had immediately reorganized the institutions of popular power from the 1905 Revolution: the soviets. The central contradiction of the February Revolution was that the upheaval from below had elevated to formal political power those pro-war political parties that possessed such profound contempt for the revolution. During the course of 1917, the institutional tension between the Provisional Government and the soviets became more pronounced as attempts to reconcile the elite prerogatives of wealth, property, and privilege and the desires of the dispossessed workers, soldiers, and peasants faltered, and then collapsed.[13]

Popular democracy emerged throughout Moscow as workers shut down factories, immersed themselves in newspapers and revolutionary literature, participated in political discussions and mass meetings, and elected representatives from their own ranks. Moscow Okhrana reports during the February Revolution confirm both workers' enthusiasm and the Okhrana's growing disorientation in the face of "urgent" events. As workers left their factories, held meetings, raised the red flag, and sang revolutionary songs, Okhrana dispatches on 28 February noted with consternation that strikers did not issue "any demands", the reports merely claimed "the cause was to protest the dissolution of the State Duma and lack of bread."[14] A few days later the Okhrana headquarters was set on fire and a large crowd prevented firefighters from stopping the blaze.[15]

The Moscow Metalworks, like other factories throughout the city, did not operate during the festive days of February Revolution. Employees attended meetings at Taganskaia Square and listened to speakers from sixteen different parties debate the issues of the revolution and war.[16] They also immediately recreated the institutions of the 1905 Revolution: factory committees and workers' councils, or soviets. When workers finally returned to the factory on 4 March, their first order of business was to elect a factory committee.[17] Four or five hundred workers hastily gathered for the committee election. Workers from "one shop after another yelled out the names of the candidates," according to the secretary of the committee, SR member V.N. Arapov. Workers' democracy was not impeccable. In one committee meeting, recalled Arapov, "Pugachev informed us that he and Kochergin were elected to the Moscow Soviet and Lebedev to the district soviet. I was extremely surprised to hear about the elections to the soviets because I knew nothing about them."[18]

With years of political experience as the only alternative to Tsarism operating in the factories, socialists dominated the elected leadership positions. The SRs' stance of refraining from political strikes because of their pro-war patriotism placed them in a position of strength, as they had been less subject to Okhrana arrests. During the factory election to the Moscow Duma in January 1917, 522 workers (of 1,477 eligible voters) elected two SR candidates.[19] The most reliable estimate states that the SRs had thirty to thirty-five members.[20] Arapov described his SR comrades as "the most active fellows."[21] Other non-SR memoirs claimed that the factory committee members "were all SRs," and even the leader of the factory Bolsheviks described the period of early 1917 as one of "SR strength." [22]

The Bolsheviks had been decimated by their audacious proclivity for hurling themselves into wave after wave of political strikes. One member claimed that in April the party had only one hundred members in the entire district and a solitary member in the factory, though a more believable account asserts that the Bolsheviks had three or four in the factory after the February Revolution. The party accumulated a handful of new recruits during the spring of 1917, though the Bolshevik secretary later wrote that there were "no more than nine people" in the cell at the time. Another party activist recalled that "members of our organization were poorly developed," and as a result they repeatedly called upon the district committee for help because "not only the Latvians, but also Simon Ivanov and other Bolsheviks were bad orators." In the first general factory meetings "the Bolsheviks were really hounded," and during their speeches they were "overwhelmed with shouts of 'Down! Enough!'" Another worker recalled that in the early meetings "the Bolsheviks were whistled at and sometimes pulled down from the podium and not allowed to speak. In our factory the SR influence dominated."[23]

Workers' failure to distinguish between different socialist parties was compounded by the diversity, commotion, and confusion among the socialists themselves in the early days of the Revolution. "Before the February Revolution," one employee recalled years later, "I had a weak understanding of the programs of the different parties."[24] Another worker explained that in his opinion, "the difference was that the SRs went into battle alone, like knights, but the Bolsheviks wanted the masses. Otherwise, their goals were the same."[25] Even the Bolsheviks' cell secretary admitted that, at the first meeting, the SRs had the advantage even though "there were not large differences between us."[26] While the SRs continued to accommodate a number of varying political tendencies, the Bolsheviks were also in a state of theoretical disarray, embracing an assortment of positions over the party's attitude toward the Provisional Government, cooperation with the Mensheviks, the war, and the role of the Soviets.[27]

Factory-wide political discussions centered on the issues of the war and governmental power. The Bolshevik *Sotsial-Demokrat* reported that one thousand employees gathered in the factory store on 12 March and resolved to support the Provisional Government on the condition that it did not delay summoning a Constituent Assembly. The paper explained that the Bolsheviks' slogan "Down with the War" distinguished the party from the "petty-bourgeois opposition" (SR), which rallied under the slogan, "Long live peace and the brotherhood of people." Workers resolved "to quickly restore relations between socialists of all countries to make preparations for peace."[28] On 23 March, the factory committee responded to a conscripted former employee's appeal against being sent to the front. In a letter to the Moscow Soviet, the factory workers' representatives requested that "revolutionary troops remain in reserve for defense of the Revolution and that the first ones sent be the police and gendarmes." An addendum to this memorandum indicated that the Soviet of Workers' and Soldiers' Deputies had taken measures to carry out these requests.[29]

Workers' direct action addressed immediate workplace grievances. Employees immediately implemented the eight-hour working day when they returned to the factory in early March. The SR and pro-war newspaper *Trud* reported that the implementation of the eight-hour day would "in no way interfere with defense work because, in the case of urgent need, the factory can organize three shifts."[30] On 21 March, the Moscow Soviet passed a resolution for the eight-hour day, which workers in many factories throughout the city had already implemented through direct action.[31] Management's 23 March factory announcement appealed to the workforce: "such a reduction of work time is contrary to the duty of the entire populace who must strain every nerve to bring the war to a victorious end. It is our duty to support our army ... in the service of guarding their country."[32] Only the Provisional Government, "which everyone has a duty to obey," had the power to make a final resolution on the question, though, "bowing to the coercion applied to it," management conceded that it would immediately implement the eight-hour day.[33] On 1 May, management complained to various Provisional Government offices that the factory committee had "forcibly introduced the eight-hour work day," unilaterally changed the nightshift to seven hours, and "took upon itself the prerogative of deciding when shifts would start and end."[34]

Throughout 1917, workers' demands became more inclusive and were distinguished by their support for previously marginalized sections of the workforce. Wage complaints focused on the gap in pay between skilled and unskilled laborers. A 23 April factory general meeting unanimously voted that skilled workers should refuse excessive wage rates and demanded that these funds be given to non-skilled employees. The administration refused, claiming that there was not enough money, but "obviously wanting to draw a distinction between workers, proposed that skilled workers get a raise to twelve rubles and non-skilled four rubles." The unresolved dispute was sent to a conflict commission of the Soviet.[35]

Management's 1 May letter to the government included a detailed summary of factory costs and income, and concluded "management considers its duty to inform you that it cannot satisfy the workers' demands, which might possibly result in a work stoppage because of a strike."[36] Still, the Factory Commission, the governmental body ruling on the issue, ordered a raise in pay. A 10 May factory announcement noted that after the increase "wages in certain categories of skilled workers are in complete accordance with the normal pay in metal factories in the Moscow area."[37]

The work slowdown over wages also led to renewed confrontation over hiring and firing, and illustrated how seemingly disparate issues overlapped as the workers' movement grew in scope and confidence. The factory committee resolved that not a single employee could be discharged without its sanction.[38] Employees then decided that they also had the right to appoint and dismiss management personnel. Management complained that on 23 May "workers in the form-casting department announced to the head of the department, Mattis, that they did not want to have him as their manager" and "immediately dismissed him from this position." The next day, bolt shop workers fired their manager. The shop manager, according to one worker account, was particularly abusive toward the women in the shop, firing women who became pregnant and forcing female production workers to wash floors.[39]

The management board argued that employees could appeal to the director or to arbitration bodies about managers, "but by no means is it possible to allow workers, on their own initiative, simply to dismiss office personnel." They warned "if workers threaten the office staff with violence, then the board cannot possibly continue operating the factory" and appealed to the factory committee to rein in the workers. "Unfortunately, the factory committee delegates declared that they could not guarantee that there would not be any violence toward the office staff."[40] Similarly, a representative from the Moscow Soviet told management that it was "now impossible to talk about methods of maintaining personal safety as was done under the old regime."[41] The new confrontation was connected to the work slowdown. "For sixteen days in April, the bolt department produced 12,000 *puds* of goods; for the entire month of May, 10,200 *puds*. The shop manager became indignant about this and demanded that they work, but workers made him leave under the threat of violence."[42]

Management's threat to close the factory led the Provisional Government and the Moscow Soviet to attempt conciliation that would resolve all problems "exclusively in a lawful manner by arbitration bodies, the decisions of which would be binding upon both sides." The conflict over the removal of managers and wage demands needed to be resolved quickly lest they "disturb the defense work at the factory." Apparently recognizing the power of the workers, the arbitrators ruled that the managers should remain suspended but asked the union to exert its influence to prevent similar incidents in the future, noting that it was "necessary to avoid undesirable excesses." Similarly, on 26 May representatives from the Moscow Soviet called for office staff to return to work, with the two managers temporarily removed, and for the Central Conciliatory Chamber to immediately investigate the issue.[43]

Arbitration failed, illustrating the more general contradictions that beset the Provisional Government as class polarization made it increasingly difficult to straddle the interests of capital and labor. The issues of pay and the removal of managers were brought before the Conciliation Chamber but remained unresolved because the board was equally composed of workers and businessmen. On 9 June, management sent a letter to various Provisional Government bodies complaining about the unrest:

> The workers' representatives declared that they are not willing to wait, that they reserve for themselves the freedom to act, and made the threat of violence against the factory administration quite unambiguously understood. The Conciliation Chamber completely refused to consider the issue of removing the office staff. This was somewhat understandable given that the workers made new threats of violence in the peacekeeping chamber.
>
> On Friday, 2 June ... at the general meeting of workers, their representatives reported that the Chamber had not satisfied the workers' demands. The workers became agitated and started to favor the immediate occupation of the factory by force and the use of the most violent measures against management and office staff living at the factory.
>
> Ensign Kolikov, the representative in charge of metal distribution, managed to persuade the workers to delay carrying out their takeover and violence at least until Monday, in order for the entire case to be considered by the Factory Commission of the Moscow Region on Saturday.
>
> The board, after they had heard of the workers unrest at the factory, appealed to the Chairman of the Factory Commission; to the head of the Security of Factories Mills, and Banks, G. Marts; and to the Government's Commissar for the City of Moscow, with the request to provide assistance and to take measures to guard the inviolability of employees.
>
> ....
>
> That the danger to management was completely well founded became apparent when Ensign Kolikov persuaded the factory director to escape from the factory. Were it not for his intervention, there is no doubt that the workers—completely unobstructed and with impunity—would have committed all kinds of violence, not only to factory property, but also to office workers. Had this violence gone further than the dragging out in wheelbarrows, beatings and other insults, then the role of Moscow administration would be limited only to registering the occurrence of such grievous excesses that, for the first time, would have taken place in the Moscow Metalworks Company.[44]

Neither management concessions nor intransigence seemed capable of stemming the tide of worker militancy. As workers had gained an acute sense of their collective power, both approaches seemed only to fuel the flames of confrontation. Significantly, the SR representatives played a leadership role in the movement, and even made threats against management in the peace-keeping chamber. Threats of violence against employers were not necessarily acted upon, however. Even though from March onward the threat of force had become a central element in labor-management relations across the empire, actual violence against management was minimal.[45]

Yet factory managers feared for their lives. The same day that management posted the above complaint, it dispatched a letter to the Moscow Police expressing a "desire to establish a staff of police to defend the factory" with sixteen armed guards. Three earlier requests for guns were not satisfied.[46] The Provisional Government's slow response to events did not help Guzhon's cause. A 17 June letter from the Ministry of Internal Affairs to Prime Minister G.E. Lvov included management's 27 May notification that the conflict between workers and management had ended and work was back to normal.[47] The letter failed to mention that the dispute was temporarily resolved and still under arbitration.[48] In sharp contrast to Guzhon management's warnings of mob action, employees' demands exude a clear sense of purpose. Economic issues were sent to arbitration, but on 19 June the factory committee submitted demands on other issues:

1. Create a permanent space for the workers' committee and for general factory meetings, lectures, and other cultural-educational activities.
2. Recognize the night shift for seven-hour working day, but pay them for the normal eight-hour day.
3. Regularize salary payments in the following form: no later than the twentieth of the month, give advances for the current month, and no later than the eighth of the next month with complete accounting for added cost-of-living bonuses.
4. Bring in air ventilation for all enclosed places where there is production work.
5. Baths and steam rooms for both sexes.
6. Sufficient temperature in all shops and washstands during the winter.
7. In all shops there should be a cafeteria or an enclosed warm place.
8. Make toilets as close as possible to the shops.
9. In all shops make a closet for workers' clothes.
10. In the sheet metal shop and construction area, bring in hot water because now it is too far away and inaccessible because of the continuous nature of work.
11. Sick pay, whether job-related or not, must be paid in full from the first day of sickness and based on the average worker's wage.
12. For women giving birth, they are to be released for two weeks before and four weeks after birth but are to be paid in full based on the average salary.

13. Medicine prescribed by private doctors should be distributed from our local clinic, and if the clinic does not have it, the factory should buy it from another pharmacist.
14. At times of stoppages because of insufficient material, pay must be issued at half the minimum wage.
15. After the birth of a child, issue twenty-five rubles; after the death of a child, give twenty-five rubles; for death of adults give seventy-five rubles.
16. Every worker who has been in the factory at least one year must be given a two-week vacation; every worker over two years or more gets a month vacation with minimum pay.[49]

The variety, clarity, and force of demands demonstrate workers' increased confidence and organization. The need for a regular meeting place shows that the employees' top priority was the strengthening of their own organization, and the special demands raised in the interest of women illustrate workers' willingness to be more inclusive. While revolutionary egalitarianism was an important factor in this process, a practical consideration also drove such demands: the prerevolutionary demographic trend toward a more diverse workforce continued, and by May 1917, the concerns of 439 women simply could not be ignored.[50]

Guzhon insisted on maintaining pay stratification, arguing that raising the wages of unskilled workers undermined the very foundations of productivity. The workers' committee demanded a minimum daily pay of 5.50 rubles for unskilled female workers and 7.20 rubles for men. Guzhon argued that, "the level of pay must directly and inseparably correspond to the productivity of the worker." Higher minimum pay was bad because "per diem rates lower productivity … shop wages should be set at a level that would be conducive for workers to switch to piece-rates to realize higher productivity on that basis." Guzhon posited that "it is generally acknowledged that the guaranteed minimum of daily pay should be at least one and one-half times less than what a worker of a particular category and specialists would earn at a per-piece job." Guzhon went on to assert that the fixing of minimum workers' pay had been an "anti-state and anti-democratic act because it creates a privileged class of people that is guaranteed its means of existence at the expense of other classes of the population."[51]

Workers, however, were more concerned with economic equality than with the logistics of running a profitable enterprise. Guzhon complained that "having learned that the Factory Commission satisfied almost all their demands," workers raised productivity for "three or four days," but production later declined to 50 or 60 percent of the normal rate. The factory committee told management that the decrease in productivity was "completely understandable" and that the best way to increase productivity would be to raise rates so that workers could earn at least one and one-half times the minimum. Guzhon included a detailed expense report that claimed such demands would lead to the factory operating at a loss of six or seven hundred thousand rubles a month.[52]

The additional demands pushed Guzhon over the brink. On 20 June he informed the Factory Commission that he intended to close the factory, and castigated the Commission on the wage dispute and the workers' dismissal of managers under the threat of violence. That the issue remained unresolved "undermines the very basis for healthy discipline, without which operating an enterprise is completely inconceivable." He accused the Commission of conducting "systematic propaganda against private industry." The Commission, he concluded, had brought "complete disorganization" to the work of the factory, and under such circumstances, he charged, it was "necessary to close the factory."[53] Two days later the board of directors issued a factory announcement that stated, "The factory has been brought to a state of complete disorganization" and appealed to the government to help resolve the financial crisis. If the government did not take immediate measures, warned management, "On 1 July the factory will close."[54]

Guzhon workers did not accept the impending closure without a fight, however. On 28 June, the factory committee reported to the Moscow Soviet that three of their members had confronted management about its attempt to shut down the factory. The director had ordered electricity cut off, but the factory committee found sufficient raw materials and fuel and ordered work to continue. Workers' representatives from the factory then asked the Soviet to intervene to make sure the electrical supply would not be cut off.[55]

In the end, Guzhon's attempt to close the Moscow Metalworks backfired. The secretary of the factory committee described the special session of defense of the Provisional Government in Petrograd that decided the fate of the factory. "We explained that Guzhon had made a large war profit, that there was a continuous expansion of the factory workforce, and at the same time an extreme drop in workers' pay."[56] The Minister of Trade, A.V. Stepanov, told *Russkoe slovo* that the Provisional Government had sequestered the factory "because it is of exceptionally important significance for the metal industry in the Moscow area."[57] The minutes from the meeting show that although several speakers argued against any concessions to the workers, the decisive issue was that 100 percent of the factory production went to defense orders.[58] Thus, the Provisional Government came to the aid of Moscow Metalworks employees not out of sympathy for their militant demands, but because of the factory's importance to the government's war aspirations.

Why did the class conflict in the Metalworks race ahead of conflicts at factories in Moscow and even Petrograd? The speed of events suggests that workers' anger exceeded the level of workers' militancy in other factories. Significantly, Guzhon persisted in upholding a more intransigent strategy than other owners, who had opted for a conciliatory approach in an attempt to diffuse labor discontent. Yet by midsummer the crisis in Russian industry led other industrialists to reverse tack and adopt a hard-line stance similar to Guzhon's. While the confrontation in the Moscow Metalworks may have temporarily outpaced events in other factories by several weeks, the escalating class confrontation throughout Russia had become irreconcilable and more political.

The Ascendancy of Bolshevism

For the Bolsheviks, Guzhon's actions were just one example of what they considered capitalist economic sabotage and, as the crisis deepened, the urgency of deciding which class would rule. Lenin lashed out in the pages of *Pravda* at those who criticized the Bolsheviks for being in "too much of a hurry" to transfer power to the Soviets. He cited the Petrograd Soviet's resolution that "the Guzhon works management is clearly disorganizing production, deliberately trying to bring the works to a standstill." For that reason, the resolution continued, "state power, left by the Socialist Revolutionaries and Mensheviks in the hands of the party of the Guzhons, the party of the counterrevolutionary capitalists who resort to lockouts, must take over the management of the works ... and provide operating funds." Lenin's response to this resolution claimed that the "government, supported by the Socialist Revolutionaries and Mensheviks, simply *obstructs* the struggle against economic dislocation," and he insisted that it was not enough for the Soviet to demand money for one factory: "Just think what a madhouse this is: the country is on the rocks, the people are on the verge of famine and disaster, there is a shortage of coal and iron." Yet in the face of an impending disaster, Lenin asserted, Minister Palchinskii had prohibited the Donets Soviet's inquiry of the mining crisis because "the Guzhons and the other capitalists, with the cooperation of the Palchinskiis, are 'deliberately' (this word is used by the Economic Department) trying to bring production to a standstill. The government is *on their side*.... Is it not high time you gentlemen realized that the Socialist Revolutionaries and Mensheviks *as parties* will have to answer to the people for the catastrophe?"[59]

By midsummer the crisis in Russian industry was generalized. Between March and July, 568 Russian factories closed. The industrialists' *Torgovo-Promyshlennaya gazeta* blamed the closures on a shortage of raw materials and fuel, "excessive" worker demands, too few orders, and declining profitability. As S.A. Smith has shown, the deepening of the economic crisis coincided with a notable rise in "the tempo of class conflict." With profits disappearing and workers becoming increasingly combative, industrialists became less willing to invest or take on new orders. In southern and central Russia, including Moscow, employers coordinated lockouts in an attempt to demoralize workers and to prove excessive workers' demands were the root cause of the crisis. Petrograd industrialists believed they had miscalculated in their earlier strategy of concessions and embarked on a much tougher labor policy, resisting wage increases and cutting back production. The government supported this more confrontational approach to labor. Under the first Coalition Government formed in May, Menshevik Minister of Labor M.I. Skobelev promised social reforms and committed himself to meeting the demands of workers and confiscating the profits of industrialists, but by June Skobelev sided with mine owners to curtail workers' demands, which he described as "immoderate," and appealed to workers to "sacrifice" in the name of "strengthening the revolution and honoring our ultimate ideals." Under pressure from industrialists, financiers, and the General Staff, the

Kerensky labor policy shifted further to the right: in August the Ministry of Labor issued directives to curtail the power of the factory committees by means of a mandate that affirmed that only employers could hire and fire.[60]

The employers' offensive against the working class coincided with the ruling classes' attempt to establish "order" in the wake of the July days in Petrograd. On 3 July four hundred thousand workers and soldiers participated in an armed demonstration under the Bolshevik slogans of "Down with the Provisional Government" and "All Power to the Soviets." While Bolshevik leaders feared a bid for power would be isolated in Petrograd, many local party activists supported the extremist mood. Loyal government troops fired on the demonstration, arrested Bolsheviks, and shut down their press.[61] Over the next few weeks, the possessing classes openly blamed the soviets for the war defeats and inflation, while the Minister of Food Supply, Peshekhonov, demanded a halt to "violent and criminal manifestations against the landlords." The SRs and Mensheviks had held the upper hand in the 6 May coalition, but in the 24 July coalition they were reduced to junior partners. The liberal Kadets led the charge against the revolution in the aftermath of the July Days, agreeing to participate in Kerensky's government only if General Kornilov's program for "the salvation of the country" was accepted and all social reforms deferred until the Constituent Assembly was convened. The antidemocratic thrust of the ultimatum became clear when elections to the Assembly itself were suspended after the Kadets recognized that they stood no chance of outflanking the socialists in a popular election.[62]

The liberals' declaration of class war shattered illusions in a "compromise" between left and right as the summer crisis escalated. Generals admitted that the June offensive in Galicia was a "complete failure" that had left fifty-six thousands soldiers dead in just three weeks, and after the fall of Riga, fears spread that Petrograd would fall.[63] In Moscow, as in other cities, the worsening food supply and rampant inflation meant that workers' living standards continued to deteriorate. Carloads of grain to Moscow dropped from 2,000 in May to 1,052 in June, and then to just 883 in July.[64] In early August, textile magnate Riabushinksy made a speech that included the infamous threat of lockouts accompanied by "the bony hand of hunger" to beat back the workers' movement.[65] While the Mensheviks continued to play both sides of the class divide, the SRs were splitting between left and right. After the July Days, the Kadets had claimed that "Bolshevism has died a sudden death," but as Alexander Rabinowitch has argued, such an assertion "failed completely to take account of the basic concerns and great potential power of the Petrograd masses and the enormous attraction that a revolutionary political and social program like that of the Bolsheviks held for them."[66]

In the Moscow Metalworks, the SRs benefited the most in the first months of the Revolution. Bolshevik speakers at a 7 July Moscow Committee (MK) meeting admitted that their influence in the city lagged behind that in Petrograd. The representative from the Rogozhskii district stated that while the situation was "extremely unfavorable," with strong Unity (Social Democrats who favored unity between the Bolsheviks and Mensheviks) and SR influence, though the party was "driving them from the factories." In

Guzhon "the majority are Socialist Revolutionaries. The mood is not good; there are often clashes." Nevertheless, the district representative claimed that among Guzhon workers "we can build a demonstration in two weeks."[67]

SR strength in the Moscow Metalworks was based on their radicalism. Workers united behind the SR secretary's proposal for a more egalitarian wage scale that gave "the possibility of subsistence not only for skilled workers, but also for all ranks of workers."[68] As workers' demands became more political, the appeal of Bolshevism became stronger. A Bolshevik interdistrict meeting in May reported that their Moscow membership was ten thousand with 1,428 in the district.[69] Two months later, at their Sixth Party Congress, the Bolsheviks claimed a citywide membership of fifteen thousand, compared to five thousand for the SRs and four thousand for the Mensheviks.[70] In the Moscow Metalworks the SRs grew from 30 to 35 in February to 180 in June, while the Bolsheviks went from a small handful to about twenty, far below their growth in the city and district.[71]

The SRs' participation in a Provisional Government that had failed to address the land and war questions, the deteriorating economic crisis, and the growing split within their ranks all contributed to the party's decline. One worker recalled that "the mass of workers in the factory were former peasants who expected that the peasants would receive land after the revolution. With the rule of Kerensky, they soon were convinced that they had been deceived."[72] The Bolshevik cell secretary, however, later asserted that the war issue was crucial in the strengthening of Bolshevism in the factory. After "Kerensky put forward the slogan 'War until Victory,' SR influence inside the factory began to weaken and the Bolsheviks' stature began to rise."[73] An SR member later also argued, "The SRs were for the war, the Bolsheviks against; this attracted workers to their side."[74] SR leaders spoke for "War until Victory," at a factory meeting of five thousand after Kerensky's offensive began in late June. A Bolshevik district leader, Rosa Zemliachka, responded, "Comrades! Many voices have rung out for continuing the war. Therefore whoever wants war should immediately sign up as a volunteer for the front lines." After prolonged silence, the SR leaders left the tribune in defeat.[75] In the late summer, Nikolai Bukharin spoke at another mass meeting of several thousand.[76]

The Bolsheviks attempted to correct their organizational weakness by dispatching talented members to the factory. One member admitted that the situation had been "difficult for us because we did not have good agitators and speakers for the large meetings."[77] Another worker wrote that the contribution of the Bolshevik Mal'kov was decisive because "from the first day of work in the factory, Mal'kov agitated against the Provisional Government and the conciliation of the SRs and Mensheviks. He energetically appealed for workers to fight for the dictatorship of the proletariat and in a short time he earned considerable respect among the workers."[78] Other SR, Bolshevik, and nonparty workers attest to the influence of Mal'kov in the factory.[79] The district committee also sent in a woman organizer who agitated effectively for revolutionary activity in the sheet metal shop.[80] Analyzing the reasons for the Bolshevik ascendancy in the Metalworks, one SR member wrote that despite their early advantage, the SRs "gave weak leadership to its members, and gave no information about the revolutionary movement, no direction." Additionally "the factory cell, which as such, did not exist. This was very different from the work of the Bolsheviks ... somebody was leading these people and gave them definite directives, even daily. The persistent pressure of the Bolsheviks," he concluded, "was astounding."[81]

While the Bolsheviks were far from monolithic, they were the extreme radicals in the factories and were united on the key political issues of the day: against the war, against a compromise with the capitalists, and for Soviet rule. Moreover, their party provided their members with organizational support and political direction. The SRs, on the other hand, were in a state of serious disarray, moving from political ambiguity to fissure based on sharp internal differences over each of the main political questions. The SR factory committee president stated that the party was split at an August district meeting, "with some factory members, including myself, on the left and others on the right."[82]

Workers' political sentiments continued to move to the left, but the Bolshevik cell was relatively weak compared to other factories. In July and August, the factory's name did not appear in a long list of workplace resolutions that called for an end to the persecution of the Bolsheviks and for the abolition of the death penalty, and against the closure of the workers' press.[83] By mid-September the district soviet noted that Metalworks was one of a small number of factories that did not have a "Bolshevik mood."[84] Tumanov claimed that by September, the Bolshevik factory organization had grown to one hundred members and had eclipsed the SRs in strength, but only at the end of the month did the decisive political meeting favor the Bolsheviks, with many young workers playing key roles.[85] In a city in which the party claimed a membership of twenty thousand by the end of the year,[86] their factory-level strength of just a hundred workers suggests that the Bolsheviks had never fully recovered from the prerevolutionary arrests.

The first signal of a shift from the SRs to Bolshevism came during the general strike on 12 August against the Moscow State Conference. The conference was an attempt to legitimize the faltering Provisional Government by balancing the "consultative" voice of the conference between the right and left. Denied entry to the conference, the Bolsheviks attempted to organize a strike against it. The 8 August MK minutes show that reports from the factories indicate the Bolsheviks were unconvinced about their capacity to overcome Menshevik and SR support for the conference. Many cells claimed that workers' inclination for strike action was favorable, but other cells reported that the mood was either ambiguous or negative. Nogin and other more cautious Bolsheviks argued against the strike, claiming it would not be a success, but the MK voted eighteen to six to agitate in the unions and district soviets for a strike. The mood in Guzhon reflected that of many Moscow factories— in the middle of the political spectrum, but moving to the left in the ideological confrontation reverberating in every workplace: "Guzhon: The masses' attitude in the factory is unfavorable. The mood is getting better: The working masses have begun to sympathize with us. The strike undoubtedly will be a success but there is hardly support for a demonstration. The attitude towards the soviet is unfavorable."[87]

The next few days provided a litmus test for the contending socialist parties. Workers in every factory, union, and soviet feverishly debated the Bolshevik call for strike action to condemn both the Moscow State Conference and the Provisional Government. On 11 August, a Moscow Metalworks general meeting voted against the Moscow Conference and for a protest in the form of a strike or demonstration.[88] Still controlled by Mensheviks and SRs, the Moscow Soviet voted 364 to 304 against the strike, yet the majority of district soviets and trade unions supported strike action.[89]

The Bolsheviks won the argument in the factories, and the 12 August strike was a profound political demonstration of opposition to the Provisional Government. Nikolai Sukhanov, a Menshevik participant at the conference wrote, "This whole working-class army was following the Bolsheviks *against its own Soviet!*"[90] *Izvestia*, the organ of the Moscow Soviet, admitted that the Soviet had resolved "to ask the Moscow proletariat not to strike" but "the attitude of the Moscow proletariat toward the conference is so hostile that late at night there was a meeting of the Central Trade Union, attended by delegates of all the wards, representing 400,000 proletarians" which voted "almost unanimously" to go out.[91] The Bolshevik *Sotsial-Demokrat* also reported that 400,000 workers in Moscow and Moscow Guberniia struck, forty-one unions supported the general strike, and 23,000 workers went out in the Rogozhskii district, including 3,300 in Guzhon. The action, according to the newspaper, showed "the revolutionary mood of the masses."[92] The SR newspaper *Trud* claimed that in Rogozhskii "the mood of the workers was very uncertain." The district soviet had issued a call for a strike but "part of the workers were for and part against a strike." As proof of this ambivalence, *Trud* reported that in Guzhon "one department, then another, then the entire factory struck."[93] The metalworkers' union reported that in forty factories, including other large plants, all members struck. The Moscow Metalworks, by contrast, was one of two factories in which part of the workforce did not participate in the action. A few metal factories did not participate at all.[94] Thus, Bolshevik influence throughout Moscow factories overcame the combined SR and Menshevik efforts to block the political stoppage, but the Moscow Metalworks was one of the few plants in which the entire workforce did not participate.

The Moscow State Conference not only failed to bridge the growing class divide; it demonstrated that civil war was imminent. Sukhanov wrote that the Bolshoi Theatre itself was divided in half: "on the right sat the bourgeoisie, to the left democracy." Kerensky threatened to put down any new attempt against the government with "blood and iron." The liberal Miliukov had been driven from his post as Foreign Minister in April after his claim that "Russia would fight to the last drop of blood" brought tens of thousands of workers to the streets of Petrograd. Now he expressed the liberals' bitter contempt for the popular revolutionary aspirations. He complained about the government's "capitulation" on five fronts: its "Zimmerwaldist" foreign policy, the "democratization" of the Army, the "utopian" demands of workers, the "extreme" demands of national minorities, and the "direct action" of peasants. The head of the armed forces, Kornilov, insinuated that a strong-man was needed to save Russia because the army had been converted into a "crazy mob trembling only for its own life," and he warned that the fall of Riga was imminent and then the road to Petrograd would be "open." [95]

Kornilov's attempted coup d'état in late August gave concrete form to the threats from the right, but also strengthened the resolve of the left. Kornilov ordered a march on Petrograd to destroy the Soviet and install himself as dic-tator.[96] The Petrograd Soviet sent agitators to fraternize with the advancing forces, and the attempted military coup dissolved without any fighting. The threat from the right, however, encouraged the formation of forty thousand Red Guards to defend the revolution.[97] Moreover, the conspiracy further eroded confidence in the Provisional Government as Kerensky's machina-tions with Kornilov became public along with the complicity of some mem-bers of the Kadet party.[98]

The attempted bourgeois coup "profoundly stirred the surface and depths of Russia," wrote Sukhanov. In the days afterwards "Bolshevism began blos-soming luxuriantly and put forth deep roots throughout the country."[99] In fac-tories and working-class districts throughout Moscow the Bolsheviks put forward resolutions to arm workers and soldiers, to disarm counterrevolu-tionary military units, to arrest Tsarist generals and liberal leaders, to close the State Duma, to expel foreign governments who gave aid to the counterrevo-lution, and to create a revolutionary dictatorship of the proletariat and peas-antry that would proclaim a democratic republic and immediately give land to the peasants. Almost ninety thousand workers participated in mass meetings that endorsed one or more of these demands.[100] The Moscow Metalworks was one of many factories in which a general meeting passed a resolution for arm-ing workers against the "Kornilov-Kadet conspiracy."[101] According to the Bol-shevik secretary, the formation of the Red Guards met with strong resistance from both Mensheviks and the SRs, who sent leading members like Spiri-donova to speak at the factory. "These were extraordinarily difficult moments whenever we found out that the SRs were going to have strong orators speak;" once again the Bolshevik Moscow Committee "sent strong comrades."[102]

By early September, democratically elected soviets throughout Russia swung to the Bolsheviks. On 31 August the Bolsheviks won a majority in the Petrograd Soviet. By 1 September, 126 soviets had requested the Soviet Cen-tral Executive Committee to take power. Over the next week soviets in Moscow (5 September), Kiev, Kazan, Baku, and Saratov passed Bolshevik resolutions.[103] As in the 1905 Revolution, the Bolsheviks adopted an "open-door" recruitment strategy, believing that workers' experience in the school of revolution more than compensated for any lack of theoretical knowl-edge.[104] Tens of thousands of the most radical workers joined the Bolsheviks, many of whom, when asked about their understanding of the Bolshevik pro-gram on their application, simply stated, "Our program is struggle with the bourgeoisie."[105] By comparison, Lenin and the Bolsheviks, with justification, continued to accuse the Mensheviks of advocating a program of "compro-mise" with the bourgeoisie.[106]

Economic discontent and a revival of labor militancy contributed to a rising tide of strikes that involved over a million-and-a-half workers in the late summer and early fall.[107] In the Moscow Metalworks, however, the 12 August political strike was the only significant work stoppage, as workers seemed content to let arbitration bodies resolve grievances—invariably in their favor. At the end of May, management fired several cafeteria workers, who nevertheless continued to show up for work. In June, an arbitrator delayed a ruling on the grievance for three weeks, by which time management had been removed.[108] In July, an arbitrator mandated a wage increase for all workers and ruled that women should receive the same pay as men for equivalent work instead of 15 percent less. Taking into account the decrease in hours since March, the arbitrator also reminded workers of their agreement to reach 85 percent production.[109] Another dispute erupted in August in the sheet metal shop over wage categories, and a union representative was posted in the factory through September to resolve the issue.[110] In early October, metalworkers' union records show that the Bolshevik Mal'kov and the SR Arapov represented five hundred workers' request for higher wage categories and the union conflict commission determined that the grievance was justified.[111] On 12 October, an arbitration judge ruled that union factory guards were entitled to the average wage of an unskilled worker.[112] Thus, strikes were avoided only because workers managed to brandish the strength of the metalworkers' union to compel arbitrators to concede to their economic demands.

The Bolshevik-dominated metalworkers' union was a focus of party members' activities in the late summer. By the middle of September the factory had three thousand dues-paying metalworkers' union members.[113] One memoir claimed, "Under Mal'kov's leadership, the metalworkers' union drew in about a thousand people."[114] The workforce's solidarity with other workers, as indicated by contributions to strike funds, shows a pattern consistent with the radicalization of Russian labor generally in 1917. On 22 July, the factory committee voted for workers to contribute a day's pay to the metalworkers' union strike fund.[115] The decision to contribute 18,237 rubles, the largest Moscow contribution of the year, to the fund was made a day before the citywide delegates resolved to deduct oneday's pay.[116] A few weeks later, the factory committee voted to contribute another day's wage per worker to striking Moscow leather workers.[117] Thus, workers, whose own financial position was deteriorating rapidly, gave material form to the theoretical abstraction of proletarian unity.

Despite their mutual animosity on larger political questions, the early nationalization of the factory encouraged Bolsheviks and SRs to cooperate in the day-to-day operations. On 14 October, workers left the factory at ten in the morning for a procession in honor of Illarion Astakhov. They marched to the bridge where he had been killed, and then to the cemetery, where they listened to speakers from the Bolshevik, SR, and Unity parties.[118] Both the SR and Bolshevik leaders claimed that in August and September the two organizations repeatedly concurred on issues concerning the control of production and procuring of raw materials.[119]

Workers in the Moscow Metalworks supported the October Revolution, as did workers throughout Moscow. Factory committee minutes show several September and October collections for Red Guard units to defend the revolution.[120] Significantly, a partial list of Red Guards shows that forty-five non-party volunteers outnumbered the nine Bolsheviks and two SRs.[121] The Bolshevik and district Soviet leader, Zemliachka, requested three to four hundred Red Guards from the factory, but because of the shortage of guns only one hundred and fifty workers volunteered.[122] At a 25 October general meeting, according to the most believable account, Tumanov requested, "Those who want to take up arms, step to the left, those who do not, to the right." "Right away," one observer recalled, "three-quarters stepped to the left and only one-quarter to the right."[123]

The factory SRs apparently divided between the left, right, and a group in the center that wavered. The Left SR factory leader Arapov enjoyed enormous authority and probably swayed many rank-and-file SRs.[124] The SRs expelled another factory leader, Kuznetsov, because he had helped organize the Red Guards, against the directives of the party.[125] As the more conservative SRs lost support to the Bolsheviks, general political discussions became increasingly hostile. One worker wrote that some SRs referred to the Bolshevik-dominated workers' councils as "the Soviet of Workers' and Dogs' Deputies" but that "every speaker against the workers' soviet was met with shouts of indignation, irritation and sharp criticism from groups of workers."[126] Other memoirs recalled boisterous meetings throughout October in which the SR factory director Weitsman had openly referred to the Bolsheviks as "swine," and other SRs denounced the Bolsheviks as "dictatorial sons of bitches."[127] The SR factory committee president, Lebedev, later claimed that he had sided with Revolution, but according to Tumanov, Lebedev had repeatedly talked on the phone with the factory director Weitsman and the Red Guards became suspicious. They wanted to arrest Lebedev but this was problematic because "he was the elected president of the factory committee," so he was merely disarmed. Tumanov wrote that he replaced Lebedev as committee president on 28 October, after the Moscow battle had begun.[128]

The Bolshevik-dominated Petrograd Soviet's Military Revolutionary Committee launched an attack upon the Provisional Government in the days before the Second Congress of Soviets. Provocative actions by the government and the right helped legitimatize the preemptive assault. Throughout October, the Kadet newspaper *Rech'* repeatedly warned against letting the Bolsheviks "choose the moment for a declaration of civil war."[129] Kerensky had already used force against the soviets on 19 October, ordering Cossacks to raid the Kaluga Soviet and arrest its leaders.[130] On 24 October, the Provisional Government ordered the arrest of the Petrograd Military Revolutionary Committee, but the following day the Committee arrested the ministers of the Provisional Government.[131] The soviet seizure of power had the support of the overwhelming majority of workers and soldiers. Throughout factories in Russia during September and October, the Bolsheviks argued for transferring power to the soviets.[132] They won this argument: 507 of 670 at the Congress of Soviets arrived in Petrograd committed to supporting "all power to the soviets."[133] As a leading contemporary opponent of Soviet power, the Menshevik Martov, reluctantly admitted that "before us after all is a victorious uprising of the proletariat—almost the entire proletariat supports Lenin and expects its social liberation from the uprising."[134]

Fierce fighting lasted for almost a week in Moscow.[135] Lack of arms meant that the majority of Moscow Metalworks workers remained passive supporters of the insurrection. During the battle, the factory cafeteria was packed as the bakery continued to feed workers from the factory and district.[136] One factory Red Guard who fought in the battle recounted frenzied, uninterrupted activity in which he did not return home for eight days.[137] For Red Guards protecting the factory, however, the weakness of the counterrevolutionary units meant that October was, in military terms, almost a nonevent. By the time guards had mustered the forces to wage an assault on the nearby cadet institute, the enemy officers had already fled.[138]

One of the more remarkable changes in workers' attitudes during 1917 was the fraternization between Russian and German-speaking workers. Two years after many Moscow Metalworks employees had participated in vicious attacks against the German-speaking citizens of Moscow, Austrian prisoners of war at the factory regularly attended general meetings and played a part in the workers' revolution. An international agreement on 1 October freed all prisoners of war, but management delayed releasing the factory's 260 prison laborers.[139] Arapov wrote that factory activists organized a "unity concert" of six hundred workers, and that fifteen to twenty Austrians actively participated in the workers' movement.[140] Another memoir claims that all eight Austrians in the sheet metal shop fought on the barricades and stormed the Kremlin, and that at least one died in the fighting.[141]

Two characteristics differentiated the 1917 Russian Revolution from other workers' rebellions of the twentieth century. First, in no society was the level of class hatred more pronounced than in Russia. The late summer crisis was not merely a consequence of a string of incompetent decisions on the part of the Provisional Government. Rather, the escalation of class conflict was the culmination of years of confrontation, war profiteering, brutal repression, and workers' rebellion that could only have ended in the forceful rule by one class over the other.[142] The second distinguishing feature of 1917 was that at the movement's decisive juncture, one political party with significant influence in the working class put forward an uncompromising stance against capitalism and for a workers' government. Socialists were the dominant political force in the factories for the previous dozen years and through their accumulated influence managed to set the parameters of the debate. While workers were sympathetic to socialism generally, it was only in the politically charged atmosphere of the late summer that they started to distinguish between different party programs. The Bolsheviks' advocacy of soviet government provided a sensible solution to the reality of unprecedented class war.

In the Moscow Metalworks the ascendancy of the extreme left did not conform to the depiction of an infallible party leading the masses later popularized by Stalinism. Workers learned for themselves through the course of class conflict, in the process gaining a visceral sense of their own collective power. Yet revolutionary *politics* contributed in tangible ways to this process. Decimated by Okhrana arrests in the prerevolutionary period, the small factory-based Bolshevik group was inept and outnumbered by the SRs. Moreover, the SRs promoted a strategy of direct action, egalitarianism, and worker unity in the early months of the revolution that was hardly distinguishable from the Leninists. Bolshevik policy only became decisive when the more fundamental political issue of state power came to the fore during the late summer. The organizational weakness of the Leninists in the factory was overcome by what Alexander Rabinowitch describes as "the relative flexibility of the party."[143] The Bolsheviks did not just react to events: instead the party provided leadership for the movement. After sending in several talented organizers, the Bolsheviks fought for—and won—the ideological argument for revolution and Soviet power, as they did among workers throughout the empire.

The Civil War Catastrophe and Personal Survival

The October Revolution did not resolve the class conflict in the Moscow Metalworks. In early 1918 workers continued to raise economic grievances in raucous factory meetings. The economic catastrophe of the Civil War, however, was not conducive to protracted labor militancy and the collective egalitarianism of the revolution was eventually displaced by the desperate politics of personal survival.

The Bolsheviks gambled that satisfying the demands of the working class and the peasantry ultimately hinged on the European revolutionary movement. As Lenin repeatedly argued after October, "If the peoples of Europe do not arise and crush imperialism, we shall be crushed ... the capitalists of all countries will stifle our struggle."[144] This perspective was no pipe dream. In response to the slaughter and deprivations of the war, the most profound social movement in European history swept across the continent during the "red years" of 1918-1919. Based on the Russian example, workers formed soviets in Germany, Austria, Bulgaria, and even Ireland, where workers moved to the center of the Irish revolt against British domination. In Glasgow's "Red Clyde" shop stewards led a general strike in early 1919 and declared "We 'British Bolsheviks' have the Russian precedent to guide us, and we believe that in the critical hours of our revolution, our rallying cry will be: 'All Power to the Workers' Committees.'"[145] British Prime Minister Lloyd George recognized the implications of this revolt from below. "The whole of Europe is filled with the spirit of revolution," he fretted. "There is a deep sense not only of discontent but of anger and revolt amongst the workingmen against the prewar conditions. The whole existing order in its political, social and economic aspects is questioned by the masses of the population from one end of Europe to the other."[146]

Workers' grievances were directed at the board of management that had been appointed by the Provisional Government. On 24 November 1917 (old calendar) the factory committee complained that minimum wage rates had already been established in other factories but not in the Metalworks because of "sabotage by the Kerensky government's board of management." A general meeting resolved to send an appeal to the Soviets for a change of management, with half of the new staff coming from the ranks of the workers.[147] On 28 November 1917, workers put forward a wage demand that complained about incorrect wage payments "for the last ten years." Union representatives, perhaps unsure of how to respond, gave the grievance to "a consulting lawyer."[148] While blaming management for wage rates, the factory committee usurped control over almost every aspect of the factory. The elected workers' representatives dealt with general production issues, sent delegates on assignment for raw materials, and hired, fired, and disciplined employees for various offenses. They also received various appeals from workers, made donations to various revolutionary causes, organized Red Guards to defend the factory, and took responsibility for workers' provisions.[149]

The board of directors attempted to resist the demise of its authority. The Moscow Soviet resolved that workers' representatives had the right to check management's sale of manufactured goods, but did not have the right to sell products, which remained a management prerogative.[150] A week later, the Moscow Soviet ordered the factory committee to stop distributing circulars to office personnel because they "may only be issued from management."[151] Management also complained about the factory committee's "tactic of discrediting management in the eyes of the office and production workers" by not allowing management to utilize one of the two factory automobiles.[152] On 6 February 1918 (new calendar hereafter), the factory committee responded to an appeal from the factory chauffeur, who complained that he had been "forced to drive Weitsman's wife around."[153]

The committee again insisted on a minimum union daily rate of three rubles, but management refused. After the Commissariat of Labor sided with the factory committee, the committee then demanded another 25 percent raise in the minimum rate. Management again refused, noting that there had not been a corresponding increase in production, but the committee blamed the drop on insufficient materials.[154] On 8 February 1918, a factory general meeting unanimously resolved that if the factory committee had not heard from the Commissariat of Labor by the morning of 12 February, the committee would assume full authority over the plant.[155]

This friction over workers' control raged throughout Russia well into 1918. As S.A. Smith has shown, the expansion of workers' control was a response to, rather than the cause of, industrial chaos, "which had its roots in the whole system of war capitalism." The discussions on workers' control centered on the division of labor between factory committees and management boards. In many factories workers' control was the norm in early 1918, with official management existing alongside the factory committee and with management orders subject to ratification of the factory committee or its control commission.[156]

By early 1918 Moscow workers' most urgent problem was the food crisis, exacerbated by continual blizzards and a breakdown of the rail system.

By February 1918, when the Bolsheviks moved the capital to Moscow, a worker's daily ration dropped to 306 calories a day—less than a tenth of what was considered necessary for a healthy diet.[157] In March 1918, the plant had received ten thousand *puds* of potatoes and the factory committee vowed that supplies "must not freeze or rot."[158] General factory meetings focused on provisions were heavily attended and boisterous. A late May 1918 session that discussed the food provisions was marked by "a stormy mood." A few weeks later, one worker criticized the proposed food-requisitioning plan and proposed alleviating the food crisis by implementing free trade with the countryside. Workers "listened attentively to the speaker, but when he called for the abolition of fixed prices and for free trade, rows of workers came alive with shouts of protest."[159] In July 1918, the factory committee authorized a half-day wage deduction from all workers to help feed the children of workers.[160]

Two management changes failed to halt the economic chaos in the factory. In March a temporary management team took over the administration.[161] In early June 1918, the Supreme Council of the National Economy (*Vesenkha*) resolved to create a new management board consisting of two workers from production, one representative from the union, and three representatives from *Vesenkha*.[162] Two strikes in May and July show that both management teams failed to halt simmering worker unrest. In late May 1918, workers in the wire stretching shop organized a nine-day strike to raise the wage rate by 130 percent. The metalworkers' union resolved not to support the action because strikes would lead to "the death of the working class at the present moment." Management threatened to fire workers who did not show up for work, but also granted a slight wage increase to end the conflict.[163] Workers in the steel foundry shop struck in late July 1918 for several days, though factory committee minutes do not record the outcome.[164]

Workers' demands exceeded what the battered Soviet state could offer. The regime inherited an economy in shambles—due in no small part to deliberate sabotage by capitalists.[165] Moreover, by the summer of 1918, Soviet Russia had shrunk to the size of the medieval Moscovy state and had lost almost all grain producing regions.[166] In July 1918 a metalworkers' representative carefully replied to workers' reiterated wage grievances "for the last ten years." He acknowledged "workers' demands from the legal point of view in principle are just, especially from 1907 to July 1917, when hiring conditions were violated all the time." The union representative told the workers that it was possible to find "thousands" of wrongdoings by management. "I pointed out to the workers that the working class, to make up for the losses that were done in the past, took industry into its hands, but is not demanding the dividing of industry among everyone, which would spell its death."[167]

The factory committee, management, and the Bolshevik cell attempted to deal with numerous problems during the Civil War. The responsibilities of the factory committee, management, and the party cell overlapped, and a high level of cooperation characterized their work. Factory committee discussions centered on workers' compensation, labor discipline, and provisions.[168] Management meetings focused on wages and securing raw materials for the factory but were also concerned with finding provisions for the workers. Joint sessions of the management team and the factory committee, including Bolsheviks and SRs, discussed these issues.[169] Bolshevik factory cell meetings discussed all issues related to the factory as well as larger political issues.[170]

Theoretically, the factory committee was the main institution for defending workers' interests, and was elected by general meetings. From the committee's inception in March 1917 to August 1918, 224 factory committee and general meetings were convened, with general meetings held about once a week and committee meetings three or four times a week. Subcommittees included commissions for provisions, sanitation, housing, education, finances, discipline, hiring and firing, and guarding the factory.[171] During the collapse of production in 1919, the committee met less frequently.[172] Operating under the auspices of the metalworkers' union, it was expected to handle economic grievances through mediation procedures rather than by strike action.[173] Factory committee resolutions were subordinate to the factory-wide meetings, regularly attended by five to eight hundred workers, that decided such matters as the firing of workers and managers, aid to families of deceased workers, holiday schedules, and contributions to various political causes.

A high level of sacrifice and discipline marked Bolshevik membership, but the organization had neither the numerical nor the political strength to combat the near-total economic collapse. Mean attendance at meetings was twenty-two in 1920 and twenty-six in 1921.[174] After the demobilization in 1921, the cell reached forty members, but only eighteen members worked in the shops.[175] Meetings voted on members' assignments, punishing reckless behavior and attempts to circumvent directives. The party expelled one member for careerism after he had forged factory committee and party signatures in order to enter an economic institute. Another party member was suspended for three months after serving in a state position without the consent of the cell. A party court punished another member with two weeks' forced labor because he had appeared at the factory drunk. Members were elected as representatives to the district and city soviets, and assigned by the party to various government posts. In May 1920, a member on assignment for Workers' and Peasants' Inspectorate (*Rabkrin*) who had gone several months without pay petitioned the cell for help because his family had been reduced to "the most pitiful existence." Party meetings during the Civil War illustrate that a high standard of political conviction, rather than the lure of material reward, defined the party's membership in this period.[176]

This high level of political commitment extended beyond the ranks of party members. Tens of thousands of young Moscow workers volunteered for the Red Army during the months after the October Revolution. On 15 January 1918, the Council of People's Commissars (*Sovnarknom*) called on all party, trade union, soviet, and Red Guard organizations to help in the task of building the "Socialist Army," and by the end of April 1918, two hundred thousand men and women had volunteered.[177] By mid-May in Moscow, more than fifty-seven thousand people, mostly workers, had enlisted.[178] Two hundred and fifty workers from the factory volunteered in January 1918, nearly all between the ages of fifteen and thirty. One volunteer, who was sixteen at the time, recalled, "thirty for us was very old."[179] In October 1919, the factory Komsomol organized another detachment of twenty-five volunteers, including fourteen-year-old Dasha Ukhova, to fight on the southern front against Denikin.[180] Volunteers wrote proudly about their combat experience, including accounts of Red Army units defending the Jewish population in the Ukraine against the White terror.[181]

While enthusiasm for joining the Red Army illustrates the breadth of popular support for the Revolution, the absence of the most committed revolutionaries from the factories had a deleterious effect on the rear guard throughout the Civil War era. By March 1918 the city party membership stood at forty thousand but only six thousand members were in the factories, and less than half on the shop floor.[182] In April 1918, the factory Bolshevik leader Tumanov complained that, "Cells have fallen apart because many comrades left for the Red Guards.... Comrades call each other saboteurs; party work has fallen."[183]

The factory party organization continued to lose cadres to the front throughout the Civil War. In January 1919, the War Commissar informed the factory cell that Political Commissar Stroikov had died at the front. "On behalf of the entire steel division, I express our deepest grief about the irrevocable loss of our dear comrade who perished with honor at his revolutionary post and, to the end of his life, honorably defended the holy communist idea."[184] The party responded to a request for two more members for the front in July 1920 that "In view that our cell has been drained of many people, and due to starting up our factory, our cell finds itself already weak with people." Having already "posted ten people from our cell to the Kafkaz front" the cell resolved to assign only one more member to the southern front.[185]

Fuel shortages also crippled the factory. The fuel crisis in the summer of 1918 forced several shops to shut down for six weeks.[186] By 1919 in Moscow, the fuel supply fell to a staggering 4 percent of the prewar level and by the summer of 1920, four hundred factories had closed—one third of all industrial enterprises in city.[187] Calculated in terms of 1914 production figures in the Moscow Metalworks, the respective percentages were 40.3 percent in 1917; 27.2 percent in 1918; 5.0 percent in 1919; 2.0 percent in 1920; and 4.9 percent in 1921.[188] From summer of 1919 till June of 1920, not a single blast furnace operated in the largest steel factory in the Soviet capital; during the next year, only one small furnace worked.[189] A party discussion in February 1921 complained that if fuel were not obtained immediately, the entire factory would have to be shut down.[190] One worker account—possibly influenced by Gladkov's popular novel *Cement*, which imbues human attributes to a factory—claims that a metalworkers' representative suggested closing the plant. "I almost got into a fight with him, but Grigorii Ivanovich Pogonchenkov held me back. I felt very sorry for the factory."[191]

Without food, many workers chose to return to their villages. The factory committee acknowledged the problem in March 1918, when many workers failed to appear after the Easter holiday, and resolved to fire those who had not returned from their villages after five days.[192] Clearly frustrated with the breakdown in factory discipline, management complained in July that "a large number of workers are the peasant element that have not broken with the countryside" and that "these elements are neither interested in the state of the factory nor even its existence, are not politically conscious, are undisciplined, and are undesirable for the factory and for the more conscious working masses at the factory."[193]

While the Bolsheviks had hoped that the European-wide popular movement would eventually come to the aid of the fledgling revolution, they also had to deal with the immediate reality that the governments of Great Britain, the United States, and a dozen other nations had come to the aid of their adversaries. By the late summer of 1918 more than 150,000 foreign soldiers were in Russia. In 1919, 200,000 foreign troops provided crucial support to the Whites' positions along the northern front, the Ukrainian and Caucasus. In just six months of 1919, Allied arms shipments to the Whites included hundreds of thousands of rifles, a thousand artillery pieces with millions of shells, seven thousand machine guns, two hundred airplanes, and a hundred tanks.[194] Most of this support came from Great Britain and France, but U.S. Secretary of State Robert Lansing convinced Woodrow Wilson to secretly funnel tens of millions of dollars to the White armies in an effort to establish "a stable Russian government" through "a military dictatorship."[195]

In response to the foreign intervention and skirmishes with the White armies, the Soviet government implemented War Communism in June 1918. War Communism entailed nationalizing almost all economic enterprises, centralizing economic policy, eventually replacing money with payments in natural wages, and making a variety of efforts to raise production.[196]Unable to solve the food crisis, the Soviet government also effectively gave workers the right and responsibility to solve their food problems themselves. In May 1918 the Moscow party and unions started organizing "food exchange" detachments from the factories that, in reality, quickly evolved into food "requisitioning" detachments.[197]

At a June 1918 general meeting, the main speaker reported that enemies of Soviet rule were not permitting grain transit and that revolutionary detachments for requisitioning grain had to be organized. Two weeks later, a general meeting elected a detachment of one hundred workers.[198] On 13 August 1918, Lenin signed a decree that gave factory committees and poor peasants the right to organize food-requisitioning detachments.[199] A few days later, the factory committee issued Vasilii Gus'kov a certificate acknowledging his election as a representative of factory Food Detachment 463 for trade with peasants.[200]

While most workers participated in rowdy factory meetings that discussed food provisions, such discontent was not politically charged—workers were far more concerned with an immediate response to desperate conditions. The percentage of workers at general meetings in which food was the main agenda item was higher than factory-wide meetings in 1917. Eight hundred (of eleven hundred) workers attended a 6 May 1919 meeting on "the critical flour situation" when the ration was reduced to one *funt* (about one pound) per worker. The meeting also resolved to donate extraordinary aid of five hundred rubles to the family of every deceased worker. A few weeks later, seven hundred workers attended a similar meeting.[201] Management responded to the food shortage by resolving to create a factory "kitchen garden."[202] Theft of the potatoes led to an August 1919 general meeting resolution to assign six men a day to guard the supply, with no rations for those who refused to stand guard.[203]

Workplace democracy extended to the shop level as workers repeatedly invoked their right to elect and instantly recall their representatives. For example, a combined meeting of the electrical and cable departments recalled a Comrade Sadov as an essential worker. "We resolve that the attitude of the factory committee is intolerable and demand an immediate response ... the department reserves the right to both elect and recall delegates sent to the committee, as this is the principle on which free elections are based."[204]

Although workers packed meetings related to food supply, only about one hundred workers cared enough to vote when the SRs won the factory committee election in May 1919.[205] In July 1919, *Rabkrin* investigated the situation after having received a complaint from three workers. The inspector found several shops closed due to lack of fuel, a shortage of skilled workers, and dissatisfaction arising from the provision crisis. He concluded that workers in the factory "live no worse than at other factories, but some individuals have a negative attitude towards Soviet power. They take advantage of every opportunity to spread rumors, to write denunciations, complaints, etc." The party cell was described as "quite weak" because "all the best party members left the factory for different Soviet institutions and the Red Army." Admitting that "there are no quick answers to many of the economic and political questions and this disturbs the workers," he urged *Rabkrin* and the Party "to pay very serious attention to the Guzhon Factory." [206]

Subsequent meetings convey the sense of despair prevailing during the deteriorating situation in the summer of 1919. A general meeting three weeks later called for the strengthening of work discipline and the combating of bourgeois "slander" against the revolution.[207] An August joint meeting of management, the factory committee, representatives from *Vesenkha*, and the metalworkers' union described the bleak situation several weeks later. Factory production was "almost zero" and most workers had not returned from the summer holiday. Of the six hundred workers who had returned, one-fourth were needed for various non-production assignments for the union. The ninety workers in the bolt shop were said to "do absolutely nothing" and had not worked since the spring.[208]

Food provision problems persisted throughout the Civil War, and the attitude of workers often depended on the short-term food supply. In the winter of 1920, provisions were extremely low and the workers' mood deteriorated after the supply of potatoes had frozen and rotted.[209] In January 1920, *Rabkrin* responded favorably to an appeal to aid the factory bakery, which supplied bread for more than fifteen hundred workers, including hundreds of workers from neighboring factories.[210] In February 1920, the party called an urgent meeting to clarify "the potato situation."[211] Because of the fuel shortage, some workers had collected peat moss and then received flour as a bonus. The party resolved that flour should not be bartered and could only be distributed through the factory clerk as compensation for work.[212] Even after the sustenance situation improved, food was still the main topic in many factory meetings. In September 1921 a general meeting again discussed "the question of potatoes."[213]

A chronic lack of heat, food shortages, and an unsanitary water supply affected the workers' health. The winter of 1919-1920 brought a devastating typhoid epidemic. In November 1919, the Moscow Soviet passed measures to combat the "catastrophic situation" caused by the epidemic.[214] Registered absentees caused by illness peaked in December 1919, with 4,208 workdays lost, figures similar to the general trend in Moscow.[215] Before the epidemic, about 8 percent of the Metalworks' workforce was listed as sick but at the end of 1919 and early 1920, a quarter of all employees were either registered as having missed work because of illness, or on sick leave.[216] During the worst period of the typhoid epidemic, wrote one worker, "Twenty-five workers died each day and carpenters could not keep up with the demand for coffins."[217] "Almost all" the active Komsomol membership perished from the typhoid epidemic, according to another account, including two leaders of the factory committee.[218] The epidemic created a shortage of graveyard space, but the factory cell asked the district party committee (*raikom*) to refrain from building a cemetery near a workers' settlement because employees feared that the "putrid smell of corpses" would make their children sick.[219] Even by the end of December 1921, the epidemic had not completely subsided, as factory management distributed a circular that encouraged workers to bathe in order to combat the most recent typhoid outbreak.[220] Moreover, sick workers were unlikely to find comfort in the district hospital. In January 1920, *Rabkrin* reported that in the district hospital "the wards are cold and damp, the patients' sheets in the hospital are changed quite rarely and most patients have parasites."[221]

The workforce was also afflicted with influenza and cholera. During the influenza epidemic in the winter of 1918, a general factory meeting resolved to give extraordinary aid of five hundred rubles to the families of dead workers. In July 1918, the sanitation commission warned workers about the cholera epidemic in Moscow and recommended boiling water before drinking.[222] The increase of sick days to 9 percent of the workforce in the summer of 1921 shows the effect of another cholera epidemic.[223] Only in the latter months of 1921, after food rations had been increased, did relative health return to the factory, with less than 5 percent of the workforce registered as sick.[224]

Workers' flight to the countryside provides a useful gauge by which to measure the hardships they endured. One worker recalled the winter of 1918-1919 as "the gloomy days of cold and hunger.... Many workers, foreseeing starvation, began to disperse to their villages."[225] Another account stated that the winter of 1919-1920 was even worse, and that "workers were completely overtaken by starvation."[226] Management complained in early 1920 that, "office workers, without authorization, fled the factory because of sickness, death, etc."[227] Conditions in the factory—illustrated by the penchant of workers for voting with their feet—indicate that the situation regressed throughout 1918 and 1919, reaching a low point in early 1920. Factory employment dropped from 2,805 to 2,169 in 1918 and while a majority of those who left had joined the Red Army, every month more workers left than arrived, including 270 workers who did not return from the summer break in 1918. The workforce fell to 1,082 workers in 1919 and again the largest drop was after the summer break, when 513 workers failed to return. Employment bottomed out in the first half of 1920, and by June only 772 workers remained on the books.

Worker absenteeism also peaked during early 1920. About 13 percent of the workforce was absent during the last four months of 1919, 14 percent in 1920, and 11.7 percent in 1921. Absenteeism was particularly high during April (34 percent in 1920, 22 percent in 1921) because workers slowly drifted back to the factory after the Easter holiday. On the Monday after the Easter break in 1920, 305 workers appeared for work but the majority of workers (373) were absent.[228] At the end of April, factory management frankly acknowledged the cause of absenteeism and worker flight because "our factory does not issue provisions. This forces them to find food outside the factory, traveling to other provinces and earning extra money in other enterprises. Therefore, management will institute a bonus system for provisions."[229]

The transition to natural wages proved essential for the further operation of the factory. In 1918 and 1919 workers in Moscow spent three-fourths of their income on food, but hyperinflation rendered wages almost worthless. By late 1918 almost half of Moscow workers received wages in kind, and two years later 93 percent of workers in the city received compensation for their labor in either food or commodities.[230] In January 1920 management asked *Vesenkha* for permission to distribute bonuses in produce.[231]

The April directive to provide bonus provisions had an impact. In June 1920 the tide of worker flight was finally stemmed, as more workers arrived in the factory than left. Thus, even under the direst circumstances in early 1920, workers had some leverage in negotiating with management, pressuring them to provide provisions to alleviate worker flight. Employment increased modestly (by 95) in the second half of 1920 and significantly in 1921—from 867 to 1,459 production workers. The factory-issued rationing amounts in 1921 show a pattern of gradual increase, with rations for bread doubling between March and December.[232]

Workers remained fairly apolitical in 1920 as securing food dominated almost every aspect of life. In May twenty workers from one of the factory's food detachments complained that they had not been paid an average workers' wage in eight months. The detachment blamed this on the factory committee and demanded that the Central War-Provisions Bureau pay particular attention to the committee "because your families are doomed to die of starvation."[233] Some workers also complained that, "The working class was boss only in 1918-1919."[234] District party reports from March to September 1920, however, repeatedly reported that the mood of the workers in the factory was "satisfactory." Reports noted "no open anti-Soviet agitation," with workers accepting resolutions to raise production. "In general, the situation is calm."[235]

While the absence of "open Soviet agitation" cannot be read as support for the regime, a minority section of the workforce continued to display a sense of civic responsibility, as evidenced by the *subbotnik* movement of early 1920. Party members were expected to participate in unpaid "voluntary" Saturday labor (*subbotnik*) that was, in fact, compulsory for party members but not for nonparty workers. Almost all the participants in Moscow during the first six months of the campaign were party members, who were ordered by the MK to participate in *subbotniki* twice a month.[236] During 1919, Moscow metalworkers contributed a total of only 140 working days to the movement and the majority of participants were party members.[237] The party reprimanded members who had yet to participate or had participated only once and resolved to expel members who had skipped *subbotniki* twice.[238] By December 1919, however, nonparty participants exceeded party members throughout Moscow, and in each of the first three months of 1920, over twenty thousand nonparty workers volunteered.[239] The voluntary movement in Moscow peaked on May Day 1920 when 425,000 workers participated, and workers contributed 4.5 million hours for the month.[240] The Moscow Metalworks contributed one thousand seven hundred workdays (three hundred by communists) in early 1920, most of which came on the May Day *subbotnik*.[241]

The economic catastrophe was not conducive to labor militancy. Workers organized several shop-specific strikes in 1920, though the distinction between a conscious strike with clearly articulated demands and employees' simple refusal to work blurred during the Civil War. Factory records show six one-day strikes in the rolled metal shop and a weeklong stoppage in the form-casting shop in 1920.[242] A January 1921 party discussion shows that workers simply refused to work, though it is questionable whether such actions should be characterized as strikes since workers issued no demands: there was simply nothing to negotiate. Lack of fuel meant production fell and "workers refuse to work." With no mittens, boots, or work clothes there was a "collapse of discipline in the factory." One member suggested organizing a general meeting "to clarify to workers that card playing in the factory is not permitted."[243]

Throughout Moscow workers used factory time and materials to produce items that they could sell in exchange for food. Such commodities included stoves, lamps, candlesticks, locks, hatchets, and crowbars.[244] An April 1921 factory announcement complained: "It has been repeatedly noticed that in different parts of the factory, during regular work hours, many workers are occupied with working for themselves, producing for their own needs such items as plows, harrow teeth, etc. Such unauthorized behavior is completely unacceptable."[245]

The most widespread method of ensuring survival was theft. In November 1917, the factory committee charged one of its members with stealing iron from his department. "He explained that he took the iron before the revolution—question not decided."[246] From the October Revolution until August 1918, the factory discussed the issue of theft on twenty-six separate occasions. Stolen items included nails, cable, metal, guns, and flour from the factory bakery.[247] The factory committee unanimously resolved to fire a worker for having threatened a Red Guard and for selling stolen flour though a Soviet court found him not guilty and ordered the factory to reinstall him with back pay.[248] In February 1918, authorities arrested three women from the factory for participating in an organized ring to send nails to their village and after an investigation, the factory committee voted fifteen to fourteen to send the women to a revolutionary tribunal instead of merely firing them.[249] The most ardent supporters of the workers' state apparently were judged the most harshly. A factory cell meeting in June 1920 reported the arrest and subsequent Peoples' Court conviction of a long-standing party member, who was sentenced to five years' imprisonment for the theft and sale of two factory shelves. His comrades deemed the sentence was too severe for a skilled worker who would "better serve the Socialist Republic at a bench" than in prison.[250]

Theft and robbery accounted for more than 90 percent of all crimes committed in Moscow during the Civil War.[251] In May 1921, a speaker at the Fourth Congress of Trade Unions claimed that workers had stolen half of all goods produced in the factories; their wages, he noted significantly, covered only one-fifth the cost of survival.[252] A district party report on the factory in May 1920 noted that "strict measures" had been taken to combat theft, including changing the factory committee.[253] A party leader admitted, "every possible abuse and theft can be observed in the factory." A June 1920 discussion on the nail shop called for "stopping the systematic theft of goods from the department," and a month later, a party meeting discussed the theft of salt. In December 1920 reports complained of "evil people" in the factory at night, and the party recommended that two cell members should be elected to stand guard.[254] A February 1921 party general meeting noted that "the systematic theft of nails" continued.[255] Workers' memoirs also describe the lenient attitude towards theft prevalent during the Civil War. "Not all the workers who brought iron from the factory were evil thieves," he wrote. "Necessity compelled them to steal. They exchanged these articles with peasants for bread and potatoes." Another account was also sympathetic: "The cause was hunger—they exchanged iron for peasant produce…. We were forced to search them at the entrance." Although many workers were sent to the People's Court, "they would get exonerated."[256]

By 1921, fines and the "shaming" of workers by posting their names on factory circulars had emerged as the principal methods of attempting to curtail factory theft, but these techniques were equally ineffective. Management in the nail shop reprimanded or fined sixteen different workers in December 1921 for attempting to steal nails from the factory, including three who were caught twice in several days. One worker was caught with fifteen pounds of nails and was fined 10 percent of his salary, but the next day he again attempted to leave work with a cache of ten pounds and was fined 30 percent of his monthly salary.[257]

The end of the Civil War encouraged rising expectations among workers. In late 1920 and early 1921 a strike wave over food provisions erupted in 77 percent of all medium and large enterprises in the Soviet Union.[258] A *Cheka* report on the May 1921 strike wave in Moscow reported that workers' political sentiments had actually improved despite widespread food and wage complaints. Earlier, workers had wavered on Soviet rule, but in early May the mood was considered satisfactory, with "no openly counterrevolutionary agitation." However, "the attitude of workers toward the VKP(b) [All-Union Communist Party (Bolshevik)] is unsatisfactory because of the low numbers in the Communist cells and the weakness of party work is such that workers remain outside their sphere of influence."[259] One worker account stated that "the factory did not work for almost the entire month of May" and that the mood was boisterous.[260] Another worker wrote that a general meeting demanded better provisions with "no difference between hot and cold shops."[261] Workers won this strike, and rationing amounts were "leveled" during the summer of 1921.[262] Factory records also show eighty workers struck from 19 to 25 October 1921.[263] MK reports indicate that the weeklong strike in the form-casting department was raucous. Workers started to take iron for themselves and, when Communists seized it, "workers hissed at them. In general, workers remained defiant."[264] Despite repeated vociferous protests, rations actually improved over the course of 1921, resulting in a corresponding increase in the number of production workers from 933 to 1,412.[265]

While the regime survived the Civil War, Soviet leaders acknowledged that the working class had been transformed by the desperate struggle for survival. Lenin went so far as to assert that the industrial working class "has ceased to exist as a proletariat." For Lenin it was the "deplorable conditions" that had driven workers to steal, to produce for themselves, and to abandon the factories. Yet this "declassed" proletariat presented a major theoretical quandary for Soviet leaders. As Alexander Shliapnikov argued at the Eleventh Party Congress in 1922, "Vladimir Ilyich said yesterday that the proletariat as a class, in the Marxist sense, does not exist. Permit me to congratulate you on being the vanguard of a non-existing class."[266]

The 1917 Revolution and the Civil War represent a single continuous upheaval. Within the factory, however, it is hard to imagine two more dissimilar periods. In the first year of the revolution, workers in the Moscow Metalworks approximated the Marxist ideal of a united, irrepressible social force. Employees learned through conflict with their employer and grew confident of their collective power. They strengthened this unity by championing the cause of less privileged workers, and by supporting workers in other factories. In the politically charged atmosphere of the late summer and early fall, the Bolsheviks in the Moscow Metalworks won the political argument for a Soviet government, as they succeeded in doing throughout the Russian empire.

While labor militancy persisted into 1918, the protracted and severe social and economic disintegration rendered any meaningful satisfaction of workers' grievances impossible. A desperate, individualistic, and apolitical atmosphere permeated factory life. Contemporary accounts from the Moscow Metalworks contradict the defective historiographical representation of a "strong state" wielding its omnipotent power against the proletariat.[267] Their flight to the countryside, their simple refusal to work, the collapse of labor discipline, and the prevalence of widespread theft all suggest that workers felt less than terrified by the weakened socialist state. The July 1919 *Rabkrin* report noted soberly that workers in the factory lived no worse than in other factories but that shortage of party members was very keenly felt. The most ardent believers in the revolution volunteered for the war effort, and the few Communists who remained had neither the resources nor the influence to combat the multitude of problems. The majority of workers fled to the countryside, while many of those who stayed in Moscow perished through famine and disease. A comprehensive social, political, and economic catastrophe did not augur well for the socialist vision of an egalitarian society. Moreover, War Communism had fractured the relationship between the Soviet regime and an exhausted, demoralized working class. Was the revolution over?

Notes

1.   Trotsky, *The History of the Russian Revolution*, 1: xvii.
2.   Smith, *Red Petrograd: Revolution in the Factories;* Rabinowitch, *The Bolsheviks Come to Power;* Mandel, *The Petrograd Workers and the Fall of the Old Regime: From February to the July Days, 1917;* Koenker, *Moscow Workers and the 1917 Revolution.*
3.   John Marot, "Class Conflict, Political Competition and Social Transformation," *Revolutionary Russia*, 7:2 (1994), offers the most thorough critique of the social historical interpretation to date, positing that the deepening economic crisis in Russia is not sufficient to explain why workers moved towards a Soviet solution. He argues that the Bolshevik political program was an integral component of the process.
4.   *Ocherki istorii Moskovskoi organizatsii KPSS, 1883-1945* (Moscow, 1966), 1:364.
5.   GARF, f. 63, op. 33, d. 1403, l. 45. Okhrana report, 9 January 1917.
6.   Figes, *A People's Tragedy*, 307-353.
7.   GARF, f. 63, op. 33, d. 1403, l. 71. Okhrana report, 28 February 1917. Reports for February Revolution are filed in the opis for 1913 (33).
8.   GARF, f. 7952, op. 3, d. 272, l. 10; d. 275, l. 54; d. 272, l. 64; d. 274, l. 24. F. I. Golikov, S. S. Leshkovtsev; N.I. Igorov; A.F. Kuznetsov memoirs.
9.   GARF, f. 63, op. 33, d. 1403, l. 90; Miasnitskii station report, 28 February 1917.
10.   GARF, f. 7952, op. 3, d. 274, l. 61. N.G. Kudrov memoir.
11.   GARF, f. 7952, op. 3, d. 257, l. 127. P.N. Klimanov recollection.
12.   RGIAgM, f. 498, op. 1, d. 305, l. 1. Factory committee meeting, 7 March 1917.
13.   Trotsky, *History of the Russian Revolution*, 1: 153-205.
14.   GARF, f. 63, op. 33, d.1403, ll. 54-90. Okhrana reports, 28 February 1917.
15.   Koenker, *Moscow Workers*, 99.
16.   GARF, f. 7952, op. 3, d. 272, ll. 66-67. N.I. Igorov memoir.
17.   RGIAgM, f. 498, op. 1, d. 305, l. 1. Factory committee meeting, 4 March 1917.
18.   GARF, f. 7952, op. 3, d. 271, l. 43. V.N. Arapov memoir.
19.   GARF, f. 7952, op. 3, d. 211, l. 1. Factory record on Duma election, 14 January 1917.

20. GARF, f. 7952, op. 3, d. 275, l. 100. O.G. Ob"edkov memoir.
21. GARF, f. 7952, op. 3, d. 271, l. 42. V.N. Arapov memoir.
22. GARF, f. 7952, op. 3, d. 272, l. 15; d. 273, l. 9; d. 275, l. 32. F.E. Golikov, P.N. Klimanov, and S.S. Leshkovtsev memoirs.
23. GARF, f. 7952, op. 3, d. 301, l. 4; d. 256, l. 37; d. 274, l. 96; d. 272, l. 68-69; d. 271, ll. 223-224; d. 273, l. 41; d. 275, l. 22. Meller, M.G. Ob"edkov recollections; S.S. Leshkovets, N.I. Igorov, I.Ia. Bredis, F.I. Karpukhin, P.V. Lavrent'ev memoirs.
24. GARF, f. 7952, op. 3, d. 276, l. 15. I.F. Toptov memoir.
25. GARF, f. 7952, op. 3, d. 271, l. 183. I.M. Belikrov memoir.
26. GARF, f. 7952, op. 3, d. 275, l. 54. S.S. Leshkovtsev memoir.
27. E.N. Burdzhalov, "O taktike bol'shevikov v marte-aprile 1917 goda," *Voprosy istorii*, 4 (1956): 38-56; "Eshche o taktike bol'shevikov v marte-aprele 1917 goda," *Voprosy istoroii*, 8 (1956): 109-114.
28. *Sotsial-Demokrat*, 16 March 1917.
29. RGEA, f. 9597, op. 1, d. 17, l. 9. M.I. Gil'berg factory history citing letter in TsGAMO to Moscow Soviet, 23 March 1917.
30. *Trud*, 22 March 1917.
31. Trotsky, *History of Russian Revolution*, 1: 242-243.
32. RGIAgM, f. 498, op. 1, d. 303, l. 1. Factory announcement, 23 March 1917.
33. RGIAgM, f. 498, op. 1, d. 303, l. 1. Factory announcement, 23 March 1917.
34. TsGAMO, f. 186 op. 1, d. 104, ll. 66-67. Management letter, 1 May 1917.
35. *Vpered*, 10 May 1917.
36. TsGAMO, f. 186 op. 1, d.104, ll. 66-73. Management letter to various Provisional Government offices, 1 May 1917.
37. RGIAgM, f. 498, op. 1, d. 307, l. 1. Factory announcement, 10 May 1917.
38. GARF, f. 7952, op. 3, d. 271, l. 43. V.N. Arapov memoir.
39. TsGAMO, f. 186, op. 3, d. 3, l. 17. Factory employment statistics; GARF, f. 7952, op. 3, d. 276, l. 46. P.I. Tarasov memoir; TsGAMO, f. 186, op. 1, d. 104, l. 60-61. Factory announcement, 25 May 1917.
40. TsGAMO, f. 186, op. 1, d. 104, ll. 60-61. Factory announcement, 25 May 1917.
41. GARF, f. 7952, op. 3, d. 191, l. 4; TsGAMO, f. 2122, op. 1, d. 248, l. 92. Factory manager letter to Provisional Government, 1 June 1917.
42. TsGAMO, f. 2122, op. 1, d. 248, l. 25. Guzhon letter to Chairman Moscow Factory Conference, 20 June 1917.
43. TsGAMO, f. 186, op. 1, d. 104, ll. 62-63. Arbitrator's letter, n. d.; Moscow Soviet decision, 26 May 1917.
44. RGIAgM, f. 1076, op. 1, d. 19, ll. 46-48; TsGAMO, f. 2122 op. 1, d. 248, ll. 98-99. Management letter to various Provisional Government offices, 9 June 1917.
45. Koenker and Rosenberg, *Strikes and Revolution in Russia, 1917* (Princeton, 1989), 137-142.
46. GARF, f. 7952, op. 3, d. 210, ll. 196-197. Factory management to head of Moscow police, 8, 24, May, 9 June 1917.
47. GARF, f. 406, op. 2, d. 204, l. 9. Minister of Internal Affairs for City of Moscow to Prince G.E. Lvov, 17 June 1917.
48. GARF, f. 7952, op. 3, d. 210, ll. 208-217. Documents of the revolution: arbitration session, 24 May 1917, Moscow Soviet session, 26 May 1917.
49. GARF, f. 7952, op. 3, d. 210, ll. 254-255 and TsGAMO, f. 186, op. 1, d. 104, ll. 74-75. The 19 June demand list continued with specific department issues.
50. TsGAMO, f. 186, op. 3, d. 3, l. 17.
51. TsGAMO, f. 2122, op. 1, d. 248, ll. 23-24. Guzhon letter to Chairman Moscow Factory Conference, 20 June 1917.
52. TsGAMO, f. 2122, op. 1, d. 248, ll. 23-27. Guzhon letter to Chairman Moscow Factory Conference, 20 June 1917.
53. TsGAMO, f. 2122, op. 1, d. 248, ll. 23-27. Guzhon letter to Chairman Moscow Factory Conference, 20 June 1917.
54. TsGAMO 2122, op. 1, d. 248, l. 176. Factory announcement, 22 June 1917.

Revolution and Counterrevolution

55. TsGAMO, f. 186, op. 1, d. 104, l. 64-65. Workers' committee letter to executive committee Moscow Soviet, 28 June 1917.
56. GARF, f. 7952, op. 3, d. 271, l. 46. V.N. Arapov memoir.
57. *Russkoe slovo*, 30 June 1917.
58. Kornakovskii, *Zavod 'Serp i Molot' 1883-1932*, 84.
59. *Pravda*, 13 July (June 30), 1917, cited in Lenin, *Collected Works*, 25: 142-145.
60. Smith, *Red Petrograd*, 168-171, 180.
61. Alexander Rabinowitch, *Prelude to Revolution: The Petrograd Bolsheviks and the July 1917 Uprising* (Bloomington, 1968), 97-176.
62. Trotsky, *History of the Russian Revolution*, 2: 113-135.
63. Trotsky, *History of the Russian Revolution*, 2: 121, 128.
64. Koenker, *Moscow Workers*, 129.
65. Trotsky, *History of the Russian Revolution*, 2: 165.
66. Rabinowitch, *The Bolsheviks Come to Power*, 51.
67. *Revoliutsionnoe dvizhenie v Rossi v iiule 1917 goda. Iiul'skii krizis* (Moscow, 1959), 106-112. MK meeting, 7 July 1917.
68. GARF, f. 7952, op. 3, d. 271, l. 43. V.N. Arapov memoir.
69. *Revoliutsionnoe dvizhenie v Rossi v mae-iiune 1917 goda. Iiun'skaia demonstratsiia* (Moscow, 1959), 38-40.
70. *Shestoi s"ezd RSDRP (bol'shevikov). Avgusta 1917 goda* (Moscow, 1958), 55, 325.
71. GARF, f. 7952, op. 3, d. 276, l. 64. E.D. Tumanov memoir.
72. GARF, f. 7952, op. 3, d. 276, l. 15. I.F. Toptov memoir.
73. GARF, f. 7952, op. 3, d. 274, ll. 94-5. S.S. Leshkovtsev memoir.
74. GARF, f. 7952, op. 3, d. 274, l. 62. G.N. Kudrov memoir.
75. GARF, f. 7952, op. 3, d. 272, ll. 71-2. N. Igorov memoir.
76. GARF, f. 7952, op. 3, d. 257, ll. 5-9. Klimanov reminiscence.
77. GARF, f. 7952, op. 3, d. 265, l. 28. Klimanov reminiscence.
78. GARF, f. 7952, op. 3, d. 274, l. 22. A.F. Kuznetsov memoir.
79. GARF, f. 7952, op. 3, d. 273, l. 43; d. 274, ll. 43, 62, 96. F.I. Karpukhin, P.L. Lavrent'ev, G.N. Kudrov, and V.I. Lebedev memoirs.
80. GARF, f. 7956, op. 3, d. 276, l. 16. I.F. Toptov memoir.
81. GARF, f. 7952, op. 3, d. 274, l. 62. G.N. Kudrov memoir.
82. GARF, f. 7952, op. 3, d. 263, l. 83. V.I. Lebedev recollection.
83. *Sotsial-Demokrat*, July-August 1917.
84. TsMAM, f. 2562, op. 1, d. 5, l. 6. Rogozhsko-Simonovskii Soviet, 15 September 1917.
85. GARF 7952, op. 3, d. 263, ll. 53-54. E.D. Tumanov recollection.
86. *Ocherki istorii Moskovskoi organizatsii KPSS*, 2: 77.
87. *Revoliutsionnoe dvizhenie v Rossi v avguste 1917 goda. Razgrom kornilovskogo miatezha* (Moscow, 1959), 379-385.
88. *Sotsial-Demokrat*, 11 August 1917.
89. Koenker, *Moscow Workers*, 124-128.
90. Nicolai Sukhanov, *The Russian Revolution* (Princeton, 1984), 494.
91. *Izvestia*, 13 August 1917.
92. *Sotsial-Demokrat*, 17 August 1917.
93. *Trud*, 13 August 1917.
94. TsGAMO, f. 186, op. 1, d. 96, l. 110. Metalworkers' summary of 12 August strike.
95. Trotsky, *History of the Russian Revolution*, 2: 160-183.
96. Rabinowitch, *The Bolsheviks Come to Power*, 94-150.
97. Figes, *A People's Tragedy*, 452-455.
98. Koenker, *Moscow Workers*, 135.
99. Sukhanov, *The Russian Revolution*, 522-523.
100. Koenker, *Moscow Workers*, 250-251.
101. *Sotsial-Demokrat*, 7 September 1917.
102. GARF, f. 7952, op. 3, d. 275, ll. 58-9. S.S. Leshkovets memoir.
103. Tony Cliff, *Lenin: All Power to the Soviets*, 313-314.
104. Lenin, *Collected Works*, 11: 359.

105. Tim McDaniel, *Autocracy, Capitalism and Revolution in Russia* (Berkeley, 1988), 390.
106. Lenin, *Collected Works*, 25: 234-241.
107. Koenker and Rosenberg, *Strikes and Revolution in Russia*, 268-275.
108. RGIAgM, f. 498, op. 1, d. 633, ll. 6-7. Management letter 30 May, Arbitrator ruling, 6 June 1917.
109. RGIAgM, f. 1076, op. 1, d. 19, ll. 97-99. Arbitrator report, 11 July 1917.
110. TsGAMO, f. 186, op. 1, d. 137, l. 16; d. 100, l. 46. Metalworkers' reports, 1917.
111. TsGAMO, f. 186, op. 1, d. 100 ll. 45-52. Demands dated 6 October 1917.
112. RGIAgM, f. 176, op. 2, d. 7, l. 1. Metalworkers' conflict commission letter, 12 October 1917.
113. TsMAM, f. 2562, op. 1, d. 5, l. 6. Rogozhsko-Simonovskii Soviet, 15 September 1917.
114. GARF, f. 7952, op. 3, d. 273, l. 37. P.N. Klimanov memoir.
115. RGIAgM, f. 498, op. 1, d. 305, ll. 1, 2. Factory committee meeting, 22 July 1917.
116. TsGAMO, f. 186, op. 1, d. 96, l. 67; d. 133, ll. 7-13. Metalworkers' report, n.d.; Metalworkers' report on contributions, January 1918.
117. RGIAgM, f. 498, op. 1, d. 305, ll. 1, 2. Factory committee meeting, n.d. August 1917.
118. *Sotsial-Demokrat*, 15 October 1917.
119. GARF, f. 7952, op. 3, d. 276, l. 67. E.D. Tumanov memoir. GARF, f. 7952, op. 3, d. 271, l. 33; V.N. Arapov memoir.
120. RGIAgM, f. 498, op. 1, d. 305, ll. 2-3. Factory committee meetings, September through November.
121. GARF, f. 7952, op. 3, d. 209, l. 216. Red Guard data in documents on the revolution, n.d.
122. M. Akun and V. Petrov, *1917g. v. Mosvke* (Moscow, 1934), 146; GARF, f. 7952, op. 2, d. 276, l. 71; E. D. Tumanov memoir
123. GARF, f. 7952, op. 3, d. 276, l. 17. I.F. Toptov memoir.
124. GARF, f. 7952, op. 3, d. 271, ll. 46-52. Memoir of V.N. Arapov.
125. GARF, f. 7952, op. 3, d. 263, l. 52. Kochergin recollection.
126. GARF, f. 7952, op. 3, d. 275, l. 101. M.G. Ob"edkov memoir.
127. GARF, f. 7952, op. 3, d. 274, l. 23; d. 276, l. 188. A.F. Kuznetsov, E.D. Tumanov memoirs.
128. GARF, f. 7952, op. 3, d. 374, l. 95; d. 276, l. 75. V.I. Lebedev and E.D. Tumanov memoirs.
129. Trotsky, *History of the Russian Revolution*, 3: 90.
130. Koenker, *Moscow Workers*, 330.
131. Trotsky, *History of the Russian Revolution*, 3: 240-275.
132. *Revoliutsionnoe dvizhenie v Rossi v sentiabre 1917 goda* (Moscow, 1961); *Revoliutsionnoe dvizhenie v Rossi nakune oktiabr'skogo vooruzhennogo vostaniia (1-24 oktiabria 1917 goda)* (Moscow, 1962).
133. Rabinowitch, *The Bolsheviks Come to Power*, 291-292.
134. Israel Geltzer, *Martov: A Political Biography of a Russian Social Democrat* (London, 1967), 172.
135. Estimates of the number of Red Guards range from six thousand (Koenker, *Moscow Workers*, 338) to thirty thousand. Rex Wade, *Red Guards Workers' Militias in the Russian Revolution* (Stanford, 1984), 296.
136. GARF, f. 7952, op. 2, d. 276, l. 71. E.D. Tumanov memoir.
137. GARF, f. 7952, op. 3, d. 276, l. 19. I.F. Toptov memoir.
138. GARF, f. 7952, op. 3, d. 276, l. 73. E.D. Tumanov memoir.
139. RGEA f. 9597, op. 1, d. 18, ll. 32-3. Guzhon factory history.
140. GARF, f. 7952, op. 3, d. 271, ll. 47-8. Arapov memoir.
141. GARF, f. 7952, op. 3, d. 276, l. 19. I.F. Toptov memoir.
142. Liberal historians continue to confuse this elementary point about 1917. For example, Mark Steinberg, in *Voices of Revolution* (New Haven, 2001), 56-57, glowingly depicts the liberals as the "obvious choice for power" who supposedly "believed in a society based on law and proper democratic procedure." Steinberg largely ignores the liberals' war profiteering, their repeated efforts to thwart popular elections, their anti-Semitism, as well as their repeated efforts to crush the revolution.

143. Rabinowitch, *The Bolsheviks Come to Power*, xxi.
144. E.H. Carr, *The Bolshevik Revolution 1917-1923, Volume Three* (New York, 1953), 17-18.
145. Donny Gluckstein, *The Western Soviets Workers' Councils Versus Parliament 1915-1920* (London, 1985), 85, 120-193.
146. John Reese, *In Defence of October* (London, 1997), 14.
147. TsMAM, f. 176, op. 2, d. 6, ll. 4-15. Factory committee meeting, 7 December; general meeting, 8 December 1917 (new calendar).
148. TsGAMO, f. 186, op. 1, d. 137, l. 18. Metalworkers' list of grievances, 28 November 1917 (old calendar).
149. RGIAgM, f. 498, op. 1, d. 305; TsMAM, f. 176, op. 2, d. 6; GARF, f. 7952, op. 3, d. 215; factory committee meetings.
150. *Vpered*, 24 December (6 January) 1917.
151. GARF, f. 7952, op. 3, d. 212, l. 74. Moscow Soviet to factory committee, 31 December 1917 (old calendar).
152. GARF, f. 7952, op. 3, d. 212, l. 90. Management letter, 20 January 1918 (old calendar).
153. GARF, f. 7952, op. 3, d. 215, l. 41. Factory committee meeting, 24 January 1918 (old calendar).
154. TsGAMO, f. 2122, op. 1, d. 236, ll.12-3. Summary of management meeting, December 1917 (old calendar).
155. GARF, f. 7952, op. 3, d. 215, l. 42. Factory general meeting, 8 February 1918 (old calendar).
156. Smith, *Red Petrograd*, 240-242.
157. Bruce Lincoln, *Red Victory: A History of the Russian Civil War 1918-1921* (New York, 1999), 59.
158. GARF, f. 7952, op. 3, d. 215, l. 69. Factory committee meeting, 12(25) March 1918.
159. GARF, f. 7952, op. 3, d. 215, l. 101, 114. Factory general meetings, 29 May, 14 June 1918.
160. GARF, f. 7952, op. 3, d. 215, l. 129. Factory committee meeting, 11 July 1918.
161. Kornakovskii, *Zavod 'Serp i Molot' 1883-1932*, x-xi.
162. GARF, f. 7952, op. 3, d. 212, l. 140; Moscow Area Economic Commission letter, 6 June 1918.
163. GARF, f. 7952, op. 3, d. 212, l. 141. Central metalworkers' meeting, 7 June 1918.
164. GARF, f. 7952, op. 3, d. 215, l. 140. Factory committee meeting, 24 July 1918.
165. Smith, *Red Petrograd*, 151, 172, 180, 237, 238.
166. Lincoln, *Red Victory*, 187.
167. TsGAMO, f. 186, op. 1, d. 104. l. 99. Report of Pavlov for metalworkers' union, 11 July 1918.
168. TsMAM, f. 176, op. 2.d. 99, ll. 1-13. Factory committee meetings, 1920.
169. TsMAM, f. 176, op. 2, d. 72, ll. 1-5. Factory management meetings, January-May 1920.
170. TsAODM, f. 429, op 1. dd. 2-4. Factory party meetings, 1919-1921.
171. GARF, f. 7952, op. 3, d. 215, ll. 3-70. Factory committee meetings, November 1917 through March 1918.
172. TsMAM, f. 176, op. 2, d. 99. Factory committee meetings, 1920.
173. TsGAMO, f. 186, op. 1, d. 96, l. 129. Moscow metalworkers' delegate meeting, 22 October 1917.
174. TsAODM, f. 429, op. 1. dd. 3, 4. Party meetings, 1920, 1921.
175. GARF, f. 7952, op. 3, d. 312, l. 2. Factory Civil War history.
176. TsAODM, f. 429, op. 1, d. 3. ll. 3, 8, 18, 20. General party meetings, 17 January, 14 February, 28 April, 12 May 1920. TsMAM, f. 176, op. 2, d. 102, l. 122. Factory announcement, 14 February 1921.
177. Mark von Hagen, *Soldiers in the Proletarian Dictatorship: The Red Army and the Soviet Socialist State, 1917-1930* (Ithaca, NY, 1990), 21-22.
178. Chase, *Workers, Society, and the Soviet State*, 32.
179. GARF, f. 7952, op. 3, d. 273, 46. F.I. Karpukhin memoir. The mean age of the party members who remained in the factory was thirty-three. TsAODM, f. 429, op. 1, d. 5, l. 2. Party membership data, October 1921.

180. GARF, f. 7952, op. 3, d. 290, 6. Factory Komsomol history.

181. GARF, f. 7952, op. 3, d. 275, l. 117-131. M.G. Ob"edkov memoir; d. 276, l. 20-22; I.F. Toptov memoir.

182. Chase, *Workers, Society, and the Soviet State*, 50.

183. TsAODM, f. 3, op. 1, d. 4, l. 160. MK discussion on work in Rogozhskii district, 20 April 1918.

184. TsAODM, f. 429, op. 1, d. 2, l. 2. Telegram dated 20 January 1919.

185. TsAODM, f. 429, op. 1, d. 3, l. 32. Factory party meeting, 10 July 1920.

186. GARF, f. 7952, op. 3, d. 212, ll. 177-181. Management meeting, 12 July 1918.

187. Chase, *Workers, Society, and the Soviet State*, 18-19.

188. GARF, f. 7952, op. 3, d. 200, l. 30.

189. GARF, f. 7952, op. 3, d. 311, ll. 1-4. Factory Civil War history.

190. TsAODM, f. 429, op. 1, d. 4, l. 5. Party meeting, 8 February 1921.

191. GARF, f. 7952, op. 3, d. 273, l. 16. P. N. Klimanov memoir. Fyodor Gladkov, *Cement* (New York, 1989).

192. GARF, f. 7952, op. 3, d. 215, l. 74. Factory committee meeting, 8 (21) March 1918.

193. GARF, f. 7952, op. 3, d. 212, l. 164. Management meeting, 29 July 1918.

194. Lincoln , *Red Victory*, 184-198.

195. David Fogglesong *America's Secret War Against Bolshevism, 1917-1920* (Chapel Hill, 1995), 87, 104. From May to December 1919 alone, the U.S. supplied $16,000,000 in arms and other materials to the White armies.

196. Alec Nove, *An Economic History of the U.S.S.R.* (New York, 1989), 37-72.

197. Chase, *Workers, Society, and the Soviet State*, 22-23.

198. GARF, f. 7952, op. 3, d. 215, ll. 110, 122. Factory general meetings, 8 and 30 June 1918.

199. GARF, f. 7952, op. 3, d. 212, l. 2. Lenin memorandum, 13 August 1918.

200. GARF, f. 7952, op. 3, d. 212, l. 24. Factory committee memorandum, 24 August 1918.

201. GARF, f. 7952, op. 3, d. 213, ll. 73, 81. Factory general meetings, 6 and 22 May 1919.

202. GARF, f. 7952, op. 3, d. 213, l. 76. Management meeting, 15 May 1919.

203. GARF, f. 7952, op. 3, d. 213, l. 113. Factory general meeting, 15 August 1919.

204. GARF, f. 7952, op. 3, d. 213, l. 35. Electrical and cable combined shops meeting, 5 March 1919.

205. GARF, f. 7952, op. 3, d. 213, ll. 87-93. Factory general meetings, 24 May, 12 June 1919. This election and SR influence during the Civil War are discussed in chapter 5.

206. TsMAM, f. 1474, op. 7, d. 126, ll.45-46. Rabkrin report, 12 July 1919.

207. GARF, f. 7952, op. 3, d. 213, l. 111. Factory general meeting, 1 August 1919.

208. GARF, f. 7952, op. 3, d. 213, ll. 116-120. Combined management and union meeting, 20 August 1919.

209. GARF, f. 7952, op. 3, d. 257, l. 122. V. Malinin recollection.

210. TsMAM, f. 2791, op. 1, d. 4, l. 74. Rabkrin report, 19 January 1920.

211. TsAODM, f. 429, op. 1, d. 3, l. 6. Party meeting 14 February 1920.

212. TsAODM, f. 429, op. 1, d. 3, l. 47. Party meeting, 24 November 1920.

213. TsMAM, f. 176, op. 2, d. 102, l. 324. Factory general meeting, 15 September 1921.

214. TsMAM, f. 2587, op. 1, d. 102, l. 1. Moscow Soviet executive committee, 1 November 1919.

215. TsMAM, f. 176, op. 3, d. 50. Monthly factory statistics; Chase, *Workers, Society, and the Soviet State*, 308. The number of deaths per thousand from 1917 to 1921 were: 23.7, 29.9, 45.6, 36.3, 25.5.

216. GARF, f. 7952, op. 3, d. 183, l. 47. Monthly factory summary of absentees.

217. GARF, f. 7952, op. 3, d. 273, l. 15. P.N. Klimanov memoir.

218. GARF, f. 7952, op. 3, d. 290, 6. Factory Komsomol history.

219. TsAODM, f. 429, op. 1, d. 3, l. 47. Party meeting, 24 November 1920.

220. TsMAM, f. 176, op. 2, d. 102, l. 483. Factory announcement, 27 December 1921.

221. TsMAM, f. 2791, op. 1, d. 4, l. 74. Rogozhsko-Simonovskii Rabkrin report, January 1920.

222. GARF, f. 7952, op. 3, d. 215, l. 73, 133. Factory committee meetings, 8 (21) March, 15 July 1918.

223. *Iunaia Pravda*, 25 July 1921; GARF, f. 7952, op. 3, d. 183, l. 47. Monthly factory summary of absentees.
224. GARF, f. 7952, op. 3, d. 183, l. 47. Monthly factory summary of absentees.
225. GARF, f. 7952, op. 3, d. 257, l. 83. V. Malinin recollection.
226. GARF, f. 7952, op. 3, d. 290, l. 7. Factory Komsomol history.
227. TsMAM, f. 176, op. 2, d. 2, l. 5. Management letter to metalworkers' union, 11 December 1920.
228. TsMAM, f. 176, op. 2, d. 50; d. 109. Factory statistics, 1920, 1921.
229. GARF, f. 7952, op. 3, d. 72, l. 1. Management meeting, 29 April 1920.
230. Chase, *Workers, Society, and the Soviet State*, 27, 37, 307.
231. TsMAM, f. 176, op. 2, d. 77, l. 2. Management meeting, n.d. January 1920.
232. GARF, f. 7952, op. 3, d. 311, ll. 1-13. Factory Civil War history.
233. TsMAM, f. 176, op. 2, d. 101, ll. 4-5. Food detachment number 817 meeting, 28 May 1920.
234. Chase, *Workers, Society, and the Soviet State*, 37.
235. TsAODM, f. 80, op. 1, d. 359, ll. 4, 13, 14, 21, 23, 30, 38, 40, 44. Proletarskii party district reports, March-September 1920.
236. Chase, *Workers, Society, and the Soviet State*, 47.
237. GARF 7952, op. 3, d. 280, l. 57.
238. TsAODM, f. 429, op. 3, d. 3, ll. 4, 9. Party general meetings, 24 January, 21 February 1920.
239. *Kommunisticheski Trud*, 9 May 1920.
240. Dewar, *Labour Policy in the USSR, 1917-1928* (London, 1956), 61.
241. Kornakovskii, *Zavod 'Serp i Molot' 1883-1932*, 121.
242. TsMAM, f. 176, op. 2, d. 84, ll. 5-6. Shop days worked, 1920.
243. TsAODM, f. 429, op. 1, d. 4, ll. 1-2. Party general meeting, 26 January 1921.
244. Chase, *Workers, Society, and the Soviet State*, 19, 24.
245. TsMAM, f. 176, op. 2, d. 102, l. 173. Factory announcement, 18 April 1921.
246. TsMAM, f. 176, op. 2, d. 6, l. 8. Factory committee meeting, 24 November 1917 (old calendar).
247. GARF, f. 7952, op. 3, d. 215, ll. 1-143. Factory committee meetings, November 1917 to August 1918.
248. GARF, f. 7952, op. 3, d. 215, ll. 38, 126. Factory committee meetings, 23 January (old calendar), 5 July 1918.
249. GARF, f. 7952 op. 3, d. 215 ll. 54, 58. Factory committee meetings 10, 14 (old calendar) February 1918.
250. TsAODM, f. 429, op. 1, d. 3, ll. 23, 26. Party general meetings, 9, 30 June 1920.
251. Chase, *Workers, Society, and the Soviet State*, 21.
252. *vserossiiskii s"ezd professional'nukh soiuzov. Stenograficheski otchet* (Moscow, 1922), 119.
253. TsAODM, f. 80, op. 1, d. 359, l. 14. Proletarskii party district report, 23 May 1920.
254. TsAODM, f. 429, op. 1, d. 3, ll. 19, 26, 28, 47-48. Party cell meetings, 20 May, 30 June, 7 July, 1 December 1920.
255. TsAODM, f. 429, op. 1, d. 4 , l. 6. Factory party general meeting, 16 February 1921.
256. GARF, f. 7952, op. 3, d. 275, l. 142; d. 274, l. 47. M.G. Ob"edkov, P.V. Lavrent'ev memoirs.
257. TsMAM, f. 176, op. 2, d. 73, ll. 459-475; d. 102, ll. 440-480. Factory announcements, December 1921
258. Chase *Workers, Society, and the Soviet State*, 49.
259. GARF, f. 393, op. 1a, d. 36, ll. 257-268. Moscow Cheka summary, 1-15 May 1921.
260. GARF, f. 7952, op. 3, d. 312, ll. 12-3. Factory Civil War history.
261. Kornakovskii, *Zavod 'Serp i Molot' 1883-1932*, 131.
262. GARF, f. 7952, op. 3, d. 311, ll. 1-13. Factory Civil War history.
263. TsMAM, f. 176, op. 2, d. 109, l. 29. October 1921 statistics.
264. TsAODM, f. 3, op. 2, d. 46, l. 190. MK information summary, late October 1921.
265. GARF, f. 7952, op. 3, d. 312, ll. 12-13. Factory Civil War history. TsGIAgM, f. 176, op. 2, d. 107. Monthly employment statistics.

266. Lenin, *Collected Works*, 33: 65; 32: 199, 411. *Odinnatsatii s"ezd RKP(b)* (Moscow, 1936), 109.

267. Aves, *Workers Against Lenin: Labor Protest and the Bolshevik State*; Vladimir Brovkin, *Behind the Front Lines of the Civil War: Political Parties and Social Movements in Russia, 1918-1922* (Princeton, 1994).

3

CLASS CONFLICT DURING THE NEW ECONOMIC POLICY

> "The trust administration drive around in automobiles, while cutting
> costs is done on the backs of workers. They trick and screw the peasants
> and this is what is called the *smychka*."
>
> — Hammer and Sickle representative at a district workers'
> conference, April 1926

The ascendancy of the Stalinist system is rooted in the qualitative change in
worker-state relations during the New Economic Policy (NEP). While militant strikes proliferated at the beginning of the era, by late NEP they were
largely an event of the past. So secure were Soviet leaders of their position in
1928 that the regime embarked on a program of draconian wage cuts to help
pay for rapid industrialization during the First Five-Year Plan—a strategy
that hinged on a speculative assessment that the formerly militant Soviet
working class had been transformed into a relatively docile social force. But
if their calculations were correct, how had the state managed to tame the
most unruly proletariat of the twentieth century?

Historians working within the narrow parameters of Cold War-driven
historiography have responded to this question by asserting either overwhelming state repression or voluntary working-class identification with
Stalinism.[1] E.H. Carr and R.W. Davies put forward an alternative, institutional argument, emphasizing the "uneasy compromise" between red managers and unions that helped avert industrial unrest.[2] While the controversy
over the central interpretive question in Soviet working-class history
persists, the decline in workers' participation in strike actions is no longer
disputable. Strikes shifted from primarily offensive demands over wage
increases in early NEP to more defensive actions (against wage cuts) by its
conclusion. Work stoppages gradually became much shorter, rarely involved
more than a single factory, and often were limited to specific departments.
The proportion of workers participating in work stoppages declined to

---

about 3 percent of the Soviet labor force during any single year between 1925 and 1928.[3]

The factory's demographic and economic recovery after the Civil War was similar to that of other high-priority metal plants in the city, but also illustrative of the limits of industrial recovery. Moscow's industrial workforce reached only 60 percent of its 1912 level by 1926, though the metal industry expanded disproportionately with the number of metalworkers (40,000) approximately double that of 1918.[4] The number of Hammer and Sickle production workers increased from 1,412 in 1921 to 2,200 by the end of 1922 and two years later exceeded (3,600) the total before the war.[5] More workers were added in 1925, but 1926 was the first year since the Civil War in which the number of workers declined, from 4,501 to 4,334.[6] Several shops added a second shift, and, at the end of NEP, the factory employed 5,000 production workers.[7] The factory's production increases were even more substantial, increasing from 4 percent of the prewar figure in 1921 to 74.5 percent in the 1925-1926 fiscal year, matching the prewar level during 1926-1927, and exceeding it by 8 percent during the last year of NEP.[8]

After seven devastating years of war, NEP was conceived initially as a temporary compromise that would permit private trade in an attempt to restore exchange relations between town and country. Lenin, at the Tenth Party Congress, expressed the logic underlying the new policy: "only an agreement with the peasantry can save the socialist revolution in Russia until the revolution has occurred in other countries."[9] From the perspective of labor, NEP was inherently contradictory. On the one hand, the Soviet state mandated that state enterprises "work without losses" and wage increases could "only be the result of higher productivity."[10] Factory managers were responsible to overseeing trusts, and in critical respects this profit and loss accounting system (*khozraschet*) meant that they were compelled to operate under terms similar to private capitalist businesses.[11] At the same time, however, the Soviet state instituted legislation very different from that of its western counterparts. The November 1922 Labor Code stipulated that wages would be negotiated through collective agreements between the trusts and unions in which workers would have a voice and the right to ratify the contracts. The Rates Conflict Commissions (RKK), composed of management and workers on an equal basis, would handle noncontract disputes; work would be limited to eight hours (six hours for youth); overtime work would be compensated at 150 percent; and women would receive sixteen weeks' paid maternity leave.[12] Such legislation did not guarantee its implementation— the fundamental tension between the pursuit of economic efficiency and the defense of workers' rights and interests would be revealed during the course of the 1920s. Here we attempt to unravel the complexities of NEP labor politics by examining the transformation of workplace institutions and class conflict.

Workplace Internationalism

Soviet labor policy cannot be analyzed in isolation from its international context. The Bolsheviks hoped, with some justification, that the meager material and technological resources available within the borders of the USSR would be augmented by a successful workers' revolution in Europe and that the coming to power of workers' governments would relieve the deprivation facing the Russian working class. But seven years of war and civil war left Soviet society devastated, in much worse shape than in 1917. Three million soldiers had died in battle or from wounds or disease, and another thirteen million civilians perished prematurely from famine or epidemic. Industrial production from large-scale industry fell to 13 percent of the prewar level.[13] Yet solidarity for international causes remained an important tenet of Bolshevik policy. The massive growth of Communist Parties throughout Europe and the German revolt of 1923 offered the Revolution a glimmer of hope in an otherwise desperate predicament.

During the 1923 German Revolution, women in the factory led a short-lived campaign to aid the children of German workers.[14] Thereafter, factory leaders attempted to build an ongoing international solidarity organization, but the International Aid Society for Revolutionary Fighters (MOPR) was in reality a paper institution, with activities organized by a handful of party members. *Martenovka* reported that hooligans regularly tore down MOPR posters and exhibits, and that the only active members (of the supposedly 1,550) were the leaders in several shops.[15] Two years later, shop leaders complained that members had not paid their dues and that the organization remained "only on paper."[16]

The failure to build an ongoing solidarity organization, however, did not accurately reflect workers' willingness to contribute to international causes. Workers donated a remarkable 26,662 rubles in support of the 1926 British general strike.[17] Incidents involving resistance to the campaign were rare, suggesting that contributions were voluntary.[18] As the Unified State Political Administration (OGPU) reported in regard to solidarity with the British general strike, "workers' sympathetic attitude is expressed in deductions often exceeding (at the initiative of workers themselves) norms established by the All-Union Central Trade Union Council (VTsSPS)."[19] Thus, despite incredible poverty compared with those workers that they were supporting, internationalism remained a powerful current in proletarian ranks.

Large mass meetings on international issues illustrate the voluntary nature of the campaign. Central Committee member Kalinin spoke at the two largest meetings in 1925 and 1926 (2,200 and 2,000 respectively), which included reports on both the international and internal Soviet situation. Three other 1926 international solidarity meetings all drew crowds of 1,200 or more.[20] Questions and comments to speakers during the British general strike convey the workers' keen understanding of solidarity, but also their utter incomprehension of the reformist logic of western social democracy, which allowed the capitalist system to remain intact. Several workers clearly thought in revolutionary terms: one asked Kalinin, "Why were not workers conscious enough to take power into their own hands and smash the House [of Parliament]? This is not correct." A second was concerned about the technicalities of an insurrection: "Comrade speaker, please tell us, what kind of guns do the English workers have?" Another worker asked, "Comrade Tomsky, if Russian workers in the year '18 had such discipline as the English workers, could we have won the revolution?"[21]

Many notes expressed exasperation over the role of the British trade union leaders. One asked: "Comrade Tomsky, tell us, if the General Council leaders betrayed the workers, then why did the workers not take the vermin-traitors out of the General Council and put workers in their place?" Another asked, "Comrade speaker, please tell us why the English Council were such cowards and sent the workers back to work." One note suggested, "Comrade speaker, I think that English workers live well in that they poorly support their strike. They need our heart and resolve." Many workers were dumbstruck by the General Council's refusal to accept Soviet support. One worker wanted to know: "Why did not they accept our financial help and who are they in the General Council, and who elected them, workers or English capitalists?"[22]

The solidarity campaigns also introduced a subversive factor into the worker-state dialogue by encouraging employees to ask comparative questions about Soviet society. One worker complained that while the speaker "talked beautifully and splendidly about these English leaders," he neglected to mention "our ragamuffin Soviet leaders who are worried about workers there, but do not have the same worries about our Soviet workers."[23] Numerous questions referred to comparative living standards. One worker asked, "Comrade Tomsky, you said that English workers live poorly, but we do not see how Russian workers can live on fifty-five rubles," and asked why British workers "did not help revolutionary workers when they were hungry." Another asked, "Comrade M.I. Kalinin, please tell us how it is possible for six people to live at the fifth wage and skill grade when they receive only fifty-six rubles, fifty-three kopecks?"[24] At a party meeting, one member asked, "Can you tell us, how is it on the one hand you put anarchists in jail, while at the same time that our union conducted protests against the execution of [American anarchists] Sacco and Vanzetti?"[25]

Soviet setbacks in the international arena had profound ramifications domestically. In December 1926 the Politburo passed a "policy of agreement" resolution that called for cooperation with industrialized countries, believing that securing of credit from abroad was a prerequisite for future economic growth. But many Western leaders rebuked the Soviet policy of seeking financial aid while the Comintern simultaneously intervened in affairs of other states. In May 1927, the British conservative government cancelled the Anglo-Soviet trade agreement, and negotiations with France, Yugoslavia, and Czechoslovakia were likewise soon halted.[26] Torn between the hope that workers' revolutions would come to their aid and a more accommodating approach that sought financial assistance from foreign capitalists, the Soviet regime received neither.

A full decade after the soviets had assumed power in 1917, the revolution was left to its own internal resources to build "socialism in one country." This isolation dampened workers' enthusiasm for international solidarity contributions, which came to be viewed as simply another tax imposed from above on rank-and-file members. After the murder of the Soviet ambassador in Warsaw in 1927, "the mood of workers in connection with international relations" took a turn for the worse, and even some party members "had become cowards."[27] For the more politically sophisticated workers, however, the Soviet Union's isolation was not just a mere inconvenience—the very hope of the revolution rested on the prospects of international socialism. Soviet leaders' exaggerations about the strength of the Europe workers' movement ultimately contributed to the demoralization of the working class. One worker challenged Commissar of Labor Schmidt's attempt to put a positive face on international events: "The results as you can see are bad. Everything is coming out badly. We are defeated everywhere and by everyone. Obviously, you are not following events well enough."[28]

The Transformation of the Party during NEP

The factory party organization changed both quantitatively and qualitatively during NEP. From just 60 highly committed members in 1921, the party grew to 240 three years later, and to 690 by November 1926. This rapid growth reflected a partial healing of the rift between workers and the state that had developed during the Civil War. By 1927, however, the party's increasingly productivist and undemocratic policies made it difficult to recruit workers, such that membership dropped to 605.[29] Membership grew marginally in 1928 by lowering the standards for those who joined, by allowing members to stay on the membership list even if they refused to pay dues or attend meetings, and by refusing members' requests to leave the party.[30]

During early NEP, the party repeatedly lent its authority to employees' grievances. In March 1922, a nonmember wanted to know "why the cell did not pay more attention to the conflict in form-casting shop?"[31] Two months later, party leaders sided with workers' complaints over provision prices, resolving that, "together with workers we demand full compensation at market rates."[32] In June 1922, after workers' complaints of form-casting shop management rudeness, the party bureau mandated that "incorrect activity by the administration should be stopped."[33] In response to a March 1923 conflict in the repair shop, the party bureau again sided with workers, calling for "clarification on the distribution of funds for workers' pay."[34] Even the factory director expressed sympathy for the economic plight of workers. In response to a Central Committee (TsK) question about wages, he stated, "Wages are too low for medium qualification workers or office personnel to survive tolerably."[35] Similarly, the party bureau acknowledged that the May 1923 strike wave had erupted over "an excessive increase in work norms" that it considered "a mistake."[36] The party also recommended nonparty workers to the Soviets, even if they were hostile to regime policy. A 1923 factory committee discussion on the party's proposed list of candidates to the

Moscow and district Soviets indicates that at least half the party's proposed candidates were "against the communists."[37]

Productivity was not yet the driving imperative in the party that it would become several years later. Thus, in June 1924, the party bureau stated that the work in many areas was being carried out poorly but that the work in the areas of production (and soviets) was "particularly bad."[38] In a nail shop discussion held in the midst of a work stoppage, the speaker attributed the strike to "the lack of discipline of certain wavering comrades and party disorganization in the shop."[39] In September 1924, the party sided with employees' demands, resolving in a factory plenum that in conjunction with the rise in productivity, "it is necessary for wage-rates not be lowered but improved."[40]

Members continued to display a high level of commitment. In January 1923, only twenty of eighty party members were without assignments, yet the party bureau resolved to call a factory plenum to distribute the work more evenly. The following month, the cell expelled several members for displaying a "passive attitude" and nonpayment of membership dues. After this mini-purge, sixty members, candidates, and sympathizers participated in a political education course.[41]

This high level of participation contrasts markedly with the low party commitment after the Lenin Levy—the mass worker recruitment campaign that followed in the months after Lenin's death in January 1924. Several months after the new membership campaign, party leaders expressed concerns about many of the raw recruits and they vowed to expel the worst offenders for "noncommunist behavior" that included failure to attend meetings, nonpayment of dues, and being so detached from the party as to be unable to name their shop organizer.[42] The purge was consistent with a party directive to rid the cell of 12 percent of "worthless elements."[43]

Party leaders faced the dual task of attempting to integrate raw recruits whose attitudes mirrored those of the workers they were expected to discipline, and breaking the sympathetic attitudes of long-standing members who identified with the egalitarian ideals of the 1917. Even some party leaders were unenthusiastic about their role as shop-floor disciplinarians. In early 1924, a district party spokesman blamed factory leaders who had known about a recent strike in the factory "but did nothing to head it off."[44] While economic "tailism" (supporting workers' grievances uncritically) was always a party concern, the majority of the cell supported a strike action in April 1924. A factory leader scolded members in a closed session: "Our task is to eliminate capitalism yet in such a difficult year we have a strike.... We rely on the organization to lead the masses, but instead it is the other way around."[45]

Rank-and-file workers noticed the shift in party policy away from labor advocacy. In September 1925, "after the lowering of wage-rates" in the rolled metal shop "workers began to exhibit a more careless attitude towards their obligations." In this early phase of the productivist turn, party activists acknowledged general "displeasure among workers that the cell supported this wage reduction" though the mood of the workers "is not so hostile towards Soviet power and the party."[46] Significantly, workers in 1925 still

expected the party to respond sympathetically to their demands and were surprised by its new wage-cutting policies that would shortly become the norm.

Party members repeatedly indulged in economic "tailism." In January
1926, the Norm Setting Bureau (TNB) ordered new piece rates in the bolt
shop. "Workers became agitated and began saying that they were being
swindled," and the shop party bureau passed a resolution condemning the
TNB position as "incorrect" and calling for a discussion of the issue in a
general factory plenum.[47] Steel foundry members complained that the shop
manager repeatedly came to work drunk and shouted profanities at workers.
They brought the issue to the unsympathetic factory director, Stepanov,
who responded that "engineers like Titov are difficult to find." At another
meeting, a member complained "the director only needs us when he wants
to implement some campaign." He went on to argue that, "the administration acts as if it is the master and the party and the trade union remain to the
side."[48] An architectural shop member sided with nonparty workers' sentiments against his comrades in the factory committee election: "I think
workers were correct to have rejected certain comrades in the reelection to
the factory committee because the factory committee is closely fused with
the administration." [49]

The changing definition of party membership also related to the campaign
against the United Opposition and the attempt to instill "iron discipline." In
practice this meant attempting to transform the membership into a passive
body that would dutifully implement the frequently changing Central Committee directives. Divergent opinion in shop cells was formally noted while,
invariably, party-sponsored resolutions carried unanimously. In October
1926, the cooperative party leaders reprimanded a member who had voted in
favor of the "regime of economy" but then "in the general open meeting of
the cell he spoke against this work."[50] The same month, the steel foundry cell
expelled five members for failing to carry out party decisions, failing to pay
dues, and drinking excessively, castigating one of them for "repeatedly criticizing the decrees of Soviet power among nonparty workers."[51] Under growing pressure to police the workforce, even the most loyal members conveyed
a sense of anxiety as the close-knit factory regime moved away from their
own rank-and-file ideals of socialism. One worker complained, "Comrade
Kalinin, please tell us, is the view from above one of complete bureaucratism
and not constructing socialism? We are seeing from below, at our place, complete bureaucratism but there is nothing we can do because they are all very
closely tied to each other. So we will either have to start over again building
socialism or erect barricades."[52]

The shop-floor membership was in such a state of confusion over its new
role that the factory director was forced to address a closed factory party
meeting at the end of 1926. "Many have spoken out here against the administration and, of course, I am obliged to respond to this question," Stepanov
told them. "Two years ago discipline was extremely weak. The factory and
shop administration have taken appropriate measures which cause a certain
dissatisfaction which has not yet dissipated."[53] Significantly, Stepanov also
noted that party members sometimes "utilized their party cards" for their

advantage in the shops, something that, he argued, "should not be a factor in production."[54] Some members increasingly viewed the party organization as a source of privilege and assumed that the tightening of discipline advocated by management applied first and foremost to nonparty workers. A bolt shop report admitted a certain "dissatisfaction of nonparty workers towards the cell, mainly about making better work available to cell members."[55]

By 1927, the formal tasks of party membership were clear, yet the party was hardly a smoothly operating productivist machine. In April, the rolled metal shop reported "cases of tailism and members falling subject to the mood of nonparty workers."[56] A November report claimed that the majority carried out the party line in meetings, but again noted "tailism" in placing shop interests above those of the factory and complained that members encouraged nonparty members to raise questions about pay. Moreover, many members had only a superficial grasp of the problems facing the party; their nonparty counterparts were frequently stronger than party members in discussions; and too many members seemed to feel "little responsibility for tasks assigned to them."[57]

The conversion of the factory party organization into an institution that would impose economic concessions and discipline the nonparty workforce confused and demoralized many members. In September 1927, the repair shop cell was in shambles. "The ideological situation in our cell is bad. There are incidents of drunken communists. Workers torment communists and their activity, but they remain silent. We have no group or individual agitation." Lamenting the dearth of discipline and political commitment among party members, the shop leaders rebuked the actions of two recent recruits who "entered the party but are against all our ideas and everything we desire."[58]

Before ascending Stalinism became strong enough to extinguish open opinion outside its ranks, many workers were unwilling to exchange free speech for membership in an organization they did not respect. In June 1928, the newspaper printed workers' explanations as to "Why We Are Nonparty." One worker complained that the cell in his shop discussed only mandated work and that "we do not want to vote for what has been predetermined." Another complained that "instead of explaining things" party members "would rather curse you out," while yet another letter protested that after losing arguments in the nail shop, the cell secretary resorted to smearing his opponents for having "white-guard views." One worker wrote that although "communists are supposed to be literate," a member held the meeting agenda upside down "and the workers laugh."[59]

Evidence suggests that the new breed of ardent party hacks came from among the most politically backward workers. A former member, Kruglova, expressed the concerns of many workers repulsed by the dramatic decline in the cell's membership standards: "Is the party a correctional institution? Why do they accept all kinds of garbage and keep those who do nasty things? Is this what Lenin willed?" One letter stated that members were "supposed to be the leadership of the working class, but unfortunately, the majority of the time this is not the case." Another worker protested that one member "spouts such nonsense that one is embarrassed for him." So strong was corruption and privilege among party members that during a bolt shop recruit-ment session, one worker explained: "I will not enter the party because communists are embezzlers and thieves."[60] In July 1928, eighty-two nonparty *aktiv* those workers theoretically the closest to the party—met to discuss party growth and "self-criticism" (*samokritika*) but several speakers spoke about the party organization in unflattering terms. One speaker complained that members were arrogant because they "do not take advice from nonparty workers.... Party members have a bad comradely attitude in the shop." Many former members complained they had been "burnt," and one warned non-party workers: "No, do not enter, even if this is what you want."[61]

The 1928 *samokritika* campaign constituted a preemptive attempt by the evolving bureaucracy to manipulate worker grievances for its own purposes and a tacit admission that the party was becoming discredited among non-party workers. In April, the head of the Central Control Commission, V.P. Zatonskii, candidly acknowledged the manipulative nature of the campaign when he argued that it was necessary to "somewhat release the pulled-up reins" and to "let the workers have the possibility of criticizing us" because "it would be much better to do so now" than later, when workers started tak-ing action on their own.[62] The literal record of workers' comments and the increasing contempt for the party, illustrated in a growing refusal to enter its ranks, attest to the failure of the campaign. *Martenovka* admitted that the "bad behavior of certain comrades" contributed to workers' "unhealthy atti-tude" toward the party. Among workers there was a "distrust of *samokritika*" and a "clear anti-party mood resulting from intensification of the working day and the politics in the countryside."[63]

The party had become so discredited and desperate for members in 1928 that it repeatedly refused to grant permission to members who applied to leave its ranks. Two members in the repair shop requested expulsion, but both were "refused and remain in the party."[64] Four rolled metal shop mem-bers refused to pay their dues debt and "demanded that they be expelled from the party."[65] A nail shop member declared at his second appeal to leave the party that "you will not keep me in the party by force."[66] A construction shop member's petition claimed that the party secretary, "instead of explain-ing things calls you a bastard and a parasite."[67] An electrical shop member requesting expulsion explained that "my views are very different and I have not paid membership dues in a long time. I cannot and will not work in the party." At the same session, another member stated, "I have not paid mem-bership dues for two years. Expel me from the party."[68] Nonpayment of dues apparently became such a widespread exit strategy in the construction shop that the party bureau suggested "canceling the debt" of five members who had not paid dues for three to fourteen months.[69] In January 1929, the party finally expelled two members in the rolled metal shop who had neither paid membership dues nor attended a single meeting in two years.[70]

The transformation of the factory party organization was astounding. During the "open door" recruitment strategy of 1924-1926, hundreds of workers had entered the party because they identified with its ideals, but by the end of NEP, the factory organization was forced to adopt a "closed door" strategy to prevent disgruntled members from leaving. Nonparty workers in the factory did not view the most hardened party loyalists as radical, but rather as "those who do nasty things," "embezzlers and thieves," or, as the Opposition characterized them, unprincipled "bootlickers and informers."[71] The party's 1928 *samokritika* campaign and OGPU reports on the mood among workers across the Soviet Union prove that the fissure between Stalinism and the working class was a general, rather than a local phenomenon.[72]

The Transformation of Union Organizations during NEP

Three positions dominated the trade union discussion at the Tenth Party Congress that convened during the Kronstadt rebellion in the spring of 1921. With famine raging throughout the Soviet Union and with the transportation infrastructure in tatters, Trotsky had converted Red Army units into "battalions of labor" and achieved impressive results in reconstructing the railways. But labor armies also incorporated civilians and, as Isaac Deutscher notes, Trotsky had turned a bitter necessity into an ideological virtue, by advocating the "militarization of labor." The Workers' Opposition justifiably noted that party and state apparatus had substituted its rule for that of the proletariat during the Civil War and had "reduced almost to nil the influence of the working class associations in the Soviet state." Their remedy for the frayed relationship between the state and working class called for "the concentration of industrial management in the hands of the Trade Unions." Lenin's middle position insisted that in industrial policy, unions should be subordinate to the party and the needs of the workers' and peasants' state—but he acknowledged that this state had become "bureaucratically deformed." Emphasizing persuasion over coercion in industrial relations, Lenin argued that unions should have a degree of autonomy for a "number of decades" to defend workers' interests. Lenin's moderate position, attempting to balance the state and workers' interests in trade union policy, won out, though it contained an implicit ambiguity regarding occasions when the interests of the state and workers collided.[73]

This dual-role of the metalworkers' union meant that it could be an important instrument for containing workers' militancy, but it also was under pressure to respond sympathetically to their grievances. The metalworkers' union advocated for a participatory membership and helped promote the usually boisterous factory-level meetings. In March 1923, the union complained that delegates met irregularly and urged them to meet more frequently.[74] A report a year later showed that this directive achieved results, as over the preceding six months the delegates and the factory committee held eleven shop meetings and nine general meetings. Throughout NEP, the delegates' sessions were the most volatile representative body because they were under the most direct pressure from rank-and-file workers and were not dominated by the party. In 1924, two-thirds of the ninety-six delegates were nonparty workers.[75] Although union meetings minutes in early NEP convey a sense of order,[76] a 1923 *Rabochaia Moskva* report on one union session

shows that these were not tranquil proceedings and that workers expected
their representatives to respond to their grievances:

> The speaker from the district metalworkers' union is giving a report on the work
> of the union for the year. He starts with a heap of figures.... The workers' atten-
> tion weakens and they begin quiet conversations. At first they talk quietly but then
> it grows louder and louder.... Someone starts to shout. He is complaining that
> they had to pressure management in order to get paid on Saturday. They talk
> about potatoes and firewood. The man sitting next to me is screaming at the top
> of his lungs. But the speaker, far from being discouraged, takes a drink of water
> and continues droning: twenty meetings, thirty sessions, and eight conferences.
> Workers are not interested in this. Reports should be connected to real life.[77]

Staffed with four full-time paid organizers by 1925, the factory committee was the main union organ within the factory, meeting with management
on a regular basis and brandishing its authority in defense of workers'
rights.[78] During "the struggle against overtime hours" the committee
coerced management to hire new workers, and a January 1926 factory
announcement noted that without union sanction, "overtime work is not
permitted."[79] Overtime hours reached 36,279 extra hours in March 1925,
but a year later monthly averages were one-sixth this amount.[80] Thus, rather
than functioning as a management tool to extend work hours—as it did during the First-Five Year Plan—the factory committee had fought to reduce
work hours. In August 1925, the committee noted that many conflicts had
arisen over repeated violations of the Code of Law, including the transfer of
workers from higher to lower wage category positions without union consultation, and nonpayment for overtime and night work. It pledged to force
the administration to post the laws in all departments and "to instruct shop
directors and accountants that infringement of the Code of Law is imper-
missible."[81] So powerful was the union organization in 1925 that the factory
director later wrote that trade union's deputies—rather than the managers—
held real power in the shops.[82]

With the support of the factory committee, workers repeatedly demanded
and received short-term loans from the factory, particularly before holidays
when they returned to the countryside. In the late summer of 1923, delegate
dissatisfaction over loans forced the issue to a general meeting of almost half
of the workforce.[83] *Rabochaia Moskva* reported that in 1924, workers were
given credit, but again in the spring of 1925 workers besieged their factory
committee representatives on a daily basis with the same question: "When
will we receive credit?"[84] Rank-and-file pressure for loans was so strong in the
spring of 1926 that factory committee party members broke discipline by
supporting workers' demands for 125 percent advances, even though the
party had mandated only 100 percent.[85]

The RKK was possibly more important than the factory committee in
terms of providing social stability. An RKK representative explained that
repeated conflicts between management and the factory committee could
not be resolved so that "it was necessary to create an authoritative commis-

sion made up of representatives of workers and management on the basis of parity."[86] Weekly sessions discussed collective and individual statements from workers, including requests for work clothes, pay issues, complaints over unfair transfers, wage category appeals, and even requests to shorten the workday.[87] For eighteen months during 1924 and 1925, the RKK handled cases involving an astounding 13,068 workers. The commission sided with 8,529 workers (65.0 percent) and against 3,918 (29.86 percent), with the remaining cases, involving 675 workers (5.14 percent), either unresolved or sent to higher arbitration.[88] Thus, far from being a state institution deployed against the working class, workers themselves viewed the union organization as an effective source of power in pressing their grievances.

The RKK enjoyed such prestige that it occasionally exceeded its formal authority. In August 1926 a party member in the bolt shop was expelled for "systematic nonpayment of dues," but appealed to the RKK and was subsequently reinstated. A party leader took exception to this interference. "The RKK must support our decisions," he complained, "so that we can raise the rate of dues payment."[89] Rank-and-file influence on the RKK is illustrated by two factory committee reports in 1925. The first summary of RKK work issued in May detailed 220 conflicts over the previous half-year involving 5,066 workers. The RKK had sided in favor of the workers 46 percent of the time and against workers 51 percent of the time. A revised report included an additional 66 conflicts—all decided in favor of the workers. The new total showed a slight majority (50.06 percent) of the 5,463 workers affected received favorable resolutions.[90]

The astounding number of industrial disputes handled by the RKKs throughout the Soviet Union shows that workers' willingness to go through official union channels to arbitrate their grievances accounts for the relatively low number of strikes. As E.H. Carr and R.W. Davies have shown, over eight thousand disputes involving over seven million workers were handled by RKKs in the last three fiscal years of NEP. They dealt with issues related to the basic wage rates, the quality of and access to state-supplied communal services, additions to wages, compensation for dismissal, procedures for hiring and firing, and protection of labor. Issues not resolved by the RKKs were sent to arbitral tribunal or conciliation courts.[91]

Sending issues to arbitration bodies apparently provided management with a means of maneuvering around workers' increased frustrations. In July 1926, workers in the nail shop requested a month off for summer holiday, which their counterparts in the hot shops already enjoyed, but the administration refused. The union transferred the issue to the Guberniia work inspector, who passed the issue on to the People's Commissariat of Labor (*Narkomtrud*). The following spring, workers' letters again appealed to *Narkomtrud*. The union newspaper *Trud* sided with the workers, arguing that it was "necessary to decide this question quickly and satisfy the justified workers' demands which are supported by the doctors' commissions."[92] Without a favorable resolution, the shop union leader and party member described the mood in the shop as "defiant," and complained that workers no longer trusted him.[93] In this incident the pro-worker metalworkers' stance collided with the harsh realities of industrial policy, though again, workers had expected a favorable response.

A level of democracy persisted in the metalworkers' union that was unimaginable a few years later. At a Mashinotrest (the trust overseeing the factory) production conference in October 1926, union representatives raised complaints about poor organization of factories, expenditures, and shortages of raw materials. The workers' delegates repeatedly spoke beyond their time limit, but when trust speakers tried to go beyond their limit, delegates called out, "Enough!"[94] At a district union conference, a Hammer and Sickle representative argued: "Pay remains the same but life is more expensive. The trust administration drive around in automobiles, while cutting costs is done on the backs of workers. They trick and screw the peasants and this is what is called the *smychka*." The OGPU reported that "the delegates' attitude towards those who spoke in this manner was sympathetic, with applause accompanying the speeches."[95]

Open expression of such sentiments became less frequent during late NEP but illustrates the paradox that beset developing Stalinism that strived to be a participatory system. Given workers' hostile sentiments towards the regime's productivist directives, it became increasingly difficult to provide a veneer of "support from below" for state policies when workers were allowed to choose their own delegates at such conferences. Workers had even more confidence when they issued complaints in the form of anonymous notes, like this one passed to Tomsky, the chairman of the All-Union Central Trade Union Council, when he spoke at the factory:

> Please remember the words of Ilyich Lenin. Why are you not conducting a cleansing of party of elements who only take up positions while not doing what they are supposed to do, but instead walk around the shops and give orders and shout at the lower class? They receive the eleventh wage and skill grade while our brothers receives only the third. They tell us, just live and prepare for war. I request you read this out loud.[96]

By 1926 party members dominated shop union positions, but the slightest suggestion of a split in the party's ranks could spark confidence among nonparty workers. In January 1926, the party leveled charges against a member because "during the adoption of the collective agreement" he had gone "against the party and criticized communists in the presence of noncommunists." Another speaker said that, "under the leadership of Comrade Runge, they buried the collective agreement in the shop" and the cell resolved to transfer the troublemaker to another shift.[97] In the form-casting shop in December 1927, a Comrade Shashkin agitated against the party, which he claimed had gone against the workers. He gained support among a group of party members, candidates, and nonparty workers and submitted "a petition from the masses." A party session subsequently discussed Shashkin's "systematic anti-party behavior" including the accusation that "while serving as general shop meeting chairman, he had helped defeat the list of candidates for the shop bureau which had been suggested by the party." Shashkin responded that he had not known about the party list and that two other party members were responsible for the meeting's disruption because while he was speaking "they tried to pull me down by the coat."[98]

Workers became more critical of the work of the union in late NEP. Repair shop workers complained that the factory committee had allowed an "incorrect lowering of wage categories" in the collective agreement and that the RKK had not decided enough issues in favor of workers. Several speakers in the repair shop reported a recent drop in work discipline and blamed this on party shop leaders who were "too busy talking."[99] At a factory conference of six hundred in December 1926, the OGPU reported that workers believed that the factory committee "did not defend workers' interests, agrees more with the administration, and does not implement the resolutions of the delegates' meetings."[100]

Factory committee summaries in the last years of NEP stopped reporting the actual numbers of workers affected in decisions handled by the RKK, but open dissatisfaction suggests a change in favor of management. From May to September 1928, the RKK handled 811 conflicts: 347 were resolved in favor of the workers and 375 against, with 89 cases sent to arbitration. Significantly, the report did not provide numbers on how many workers (of 3,996) were affected by decisions.[101]

Throughout NEP, workers continued to pay dues and to appeal to the union for support. After 1922 union membership in the Soviet Union was voluntary, but almost 90 percent of Soviet workers chose to join the unions because of such benefits as sickness insurance, access to housing, and priority in hiring in case of layoffs.[102] Significantly, even in late NEP, production remained a relatively minor issue in union meetings, especially when compared to its single-minded pursuit during the First Five-Year Plan. From May 1926 to May 1927, production was broached only six times among 252 issues in forty factory committee meetings, only once in delegates' meetings, and once in general factory conferences.[103] In January 1927, 97 percent of more than four thousand workers were members of the union, indicating that despite their criticisms, the overwhelming majority of workers were willing to pay membership dues to receive union benefits.[104] Three thousand workers participated in the 1927 vote that elected 51 shop bureau members including twenty-two nonparty workers and three women. The delegates were under even less control of the party, electing 139 of 195 nonparty workers as delegates, including eleven women.[105]

Delegates continued to press for wage increases on an egalitarian basis. In December 1927, delegates resolved that, "the line must be taken to raise the pay of the most poorly paid and lagging behind workers, while mostly preserving regular wages in the factory."[106] Pressured by factory delegates and union representatives, the wage increase (excluding inflation) in 1927 of over 20 percent for third and fourth wage and skill grade workers was ten times that of the more highly skilled workers.[107] In negotiations between management and the metalworkers' union, the union backtracked on many issues and sent others to arbitration. For the 1927 wage scale, the union wanted 5 percent more than was offered by the trust and wanted to raise productivity by only 1 percent, versus the trust's demand of a 6.8 percent increase. The trust won on the wage rate issue but, perhaps sensing the volatility of worker grievances, asked for only a 2.5 percent raise in productivity.[108] To reduce overall wage costs without explicitly lowering wages, management also sought to reclassify the wage and skill categories of almost a thousand employees. The union resisted, and the new classification resulted in a net reduction for 327 workers, rather than the 943 that management had wanted.[109]

The retreat of the unions was generalized throughout the Soviet Union. As Carr and Davies have argued, from 1925 "the destiny of the worker had rested on the uneasy compromise" between *Vesenkha* and red managers on the one hand, eager to increase the efficiency of industry and to cut down costs, and the trade unions still concerned with "the immediate material interests and welfare of the workers." Yet, "as the drive for industrialization became more intense, the trade unions fought a losing battle; the needs of industry were the paramount consideration." Trade union leaders such as Tomsky "had been content to conduct an orderly retreat, saving what he could on the way."[110]

Union activity in the Hammer and Sickle Factory illustrates the demise of this "uneasy compromise." Workers repeatedly appealed to their union for help and expected a favorable response. By the end of NEP, however, workers were acutely aware that their union organizations had conceded considerable ground to management. Nevertheless, they continued to believe that they could compel their representatives to fight on their behalf. Workers' hope for reform *within* existing factory institutions was crucial to the transformation of labor relations in NEP and helps to explain why workers did not build new independent networks that could have challenged the harsh anti-labor policies later introduced by the state. Given that the metalworkers' union had previously defended their interests and continued to do so nominally even at the end of NEP, such hopes were quite rational.

Workers' Grievances and Strikes during NEP

The contours of labor conflict and management's strengthened position against the workforce are reflected in trends in workers' wages. Real wages rose during early NEP to 1924-1925, and declined each year thereafter. Although wages constituted only about 23 percent of overall production costs—the majority of expenditures were for fixed capital costs such as raw materials and fuel—it was the variable costs of production that directly pitted management against the workforce.[111] *Martenovka* printed the average workers' wages as a percentage of prewar (1913-1914) rubles for several years and incorporated inflation into its calculations. The average real wage rose from 79.6 percent of the prewar wage in 1923-1924 to 93.9 percent in 1924-1925. A year later, the average wage had increased 10 percent, though the factory newspaper acknowledged that with inflation, it had actually dropped 6 percent. The average wage without inflation increased 14.6 percent in

1927, suggesting a slight decrease in real wages. In the last year of NEP, wages increased 6.2 percent—a real wage reduction of about 4 percent according to *Martenovka*, though the actual decrease was more substantial as official figures underestimated the rate of inflation.[112]

Strike activity began rather modestly in 1922. On 6 June, 125 workers in the bolt shop struck because they had not received overtime pay for the second half of May. The next day, 65 workers in the rolled metal shop stopped work for a half-hour and demanded clarification on work norms.[113] The factory director reported that there was "a conflict with all production shops (simultaneously) in November 1922 on the question of production norms, which had been raised in connection with the pay increase." The dispute ended in favor of management when the district metalworkers' union intervened and sanctioned the increased norms.[114]

Complaints about food and delays in payment of wages dominated workers' grievances during 1922 and 1923. A May 1922 factory meeting discussed "the flour question," resolving to demand full compensation of flour for all workers at the market rate.[115] So rampant was hyperinflation that a factory announcement listed monthly payments in million of rubles—11,750,000 for the lowest level and 28,000,000 for the eighth wage and skill category worker.[116] Moscow Soviet reports show that employees' most frequent grievance during the period of hyperinflation was concern over delays in wage payments.[117] Occasionally work stoppages were avoided when management acquiesced to employees' grievances. For example, "worker dissatisfaction in the Hammer and Sickle Factory (formerly Guzhon) caused by nonpayment of wages for January" was "liquidated by issuing their pay."[118] The GPU reported "a sharp deterioration of the situation in industry" throughout the Soviet Union with workers' complaints about "late payment of wages" continuing until the fall of 1923.[119]

An unprecedented strike for the six-hour day illustrates early NEP labor militancy. On 22 February 1923, the factory committee, union representatives, and management discussed the implementation of a six-hour day, and agreed to consider two categories of workers but rejected others, including workers in the wire pulling shop. On 26 February, sixty wire pulling shop employees struck after their petition for a six-hour day had been refused. On 1 March, metalworkers' leaders proposed that workers return to work under the old conditions because they could not support the demand for the six-hour day, and warned that they would not object if management fired workers and brought in replacements.[120] Under this threat, workers met and agreed to return in unison at 1:20 that afternoon, though they insisted that the entire shop be taken back without victimizing "specific persons" and demanded that officials and shop representatives discuss the possibility of implementing the six-hour day.[121] Even in defeat, the strike shows a high level of workers' confidence and organization, fueled in part by rising expectations of economic recovery. They put forward offensive demands for a six-hour day, convened meetings in which they could determine their own strategy, returned in unison, and organized collective defense against victimization. Many workers in 1923 had not forgotten the strength and tactics of collective action learned during the prerevolutionary years, and their high level of organization contrasted with that of later in NEP.

Three shops struck in May 1923 against an increase in production norms. On the evening of 4 May, a delegates' meeting complained about increased norms and elected four representatives to talk with Mashinotrest. Reports on 7 and 8 May noted widespread complaints in the factory over raising work norms. The union transferred the issue to the Protection of Labor on 14 May, but the rolled metal and form-casting shops struck the next day, spreading the action to the wire pulling shop. Several speakers at a delegates' meeting on 15 May spoke in favor of continuing the strike action, even seeking formal union support for the stoppage—again indicating workers' high expectations of the union in early NEP. Other workers denounced the excessive norm increases, but conceded that the Moscow Soviet had to resolve the dispute. A factory-wide meeting that afternoon failed to resolve the issue, and another report on 18 May noted that "Italian" strikes continued in two shops and warned that the workers' mood was such that, if the norms were not lowered the next morning, all shops would stop work. The report stated that the strike was launched in solidarity with two other factories in the district that had gone out over the raising of production norms. The strike apparently ended in a compromise, raising norms from 3.6 to 10 percent.[122]

Mass workers' meetings also attest to a rising tide of worker militancy during early NEP, with reports repeatedly describing Hammer and Sickle meetings in 1923 as "stormy" and numerous threats to stop work. On 1 August, 1,500 workers (of 2,352) attended a "quite stormy" meeting during another strike over lowering wage rates. Fifteen speakers denounced the reductions in a raucous session and some workers, according to the report, were in "an inebriated state." The proceedings turned particularly tumultuous when a Mashinotrest representative told workers that the trust had explored the possibility of closing the factory with the aim of concentrating production. The workers voted to ask the union to reexamine the wage rates and returned to work the next day, but "their mood continued to be unsatisfactory." A week later, several shops again struck, with the possibility of the entire factory halting work. A dispatch the following day reported another mass meeting: "At the time of printing the report, the meeting continues and is stormy." Another general meeting in August became unruly when management proposed to pay part of workers' wages in state bonds. Stoppages continued in several shops until 16 August.[123]

In November 1923, workers in two shops initiated another round of strikes over piecework rates. A 15 November delegates' meeting voted to accept an 11 percent raise in rates, but workers in the rolled metal shop voted against the proposal and 504 employees struck, joined by 150 nail shop workers on 6 December. On 10 December, management threatened to bring in replacements against the unsanctioned strikers, but fifty-six rolled metal workers continued to strike. The strike collapsed before the holiday (22 December) when twenty skilled workers signed an agreement to return to work.[124]

By the spring of 1924, labor dissatisfaction had again escalated. *Tsekhovsh-china* characterized the strike movement as localized shop-based stoppages spilled over into other departments. The lowering of wage-rates and increased work norms in metal factories met with "strong dissatisfaction."[125] This round of strikes started in the predominately female nail shop, where workers demanded higher wages and lower production norms, and again workers convened their own meeting. "Strikers did not permit anyone from the administration, the factory committee, the cell, or even workers from other shops to enter their meeting." On the second day of the strike, with negotiations under way, the mood in the nail shop was marked by "extreme discontent." The stoppage then spread to the wire pulling shop, and speakers in a stormy meeting threatened to shut down the entire factory. Unrest was becoming endemic in the factory. "Work stoppages in one shop, then another, appear chronic," the report noted.[126]

Although less political, this renewed workplace militancy was reminiscent of the post-Lena economic strikes with industrial expansion encouraging rising expectations and demands. Similarly, sectional divisions within the workforce also reemerged, particularly *tsekhovshchina*. Disagreements over the length of holidays also led to friction between ex-peasants and urban workers. A December 1922 "city and countryside" general meeting led to "a victory for the villagers." Workers received a weeklong break so that they could return to the countryside, rather than the three days urban workers preferred so as not to lose additional pay.[127] Several participants in an October 1924 factory party discussion on "raising the productivity of youth" were frustrated by the skill level and work habits of younger workers. One speaker complained that "the young have a careless attitude towards work" and another speaker blamed younger workers because "machines and tools are broken every day."[128]

The Civil War era rift between the state and Hammer and Sickle workers was partially healed by the early NEP economic recovery, substantial wage increases, and the party's sympathetic position toward workers' concerns. Workers' proclivity for strike action did not continue throughout NEP: no more strikes were reported after the early 1924 unrest and only one for all of 1925. Given both the persistence of economic grievances and the absence of any evidence of state repression, this conspicuous intermission in labor activism can only be explained by the state's success in co-opting labor grievances through official union channels. By early 1925, workers' relative satisfaction with the regime appears to have reached its apex, a sentiment reflected in hundreds of workers joining the party membership. A party bureau report for March 1925 stated that production and wages were going up and found "the mood of workers satisfactory, the only dissatisfaction is with housing."[129] Another report again claimed that the mood in the factory was still "sufficiently satisfactory" except with regard to the housing shortage.[130]

Complaints over housing persisted throughout NEP. On the sixth anniversary of the revolution, the factory newspaper demanded "Give Workers Housing."[131] In early 1924, the first reports that workers were spending the nights in the shop appeared.[132] The factory had its own housing cooperative whose 360 members helped to build apartment complexes near the fac-

tory.[133] In 1924, 66 percent of the new housing in the district went to workers, 10 percent to demobilized soldiers, 5.5 percent to unemployed persons,
5 percent to office workers, and only 4 percent to members of the party organization.[134] Despite this, in August 1924, eight hundred workers were without adequate housing.[135] An MK report on the factory from early 1925
claimed that a shortage of apartments for seven hundred workers and their
families was "reflected in the mood of workers and in problems in implementing increased productivity."[136] By September 1925, this figure had
reached fifteen hundred, though the urgency of the housing problem gave
way to new concerns with economic and shop-floor grievances.[137]

The only significant political criticism expressed during these years concerned the regime's rural policy. In April 1923, a Moscow Soviet report
noted "dissatisfaction" among "workers with ties with the countryside"
because of the large tax on the peasants.[138] A 1924 factory party report again
reported "a village mood" and complaints about higher taxes in the countryside.[139] Several speakers in a 1925 shop discussion on party work in the
countryside stated that conditions in the countryside had improved, but
complained about kulaks, who were "oppressing poor peasants."[140]

The collective agreement in June 1925 was the first major test for evolving Stalinism and indicated that management would begin implementing a
harder line against the workforce. It also shows how the threat of unemployment became an increasingly powerful weapon with which management
could threaten the workforce. Two closed general party sessions were
devoted to new 11 percent wage reductions—the first new collective agreement since 1923. Party leaders complained that production had dropped
after the wage cut, reminding members that it was their duty to help the factory administration implement the new agreement in order to strengthen the
link between the town and country (*smychka*). A week later an MK speaker
defended the wage cut, reporting ominously that unemployment in Moscow
had doubled to ninety-six thousand in the preceding five months, with seven
thousand unemployed metalworkers. The economic crisis during the latter
part of the NEP strengthened the position of the state against the working
class, but in April 1925, open dissent was still very much alive in the party as
at least four speakers condemned the proposed wage reduction.[141]

A June 1925 party bureau discussion on problems in the nail shop noted
that several members "have bad relations with the administration." Real
wages had been lowered by about 11 percent, and this was "reflected in the
mood of the workers. Currently we have protests in the ranks against the new
wage-rate." Workers in the rolled metal shop signed a declaration for a wage
increase and sent it to the RKK. Factory party leaders complained that many
Lenin Levy recruits, rather than curtailing such actions, were "tailing the
masses," and resolved to pay more attention to this "intolerable situation."
Nevertheless, the leaders believed that, with the exception of the form-casting and rolled metal shops, the workers' mood was satisfactory.[142] A report
sent to the Central Committee also condemned Lenin Levy recruits' "tailism," and warned that the reaction to the wage cut in the rolled metal shop
"nearly took the form of a strike."[143]

Implementing the new wage-rates was problematic for factory leaders. Two hundred workers from several shops signed another petition to RKK demanding reestablishment of the old norms. On 17 June seventy workers in the rolled metal shop demanded an immediate reexamination of the wage-rate. The strike lasted only an hour and a half, as the factory committee and administration intervened and, according to the OGPU, "satisfied the demands of the workers."[144] The new factory directory, Petr Stepanov, later wrote that enraged rolling mill workers marched to his office with their tongs and that management assistants had "gathered around to defend their director—they feared excesses."[145] Rather than workers being intimidated by a "strong state," as depicted in the pre-archival Cold War historiography of the Soviet working class, an increasingly unruly workforce threatened the most ardent state loyalists.

Yet factory leaders proved to be adept "firefighters," straining themselves repeatedly to contain simmering discontent. Significantly, they were allowed tremendous flexibility in allocating wage increases, which ranged from 0 to 12 percent per department. In 1925, management responded favorably to shop-based grievances: departments that reported the most problems (the form-casting and rolled metal shops) had received the highest wage increases in the December collective agreement. Party leaders implemented wage increases "by carefully taking into consideration the mood and demands of the workers" and "distributing the percentage of increase in particular shops."[146]

In early 1926 *Vesenkha* launched a "regime of economy" campaign to intensify the work process, lower costs, and promote industrialization. Having reached prewar levels of production, the campaign attempted to obtain resources for the "new phase" of industrialization to construct and re-equip factories. Theoretically, a reduction in costs would reduce prices to strengthen the "link with the peasantry." Stalin and Kuibyshev drafted a 25 April 1926 appeal, "The Struggle for a Regime of Economy," that frankly admitted an "extreme shortage of capital," which meant that further industrial expansion would have to "rely only on internal factors and resources." As Carr and Davies note, the regime of economy was essentially an attempt "to cut costs by the simple device of increasing the output of the worker while holding down his wage and depressing his work condition."[147] *Martenovka* stated that the "regime economy" strategy meant "we must complete the party and government directives to lower costs by 6 percent."[148] From a management perspective, the campaign was a success. With a smaller workforce, productivity increased 18 percent while wages went up only 10 percent, less than the rate of inflation.[149] With the threat of unemployment looming, management directed their cost-cutting efforts against the highest paid workers. The OGPU claimed that wages for skilled workers in the Hammer and Sickle Factory declined by 35 percent and characterized efforts to lower the pay of skilled workers in the metal industry as being of a "mass character." Such wage reductions resulted in some workers believing that the "regime of economy was being carried out at their expense."[150]

Workers repeatedly complained about managerial efforts to raise production, though they often perceived shop-floor tensions as misunderstandings.

During a shop cell discussion to reduce defective output (*brak*) in late 1926, a member argued that the administration displayed a "bad attitude towards production." Another member argued that "pay is low" and suggested management increase wage rates because "then workers will pay attention and not be in such a hurry." One member characterized the administration's role in production as "counterrevolutionary." After venting these grievances, the cell resolved to "strengthen the struggle against *brak*."[151] In April 1927, the repair shop cell reported incidents of "engineers' rude attitude towards workers." This was attributed to a "lack of experience and knowledge of workers' psychology," which meant that bosses "absolutely do not know how to approach them which creates hostility on the part of the workers."[152] A 1927 party report noted an "abnormal" relationship in some shops between the administration and shop union representatives. "It is clear," claimed the report, "that the administration does not understand these organizations."[153]

Factory management attempted to strengthen its position by fomenting divisions among workers. In January 1926, the OGPU reported strong dissatisfaction over the lowering of rolling mill workers' piece rates. Some rolling mill workers were paid about 250 rubles a month, while the remaining workers in the shop averaged eighty rubles.[154] Subsequently, rolling mill operators in the fourth mill submitted a petition for a pay raise because of their difficult work, but management suggested that to implement this raise, they lower the pay of remaining workers—a suggestion that met with "objections on the part of the workers." Management then announced that the rolling mill operators would alternate locations with the goal of leveling wages, but this also met with "sharp dissatisfaction on the part of workers."[155]

One ploy in management's "divide and conquer" strategy was to punish workers who raised grievances or who failed to meet production quotas. In 1925, the party had responded to dissident activity in the form-casting and rolled metal shops by allocating extraordinary raises. By the end of 1926, the factory party leadership reversed this strategy and punished resisting shops. Apparently because of material shortages, workers in the fourth mill of the rolled metal shop did not fulfill their quotas, and management lowered their pay by 31 percent.[156] In October, the OGPU reported that workers in the fourth mill complained that, under the collective agreement, their pay would not increase and would instead fall relative to that of other workers.[157] In December seventy workers in the fourth mill expressed dissatisfaction with management's refusal to pay for idleness, and petitioned the RKK. A few days later, the OGPU again reported workers' complaints in the fourth mill because they had received 150 rubles while other mills received 170 to 190 rubles.[158]

Though complex wage scales with variations between and within shops promoted the reemergence of *tsekhovshchina*, workers' representatives resisted parochial shop interests. A November 1925 delegates' resolution, with 133 for and only seven against, called for the leveling of wages, raising them in some shops while abstaining in those departments that received overtime compensation.[159] In 1927 and again in 1928 factory delegates again pressured management for more equalization in the wage rates.[160]

Management's strengthened position allowed it to transfer workers. Because of the stagnant market for bolts and nails, fifteen workers were reassigned to other shops in early 1926. "Workers categorically refused the transfer and threatened to leave the factory," but no strike action was reported.[161] A shortage of materials in the construction shop led management to reduce the number of workers and transfer some to other work.[162] In August sixty workers in the rolled metal shop submitted a petition to the RKK because their transfer had led to a wage reduction from 145 rubles to 95. A few weeks later, seventy-five workers in the same shop appealed to the RKK, asking them to raise their wage and skill grade.[163]

The threat of unemployment became an important weapon for the state-management offensive against the working class. Official unemployment figures show that 113,898 Moscow workers were registered as unemployed in July 1925, but that the number steadily increased to 223,549 three years later.[164] Unlike unemployment in the West, however, Soviet NEP unemployment increased simultaneously with a growth in overall employment, as the mass rural-to-urban migration outpaced industrial expansion.[165] In early 1926, the lack of raw materials and fuel in the metal industry in Moscow spurred fears of layoffs. The OGPU reported that among metalworkers in Moscow, there were "observed all kinds of rumors concerning the reduction of the workforce.... Naturally workers express dissatisfaction and blame the factory administration and trusts for mismanagement."[166] A few months later, the factory committee was not informed about the layoff of four painters in one department and even the shop cell complained that the "shop administration is not coordinating with us and is playing with workers and members of the bureau cell."[167] An architectural shop party member complained about the strength of the shop manager, who exhibited a "bad attitude towards workers, and ... threatens to fire them. Workers have to submit to him in everything."[168] In August, the main speaker in a maintenance shop party meeting asserted that the position of the Central Committee was "in general correct," but expressed fears of growing unemployment and warned, "life would be more difficult with lower pay."[169] In November several more painters were again laid off without notifying the union. One member argued that the "administration of the shop has a bad attitude towards the trade union representatives."[170] In April 1927, *Trud* reported widespread discontent in the nail shop over layoffs. The market for nails had been depleted, but the trust only recognized the problem when the warehouse was full. "You are in a position to plan production," workers complained, "but because of your 'planning' workers are thrown on the street."[171] While fear of being let go curbed workers' willingness to speak openly, layoffs had the opposite effect among those already fired. At a May 1927 rally of unemployed in Moscow, speakers claimed "the Communist party has established its dictatorship over the working class and over the entire country," and that soviet power was "nothing but a system for the deceit and exploitation of workers."[172]

The Soviet government's "rationalization of production" campaign, inaugurated in the spring of 1927, was very similar to the 1926 "regime of economy." It was another attempt to cut costs and raise production by increased use of machinery and transport within works, a higher division of labor, and rationalized utilization of fuel. At a time of mounting unemployment, the plan raised concerns among workers. The chairman of *Vesenkha*, Kuibyshev, frankly admitted, "Rationalization of production inevitably brings about a reduction in the amount of labor power required to produce the same output. Otherwise it would not be rationalization." Unlike the "regime of economy," the rationalization plan actually succeeded in holding down costs. According to *Vesenkha*, these fell by more than 6 percent during the 1927-1928 fiscal year. This success was based on a 13.5 percent increase in productivity.[173] The intensification of the labor process, real wage reductions, and the exploitation of the Soviet worker were no longer temporary strategies to ameliorate an immediate crisis, but henceforth became integral components of the Stalinist industrialization strategy.

Workers continually raised grievances over wages and norms during late NEP. In early 1926 conflicts arose "every month over the piece rate."[174] After a November 1926 strike in the form-casting shop, a party bureau member asserted that among workers in the department, "there is a constant mood favoring an Italian strike." A few weeks later, the bolt shop mood "was not completely healthy because of the piece rate."[175] Rolled metal shop meetings in April and May 1927 noted strained relations with management because of the wage rate.[176] A later report from the shop detected no anti-Soviet mood among workers, but noted that they raised many questions about pay and the delay in lowering consumer prices.[177]

Two short strikes in the winter of 1926-1927 involved small numbers of workers, were isolated to a single shop, and lasted only a few hours. On 15 November 1926, seventy casters and cutters in the form-casting shop organized a two-and-a-half hour "Italian" strike after management ruled they would have to pay for *brak*. Workers, claiming that management had no right to penalize them under the collective agreement, halted work at 7:30 in the morning. Communists in the shop "took little part in stopping the strike and adopted a passive stance except for the cell secretary, the union representative, and one party worker." The RKK halted the stoppage by siding with the workers and ordered management "to change temporarily the payment system back to the old method."[178] Backed by the word of the collective agreement, workers successfully resisted management attempts to force employees to pay for *brak*.

A January 1927 strike ostensibly developed over a lack of heat in the shop, but in reality centered on wage distribution. Workers insisted on compensation for work performed during the holiday, but management argued that they did not have the money, and that pay would be distributed on the fifteenth of the month. At mid-morning on the fourteenth, some thirty-five workers (including party members) stated that they could not work because of inadequate heat. The oppositionist Zhirov and another worker went to the factory office to explain the situation. The factory committee president and another committee member then entered the shop and asked nonparty workers if it was possible to work. The idle workers pointed to a group that included party members and said, "Just like them," meaning that action had been sanctioned as they were merely following the lead of party members. Union members suggested transferring workers, as mandated by the collective agreement, but the workers refused the transfer, returning to work at 2:30. Party leaders noted that, "unfortunately, the leaders of this stoppage appear to be party members Zhirov and Koptev" and issued reprimands, but none of the members who participated in the action were expelled. They also reported that 60 to 65 percent of the strikers had "ties with the village" but noted "no petty-bourgeois speeches."[179]

During the next shop cell meeting, several members challenged their leaders. One member protested against the notion of party members acting as strikebreakers. "To work was impossible. If workers got up and party members worked, this would not do," he asserted. Moreover, the same member argued, "individual comrades should not be blamed. The factory bureau decision is incorrect." Another member argued that there were "many stoppages" in the shop, indicating that short strikes over specific issues were never reported to the factory party leaders, much less to the MK.[180]

Official union channels—rather than state repression—ended these disputes. Significantly, an oppositionist, whom the state would brand as "counterrevolutionary" a few months later, was one of the leaders of the second strike and was not expelled, much less arrested. Archival research on strikes has uncovered little evidence of arrests of striking workers.[181] Mass arrests of dissidents, particularly Trotskyists, began only in the second half of 1927—after the demise of widespread strike activity. Indeed, during mid-NEP the Soviet Union incarcerated very few of its citizens. The entire Soviet prison population was no higher than 150,000, with a tiny minority imprisoned for political offenses.[182] Union intervention and the letter of the collective agreements were instrumental in resolving strikes. Aggregate data from Eighth Congress of Trade Unions in December 1928 show that more than one-third of labor conflicts during 1926, 1927, and the first half of 1928 were settled in arbitration in favor of workers, less than one-third in favor of management, and the remainder had compromise results.[183] Recently published OGPU summaries from 1922 to 1928 include reports on over three thousand strikes, but mention only six incidents in which authorities arrested striking workers, and only five other strikes in which they used or threatened to use force.[184] Strikes ended by union intervention and clarification (often on the side of the workers), management satisfying some or all of the workers' demands, the dispute being sent to arbitration, all sides agreeing to revisit the disputed issues, or, in some cases, management firing workers or threatening to close the factory.[185]

In both Hammer and Sickle strikes in the winter of 1926-1927, workers understood the details of the collective agreement. In the first strike, they realized that management had gone beyond the bounds of the contract and believed with justification that the powerful RKK would side with them. The second strike was ill-conceived in terms of the collective agreement. In both strikes, party members either passively or actively supported the actions and party participation gave the stoppages an umbrella of legitimacy. In both strikes union representatives understood that their task was to resolve the issue as quickly as possible, but they were not merely management dupes: all concerned recognized the importance of the collective agreement. The scrutiny devoted to the official investigation of the 1927 strike reveals the seriousness with which the party viewed strike action. Party members were nevertheless caught in the contradictory role of trying to be both loyal party members and shop-floor leaders at a time when state policy was moving more decisively against the interest of labor.

To facilitate the implementation of wage cuts, collective agreements were no longer openly discussed in large mass meetings. The seventh Trade Union Congress in December 1926 called for keeping workers "informed" about the negotiations between trusts and unions while the United Opposition advocated that "collective agreements shall be made after real and not fictitious discussions at workers' meetings."[186] In November 1927 one worker responded to Tomsky's accusations against the British trade union bureaucracy by asking, "Comrade Tomsky, tell us why, in finalizing the new collective agreement, Hammer and Sickle Factory workers did not know about it and why was it not discussed in the general meeting?"[187]

The Decisive Year: 1928

The final year of NEP was potentially the most explosive. In the countryside, the specter of famine returned after the back-to-back poor harvests in 1927 and 1928. In early 1928, under the pretext that "kulaks" were hoarding grain and with a shortage of commodities to offer in return, the regime returned to a policy of grain requisitioning similar to war communism. By the summer, peasants had revolted in 150 different villages, slaughtered cattle, and beat and murdered local officials. The crisis in the countryside resounded in the cities as shortages led to the reintroduction of rationing. By May, food riots were reported in many cities, including Moscow. As Michal Rieman has argued, the crisis was much deeper than a temporary phenomenon—it was the result of deep structural problems of the financially strapped Soviet system, of a society that lacked internal resources for industrial expansion beyond restoration to the prewar level.[188] By the end of NEP, the breakdown of outdated industrial machinery and equipment had become endemic. After production fell dramatically in the last two months of 1927, Kuibyshev described the economic situation as "disastrous." The more aggressive rural policy was matched in the factories as party leaders embarked on a risky solution by mandating further sacrifices. Near the end of 1927 *Vesenkha* and VTsSPS issued a directive "On Overcoming Low Production Quotas" to raise intensity of work, to lower qualifications of workers, and to cut wages. This renewed offensive against the working class did not go unchallenged; strikes broke out in several large factories including the Putilov works in (now renamed) Leningrad, and the Hammer and Sickle Factory.[189]

Top secret 1928 reports include hundreds of pages of lists of protests across the country. By the fall of 1928, as Vladimir Brovkin concludes, "The temperature of frustration at the factories and plants rose, ready to boil over."[190] Recently published monthly OGPU reports confirm this assessment. While the OGPU reported "anti-Soviet" worker sentiments throughout NEP, by 1928 workers' grievances had become more political and brazen during labor conflicts, with openly anti-party speeches and workers shouting down party loyalists—widespread working-class anger not seen since 1921-1922. By the summer, the deteriorating food supply strengthened workers' receptiveness to oppositionist and anarchist agitation. The OGPU also reported repeated disturbances of unemployed workers at labor exchanges throughout the Soviet Union. By September, workers' factory meeting speeches expressed strong dissatisfaction against the policies of the party and food cooperatives. The next month the mood of workers in the majority of enterprises with supply difficulties worsened, while oppositionists stepped up their agitation as the collective agreement campaign began.[191]

The two short economic strikes at the Hammer and Sickle in early 1928 indicate workers' increased frustration with party and management tactics. Workers struck on February 6 and again on March 15 against the lowering of wages by 20 percent. These, the last two known stoppages in the factory, follow the general trend of strikes at the end of NEP and contrast with the offensive actions during early NEP when the working class, rather than the state, was on the offensive. Reports elsewhere reflect this pattern of continued low-level participation in strike activity. Stoppages lasting more than a day were rare: the overwhelming majority lasted a few hours, and some only fifteen minutes. Aggregate strike data from 1926 and 1927 also show isolated, short stoppages with very few participants.[192]

The first strike in the bolt shop shook the party organization. The cell secretary reminded members that in the event of a conflict, it was necessary to go through the proper channels. One member challenged this notion, charging that the "factory committee is to blame for the strike because they had failed to pay attention to workers' petitions over the preceding five months."[193] A detailed report on the stoppage and the mood of workers shows that sixty press operators stopped work for one and a half hours because of dissatisfaction over piece rates. After the director's assistant explained to them that the rates would be taken up as the top priority in the forthcoming collective agreement, all the press operators returned to work. The party organized a commission to investigate the strike and called a meeting for 18 February. Three days before the meeting, management decided to dismiss one of the strike leaders, Stepanov, under the pretense that he had refused transfer to another press. A member of the commission suggested postponing Stepanov's dismissal "because the workers could interpret it as a reprisal against one of the leaders of the conflict." The administration refused, and Stepanov received his dismissal pay on the day of the meeting. Sixty people, but only ten of eighty communists, attended the extraordinary shop meeting.

Workers who spoke up placed all the blame for the stoppage on the factory committee and administration. A candidate party member justified the stoppage and

threatened to repeat the strike if the many deficiencies in the shop were not eliminated (ventilation, etc.). Workers listened to speeches by the director and cell secretary but without approval. I wrote the draft resolution with three main points:
1. Admitting the incorrect path that workers chose to resolve the conflict. 2. A
thorough investigation of the RKK member's behavior towards workers' complaints. 3. A reexamination of the per-item rate.

   This resolution did not receive a single "for" vote. Many workers spoke up and
said that the resolution judged workers' behavior incorrectly. Many of them
stressed that Stepanov's dismissal is the factory organizations' answer to the justified demands of the workers. The shop cell secretary and the union representative
who chaired the meeting did not help change the mood of the meeting by their
speeches and even made it worse. Some of the workers attempted to put to a vote
the question of whether the dismissal of Stepanov was correct but we succeeded in
avoiding the vote.[194]

The state-loyalist orchestrated session managed to maintain control of the
festering hostility. Though workers attempted to resist management's dismissal of one of the strike leaders, they simply did not have the confidence to
take over the meeting and resist victimization as they had in early NEP. The
regime became more adept at isolating and neutralizing strike action, and it
was partially successful at preventing inter-factory and intra-factory solidarity.
By 1928, the state offensive had not attained the effectiveness it would later
acquire in preempting strike action, but it had succeeded in shifting the collective agreements in favor of the state.

   Widespread discontent over wage reductions resurfaced in a March delegates' meeting. A representative from the electrical shop, Torkunov, turned
to factory director Stepanov and said, "You should remember that when you
paid us poorly, we worked poorly and engines were damaged every day." The
director branded this statement "counterrevolutionary" and the issue topped
the agenda at the next electrical shop meeting. Torkunov attempted to
explain his behavior in the delegates' meeting to his shop mates. He stated
"when the wage and skill grades go down, the workers get completely over-
worked and everyone will not work as well chasing after rubles. Besides, I
spoke for myself and not for the whole shop." The next speaker asserted,
"Torkunov did not speak just for himself, but for the entire shop." Several
party loyalists challenged this point, and the shop meeting, wary of the implications of such an open challenge to the administration, ultimately passed a
resolution that "resolutely protests against such speeches" and sent a copy of
the declaration to the director.[195] While the resolution contradicted workers'
sentiments, it also shows employees' increasingly silent frustrations and their
lack of collective resolve to challenge the loyalists. A 1928 MK report noted
numerous similar cases of "direct acts of violence" or threats of violence
against foremen, technical personnel and directors, which it characterized as
"a terrorist atmosphere in the factories and plants."[196]

   Individual threats, rather than collective intimidation as in 1917, indicate
the weakness of the workers' position as party functionaries were able to
control delegates' meetings, and repeatedly passed resolutions against workers' material interests. Thirty written questions posed to the speaker at

another delegates' meeting focused on the management's lowering of wage categories and the twenty-three point collective agreement, which apparently was presented in a confused manner. One delegate asked the speaker to simply state the wage rates and the percentage difference with the previous rate. Another asked, "Why are the wage and skill grades being immediately lowered by three categories, when Moroz said at the factory conference that they would only be lowered by two, but we see ninth lowered to sixth, eighth to fifth, and seventh to fourth category?" Only eight of the thirty questions referred to the general collective agreement; the remainder concerned trade, shop, or even individual issues, illustrating the complexity of the collective agreement, but also the retreat on the part of workers. Three workers were concerned about staff reductions, and one asked, "If a worker was ill for three months but his sickness was the fault of the factory, not his, would he be fired?" Another delegate's question shows the individual rather than collective concern of many workers: "If they lowered the wage and skill grade of a worker and he did not want to work at this rate but wanted to leave the factory, would they give him two weeks' pay?"[197]

Party members' economic "tailism" continued throughout 1928. In February, a party bureau speaker warned against further pay reductions in the bolt shop, where repeated incidents "prove that the *aktiv* are weak." Complaints about lowering the wage and skill grades of hundreds of workers were noted, "even among party members" and the next month party leaders vowed "to liquidate doubts and wavering of certain comrades" on questions related to the Fifteenth Congress, grain procurement, and the "tailism" on the collective agreement.[198] In May, workers in the rolled metal shop petitioned the RKK for a 10 percent wage increase. The RKK refused but the director, factory committee, and cell all backed down and offered a 5 percent increase. Workers remained unsatisfied, threatening to strike in three days if they did not receive 10 percent, but a stoppage was averted. At the next bureau meeting, the speaker depicted the behavior of party members in the rolled metal shop as "disgraceful" and called for a "closed session of the entire cell to clarify whether mistakes had been made in carrying out the collective agreement."[199] In November, several bolt shop members rejected the party line in the department and other members reportedly "wavered."[200]

The leader of a small revolt in the steel foundry shop in December 1927, Shashkin, sparked another protest in August 1928. The conflict arose there because "some workers were dissatisfied with the strengthening of discipline." A group of workers "attempted to incite a bad relationship between party and nonparty" and "spoke against the party and Soviet government." The shop cell resolved to expel Shashkin, whom the cell admitted, enjoyed "authority among nonparty workers."[201] At an August delegates' meeting, several representatives spoke against managers in their shops. A rolled metal shop delegate argued, "The administration in the shop has a very bad attitude toward the delegates and sometimes swears at them. This simply cannot be allowed." A representative from the bolt shop said, "There were times when our shop manager was called to the union office where he was tongue-lashed. Since that time, he has not been an obstacle." Thus, some workers continued to believe the union still exerted considerable leverage over management. A nail shop delegate reported a conflict with the shop manager, but noted that "we explained to him the rights of delegates and representatives and since then there was no problem."[202]

Workers expressed increased frustration with their trade union representatives. Bolt shop dissatisfaction over wage scales for the new second shift led to several attempts to stop work.[203] Fire brigade members blamed the factory committee for ignoring their concerns and wanted to know "why we receive lower pay than other workers."[204] One brigade worker suggested that the "factory committee, has lost or has almost lost its authority among workers in regards to the wage-rate policy. Thanks to this, the mass of workers' interest is weak."[205] Many speakers in a September nail shop meeting criticized the work of the RKK, the factory committee, and the "insufficiencies" in the collective agreement, particularly in "raising the pay of lower workers." Numerous "misdeeds" of the RKK caused "many workers to suffer," according to one worker, while another speaker asserted that "members of the factory committee and representatives fall in line with the administration and are afraid to stand firm and defend workers' interests." Several bolt shop speakers raised similar criticisms about the "foot dragging" of the RKK and complained about the low piece rates.[206] In October, a speaker in the form-casting shop attributed flagging support for the factory committee to "the large number of declarations from the workers, more than half of which were decided against them." Moreover, employees' production suggestions were not carried out. "This says that the factory committee does not always consider the opinions of workers and therefore they are not active."[207] In the steel foundry, one worker complained that "food prices are going up and pay is not, it has become difficult for workers to live." Another protested that, "in 1926 we re-negotiated the collective agreement and we worked less but received more" and proposed that the "factory committee should devote serious attention to this in negotiating the agreement." Other workers criticized the RKK, noting that the majority of conflicts were decided in favor of management.[208] Similarly, six speakers in a November 1928 form-casting shop meeting criticized the work of the RKK and factory committee.[209]

The expelled United Opposition led the most organized challenge to the Stalinist section of the party in 1928, despite the rapid escalation of state repression. Oppositionists operated with a fearless abandon reminiscent of revolutionary activity in the late Tsarist period. The Secret Police convictions in 1928-1929 exceeded the combined total for the six previous years, and the 1930 total (208,069) exceeded that for 1922-1929.[210] Trotskyists estimate that state forces arrested or deported at least eight thousand supporters by 1928.[211] Yet oppositionists agitated successfully around economic and political issues and created strong organizations in the Donbass, Ivanovo-Voznesensk, Tula, Dnepropetrovsk, Saratov, and many Ukrainian cities. In Moscow, Trotskyist supporters put forward resolutions for free elections to the Soviets, against the *samokritika* campaign, for the rescinding of the deportation of oppositionists, for collective agreement wage increases, and supporting striking workers. Trotskyist support in Moscow was so widespread that many non-oppositionist workers throughout the city distributed and posted tens of thousands of their leaflets.[212]

Opposition strength in the factory reached its zenith in the fall. A party report claimed that six Trotskyists and unnamed supporters "spoke very energetically in the collective agreement campaign under one slogan: raise workers' pay."[213] In November, *Martenovka* complained that Bakanov "still tries to fill other workers' heads with Trotskyist ideas."[214] In the steel foundry shop, oppositionists argued for wage increases and a party loyalist admitted, "The authority of Lebedev quickly increased. In the first shift there was a large group of oppositionists."[215] *Trud* reported that, "In the Hammer and Sickle Factory, Trotskyists called for supporting workers in other factories who have raised demands for wage increases."[216] Support for the Opposition included the union bureau chairman of the form-casting shop and a factory committee member. The United Opposition activity expanded in the factory to the point at which "recently the opposition group have developed their work up to creating cells" and even called their own meeting in late December.[217]

Trotskyist agitation over bread-and-butter issues gave other workers confidence during the collective agreement campaign. A report to the Central Committee complained that "counterrevolutionary elements" were "not always given a rebuff by the party." Trotskyists agitated for wage increases and against an increase in production. The cable shop unanimously agreed to the oppositionists' resolution to raise pay, "while leaders who were present were stubbornly silent." The steal foundry also accepted an oppositionist resolution to raise pay by 5 percent. The GPU reported that even party members in the Hammer and Sickle Factory spoke "against the party line" during the collective agreement discussions. Hard-line state loyalists had to resort to heavy-handed measures, and the resolutions were rejected only after "repeated clarification of the question."[218] A December delegates' meeting gives an insight into the role of Stalinist supporters and shows that their assertions did not go unchallenged:

> Comrade Kochin: (repair shop) ... Is it correct to raise the question of raising pay? I think it would be incorrect. We should increase productivity and thus we will lower the costs of production. Our comrades who are former oppositionist now call for raising wages. They seek every possible way to disrupt our collective agreement ...

> Comrade Chernyshev (form-casting shop): On the question of pay, Comrade Kochin is not correct that in the form-casting and rolled metal shops that this was proposed by former oppositionists. In our shop this question was put forward because there are large discrepancies between shops on wage and skill grades. It is this very disparity that workers suggested adjusting ...[219]

Many workers' complaints focused on supplies and relations with the countryside. The year before, three-fourths of the workers had holdings in countryside, though "recently, it can be noted that workers are breaking ties with the village" and had moved their families to the city.[220] One worker argued that while "horse drivers feed bread to the horses, workers do not have enough."[221] Private notes to speakers reveal widespread rank-and-file party discontent. Thirty of thirty-three questions to the speaker at an August party plenum concerned either provisions or relations with the peasantry. One member agreed with the speaker's claim that kulaks had disrupted grain collection the preceding year, but then stated, "The government was also at fault because they did not prepare goods in time. To make such mistakes is inexcusable." Two members asserted that the grain supply was so depleted that peasants were mixing bread with additives such as fur, and complained that while the speaker "talked a lot about supplying bread to the cities," the state neglected to make provisions for "supplying poor peasants with bread. Where would the poor peasants find seven rubles for one *pud* of flour? They are now in a situation like 1919." Another member suggested that, "poor peasants in the village are dissatisfied with Soviet rule." One member wanted to know "why has the *volost* committee not taken measures? The poor peas- ants are hungry." Three questioned the speaker on Soviet grain exports, one member asked how much was exported in the previous year, and another wanted to know: "How much grain will be exported in 1929?" An inquisi- tive member asked, "You said that grain was not exported last year, but then where did all the grain go?" One member insisted it was "necessary to stop feeding the horses with grain." Another note requested that the speaker "Tell us whether or not there will be bread reserves in case of need." Two months later, party members complained about bread lines. "Who and what," asked one member, "caused the food shortage?" Another note asked, in reference to the grain collection campaign, if "grain will be taken forcibly from the peasants again."[222]

GPU summaries from around the Soviet Union affirm workers' sympathy with the plight of the peasantry during the crisis of late NEP.[223] Two ques- tions from Hammer and Sickle workers were provocative enough to reach the Central Committee information department. "Tell us comrade," asked one worker, "what is the danger of organizing a peasant union, and will it be organized?" Another worker from the factory wanted to know if "there will be equality for everyone living in the Soviet Union and if so, when?"[224] Sev- eral anonymous notes passed to Central Committee member Mikoyan in March conveyed extreme hostility towards the regime. "Peasants shout: the king is a plunderer!" one noted. "But even workers have no life." Another worker objected to the regime's definition of the term 'kulak.'

> Comrade speaker, at every meeting all we hear from you is that the village has kulaks. It seems to me that Soviet power has existed not just for ten days but for ten years, everything has been equalized, but even if a peasant has one horse, one cow, or several sheep then you consider him a kulak. If you examine the villagers and then estimate your possessions, the figures will show who is the kulak based on possessions.[225]

Such hostile private notes again show how the threat of unemployment affected workers' behavior. *Martenovka* acknowledged that some workers "are afraid to utter a word" because they believed that "if you say something, they will show you the gate" while other workers were "apathetic about everything." While some workers had become more political in their statements, for many others the threat of unemployment, political apathy, and individual rather than collective solutions acted as barriers to collective solidarity. The newspaper challenged the assertion that anyone could be fired for expressing their opinion and urged nonparty workers to participate in the *samokritika* campaign because they have "a lot to say about undisciplined members."[226]

Workers failed to overcome the divisions within the workforce that weakened their resistance. Whereas early NEP *tsekhovshchina* was partially overcome as stoppages spread to other shops, all four of the four late NEP strikes included only part of the workforce in one shop—from strike reports this was the norm throughout the Soviet Union. Similarly, a raucous factory committee election in the rolled metal shop was split along generational lines, with older male workers placing particular blame for problems in the shop on women.[227] Such generational divisions also surfaced at factory production conferences, with overwhelmingly older male participants and with less than 3 percent of young workers participating.[228]

Speakers at a December union meeting challenged the form and content of the collective agreement. Party loyalists held the line and pushed through the agreement by "repeated clarification" of questions. One dissident argued that the campaign was conducted "too hurriedly," while another complained, "workers do not understand the new plan of remuneration." Several workers addressed the underlying issue, one complaining that production savings were "being taken out of workers' pockets."[229] The party reprimanded two members for breaking party discipline during a production meeting, one of whom had complained: "They squeeze and oppress us, and suck our blood dry."[230] Such were the sentiments of outspoken party members, theoretically those most sympathetic to the regime's aspirations.

Late 1928 recalls the crisis of the summer of 1915: a rapidly deteriorating political and economic emergency that suddenly called into question the regime's ability to rule; rampant food shortages with unruly unemployed on the streets; widespread discontent in the armed forces; and the reemergence of an "us against them" *mentalité* amongst a significant section of the working class—with revolutionaries playing a catalytic role in sparking protests. But the return to workers' activism in 1915 took place within the larger context of a long-term trend towards militancy and activism only briefly interrupted by the war, whereas the 1928 crisis occurred within the framework of a generalized retreat, with many workers continuing to look for reform within existing workplace institutions. Moreover in 1928 there was no incident similar to the Lena massacre, the proroguing of the Duma, or even one significant strike in the capital that might have reverberated as a "call to action" among wider groups of workers. That emerging Stalinism managed to weather the storm has tended to obscure what is now discernible: a narrow gap between widespread working-class resentment and open revolt.

The demise of workers' militancy is the central issue of early Soviet labor history. More than a decade after the opening of the archives of the former Soviet Union, no one today could possibly echo the "speculative" revisionist argument that Stalinism was able to draw on significant working-class support. Similarly, we now know that state repression during NEP was in no way comparable to the regular Okhrana roundups of shop floor militants during late Tsarism—a period when the workers' movement was on the upswing, despite arrests. To be sure, when rolling mill workers marched to the director's office with their tongs they were hardly intimidated by the early Soviet regime. The opening of the archives allows us to move beyond the Cold War mythology that rested on fundamentally flawed misunderstandings of how the early Soviet system functioned. Workers were neither terrorized by the early Soviet state nor impressed with evolving Stalinism.

Workers' words and actions show that the decline in strike action can only be explained with reference to the transformation of workplace institutions and workers' collective loss of confidence. At the beginning of the era, workers knocked the state on its heels and aggressively articulated their demands in boisterous mass meetings. They convened their own meetings in which they could determine their own strategy and organized collective defense against victimization. Early NEP strikes were not simply driven from below—party and union organizations championed the cause of labor. Moreover, in order to contain rank-and-file anger and prevent work stoppages, favorable collective agreements, and RKK decisions had to reflect sympathy with workers' concerns. This "uneasy compromise," as first noted by Carr and Davies, accounts for the cessation of strike activity during NEP. Yet the truce between workers and state gradually eroded, as the state's increasingly productivist labor policy became less tolerant of party and union members who did not conform to the state's objectives. Factory management also benefited indirectly from the economic crisis of late NEP because many workers became increasingly defensive and sought individual rather than collective solutions to their problems. The threat of unemployment, as in many societies, helped shift the balance in favor of management.

By the end of NEP, discontent reverberated in the factory. Workers no longer wanted to join the party, many discontented members wanted to leave, and grievances that had been almost exclusively economic became more politically charged. Such sentiments reflected the state's failure to deliver on its egalitarian promises and the decision by the Stalinist leadership to make workers pay for industrialization and silence dissent. However, a gap developed between workers' increasingly hostile attitudes towards the party and state and their own confidence to take action. State loyalists managed to control meetings, victimize dissidents, and use the threat of unemployment to discipline the workforce. Nevertheless, the history of the Russian working class in first third of the century was marked by volatile shifts in working-class moods, with festering hostility often escalating to revolt—the regime's triumph over the working class was not a foregone conclusion. Moreover, the state and its loyalists were far from invincible. To be sure, the Stalinist movement aspired to omnipotence, but it was burdened with deep cracks in its ranks and, paradoxically, benefited from the failure to implement "iron unity." Even nonparty workers repeatedly looked to party dissenters for leadership and change within the existing factory system. This hope for reform explains the failure of workers to build new independent networks to challenge the increasingly antilabor state policy. Given that workplace institutions had earlier responded sympathetically to their concerns, workers' expectations that they could pressure them to do so again were quite logical.

Notes

1. For example, Andrew Pospielovsky, in "Strikes During the NEP," *Revolutionary Russia*, 10, 1 (1997) notes that after 1922 reports of worker arrests were rare but asserts that it is "likely that leading shop-floor organizers were arrested in the general roundups of 'anti-Soviet' elements" such as SRs and Mensheviks. William Chase, in *Workers, Society, and the Soviet State*, 299, takes a diametrically opposed view, asserting that workers were impressed with Stalinism such that by 1928-1929 "the party and workers, especially urban workers, reforged the old alliance of 1917-1918."
2. Carr and Davies, *Foundations of a Planned Economy*, 1: 544.
3. Pospielovsky, "Strikes During the NEP."
4. Chase, *Workers, Society, and the Soviet State*, 105, 107, 312.
5. TsMAM, f. 176, op. 2, d. 107. Employment statistics.
6. TsAODM, f. 429, op. 1, d. 62, l. 36. Party report, n.d. September 1927.
7. *Martenovka*, 3 January 1929.
8. GARF, f. 7952, op. 3, d. 200, l. 30. Production figures from 1913 to 1932.
9. *Desiatyi s"ezd RKP(b)* (Moscow, 1963) 404.
10. Dewar, *Labor Policy in the USSR*, 211. Although NEP is often associated with private capitalism, at the height of NEP only 18.8 percent of wage earners were employed in the private sector. Isaac Deutscher, *Soviet Trade Unions* (London, 1950), 67.
11. Lewis Siegelbaum, *Soviet State and Society Between Revolutions, 1918-1929* (Cambridge, 1992), 101.
12. Dewar, *Labor Policy in the USSR*, 228-234.
13. R.W. Davies and S.G. Wheatcroft chapter "Population," in *The Economic Transformation of the Soviet Union, 1913-1945* (Cambridge, 1994) eds. R.W. Davies, S.G. Wheatcroft, and Mark Harrison, 62-63.
14. TsMAM, f. 176, op. 2, d. 174, ll. 29-30. Combined women's and delegates' meeting, 6 December 1923 and women's general meeting, n.d. December 1923.
15. *Martenovka*, 21 November 1925.
16. *Martenovka*, 23 December 1927.
17. TsMAM, f. 176, op. d. 568, l. 94. Factory committee report, April 1926 through April 1927.
18. For example, *Martenovka* denounced one member in the bolt shop who had refused to give a day's wage in support of the British general strike, but at the request of the party bureau, he agreed to acknowledge his "error" in the factory newspaper. *Martenovka*, 12 June 1926, TsAODM, f. 429, op. 1, d. 49, ll. 33-34. A bolt shop party bureau meeting, 26 July 1926.
19. TsAODM, f. 3, op. 7, d. 54, l. 117. OGPU information summary, 9-12 May 1926.
20. TsMAM, f. 176, op. 2, d. 403, l. 24; d. 545, ll. 5, 6, 9, 11. Factory general meetings, 25 March 1925, 7 May 1926, 6 July, 17 August 1926, 14 September 1926.
21. TsMAM, f. 176, op. 2, d. 403, l. 24; d. 545, ll. 5, 6, 9, 11. Factory general meetings, 25 March 1925, 7 May 1926, 6 July, 17 August 1926, 14 September 1926.
22. TsMAM, f. 176, op. 2, d. 403, l. 24; d. 545, ll. 5, 6, 9, 11. Factory general meetings, 25 March 1925, 7 May 1926, 6 July, 17 August 1926, 14 September 1926.

23. TsAODM, f. 429, op. 1, d. 56, l. 56. Party plenum, 6 November 1927.

24. TsMAM, f. 176, op. 2, d. 403, l. 24; d. 545, ll. 5, 6, 9, 11. Factory general meetings, 25 March 1925, 7 May 1926, 6 July, 17 August 1926, 14 September 1926.

25. TsAODM, f. 429, op. 1, d. 56, l. 56. Party plenum, 6 November 1927. Nicola Sacco and Bartolomeo Vanzetti were anarchists arrested for robbery and murder in South Braintree, Massachusetts during the "Red Scare" of 1920. They were convicted based on superficial evidence and executed in 1927. The Sacco-Vanzetti defense movement attracted attention around the world. See James Green, *The World of the Worker* (Champaign, 1980), 113-114.

26. Reiman, *The Birth of Stalinism*, 10-12.

27. TsAODM, f. 429, op. 1, d. 67, l. 20. Nail shop party report, 14 September 1927.

28. TsAODM, f. 429, op. 1, d. 56, l. 13. Factory party meeting, 23 May 1927.

29. *Martenovka*, 7 November 1927.

30. *Martenovka*, 7 November 1928, 21 January 1930; TsAODM, f. 429, op. 1, d. 129, l. 7. Party secretary report on the first Five-Year Plan, 27 February 1933. The factory newspaper did not include membership figures on 7 November 1928 but over two years later claimed 128 workers had entered the party in 1928. A 1933 report states that membership increased to approximately 700.

31. TsAODM, f. 429, op. 1, d. 7, l. 8. Open party meeting, 1 March 1922.

32. TsAODM, f. 429, op. 1, d. 6, l. 8. Party bureau discussion, 4 May 1922.

33. TsAODM, f. 429, op. 1, d. 6, ll. 14-15. Party bureau meetings, 19, 24 June 1922.

34. TsAODM, f. 429, op. 1, d. 10, l. 26. Party bureau meeting, 7 March 1923.

35. TsMAM, f. 176, op. 2, d. 133, l. 2. Survey response from factory director to TsK, n.d. 1923.

36. TsAODM, f. 429, op. 1, d. 10, l. 38. Party bureau meeting, 19 May 1923.

37. TsGAMO, f. 186, op. 1, d. 950, l. 18; Factory committee meeting, 26 November 1923.

38. TsAODM, f. 429, op. 1, d. 15, l. 27. Party bureau meeting, 6 June 1924.

39. TsAODM, f. 429, op. 1, d. 24 l. 47. Nail shop party meeting, 12 April 1924.

40. TsAODM, f. 429, op. 1, d. 15, l. 57. Factory party meeting, 10 September 1924.

41. TsAODM, f. 429, op. 1, d. 10, ll. 12, 13, 34. Party bureau meetings, 31 January, 6 February, 17 April 1923.

42. TsAODM, f. 429, op. 1, d. 15, l. 39. Party bureau meeting, 5 August 1924.

43. TsAODM, f. 429, op. 1, d. 17, l. 46. Party general meeting minutes, 3 December 1924.

44. TsAODM, f. 80, op. 1, d. 137, l. 8. Rogozhsko-Simonovskii party conference, 3 January 1924.

45. TsAODM, f. 429, op. 1, d. 17. l. 18. Closed party meeting, 16 April 1924.

46. TsAODM, f. 429, op. 1, d. 37, l. 58. Rolled metal shop party meeting, 25 September 1925.

47. TsAODM, f. 429, op. 1, d. 49, l. 13. Bolt shop bureau meeting, 26 January 1926.

48. TsAODM, f. 429, op. 1, d. 49, ll. 87, 118. Steel foundry shop party meetings, 22 September, 4 October 1926.

49. TsAODM, f. 429, op. 1, d. 48, l. 12. Architectural shop party meeting 16 July 1926.

50. TsAODM, f. 429, op. 1, d. 50, l. 19. Factory cooperative party bureau meeting, 20 October 1926.

51. TsAODM, f. 429, op. 1, 49, l. 112. Steel foundry shop party meeting, 4 October 1926.

52. TsMAM, f. 176, op. 2, d. 545, l. 8. Factory general meeting, 5 July 1926.

53. TsAODM, f. 429, op. 1, d. 40, l. 140. Closed factory party meeting, 8 December 1926.

54. TsAODM, f. 429, op. 1, d. 40, l. 140. Closed factory party meeting, 8 December 1926.

55. TsAODM, f. 429, op. 1, d. 48, l. 94. Party report on bolt cell, June 1926.

56. TsAODM, f. 429, op. 1, d. 52, l. 17. Rolled metal shop party report, 1 April 1927.

57. TsAODM, f. 429, op. 1, d. 62, ll. 10-11. Party report, September 1927.

58. TsAODM, f. 429, op. 1, d. 70, l. 5. Repair shop party meeting, 12 September 1927.

59. *Martenovka*, 30 June 1928.

60. *Martenovka*, 7 November 1927, 30 June, 19 February, 6 September 1928.

61. TsMAM, f. 176, op. 2, d. 810, l. 78. Nonparty *aktiv* meeting, 29 July 1928.

62. Hiroaki Kuromiya, *Stalin's Industrial Revolution, Politics and Workers, 1928-1932* (Cambridge, 1988), 36.

63. *Martenovka*, 12 October 1928.

64. TsAODM, f. 429, op. 1, d. 87, l. 8. Repair shop party bureau meeting, 18 January 1928.

65. TsAODM, f. 429, op. 1, d. 86, ll. 56, 111. Rolled metal shop party meetings, 17 October, 26 November 1928.

66. TsAODM, f. 429, op. 1, d. 85, l. 8. Nail shop party meeting, 14 March 1928.

67. TsAODM, f. 429, op. 1, d. 87, l. 67. Construction shop party meeting, 14 May 1928.

68. TsAODM, f. 429, op. 1, d. 90, ll. 67, 80. Electrical shop party bureau meetings, n.d. 1928.

69. TsAODM, f. 429, op. 1, d. 87, l. 80. Construction shop party bureau meeting, n.d. 1928.

70. TsAODM, f. 429, op. 1, d. 103, l. 12. Rolled metal shop party bureau meeting, 2 January 1929.

71. RGASPI f. 17, op. 85, d. 237, l. 55. MK information summary, May 1927.

72. Vladimir Brovkin, *Russia After Lenin: Politics, Culture, and Society, 1921-1929* (New York, 1998), 185-186. *Sovershenno Sekretno: Lubianka-Staliny o polozhenii v strane (1922-1934 rr.)* (Moscow, 2002) Editors: A.N. Sakharov, G.N. Sevostianov, V.S. Khristoforov, V.K. Vinogradov, T. Vihavainen, M. Kivinen, A. Getty, T. Martin, L. Viola, L.P. Kolodnikova. Vol. 6: 31, 34-41, 44-45, 75-79, 102-113, 142-147, 162-169, 196-199, 207-213, 237-238, 258-267, 508-515, 563-571, 608-618.

73. Deutscher, *Soviet Trade Unions*, 33-74.

74. TsMAM, f. 176, op. 2, d. 171, l. 7. Metalworkers' union instruction, March 1923.

75. TsGAMO, f. 186, op. 1, d. 950, l. 27. Factory committee report to general meeting, 14 March 1924.

76. TsGAMO, f. 186, op. 1, d. 744, ll. 1-69; d. 950, ll. 1-62. Union meeting minutes, 1923, 1924.

77. *Rabochaia Moskva*, 3 November 1923.

78. TsMAM, f. 176, op. 2, d. 344, l .1. Factory committee report, January 1925.

79. TsMAM, f. 176, op. 2, d. 129, l. 57. Factory announcement, 12 January 1926.

80. TsMAM, f. 176, op. d. 568, l. 33. Factory committee report, May 1926.

81. TsMAM, f. 176, op. 2, d. 402, l. 41. Factory committee meeting, 15 August 1925.

82. Straus, *Factory and Community in Stalin's Russia*, 248.

83. TsGAMO, f. 19, op. 1, d. 62, ll. 215, 238. Reports to Moscow Soviet, 6 and 29 September 1923.

84. *Rabochaia Moskva*, 6 April 1925.

85. TsAODM, f. 429, op. 1, d. 41, l.28, Party bureau meeting, 21 April 1926.

86. GARF, f. 7952, op. 3, d. 255, ll. 51-52. Dimitriev recollection.

87. TsGAMO, f. 186, op. 1, d. 950, ll. 63-99. Factory RKK meetings, 1924.

88. TsMAM, f. 186, op. 2, d. 216, ll.5-6; d. 220, ll. 15, 16; factory committee reports, 1924, 1925.

89. TsAODM, f. 429, op. 1, d. 48, l. 45. Bolt shop party bureau meeting, 16 August 1926.

90. TsMAM, f. 176, op. 2, d. 254, ll. 45-47. Factory committee reports, 1925.

91. Carr and Davies, *Foundations of a Planned Economy*, 1: 600-601. The figures for 1925-1926 are 2,426 disputes involving 3.2 million workers; for 1926-1927: 3,155 disputes involving 2.46 million workers; 1927-1928: 2,661 disputes involving 1.87 million workers.

92. *Trud*, 29 July 1926, 10 April 1927.

93. TsAODM, f. 429, op. 1, d. 67, ll. 18-19. Bolt shop party bureau discussion, 14 September 1927.

94. TsAODM, f. 3, op. 7, d. 56, l. 46. MK information summary, 23-26 October 1926.

95. TsAODM, f. 3, op. 7, d. 54, l. 83. OGPU information summary, 1-3 April 1926.

96. TsMAM, f. 176, op. 2, d. 545, l. 10. Factory general meeting, 12 August 1926.

97. TsAODM, f. 429, op. 1, d. 51, l. 3. Rolled metal shop party meeting, 14 January 1926.

98. TsAODM, f. 429, op. 1, d. 68, l. 27, 54-55. Steel foundry shop party meetings and closed party meeting 20, 21 December 1927.

99. TsMAM, f. 176, op. 2, d. 785, ll. 13-18. Repair shop meetings, October and November 1928.

100. TsAODM, f. 3, op. 7, d. 56, l. 120. OGPU information summary, 11-13 December 1926.

101. TsMAM, f. 429, op. 1, d. 812, ll. 66-67. Factory committee report, September 1928.
102. Deutscher, *Soviet Trade Unions*, 122. That union membership was voluntary is illustrated by 27.4 percent of Soviet workers who chose not to join unions in 1931. Hoffman, *Peasant Metropolis*, 194.
103. *Martenovka*, 10 May 1927.
104. TsAODM, f. 429, op. 1, d. 62, l. 36. Factory party report, September 1927.
105. TsGAMO, f. 186, op. 1, d. 2394, l. 128. Factory committee election summary, 4 May 1927.
106. TsMAM, f. 176, op. 2, d. 693, l. 28. Delegates' meeting, 8 December 1927.
107. In 1923, 92 percent of the workforce fell between the 1.2 and 2.4-coefficient wage range. *Martenovka*, 7 November 1925, 7 November 1926, 12 February, 26 October 1928.
108. TsMAM, f. 176, op. 2, d. 718, ll. 1-3. Metalworkers' information bulletins, December 1927.
109. TsMAM, f. 176, op. 2, d. 812, ll. 66-67. Factory committee report 1928.
110. Carr and Davies, *Foundations of a Planned Economy*, 1: 544.
111. TsMAM, f. 176, op. 2, d. 210, l. 116. Production program statistics for 1926-1927.
112. *Martenovka*, 7 November 1925, 7 November 1926, 12 February 1928, 26 October 1928. On inflation and decline in real wages in 1927 and 1928 see Reiman, *The Birth of Stalinism*, 37, 38, 54.
113. TsGAMO, f. 19, op. 1. d. 21, ll. 249-250. Reports to Moscow Soviet, 6, 7 June 1922.
114. TsMAM, f. 176, op. 2, d. 133, l.5. Survey response from factory director to TsK, n.d. 1923.
115. TsAODM, f. 429, op. 1, d. 6, l. 8. Party bureau discussion, 4 May 1922.
116. TsMAM, f. 176, op. 2, d. 102, l. 635. Factory announcement, 1 April 1922.
117. TsGAMO, f. 176, op. 1, d. 21, ll. 244, 53, 85, 156, 209, 245, 250. Report to Moscow Soviet, 11 June 1922 and other 1922 reports.
118. TsGAMO, f. 19, op. 1, d. 62, l. 21. Report to Moscow Soviet, 26 January 1923.
119. Brovkin, *Russia After Lenin*, 174-175.
120. TsMAM, f.176, op. 2, d. 175, l. 1. TsGAMO, f. 19, op. 1, d. 62, ll. 46, 56, 58, director registration form for strike to Mashinotrest, 26 February 1923, Report to Moscow Soviet, February 1923.
121. TsMAM d. 137, ll. 7, 9-16, 24. Wire pulling shop meeting, 1 March 1923.
122. TsGAMO, f. 19, op. 1, d. 62, ll. 115-129; TsMAM, f. 176, op. 2, d. 169, ll. 1-2. Reports to Moscow Soviet, May 1923. Delegates' meeting, 15 May 1923.
123. TsGAMO, f. 19, op. 1, d. 62, ll. 187-194. Reports to Moscow Soviet, August 1923.
124. TsGAMO, f. 19, op. 1, d. 62, ll. 284-287, 300, 302, 306, 317. Reports to Moscow Soviet, November, December 1923.
125. TsGAMO, f. 66, op. 22, d. 87, l. 45. Report to Moscow Soviet, April 1924.
126. TsGAMO, f. 66, op. 22, d. 87, l. 45. Report to Moscow Soviet, April 1924.
127. *Trud*, 4 January 1923.
128. TsKhDMO f. 1, op. 23, d. 260, ll. 48-49. Komsomol general meeting, 3 October 1924.
129. TsAODM, f. 429, op. 1, d. 27, l. 29. Party bureau report, 24 March 1925.
130. RGASPI f. 17, op. 16, d. 563, l. 251. Factory Party summary report for March to May 1925, June 1926.
131. *Nasha gazeta*, 7 November 1923.
132. TsAODM, f. 429, op. 1, d. 17, l. 1. Factory general party meeting, 2 January 1924.
133. TsMAM, f. 176, op. 2, d. 254, l. 50. Factory party summary, September 1924.
134. TsMAM, f. 176, op. 2, d. 405, l. 5. Delegates' meeting, 29 January 1925.
135. TsAODM, f. 429, op. 1, d. 15, l. 40. Factory party bureau meeting, 12 August 1924.
136. RGASPI f. 17, op. 16, d. 563, ll. 229-230. Factory party report for May through December 1924, January 1925.
137. TsAODM, f. 429, op. 1, d. 27, l. 85. Factory party bureau meeting, 22 September 1925.
138. TsGAMO, f. 19, l. 1, l. 62, l. 107. Report to Moscow Soviet, 23 April 1923.
139. RGASPI f. 17, op. 16, d. 563, ll. 229-230. Factory party report, May through December 1924.
140. TsAODM, f. 429, op. 1, d. 34, l. 10. Form-casting shop union meeting, 1 July 1925.

141. TsAODM, f. 429, op. 1, d. 28, ll. 25-26. Closed party general meetings, 8, 15 April 1925.

142. TsAODM, f. 429, op. 1, d. 27, ll. 48-49. Party bureau meeting, 5 June 1925.

143. RGASPI f. 17, d. 16, d. 563, ll. 183, 195. Party bureau meeting, 5 June 1925.

144. *Sovershenno Sekretno: Lubianka-Staliny o polozhenii v strane*, Sevostianov, Sakharav, et al. eds. Vol. 3, part 1: 359, 378-379.

145. Straus, *Factory and Community in Stalin's Russia*, 247.

146. TsAODM, f. 429, op. 1, d. 27, l. 127. Combined factory and shop bureaus party meeting, 1 December 1925.

147. Carr and Davies, *Foundations of a Planned Economy*, 1:357-362.

148. *Martenovka*, 15 March 1926.

149. *Martenovka*, 7 November 1926; GARF, f. 7952, op. 3, d. 200, l. 30.

150. *Sovershenno Sekretno: Lubianka-Staliny o polozhenii v strane*, Sevostianov, Sakharav, et al. eds. Vol. 4, Part 1: 526.

151. TsAODM, f. 429, op. 1, d. 73, l. 25-26. Form-casting shop party meeting, 16 December 1926.

152. TsAODM, f. 429, op. 1, d. 69, ll. 20-22. Rolled metal shop party meeting, 2 April 1927.

153. TsAODM, f. 429, op. 1, d. 62, l. 8. Party report, September 1927.

154. TsAODM, f. 3, op. 7, d. 54, l. 3. OGPU information summary, 1 January 1926.

155. TsAODM, f. 3, op. 7, d. 54, l. 29. OGPU information summary, February 1926.

156. TsAODM, f. 3, op. 7, d. 54, l. 56. OGPU information summary, 10-13 March 1926.

157. TsAODM, f. 3, op. 7, d. 56, l. 40. OGPU information summary, 23-26 October 1926.

158. TsAODM, f. 3, op. 7, d. 56, ll. 126, 135. OGPU information summaries, December 1926.

159. TsMAM, f. 176, op. 2, d. 405, l. 31. Delegates' meeting, 26 November 1925.

160. *Martenovka*, 12 February, 26 October 1928.

161. TsAODM, f. 3, op. 7, d. 54, l. 26. OGPU information summary, February 1926.

162. TsAODM, f. 3, op. 7, d. 54, l. 71. OGPU information summary, 28-31 March 1926.

163. TsAODM, f. 3, op. 7, d. 55, ll. 67, 88. OGPU information summary, 24-27 August, 8-10 September 1926.

164. Chase, *Workers, Society, and the Soviet State*, 139.

165. E.H. Carr, *Socialism in One Country*, 2 vols. (London, 1973) 1: 363.

166. TsAODM, f. 3, op. 7, d. 54, l. 22, OGPU information summary, January-February 1926.

167. TsAODM, f. 429, op. 1, d. 48; l. 3. Architectural shop party bureau meeting, 9 July 1926.

168. TsAODM, f. 429, op. 1, d. 48, l. 12. Architectural shop party meeting, 16 July 1926.

169. TsAODM, f. 429, op. 1, d. 55, l. 66; Maintenance shop party meeting, 18 August 1926.

170. TsAODM, f. 429, op. 1, d. 48, ll. 20-22. Architectural shop party meeting, 1 December 1926.

171. *Trud*, 20 April 1927.

172. Brovkin, *Russia After Lenin*, 184.

173. Carr and Davies, *Foundations of a Planned Economy*, 1: 362-370.

174. TsMAM, f. 176, op. 2, d. 544, l. 8. Factory committee meeting 3 March 1926.

175. TsAODM, f. 429, op. 1, d. 40, ll. 130, 140. Factory bureau meeting 19 November, closed general party meeting 8 December 1926.

176. TsMAM, f. 176, op. 2, d. 699, l. 3. Rolled metal shop meetings, 14 April, 14 May, 1927.

177. TsAODM, f. 429, op. 1, d. 52, l. 17. Rolled metal shop summary for January 1926 to April 1927.

178. TsAODM, f. 429, op. 1, d. 62, ll. 13-15. Factory party report, September 1927; f. 3, op. 7, d. 53, l. 149, MK summary 20 November 1926; d. 56, l. 74, MK summary, 10-12 November 1926. *Sovershenno Sekretno: Lubianka-Staliny o polozhenii v strane*, Sevostianov, Sakharav, et al. eds. Vol. 4, Part 2: 832.

179. TsAODM, f. 429, op. 1, d. 62, ll. 40-41; d. 57, ll. 117-118. Factory report, September 1927; Factory party bureau meeting, 9 February 1927.

180. TsAODM, f. 429, op. 1, d. 55, ll. 21-22. Form-casting shop cell meeting, 16 February 1927.

181. Brovkin's archival study of the Soviet Union from 1921 to 1929 (*Russia After Lenin*, 173-189) includes only two references to state arrests of strikers.

182. Vadim Rogovin, *Vlast' i oppozitsii* (Moscow, 1993) 10. These figures are consistent with *Obshchestvo Memorial: Sistema ispravitel'no trudovykh lagerie v SSSR, Spravochnik* (Moscow, 1998), 17, which states there were 200,000 prisoners in the middle of 1927. Arch Getty and Oleg Naumov found records that prove that the annual number of GPU, OGPU, and NKVD convictions from 1922 to 1926 were low: 6,003; 4,794; 12,425; 15,995; 17,804. *The Road to Terror* (New Haven, 1999), 588.

183. Carr and Davies, *Foundations of the Planned Economy*, 1: 603.

184. *Sovershenno Sekretno: Lubianka-Staliny o polozhenii v strane*, Sevostianov, Sakharav, et al. eds. Vol. 1: 274, 771, 890, 933, 957-958; Vol. 4: 129, 563-564, 841, 843; Vol. 5: 557.

185. *Sovershenno Sekretno: Lubianka-Staliny o polozhenii v strane*, Sevostianov, Sakharav, et al. eds. Vol. 1: 89-90, 96-121, 129-163, 166-188, 204-206, 221-247, 257-259, 269-279, 300-305, 307-471, 475-476, 486, 491-867, 886-892, 909-911, 932-936, 952-960; Vol. 2: 22-26, 40-43, 57-60, 72-76, 93-98, 113-117, 139-143, 161-165, 195-198, 218-223, 253-259, 282-283, 316-318, Vol. 3: 36-38, 49-56, 120-121, 137-140, 177-181, 194-198, 226-232, 249-255, 285-294, 310-322, 357-361, 375-382, 408-413, 423-429, 455-458, 468-476, 497-503, 516-533, 568-573, 593-608, 651-655, 665-681, 707-712, 726-742; Vol. 4: 24-30, 47-63-90-96, 117-137, 169-175, 191-207, 230-235, 264-270, 308-312, 323-336, 372-377, 392-404, 445-452, 468-483, 526-533, 553-571, 622-629, 646-665, 705-710, 731-747, 803-811, 832-847, 906-912, 938-954; Vol. 5: 22-27, 50-60, 126-135, 159-174, 234-243, 263-273, 309-315, 335-340, 357-363, 380-391, 415-421, 444-450, 485-492, 511-518, 557-564, 585-586, 592-593, 611-612, 637-638, 646-647, 655-667; Vol. 6: 31, 34-41, 74-80, 102, 105-113, 142-147, 162-168, 196-199, 207-210, 237-239, 258-265, 323-327, 378-382, 420-425, 460-466, 508-515, 563-570, 608-618.

186. Carr and Davies, *Foundations of a Planned Economy*, 1: 560, 562.

187. TsAODM, f. 429, op. 1, d. 56, l. 56. Party plenum, 6 November 1927.

188. Reiman, *The Birth of Stalinism*.

189. Reiman, *The Birth of Stalinism*, 51-84.

190. Brovkin, *Russia After Lenin*, 185-186.

191. *Sovershenno Sekretno: Lubianka-Staliny o polozhenii v strane*, Sevostianov, Sakharav, et al. eds. Vol. 6: 31, 34-41, 44-45, 75-79, 102-113, 142-147, 162-169, 196-199, 207-213, 237-238, 258-267, 508-515, 563-571, 608-618.

192. RGASPI, f. 17, op. 85, d. 311, ll. 4, 7. Strike statistics for 1926, 1927. ll. 59, 94. Strike summaries for February and March 1928. The February Hammer and Sickle strike was one of seven in Moscow and twenty-two around the Soviet Union, yet the combined total of strikers was only 3,156. The March strike was one of fifteen, with 6,723 participants. Given that one strike in Leningrad had four thousand participants, the other strikes could have involved no more than several hundred workers each. The 826 strikes in 1926 involving 101,572 workers, or an average of 123 per stoppage, and 905 strikes in 1927 involved 80,784 workers, or an average of 89 workers per stoppage. OGPU strike statistics for the last quarter of 1927, for those stoppages reporting data, show that only 5 of 50 strikes across the nation lasted more than a day, and that the majority (33) lasted less than a day.

193. TsAODM, f. 429, op. 1, d. 84, l. 101. Bolt shop party meeting, 15 February 1928.

194. TsAODM, f. 429, op. 1, d. 84, ll. 135-138. Secret party report by R. Novin, 18 February 1928.

195. TsMAM, f. 176, op. 2, d. 797, ll. 3-4. Electrical shop meeting, 28 March 1928.

196. Brovkin, *Russia After Lenin*, 187.

197. TsMAM, f. 176, op, 2. d. 780, l. 10. Delegates' meeting, 1 March 1928.

198. TsAODM f. 429, op. 1, d. 74, ll. 70-71, 100-102. Factory party bureau meeting, 23 March 1928.

199. TsAODM f. 429, op. 1, d. 75, l. 50; d. 81, l. 17. Party bureau meeting, 15 May 1928, party factory committee fraction meeting, 11 May 1928.

200. TsAODM, f. 429, op. 1, d. 84, l. 40. Bolt shop party meeting, 14 November 1928.

201. TsAODM, f. 429, op. 1, d. 85, l. 116. Steel foundry party meeting, 18 August 1928.

202. TsMAM, f. 176, op. 2, d . 780, l. 18. Delegates' meeting, 23 August 1928.

203. TsAODM, f. 429, op. 1, d. 84, l. 40. Bolt shop party meeting, 14 November 1928.

204. TsMAM, f. 176, op. 2, d. 791, l. 14. Fire brigade union meeting, 9 September 1928.
205. TsAODM, f. 429, op. 1, d. 40, l. 119. Party bureau meeting, 22 October 1926.
206. TsMAM, f. 176, op. 2, d. 792, ll. 24-25. Bolt and nail shop union meetings, 26, 28 September 1928.
207. TsMAM, f. 176, op. 2, d. 790, l. 16. Form-casting shop meeting, 2 October 1928.
208. TsMAM, f. 176, op. 2, d. 789, ll. 72, 73. Steel foundry shop union meeting, 2 October 1928.
209. TsMAM, f. 176, op. 2, d. 789, l. 87. Steel foundry shop union meeting, 15 October 1928.
210. Arch Getty and Oleg Naumov, *The Road to Terror*, 588.
211. Victor Serge and Natalia Trotsky, *The Life and Death of Leon Trotsky* (London, 1975), 158.
212. Isabelle Longuet, "L'Opposition de gauche en 1928-29," *Cahiers Leon Trotsky*, 53, April 1994.
213. TsAODM, f. 429, op. 1, d. 129, l. 8. Party report on the First Five-Year Plan, 27 February 1933.
214. *Martenovka*, 16 November 1928.
215. TsAODM, f. 429, op. 1, d. 105, l. 50. Steel foundry shop party bureau meeting, January 1929.
216. *Trud*, 18 December 1928.
217. TsAODM, f. 429, op. 1, d. 104, ll. 54-55. Repair shop party meeting, February 1929. TsAODM, f. 429, op. 1, d. 105, l. 76. Party bureau report, 9 January 1929.
218. RGASPI f. 17, op. 32, d. 183, l. 3. TsK Information department bulletin, 28 September 1928. *Sovershenno Sekretno: Lubianka-Staliny o polozhenii v strane*, Sevostianov, Sakharav, et al. eds. Vol. 6: 565, 614.
219. TsMAM, f. 176, op. 2, d. 780, ll. 30-32. Delegates' meeting, 13 December 1928.
220. TsAODM, f. 429, op. 1, d. 62, l. 36. Factory party report, January 1927.
221. GARF, f. 1235, op. 140, d. 1107, l. 62. VTsIK information summary, 21 September 1928.
222. TsAODM, f. 429, op. 1, d. 77, ll. 15, 49-50. Party meetings, 15 August, 10 October 1928.
223. Brovkin, *Russia After Lenin*, 185.
224. RGASPI f. 17, op. 85, d. 67, ll. 14, 16. MK information summary, summer 1926.
225. TsMAM, f. 176, op. 2, d. 779, l. 39. Factory general meeting, 21 March 1928.
226. *Martenovka*, 6 September 1928.
227. TsMAM, f. 176, op. 2, d. 795, ll. 22, 29-31. Rolled metal shop meeting, 2 October 1928.
228. *Rabochaia gazeta*, 30 March 1929. Of the 2,500 attendees at a March 1929 production conference, only eighty were characterized as "youth" and only seven were women.
229. *Martenovka*, 7 January 1929.
230. TsAODM, f. 429, op. 1, d. 84, l. 19. Architectural shop party meeting, 27 December 1928.

4

EVERYDAY LIFE UNDER
DEVELOPING STALINISM

"Often because of our inability to conduct a sensible discussion, they leave
believing [in God] even more strongly."
—Party report on antireligious work among women, March 1927

The October Revolution had promised fundamental changes not only in the
realm of politics but also in everyday life (*byt*). The harsh realities imposed by
the Civil War had relegated the hopes of a more egalitarian society to the
future, yet as the economic recovery extended into 1923, Bolshevik leaders
welcomed a renewed dialogue on "cultural work." Trotsky wrote a series of
articles on "Problems of Everyday Life" that inaugurated a wide-ranging
public discussion.[1]

The creation of a new culture and the transformation of everyday life were
viewed not as independent tasks to be carried out separately from economic
and political work. As Marxists the Bolsheviks believed that the ideas, habits,
and accumulated knowledge of a society were based on its class nature.
Whereas the rulers of class societies had utilized culture to their own benefit,
the crucial task of the Cultural Revolution would be to raise the "cultural
level of the masses," to change "the conditions of life, the methods of work,
and the everyday habits of a great nation, of a whole family of nations." Technological advances would be central to this voluntary and collective progress.
Continual improvement in the process of production would raise the cultural
level of Soviet citizens and in turn would encourage further technological
progress and help overcome the cultural backwardness inherited from the
Tsarist era. As Trotsky argued in 1926, "Improved technology and morals
will advance us along the road to a social order of civilized co-operators, that
is, to socialist culture." Yet the long-term objective of constructing a classless
society that would transform everyday life and end the oppression of women,
popular faith in the supernatural, and rampant alcoholism necessitated both
time and resources: "The lack of the necessary good things in life still sets its

mark heavily on our life and our morals, and will continue to do so for a number of years," Trotsky acknowledged.[2]

With the state as employer, issues related to everyday life were inextricably linked to industrial strategy. Much of the regime's efforts to transform *byt* focused on the role of women, religion, and alcoholism. At the factory level, the approach remained progressive and flexible until the crisis of late NEP when party leaders began to adopt "extremist solutions" that served the interests of the regime rather than those of ordinary Soviet citizens.[3] The drive for productivity saw the state undertake aggressive intervention in almost every aspect of workers' daily lives. Increasingly, Stalinist loyalists at the factory level viewed attempts to ameliorate the plight of workingwomen, continued tolerance of Orthodox work holidays, and rampant alcoholism as impediments to the drive for industrialization. Here we examine these three crucial aspects of *byt* during NEP in the Hammer and Sickle Factory.

Women and NEP

Early Soviet laws placed the regime at the forefront of progressive legislation for women's equality. In 1917 Soviet legislation mandated that women had full legal and political rights and unrestricted freedom of divorce. Women received sixteen weeks' paid maternity leave, and in 1920 the Soviet Union was the only nation in the world to guarantee women the right to free abortion on demand.[4]

The Bolsheviks had no illusions that progressive laws alone would suffice to end women's oppression, and the goals of the Communist Party and its women's section, the Zhenotdel, were ambitious. As Wendy Goldman has argued, the tasks of the Zhenotdel were twofold: to train women cadres and to "transform the very nature of daily life (*byt*)." Women's liberation could only be achieved on the basis of their full participation in public life, and in practical terms this meant attempting to free women up for such participation by shifting the domestic burden from the individual home to communal laundries, dining halls, and day care centers. By purging personal relationships of all forms of economic dependence, the Bolsheviks believed, the radical transformation of daily life for both women and men would lead to the gradual "withering away" of the family.[5]

While historians have produced a wide range of general works on Soviet gender issues, no systematic analysis of women's experiences in the factories during NEP has yet been published. Studies influenced by postmodernism have chosen to focus on the regime's language and symbols, with minimal attention to workingwomen's own experiences and activism.[6] This method is at odds with the approach of Communist women activists themselves, who emphasized proving oneself through action, rather than through rhetoric, a practice that became known as "agitation by the deed."[7] What were the practical activities of "agitation by the deed" introduced by advocates of women's liberation, how did this change over time, and how did workingwomen themselves respond to these efforts?

The sharp fluctuations in female production employment in the Hammer and Sickle Factory reflected dramatic changes in social conditions and state industrial policy. The shortage of male metalworkers during the war had led to an increase of women workers, such that by November 1917, there were 456 women. The economic collapse adversely affected women, and by February 1920 only 71 women worked in the factory. Yet women were proportionately overrepresented during the factory's economic and demographic recovery in early NEP, with 226 women constituting 10 percent of the workforce at the end of 1923.[8] By the spring of 1925, 300 women engaged in production work,[9] but unemployment during latter NEP affected women disproportionately and the factory employed older women with more family responsibilities and less time for political activism.[10]

The unity between women and men during the revolutionary *élan* of 1917 did not survive the Civil War. Attempting to regain the trust and confidence of women was no simple task, but both the party and the metalworkers' union acted on issues of particular concern to women, even during the catastrophe. In the dismal winter of 1919-1920, the party assigned an additional male member to help because "the organizer was overloaded with work."[11] Women's issues were given high priority on the party meeting agenda eight times in 1920 and 1921, excluding other pertinent discussions that arose during routine business.[12] After the Civil War, the metalworkers' union warned that the new economic conditions in private industry and self-financing state enterprises "create conditions for the displacement of women's labor in certain branches" and for greater exploitation of women. The union claimed that systematic work over the previous half year had begun to pay off, but also called for further measures, including more female representation on union bodies and that industrial enterprises with three paid union members and 250 women should have a paid woman organizer.[13] In March 1923, the metalworkers' union again instructed representatives to extend their work among women, to assign an instructor from the organizational secretariat, and to prepare for a women's conference in April that would consist of female factory representatives and factory committees.[14]

The combination of women's rank-and-file pressure and the special efforts by the party and union reactivated women's work. The women's organizer's November 1922 report shows that women's main concern expressed at the eight women's meetings was low wage and skill grades. The 283 female production workers earned slightly less than the third of nine grades for production workers, but the party pressured management to advance eighty-one women in three departments from the second to the third wage grade.[15] Women advocates addressed other issues of concern to female workers. A factory announcement in October 1922 noted that women had the right to take off two hours a day to feed their babies.[16] In July 1923, the factory committee recommended removing the clinic women's doctor after receiving an appeal from women who had complained about his "bad attitude towards his obligations."[17] In November 1923, eight women representatives resolved to ask the RKK to give a report at the next factory meeting on pending claims involving women.[18] Backed by the sympathetic attitude of the RKK, this pressure helped to ensure favorable resolutions of almost all the cases involving eight hundred women in the winter of 1923-1924.[19]

Such "agitation by the deed" brought positive results for women's work in the Hammer and Sickle Factory. Additionally, both the party and factory committee prioritized women's work while encouraging female representation and participation. The party bureau discussion on the factory committee slate in July 1923 noted the need for women's representation in its work, a suggestion that was subsequently acted upon.[20] By the end of 1924, the party bureau reported that of 282 women in the factory, sixteen were members and candidates, forty were actively participating in the campaign to liquidate illiteracy, ten were involved in a political circle, and forty-five took an active part in party work.[21] Similarly, the factory committee's April 1924 plan for specific areas of activity prioritized women's issues and included reorganizing the delegates' meetings so that they took place twice a month, launching a literacy school for women, involving women in a factory training school to raise their skill level, and expanding the kindergarten.[22]

The district Zhenotdel also acted as a catalyst, arguing for regular women's general and delegates' meetings. A Communist International thesis on women's work sent to the factory organizer claimed seven hundred thousand workingwomen participated in the movement—illustrating that early NEP was the heyday of women's liberation activity in factories throughout the Soviet Union.[23] At an October 1924 meeting, one of the first women delegates accepted, on behalf of her comrades, a set of books donated by the party cell, and noted the party's critical role in efforts to fully involve workingwomen in public life. "A year ago we were elected delegates," she recalled. "Some of us were totally illiterate and the others were semi-literate. During the year of our delegacy, the RKP(b) cell, and factory committee helped us become more politically conscious and active, and these books will help us to become even more clear about everything."[24]

The annual International Women's Day (8 March) meetings provided a focus for this activity. A week before the 1922 holiday, the women's organizer announced that the factory would open a kindergarten for twenty-five children and that women could leave work an hour early.[25] Two days later, the women's organizer and a delegation of five women appeared at a party bureau meeting and again demanded, unsuccessfully, release for the entire day.[26] On International Women's Day 1923, women left work two hours early.[27] The event the following year also attracted male employees, as the celebration of "women workers and workers" drew eight hundred people, three times the number of female employees.[28]

Women's voluntary participation in such meetings proves that they believed this activity was important. Attendance at the twice-monthly regular meetings varied between 100 and 120 (of 216). Autumn meetings to elect women delegates and district soviet representatives brought out 180 and 200 women respectively.[29] Two 1924 meetings that elected women union representatives and delegates each drew 190 participants, with the October meeting ending with a call "Long live the Communist Party and Soviet rule!"[30] To be sure, the party did not counter pose membership recruitment to this "agitation by the deed." Women members used this work to promote party policies and recruit women—by May Day 1925 thirty women had joined the factory cell.[31]

Large numbers of workingwomen consistently attended women's meetings because the sessions provided an arena in which they could openly air their grievances and enact measures to resolve issues of special concern to them. In February 1924, women from the bolt shop issued an oral complaint about heavy lifting conditions. The session passed a resolution to take up the issue with both the Protection of Labor and management.[32] At another session, a woman complained about "the cafeteria director's unfair attitude, intimidation, and firing of waitresses" and the meeting resolved to bring it to the attention of the party organization. Women from different shops repeatedly issued complaints about lack of work clothes and the meetings resolved to take action by pressuring either the party or union.[33] With representation and with the union's sympathetic policy, women expected a fair hearing on the factory committee. In November 1924, the women's organizer received support from a factory committee meeting after complaint about poor supplies and the need for repairs in the kindergarten.[34]

Women also raised grievances in the popular press. *Rabochaia Moskva* reported that yard crew women complained that their foreman had sexually harassed them and accused him of imposing unjust fines against those who rebuked him. While the majority of women despised the foreman, a few who played up to him had been rewarded with favoritism, including transfers to lighter work. Women argued that he ruled over women "like a lord in his castle" and that he needed to be "reined in."[35] Bolt shop women also aired grievances against their manager in *Rabochaia Moskva*. They accused him of miscalculating their hours during a power failure when their machines had been idle. A conflict arose when the manager, unaware of the power failure, accused the women of organizing an "Italian" sit-down strike, to which the women responded, "What kind of Italians are we? Fascists or something?" The women complained that they had not received their full wages and the reporter suggested that the factory committee and party teach the foreman "a lesson once and for all."[36]

The short-term success of women's work rested in part on the organizer's efforts, talents, and health. In March 1923, the women's organizer asked to be relieved. The new organizer, Arakova, complained two months later that the previous organizer had left many deficiencies, especially concerning food supplies for the nursery. Due to Arakova's absence, argued one party leader, the women's activity had taken a turn for the worse and that another member had been assigned to help.[37] In January 1924, Arakova reported modest successes, including a literacy circle and aid to women with children, but complained about the low job classifications assigned to women. She revealed plans to involve men in women's work and to create a sewing circle. Arakova argued that her tasks required a full-time organizer and requested compensation at the fourth wage category.[38] The cell agreed and the factory committee decided to pay her at the seventh-level rate.[39] However, Arakova requested a leave after giving birth in February. When the women's organizer fell ill in August 1924, two male members were assigned to help and the factory party bureau subsequently resolved to ask the district Zhenotdel for support.[40] Again in March 1925, party leaders expressed concerns that "because of Comrade Potapova's sickness, the work among women is carried out poorly" and passed a resolution assigning another member to help with the work.[41]

The promotion of female organizers also had an unexpected detrimental impact on women's political activism. The talented Potapova was assigned to the district committee of the party in May 1925 and the following month the party bureau acknowledged that in youth and women's work "we have a feeling of certain weaknesses."[42] In an August general party meeting, the new organizer, Sidorova, admitted that the work was conducted irregularly and blamed the failures on the summer break and on the low literacy level among women in the factory—a common theme for problems in women's work in late NEP, but an excuse that the previous organizers had not relied on.[43] Similarly, speakers at delegate meetings during 1925 began to express their own frustrations that the low level of women's literacy made it "difficult or even impossible to agree with them on some issues and draw them into work."[44]

Yet even with the support of the press, the Zhenotdel, the metalworkers' union, and the party, women faced many obstacles. For example, the passage of progressive Soviet legislation, like that which allowed for four months' paid maternity leave, did not necessarily mean that the laws were implemented at the factory level. A 1924 letter signed by "Worker Nadia," entitled "Need to Fix the Mistake" indicates that issues related to child rearing became more important to women as they started families. "Women workers' life is not easy," Nadia noted.

> Unskilled, trapped in a low wage and skill grade, they barely earn enough to eat. Widows who are weighed down by their families live particularly poorly. That is why it is difficult to be quiet when there is such 'state-sanctioned' robbing of workers, as in … cases involving women workers from our factory, 'Hammer and Sickle': Panka Chernysheva was given one month off before giving birth, Luda from the yard shop also a month, and others too. But women workers talk of cases in which one was given only a few days off before birth and here is why. During her clinic appointment, the woman doctor told her how she was reprimanded for letting one of the women off work…. The insurance office refuses to pay for the fourth months. This is not only a violation of the law but also a loss of health. The insurance office should catch up. They should have seen a long time ago from the medical release statements how maternity leaves are being unfairly cut. They should have paid attention to this a long time ago.[45]

Attempts to overcome male prejudices presented women workers with enormous difficulties. During the new marriage code discussion in 1925, the All-Union Central Executive Committee of Soviets (VTsIK) invited popular responses to the proposed legislation.[46] *Martenovka*, however, printed only a male worker's letter that complained of having to give up one-third of his wage for child support. "We need to have a law so that women do not change men like gloves. They should settle on a certain man and together create a strong and harmonious family life."[47] Yet some male party members were explicitly sympathetic to women's plight. For example, a speaker in the bolt shop reported on his recent village vacation, in which he claimed to have witnessed rampant alcoholism among leading party members. He also noted "the very bad situation with women and childbirth" in which they had to return to work "the day after giving birth."[48]

Women's activity continued into 1925, but was beset by serious obstacles. By May, *Martenovka* claimed thirty women party members, eleven Komsomol members, forty-five participating in study groups, twenty-five in a sewing school, and thirteen involved in union work. Political activity had been hampered, according to the article, because the majority of the women had large families or were widows, were concentrated in the lowest qualification and pay levels, and were burdened with heavy physical work. The factory employed "very few young women, and the older women with the exception of a few still have deep-seated religious illusions and old prejudices."[49] The Zhenotdel organizer in the bolt shop complained, "Women's work in the shop has been impossible to expand because every woman is extremely busy with home obligations." In the same discussion, a male member argued that less priority be given to women's issues: "It is completely impossible for the bureau to conduct work among women because it is overloaded."[50] While the party started to backtrack, the union continued to defend women. A 1925 factory Protection of Labor report on "conditions of work among women and adolescents" noted that the legal norms for women workers were not in effect in the bolt shop, and pressed management to take action.[51] Women with children in the third-wage category routinely received short-term advances on their paychecks.[52] Moreover, throughout 1925, women from the shops repeatedly presented wage, skill grade, and other grievances to the women's delegate meetings, from which they expected a fair hearing.[53]

The party's de-emphasis on women's issues coincided with management's increasingly productivist aspirations. In November 1925, the factory director, Stepanov, stated that women workers were not profitable and not needed because they were less productive. Moreover, Stepanov complained, women had to be given four months for childbirth, and because of breastfeeding they often had to leave early.[54] The director's confidence that such comments would go unpunished reflected the productivist shift in state policy and presaged the "regime of economy" that would be mandated a few months later.

Party leaders expected the Zhenotdel to encourage workingwomen to participate in the "regime of economy." Central Committee member Artiukhina implored women to "fight against wreckers in the national economy." Yet in their own meetings, Zhenotdel leaders admitted widespread resistance to the rationalization campaign among women workers. Artiukhina noted "mistakes" in its implementation, including the decisions to cut back on work clothes for women and on kindergartens and nurseries. Particularly harmful, in her opinion, was the decision to remove nursery funding from collective agreements between management and workers.[55]

The party's retreat on women's issues led to double standards and inactivity. In October 1925 the party bureau summoned a female member to explain her "drunkenness and promiscuous behavior"; when she refused to attend she was expelled for being a "demoralized element."[56] In February 1926, the women's group organized several meetings among housewives, but their elected representatives had yet to do anything, remaining merely "on paper," and, according to *Martenovka* "the women's section is disorganized."[57] The most outspoken women criticized factory leaders' lack of concern for their grievances. At a general party meeting in April 1926, a female member criticized the party faction of the factory committee because the committee provided "insufficient leadership in women's work."[58] Two speakers at a factory conference in November 1926 rebuked the main speaker for not having mentioned women's work.[59] At another factory-wide meeting, the women's organizer complained about the low pay of women in the bolt shop.[60]

The factory committee soon followed the party's retreat on women's issues. The change in committee priorities can be gauged by its reports. For the first half of 1923, the second area of activity mentioned after the organizational section was women's work, noting women's representation on the factory committee, monthly general and delegate meetings, a political education circle, and the factory nursery. Significantly, it did not mention raising productivity.[61] In contrast, factory committee reports for April 1926 to April 1927 included regular sections on organization, finances, youth, Protection of Labor, cultural work, and production conferences and sessions, but not a single section on women.[62] Thus, by 1927, both the party and union viewed workingwomen primarily from a productivist perspective, with their specific concerns either sharply de-prioritized or forgotten altogether.

Responding sympathetically to women's concerns had provided the basis of unity between women workers and the proletarian state during early NEP. With the serious obstacles faced by women's advocates in the austere conditions of early Soviet rule, even a minor shift in state policy away from a commitment to women's work and toward a more productivist ethos increased the growing sense of isolation and frustration among women activists:

Cell, Help!

The women's delegates' meetings were well attended. Now their enthusiasm has been crushed. Little attention is devoted to them. Everywhere they turn for help they are turned down. For example, women busied themselves and solicited many appeals in order to secure a doctor for women but nothing came of it. So now the delegates say, "What is the use of going? It just wears your feet out. Nothing will come of it anyway." It is the cell's duty to turn their attention to this and help women workers.

Rabkora [worker-correspondent] Luda[63]

Subsidies for day care and the factory kindergarten were of paramount importance to women, as expressed at a factory conference in October 1925. "The most important question for women workers," one female delegate argued, "is to quickly expand the kindergarten and day care nursery. Many applications have been submitted, but still no room has been made to place them." The other fifty women were reluctant to speak in such a large meeting (1,270 attendees), but the submission of nine (of sixty-four) notes to the speaker that directly concerned women's issues suggests that workingwomen were concerned about their deteriorating position. Two notes asked about the women's sewing club, and one advocated raising the skill level of women. Six of the nine notes raised issues about the kindergarten and nursery. "Tell us, why are we assessed six rubles per child for day care?" one woman inquired. "I have three children, have no husband, and I am in the third-level wage and skill grade. I do not have the means to pay."[64]

The day care issue was again a focus at the International Women's Day in 1926. Four hundred workers attended the gathering, which included a lecture on abortion, a film, and a report on the nursery. "Many women workers spoke up about the nursery report," *Martenovka* reported.[65] Factory leaders, however, apparently ignored such concerns. In March 1928, *Martenovka* claimed that fifty children were in the factory kindergarten but acknowledged "conditions are extremely unsanitary."[66] A speaker at a women's delegate meeting in 1928 protested that "the children's situation is awful because of the small quarters."[67]

Women viewed their representation, and the solidarity with men on the factory committee who supported them, as very important. One woman argued at a factory general conference in June 1926 that if it had not been for the efforts of one representative, "we women would now still be in the third wage and skill grade."[68] At a factory general conference in May 1927, a female speaker criticized the factory committee for its failure to take up women's issues and their underrepresentation: "We have 320 women in the factory, but there are no women freed from work obligations on the factory committee. They work a lot, but little attention is devoted to them." A female member complained in a party meeting that the cell had "forgotten about women's work. If it continues further, the problems will not be liquidated." Another noted similarly that the "factory committee pays little attention to women's work. Representatives are very bad at conducting clarifying discussions on the rights of women as industrial workers." A third speaker blamed the situation on women, arguing "the low political consciousness and ignorance of women, and their economic and family situation."[69]

Ominously, *Martenovka* also began to blame female employees themselves for the problems with the women's activities. On 7 November 1926, the factory newspaper argued that it was "impossible to say many pleasant things about women's work. First blame should be assigned to women workers themselves for their inactivity." The article suggested that the secondary fault lay with "the women's commission," which "has not been active enough." The productivist approach to women's work elicited the telling observation that "the worst thing is that questions about production, which would involve women, have not been raised," and lamented that there were either no shop meetings or meetings only once a year.[70] At a party meeting, the women's organizer argued that few women entered the party because of their low level of literacy.[71]

By 1927, the party was compelled to acknowledge continual problems with women's work. In February, the organizer's report admitted many shortcomings and seemed to attach some importance to the increased average age of the female workforce. She claimed that there were thirty-nine *aktiv* but noted that they had no representation on the factory committee, that their representation and ties within the shop cells were weak, and that the three previous meetings were poorly attended, with an average attendance of just seventy. She further charged that, "One of the main causes for this weakness is that little interest is devoted to women's work by factory organizations."[72]

The party's reversal on women's issues coincided with the economic crisis of late NEP, which particularly affected women. In 1926, for the first year since the Civil War, the number of workers declined by 165 with the number of women decreasing from 284 to 254.[73] Moreover, only a handful of women advanced to skilled positions during this period. By May 1927, four women had transferred to skilled positions, and three women had enrolled in a technical course. Ten months later, however, two of the women had dropped out of the course. In March 1928, one woman asserted in the factory newspaper that, "We criticize the factory committee and management for good reason. When a machine on which a woman could work frees up, they put a man there." The result was that "the question of advancing women to more skilled work is still stuck in the mud." In June 1928, *Martenovka* responded to women's complaints that only three women had advanced to skilled positions in the rolled metal shop. "Let us see how they show for themselves, and then raise the question of broader advancement for women," the newspaper suggested.[74]

On the rare occasions in late NEP in which the party addressed women's issues, the discussions were dominated by productivist concerns. A party proposal for factory committee activity focused on production, organizational work, and finances, and made no mention of women's work.[75] In April 1928, party leaders mandated that the bolt shop cell should "turn particular attention to working with women and drawing them into the social-production life of the shop." Several weeks later, when a bureau member complained of "insufficient participation of women in the production commission," a woman speaker countered that "in the shops there is insufficient attention to the women's work," with no female representation on the shop union bureaus.[76] Another female member chastised the main speaker in a nail shop discussion for not having mentioned women, despite the fact that there were sixty-five women in the shop.[77] Another outspoken female critic placed the blame on male members, and cited "incidents in which Communists did not defend party women who were completely innocent, and by doing so undermined them in front of nonparty women."[78]

An incident a few days later illustrates the claim about male party members. Dronnikov accused Beleberdina of slandering him by asserting he had blocked her transfer to another shop after she had refused his advances two months earlier. One speaker asserted that "it is impossible to call Beleberdina an exemplary member because she does not pay dues" and another added that "not only does she not pay her dues, but she completely refuses to attend the war circle." The shop cell voted to reprimand Beleberdina for her "slander" of Dronnikov.[79]

The promotion of even a few women incited resentment among some skilled male workers. A rolled metal shop worker complained that women had been assigned to operate machines and proposed "measures should be taken to remove them." The reelection of Chubikov, a former Trotskyist, as union representative in the rolled metal shop suggests that there was a generational split on attitudes to women's advancement. A factory committee representative argued that the disgruntlement was due to age differences and male workers' resentment of Chubikov's bold stand in favor of women's equality. A woman speaker noted that "older machinists do not support women; the skilled workers have no pity on us. Only Chubikov defends us." One worker admitted that though male workers drink, "they do not make such mistakes as women who really mess things up." The shop reelected Chubikov as representative by a vote of twenty-seven to twenty, indicating that younger male workers cast their votes for him in spite of the complaints from their elders.[80]

Rising unemployment in late NEP exacerbated these divisions between male and female workers. In May 1925, the party bureau reported twelve thousand unemployed workers in the district, including twenty-five hundred union members and two hundred Red Army veterans. Hiring practices mandated that top priority be given to the Red Army veterans, followed by union members—a policy that negatively affected women.[81] By December 1927, the number of registered Moscow unemployed reached 177,476, with the majority (51 percent) women.[82]

The desperation that accompanied increasing unemployment and underemployment drove working-class women to prostitution during NEP.[83] In an articled entitled "The Path to Prostitution," *Martenovka* claimed that teenagers and children as young as ten had engaged in "outrageous behavior" until two o'clock in the morning in a cooperative near the factory. The "outrage" in this case seems to have consisted only of playing music, singing, dancing, making noise, and shouting, but the resort to a sensationalized linking of such behavior with paid sex made some sense for a regime increasingly unable to offer material solutions to widespread desperation.[84] Questions to speakers indicate that prostitution was becoming a reality in working-class life during late NEP. At a February 1928 meeting on crime and hooliganism, four questions referred to prostitution, and one challenged the speaker's assertion that prostitution had declined by 75 percent: "Go to the city center and then say that there is less."[85] At a women's meeting in May 1928, a speaker remarked that because of staff reductions "we have the appearance of prostitution."[86]

Women's delegate and general meetings in 1928 show obvious tensions. Women expressed numerous grievances at a women's general meeting of one hundred in October 1928. They argued that there were not enough women accepted into the factory technical school, that the factory committee paid little attention to their concerns, that unskilled women were receiving lower pay than men for the same work, and that they were underrepresented on the committee.[87] At a May delegates' meeting, a speaker complained that she had not been informed about the latest staff reduction and requested advance notice in the future. The promotion of a woman from the Red Army to a skilled position caused resentment in the cable shop. One delegate complained that, "We have woman workers who have been in the shop ten to fifteen years and who cannot get onto a machine." Another delegate stated that the administration took into account her family situation, but "for others in need, they do not take this into consideration."[88]

Such accusations illustrate the tendency for sectional divisions to be strengthened as working-class activism declined. The continued weakening of class solidarity during the crisis of 1928—when the state was moving on the offensive—would prove costly for Soviet workers. Just as male workers blamed female workers, women also started to blame other workers, including this female Red Army veteran, for their own deteriorating position. Stalin and other party leaders tolerated open anti-Semitism in the party's campaign to defeat the United Opposition, and only after the expulsions did the factory cell begin to confront such prejudices, with the first factory discussion on anti-Semitism organized among women. As with many women's meetings in late NEP, it was composed almost entirely of housewives, with only fifteen workers among the 150 participants. The women complained that "Jews have all the good positions," "shun heavy work," and "get new apartments without waiting in line." The speaker countered that there were very few Jews in the district, that they constituted 8 percent of the government apparatus, that Jews received only 3 percent of new housing, and that in many places such as Kharkov, industry relied almost exclusively on Jewish labor.[89]

Women workers expressed similarly hostile sentiments against peasant laborers. During a discussion on women's unemployment in May 1928, the union representative attributed the rise in women's unemployment to a massive influx of arrivals from the countryside. One laid-off woman with eight years' experience reported that she had been promised a work guarantee, but that when she had gone to the Labor Exchange, they would not enrol her. The focus of the meeting, however, was against the newly arriving peasant laborers. The 146 women in attendance attributed the rise of unemployment to the "influx of the peasant population," and passed a resolution "to stop registering the unemployed arriving from the village except for seasonal workers."[90]

Women also noticed the party's change in priorities, its double standards, and the clampdown on democracy. Only eight women (out of 199 new members) joined the party in the recruitment drive in late 1927 and early 1928, prompting the speaker at a general party meeting to comment that "work in this area needs to be strengthened."[91] At a women delegates' discussion on the recruitment campaign, the first speaker argued that workingwomen "do not go into the party because Communists themselves do not attract them but discourage them."[92] A note in a May 1927 party meeting complained that although a member had sexually assaulted a woman and had taken bribes, he "remains unpunished and was transferred to better position. I think that one should be punished more severely, then there will be order."[93] Another party meeting note in August 1928 asked, "Why has Kitashev still not been removed from work and sent to jail for killing a woman. During his vacation, he got drunk and shot a woman. The cell knows about it, but is silent.... He continues to thrive and laugh at workers—kick him out!"[94] A June 1928 *Martenovka* letter again complained that the director's attitude toward women was that they were "manure" and that it would be better if they simply left the factory.[95] In another article entitled "Why we are Nonparty," three women from the bolt shop wrote that they refused to enter the party "because our tongues are whole," and posited "only those who swallow half their tongues beforehand are met with open arms."[96]

The most conspicuous result of the changed perspective on women's work in late NEP was that female workers simply stopped going to the monthly meetings and housewives with more time attended instead. On 7 March 1928, *Martenovka* claimed thirty-five *aktiv* among 325 women in the factory, but then noted that attendance at the four preceding mass meetings had drawn an average of 110 housewives and only ten women workers. The article claimed that only the party took women's work seriously and that the factory committee and management did not—a dubious assertion given that the party dominated both the committee and management.[97] In June 1928, women delegates discussed the failure to involve working women in various activities. One speaker acknowledged that the "work has bypassed our leadership, and is our fault" and argued that "the work is organized without adjusting to women's workload and it needs to be reorganized. During the year, the work was left to its own devices."[98] "Not long ago," the factory newspaper lamented several weeks later, "we read in our newspaper that in mass women's meetings 200 participated, and we used to take pride in this." At a May 1928 women's meeting, eighty-one women signed up for club membership but just twenty-one were workers.[99] Judged by workingwomen themselves, the party's "agitation by the deed," earlier considered a success, was now deemed a failure.

One clear sign of the increasing disaffection among women was the unofficial protest they organized during the factory's International Women's Day in 1928. Two days before the event, a rolled metal shop union meeting focused on the role of women in production and contrasted their position in the Soviet Union with that of women in capitalist countries, but women in the department issued a declaration that "women's pay in the shop is very bad" and the meeting resolved "to bring this to the attention of the representative and the factory committee."[100] The factory-wide event of 520 workers listened to a male speaker, Karpukhin, attempt to present women's work in a positive light.[101] In a remarkable show of defiance, however, *Martenovka* reported that the former factory committee member, Shirakova, and a candidate member, Karpova, gathered a group of women from the bolt shop and organized a boisterous protest at the event. Supposedly "as drunk as old shoemakers," they burst into the celebration during the main speech "swearing like horse drivers," and were forcibly removed. Shirakova had organized a similar protest of workingwomen at the 1927 celebration and the factory newspaper warned that, "This is not the correct path for proletarian women."[102] Whether the women were drunk during the protest is questionable, but the demonstration was large enough to be the main theme of the article. On International Women's Day 1927 and 1928, Hammer and Sickle women boldly ridiculed the hypocrisy of official rhetoric in the face of factory leaders' actual retreat on women's issues.

The sharp contrast between the priorities of workingwomen and factory management in the male-dominated metal industry during late NEP illustrate the evolution of a productivist state policy and the decline of egalitarianism. During the 1917 Revolution, a united working-class movement championed the concerns of women. After the Civil War, Bolshevism remained committed to women's emancipation and the overcoming of male prejudice. Rather than emphasizing "the destruction of the family," however, state policy at the factory level promoted the more pragmatic organization of women around issues that specifically affected them, while factory party and union leaders promoted women's activism and responded sympathetically to their concerns. Significantly, the majority of Hammer and Sickle women actively participated in meetings in which their grievances were addressed. By mid-NEP, however, party leaders at the factory level perceived the special emphasis on women's issues as an obstacle to the pursuit of their main priority. Pressured from above to meet production quotas, management and the party apparatus started to view the female workforce strictly in productivist terms and, therefore, as a problem. In response, working women simply stopped attending meetings.

To be sure, the state change in policy entailed a fundamental break with the Marxist position of promoting women's liberation. The abolition of the Zhenotdel in 1930 marked the end of the proletarian women's movement.[103] That Stalinism dropped even the pretence of women's emancipation is no longer disputable, but an exclusive focus on the decline obscures the proletarian state's efforts to raise the position of workingwomen. What makes this movement all the more impressive is that it took place in a society devastated by seven years of war and foreign intervention. Hammer and Sickle women were among the seven hundred thousand active participants in this remarkable movement that remains largely hidden from history.

Orthodox Belief

Orthodox belief remains a relatively unexplored topic for historians of Soviet labor—a peculiar omission given that workers' belief in the supernatural remained so strong, with religious ceremonial practices continuing among the urban population well into the 1920s.[104] Conservative historians of religion during the Soviet period have attempted to draw a straight line from the relatively lax approach immediately following 1917 to the repressive regime of high Stalinism.[105] More recent scholarship emphasizes the ineffectiveness of state antireligious work.[106]

For the Bolsheviks the battle against religion was not an isolated objective, but one component in a more comprehensive campaign to improve *byt* and to raise the cultural, political, and education level of Soviet citizens. As Marxists, they asserted that under Tsarism the ruling classes had quite consciously perpetuated both low levels of literacy and belief in the supernatural in order to stifle popular unrest while enriching themselves. The advent of socialism would end the myriad social ills associated with nonscientific thinking such as alcoholism, the subjection of women, anti-Semitism, and belief in the supernatural. The ultimate victory of the "struggle for a new lifestyle" rested on a long-term attempt to recast Soviet citizens' worldview through the widespread application of reason and the practical utilization of science and technology as the principle vehicles for mass acceptance.[107] Rather than a system based on exploitation, mutual cooperation in the factories would advance humanity's conquest over nature by constantly improving the process of production; delivering continual improvements in workers' material well being while also undermining the belief that supernatural forces controlled destiny.

Orthodox belief was strong before the Revolution. Workers' memoirs mention icons in every shop and large prayer services in the factory and assert that, "The workers, for the most part, were religious."[108] Of the twenty-two holidays before the Revolution, only the New Year and peasant liberation days were nonreligious.[109] For many workers, religious holidays were a time for alcohol. "We drank for any reason and for no reason at all—when starting a job, on religious holidays, etc."[110]

Sources during the revolution conspicuously omit mention of Orthodoxy or the church. The only overt reference was an early 1918 factory meeting resolution that associated clerics with enemies of the workers' state: "If there is not peace, then mobilize the entire bourgeoisie, monarchists, and priests who oppress working people ... into the first row of the trenches."[111] Significantly, the tradition of religious holidays persisted, as even a Bolshevik organizer acknowledged returning to the countryside for the Easter 1917 break.[112]

The factory continued to honor religious holidays after the October Revolution. A general factory meeting on 18 December unanimously resolved a "red present" of half a day's pay, and the factory closed from 21 December to 8 January.[113] In February 1918, the factory committee voted to close the factory for Maslenitsa (Shrovetide) and two months later the factory shut down for three weeks for the Easter holiday.[114] In 1919, a general meeting again resolved to close the factory for the Easter holiday.[115] As we saw in chapter two, many workers returned to the countryside for the holiday, with over half the workforce absent "without just cause" after the 1919 Easter break. Two years later, "in view of workers' expressed desires," the factory again closed for Easter week, though workers were expected to work overtime to compensate for the lost time.[116] During early NEP, moreover, icons continued to be displayed in shops.[117]

An exception to such leniency came in the spring of 1922. Lenin and the Bolsheviks believed that the Orthodox Church's policy of placing a higher priority on its own valuables than on human life during the famine of 1922 placed the church in a precarious position, and they ordered a campaign to seize church valuables.[118] The Moscow Soviet reported that four hundred Hammer and Sickle workers attended a meeting on the seizure of church valuables and a resolution in support of the confiscations passed "almost unanimously."[119] The low turnout as compared with other factory-wide meetings in early NEP indicates that workers were less concerned with the church relics than with religious practices. Five members from the factory participated in the confiscations. One participant recalled:

> I had already entered the party in 1920. I would have entered earlier, in 1918, but my wife was religious and she swore at me: "Bolshevik." In 1919 she died of pneumonia. I joined in 1920. The cell was small with no more than twenty members. In 1922 I married a second time. Her first husband worked in our factory but he died in 1918.... In 1921 the district committee called for five people to withdraw valuables from churches. Gus'kov, Timofeev, two others (whose names I cannot remember), and myself went. Communists were summoned from all the factories for this activity.... We were delayed till seven o'clock. A lot of people gathered and they swore at us. We took seventeen *puds* of silver and one large diamond.[120]

Workers' primary religious concern was their religious holidays. Workers in the rolled metal shop (650 people) and nail shop (250 people) submitted a joint statement to the factory committee in December 1923 with a demand for a Christmas holiday based on the old-style calendar, while other shops asked for the break based on the new calendar.[121] The factory committee deferred the issue to a delegate meeting, which subsequently resolved that individual shops should decide the date of the Christmas holiday. The rolled metal and nail departments opted for the old-style calendar, while other shops chose the new calendar. Four hundred workers attended the rolled metal shop meeting (the same number in attendance at the factory-wide session on confiscations) and two hundred workers were present when the bolt shop opted for the old-style calendar.[122] Workers could also extend their religious holidays by working Saturdays before the holidays, and several shops voted for resolutions to do so.[123]

Rank-and-file worker pressure for the Christmas holiday in 1923 forced a frank discussion about religion in the party organization. The controversy revealed rampant confusion on the issue and no clear policy. Several speakers merely noted that religion was a "very serious" matter, but one member ignited a controversy when he stated that almost all members had icons in their homes. The next speaker took issue with this assertion. "When Comrade Lavrenov says that almost all of us have icons at home, this, comrades, just will not do," he responded. "If we, the advanced guard, are still under this drug, then I think we have an insufficient understanding of V.I. Lenin's legacy." Another speaker argued that members with icons in their homes should read Comrade Trotsky because "he shows the way to fight religion." He suggested organizing a "burning of the gods" and urged a consultation with the party center about resolving the question. The discussion shows that party cells, even in the socialist capital, were left to their own devices on the issue. A Comrade Voronin called for restraint:

> The question of religion is very serious. The point about burning is not new—this was done in ancient times. I think we should not get too hot and talk about

destroying things. The question is serious but it will be resolved according to the level of development of the workers. This development has already begun, and thus, religion will gradually leave workers' heads—but this will take a long time.[124]

The admission that "almost all" experienced party members had icons in their homes was certainly at odds with Trotsky's assertion a few months earlier that "religiousness among the Russian working classes practically does not exist."[125] The Lenin Levy a few months later further strengthened religious belief within the party's ranks. The Bolsheviks recruited believers in the hope that their convictions would later change, but the party placed restrictions on open worship—limits to which nonparty workers were not subject. Yet in 1924 the party continued to avoid religious issues. In December 1924, a party leader admitted that, "Often party members do not know how to approach nonparty workers about religious questions."[126] Significantly, religious practice rarely resulted in expulsion; the party continued to tolerate members who believed in the supernatural. The party reprimanded one member who had returned to his village, "went to church and read the book of the Apostles."[127] The party also tolerated shifting attitudes to religion among its members: a four-year member who had been expelled for marrying in a church reapplied, and the shop bureau simply decided to "find out his leanings at the current time."[128]

Party expulsions for religious belief were invariably combined with other offences. An unusual incident concerned a member threatened with expulsion for "going to church and snorting cocaine." The accused did not deny the charges, and the bureau reported, "Lartsev considers this his personal business."[129] The party expelled another member for not paying his party dues for twelve months, for not going to party meetings, for not breaking with his religious convictions, and for being married in a church.[130] While believers could pray openly in the shops, such practices were frowned upon for party members. When the party informed one member of his expulsion, he pulled out an icon. "Well thank you Lord! Now I can at least pray in the open because for the last two years I have not been praying the way I should. I used to bring out an icon, do some praying, and then put it away again."[131] Another member submitted a request to release him from the party "because he cannot overcome the religious mood in his family."[132] The party strategy of gradual atheistic transformation failed for another member:

> The bureau notified her many times to appear before the bureau, but she answered, "Go to hell, I'm tired of you." Comrade Kruglova has been a candidate member for three years but does not go to meetings and does not pay membership dues. She is religious with strong beliefs. She has already said that she does not want to be a member and we are dragging her into the party almost by force. Resolution to expel from the party.[133]

The Union of Godless, the Soviet atheist organization, was largely an ineffective paper organization, repeatedly criticized by factory party leaders. In May 1925, the Godless claimed 325 members but the report admitted that weak leadership in the shops made the work careless, unsystematic, and sluggish, with only two general meetings and no distribution of antireligious propaganda.[134] In the repair shop in January 1925, the Godless organizer pleaded to strengthen antireligious activity among party members.[135] In September 1925 the factory newspaper chastised the Godless because a cross and icon had hung openly in the warehouse.[136] In March 1926, the nail shop party bureau also characterized the Godless work as weak.[137] A few weeks later, a bolt shop report claimed 60 Godless members but "no leadership."[138] A year later, the factory newspaper complained that "the Godless are asleep" in the pattern shop because Nikitin "gathers young and old workers" to read aloud from the Gospel.[139] In May 1927, the Godless claimed that the group had 296 members but party speakers admitted the group's ineffectuality in combating the influence of priests and sectarians.[140] During the Christmas season of 1927-1928, *Martenovka* noted that, "New religious sects have appeared" in the district, and accused the nail shop Godless of being particularly lackadaisical in combating the new phenomenon.[141] In the form-casting shop, the Godless failed to organize a single general meeting in three months and generally did "nothing."[142]

The Godless did organize some successful events. On the Saturday before Easter in 1928, thirteen hundred workers and their families had attended an antireligious evening in the club with films, dancing, games, and discussions continuing until 7 a.m. The newspaper conspicuously omitted absentee figures for the following Monday; yet 3 percent of the workforce failed to show up for work on Tuesday, which showed that "religious traditions have a strong hold on the minds of the workers."[143]

The Godless were particularly concerned about the hold of religious mysticism among women. In 1925 the factory youth group organized a "Komsomol Christmas" in the club and included a lecture on "natural history" in which "every woman worker and worker's wife can ask questions that interest them and they will have them answered."[144] The Godless "often forget about their families. Women, housewives, in particular, are not drawn into social work." The article implored the Godless to "break the wife from this darkness and bring her to the club for an evening of speeches, develop her by the reading of books and journals, and make her your comrade."[145]

The effectiveness of such club lectures is questionable. A report on the Godless work in the sheet metal shop in March 1927 (which probably underestimated religious belief) claimed that two hundred workers in the shop were nonbelievers, 90 were "fanatical believers," and 150 were "wavering" on the issue. Nonbelievers, "particularly women," were reluctant to participate in Godless lectures and when they did go, a party leader admitted, "often because of our inability to conduct a sensible discussion, they leave believing [in God] even more strongly."[146] This persistence of religious belief in the factory is consistent with figures for Moscow where religious practice remained strong. The number of religious births and funerals actually increased from 1925 to 1928, while the number of civil marriages declined slightly.[147]

With religious practice, as with many issues in late NEP, a double standard prevailed between party leaders and the rank-and-file members. A note to the main speaker at a May 1928 meeting complained: "You spoke of party discipline and antireligious propaganda, and you touched mostly upon the rank-and-file members, but you failed to mention certain factory bureau members who show an example of how to celebrate Easter rituals by making Easter bread, like Pritamanov."[148]

Although party and state policy focused more attention on productivity and factory leaders became less tolerant of multiple religious work holidays, workers continued to observe their own schedules with or without state sanction. A 1927 MK report on work discipline and the struggle with absenteeism in Moscow asserted that the three main causes for missed work were vodka, church holidays, and excursions to the countryside. The factory was singled out for days missed because of religious holidays, with twice as many absentees on old Christmas and five times as many on Maslenitsa.[149]

The 1928 campaign to require work on the Christmas holiday was a litmus test of the relative strength of the state's increasingly productivist ethos vis-à-vis Orthodox belief. Different department resolutions illustrate the party's unevenness: its influence was simply not yet strong enough in all shops to intimidate opposition to party-sponsored resolutions. The majority of speakers in the nail shop spoke in favor of working on Christmas, but two speakers challenged the resolution. One speaker against the holiday work used anti-Semitic terms: "They are taking away our holidays such as Christmas and New Year, but the Jews get to celebrate their holidays." The resolution for Christmas work failed, with nineteen in favor, thirty-five against, and twenty-three abstentions, a result indicative of the discrepancy between the majority of loyal speakers and rank-and-file workers' silent sentiments.[150] The speaker in the maintenance shop stated that women in the bolt shop had already agreed to work on Christmas and another union leader argued, "Women workers always welcome positive initiatives." The shop passed a qualified resolution to work only if other shops did so.[151] In several other shops, party and union loyalists prevailed. In the cable shop meeting, for example, only twelve of fifty-five voted against working on Christmas.[152]

The 1928 state campaign to work through Christmas was a failure. Because of the disparities between shops, delegates met on 14 December to decide the issue. A factory announcement on 17 December 1928 mandated that in accordance with the delegates' meeting, the Christmas holiday would start on 22 December.[153] Moreover, because the Russian Orthodox Church did not adopt the new calendar, many workers were absent on the old calendar Christmas. For example, seventy-two workers were absent from the bolt shop, twenty-six without just cause.[154] This pressure from below was apparently replicated in other Moscow factories. Responding to "ten different suggestions" on the holiday issue, the Moscow City Central Trade Union Council backtracked and declared December 24th to 29th a holiday.[155] A note to a speaker in early 1929 indicates that workers in the district recognized the duplicity of union policy: "Why did the unions agitate that workers should work on Christmas—which of course we did not—while the central organs of the union and administration institutions did not work? They cannot agitate against it and at the same time celebrate."[156]

Factory policy on religion during the early years of the revolution was marked by leniency and tolerance. Workers decided their own holiday schedule and openly worshiped in the shops. Antireligious work was practically nonexistent as the Union of Godless had little influence. Moreover, the majority of party members held religious beliefs and did not consider their belief in the supernatural to contradict their own commitment to socialism. Given a choice between the productivist ethos and their religious beliefs during Christmas 1928, workers opted for the latter. Thereafter, Stalinism became less tolerant of religious values that challenged the industrialization drive, and abandoned the pretence that workers' opinions mattered.

Alcoholism, Fighting, and Hooliganism

No issue illustrates the frustrations of the state's social engineering efforts more than the persistence of alcohol abuse and hooliganism. Alcoholism was rampant during the prerevolutionary years and management tried to discipline employees by fining them one ruble for fighting or appearing at the factory in a drunken state.[157] Such methods of social control were ineffective. "On payday," one worker wrote, "wives often stood guard at the gate to grab the wages and to keep them from going to the tavern."[158] Because of a prohibition on hard liquor, "workers drank different substitutes, such as purified denatured alcohol and varnish. Every day we stayed in the evening as if for overtime work, but in reality we played card games."[159] "Women and men drank wine together in the shops," wrote one woman. "Almost everyone drank in the morning and at lunch. They smuggled it in their clothes and pockets. Only after the revolution did all this stop."[160]

Alcoholism did not miraculously halt after the October Revolution, nor was it limited to rank-and-file workers. In early 1918, the factory committee leaders Tumanov and Dimitriev created a scandal when they got into a drunken confrontation with factory Red Guards. The factory committee organized a trial that found Tumanov innocent but Dimitriev guilty, and he was thrown off the committee.[161]

Early Soviet prohibition on alcohol production gave way to pragmatic financial concerns. The Soviet government prohibited the sale of strong alcohol in December 1919 but consumption fell during the Civil War due to the grain shortage rather than state policy. During NEP, prohibition proved ineffectual: fully one-third of rural households distilled alcohol, and prosecutions strained the court system. Prohibition ended gradually, as the strength of permissible alcohol steadily increased. State alcohol production became an important source of Soviet revenue, accounting for 12 percent of state income by the late 1920s.[162]

Alcoholism in the factory followed this general trend, declining and then increasing with the grain supply. Civil War sources rarely mention alcoholism and contrast markedly with evidence from NEP. In December 1924, *Rabochaia Moskva* reported that unexcused absences increased significantly after payday because of drunkenness. In the rolled metal shop, the average number of absences due to illness and other causes was sixty-five, but after receiving pay, the average was eighty-seven.[163] By October 1925 party leaders addressed "the struggle with drunkenness in the factory" and pointed out that on the eighth, ninth, and tenth of the month, seven hundred workers were absent without just cause.[164]

The Lenin Levy apparently increased the number of alcoholic members. In August 1924, the party bureau and factory committee resolved that, "If a comrade appears in the factory in an inebriated state, then the question will be brought before the general meeting of workers."[165] The main speaker in a September 1925 factory party meeting claimed "at the present time this is the most important question." He noted that party members were not attending meetings and were often intoxicated while at work. Nor was this a rank-and-file phenomenon, because "even bureau members" appeared in the factory drunk. The meeting subsequently resolved to take "extreme measures."[166] In October 1926, the party expelled five members for not carrying out work, not paying their dues, and habitually showing up for work "in an inebriated state."[167]

As with religious belief, party expulsions for alcoholism were almost always combined with other offences. The party expelled a long-term member in the bolt shop for nonpayment of dues and habitually drinking on payday.[168] The party only reprimanded seven older members for repeated drunkenness at work.[169] The nail shop bureau summoned a candidate member, Semenov, four times because of drunkenness. After three years of candidate membership, the bureau concluded that "he promised to straighten out, but he is not getting any better." Semenov argued that he "drinks because of his wife," but the party expelled him for repeated drunkenness and nonpayment of party dues. The nail shop cell merely reprimanded another member after it received a police report on his "violation of public order in an intoxicated state," even though he had been expelled earlier for drunkenness and nonpayment of dues.[170]

Only the most outrageous drunken behavior led to expulsion. In 1927, on Unity Day with the Red Army, "Comrade Ivanov (cable shop) was in an inebriated state." Ivanov supposedly walked up to a soldier and taunted him: "You're only making one and a half rubles? That is nothing! I would not serve in the army if I were you." Other workers told him that this was "not permissible talk" and after rumors of the incident spread, Ivanov was brought before a general party meeting and expelled.[171] Another member was expelled before the entire factory organization because of his previous outburst when Lenin's sister spoke at the factory: "In the factory cell plenum during Maria Ulianova's report on the Seventh Plenum of the Moscow Committee and the related report on the Moscow Control Commission, he, in a drunken state, began shouting at her, 'Enough talk!' ... despite the fact that Maria Ulianova had spoken for no more than ten to fifteen minutes. Because of this outburst he was removed from the meeting."[172]

Alcoholism was not limited to male employees. Increased alcoholism among female production workers appears to have coincided with the demoralization and collapse of women's work. A bolt shop report on women's work in May 1926 estimated that 30 percent of women drank.[173] In May 1928, a party bureau speaker noted "recently a noticeable drunkenness among women."[174] The bolt shop cell reprimanded a female member because "she came to work drunk and had to be removed from the shop for a while."[175]

Women members with drinking problems faced double standards. The party expelled one member who had penned three articles for *Martenovka*, including two on women's issues and one against religion, before Christmas in 1925.[176] The shop bureau noted that "she is a good worker, but she drinks" and specified "she will keep herself in check." A candidate, she was elevated to full membership but within a month male members complained that, "She does not carry out the work of distributing literature in the shop, and is often absent and drinks." The shop bureau resolved to remove her from the distribution assignment. Three months later she was expelled because "her drinking activity was demoralizing nonparty workers."[177]

Drunkenness, fighting, and hooliganism took place in many arenas in and around the factory. In March 1922, the party bureau discussed the behavior of one member involved in "an incident in the theatre." The meeting minutes do not describe the details of the incident, but the bureau resolved to immediately remove the strong drinks sold at the theatre buffet.[178] Two months later, a party meeting resolved to pressure the factory committee "to take measures to stop outrages in the theatre."[179] Another arena of rowdiness was the factory cafeteria. *Martenovka* claimed, "In our cafeterias there are rows and scandals almost every day" and referred to the canteen as "the hooligans' den." In addition to fistfights, the newspaper complained that some workers, "particularly when they need a drink," would sell their lunch tickets to "derelicts."[180]

The focal point of hooliganism was the factory club. Ironically, the factory's first newspaper, *Nasha gazeta* (Our Newspaper), had called for the creation of the club because "in their free time workers are drawn to the pub and sometimes even to church." A factory club would help "to raise cultural-educational work."[181] In February 1924, a combined meeting of party and delegates discussed measures for combating hooliganism in the club. One representative suggested enlisting the Komsomol to prevent club disorders, but another speaker countered that it was "not possible to restore order in the club through the Komsomol because the hooligans are armed with guns and hand weapons."[182] In January 1925, *Rabochaia Moskva* reported that the hooligans had the upper hand against those who tried to restore order in the club, including repeated incidents of hooligans beating up club officials and factory committee members. Calling the militia by telephone was ineffective because "either the militiamen are busy, or if only one person shows up, he will likely be unable to deal with it." Moreover, warned the newspaper, the "hooligans, sensing that the club administration cannot handle them, are getting more brazen."[183] By November 1925, *Martenovka* reported that the factory club "rarely had a night without a fight or a scandal."[184] In December 1926, the factory newspaper called on the Komsomol to help defend the club from hooligans.[185]

Expecting the youth organization to stem rowdiness in the club was problematic. A Komsomol leader acknowledged drinking and hooliganism among
about half the membership, but claimed that it was nothing serious. He also
claimed that the Komsomol had created guard units of five persons for the
club, five for the factory, and five for the surrounding area.[186] The same
leader later admitted Komsomol passivity and hooliganism but claimed they
had helped to rehabilitate many former youth bandits.[187] Another 1926 factory Komsomol report noted "unhealthy phenomena" that once again
included drunkenness and hooliganism.[188] The MK reported that the factory
Komsomol secretary himself "actively participated in forming a hooligan
group." The group's activities included "drunkenness and armed assaults on
passers-by." The arrest of the cell secretary ended a bitter, apparently apolitical nine-month fight for control of the Komsomol organization in the factory.[189] In March 1927, the new Komsomol leader reported, "It is true that
there have been incidents of drunkenness and hooliganism, but in general the
masses are healthy."[190]

Komsomol guards' failure to combat rowdiness in the club led authorities
to attempt more stringent measures. In September 1926, factory leaders
organized a show trial against eight hooligans, including one Komsomol
member. According to one militiaman, they had arrived to quell a distur-
bance at the club but the hooligans outnumbered the militia. "The hooligans
became enraged, beat and grabbed the militia by their throats, pushed their
backs to the fence and while punching shouted, 'Beat the militia!'" Only after
a Red Army detachment arrived did authorities restore order. The trial ultimately sentenced the accused to serve from four to eighteen months in
prison.[191] Show trials, however, did not end disturbances in the club. In
March 1928, the factory cultural commission leader argued, "The way the
administration conducts the struggle with hooliganism is too soft and it is
necessary to adopt the most severe measures."[192]

Brawling on the shop floor was also a frequent occurrence. Management
repeatedly issued factory-wide announcements that included the combat-
ants' names in a futile attempt to embarrass them. "Shaming" as a method of
social control started modestly. Management issued only one reprimand in
1923, indicating that the fight in question was rather vicious.[193] In December 1925, management reprimanded a worker in the steel foundry shop for
wounding another worker with a shovel.[194] In February 1928, management
reprimanded a worker in the wire pulling shop "for punching the technical
control worker in the face."[195] An unusual strike in April 1924 illustrates the
shop-floor disorder but also the strength of worker activism and the relative
weakness of the state during early NEP.

On 24 April there was a strike because of the following: On 7 April a worker in the
repair shop hit another worker over the head with a bottle. A few days later the
wounded worker died and the militia arrested the killer. On 24 April he again
appeared at the factory and his presence caused strong indignation among workers. Workers returned to work only after the factory committee promised to legally
pursue the matter. The next day, 25 April, was again marked by strong worker dis-

satisfaction, this time in the rolled metal shop (514 workers) because of the following. A worker in the rolled metal shop, Vavilov, in an inebriated state, badly beat Baranov from the rolled metal shop, who was sent to the hospital unconscious. In response to this, workers said: "Why was a worker such as Vavilov again accepted back at work after he had already been fired from the factory for brawling and fighting?" Vavilov was arrested.[196]

If workers were outraged by the murder of one of their comrades, they also defended their right to brawl on the shop floor. Dismissal for fighting alone was such a rare occurrence that when management fired employees, their colleagues often challenged it. Several men in the mechanical shop were fired for fighting and the shop party bureau supported the firings, but "among workers there began a movement to have the firings overturned." Several rank-and-file party members "took the lead of the workers' movement and insisted on submitting a petition to have the workers reinstated."[197]

Party members participated in shop floor brawls. Repeated shouting and fighting between two repair shop members, according to shop party members, created "a nervous mood in the shop and lowered the cell in the eyes of the workers."[198] In May 1925, a factory party leader reported on "unhealthy phenomena" among members, and ranked fighting behind theft, but ahead of absenteeism and economic tailism.[199] In December 1925, a fight between party members in the rolled metal shop erupted after they doused each other with water. "A Communist is not like Christ, who turned the other cheek, so instead he hit Anulevich on the forehead with a mug, wounding him and sending him to the clinic. It is not good for older workers to practice hooliganism; just the opposite," argued *Martenovka*. "They should set an example for our youth."[200]

The few party reprimands and expulsions for violent behavior against women probably underestimate the number of assaults on female employees. In May 1925, the factory party bureau reprimanded—but did not expel—a member for drunkenness and beating his wife.[201] *Martenovka* accused two workers of regularly beating up women, particularly on payday.[202] Another article demanded that the party should expel a wife-beating candidate member.[203] A party report for 1927 noted that one of the insufficient areas of party work was among women and cited members' "non-communist behavior, including drunkenness and wife beating."[204] *Martenovka* also reported one gruesome incident in which Plekhanova, described as a "good worker," started a relationship with a married employee and became the victim of his enraged peasant wife. The wife heard gossip about the relationship, sold the family's belongings, travelled to Moscow, and threw acid in Plekhanova's face, blinding her.[205]

A February 1928 factory discussion on hooliganism indicates the level of lawlessness and disorder in the district. Seventy-three questions to the speaker, a member of the district militia, suggest a deteriorating situation and frustration over the authorities' inability to curb the problems. One worker wanted to know "why do we have such a strong development of hooliganism in the USSR, and why was it less developed under Tsarism?" Another worker asked: "Comrade, why do we have such disorders in the Russian republic? I notice that at twelve o'clock at night it is impossible to walk the street." One note claimed "an increase of theft in the lines at the district cooperative." Many notes recommended stronger police presence and more severe measures, such as higher fines, though another complained that fines were useless. One worker complained that a newspaper article said that a hooligan was sentenced to jail for only one month, while others suggested "Beat the hooligans," and "Why don't the militia shoot?" Another worker asked, "Why don't we have hooligan trials in the club?" Many notes blamed the militia for incompetence, and several suggested that the militia were "simply afraid of the hooligans." Another worker asked why it was that "when there are fist fights and knife fights in the club, and you go to the militia post, he refuses to come and says, 'I'm not going, let them kill each other'?" Several notes blamed the problems on alcohol. One proposed to close taverns on payday, and another suggested: "Comrade speaker, don't you think that if we banned vodka altogether we would get to socialism much faster?"[206]

Increased alcoholism and hooliganism appears to have been generalized throughout late NEP Soviet society. A 1927 survey of Moscow Komsomol members found "apathy, disillusionment, and decadent attitudes" among youth and Komsomol leaders. The report claimed a "growth in manifestations of malaise such as drunkenness, hooliganism, and suicide."[207] The United Opposition platform complained that the "swiftly growing consumption of alcoholic liquor … takes away from the working class budget" while leading to an "increase of absenteeism, careless workmanship, waste, accidents, fires, fights, injuries, etc."[208]

Declining party morale during late NEP contributed to alcohol-induced outbursts against the regime. The new practice of members reporting on the utterances of other members applied foremost to political remarks and coincided with party loyalist reports on Oppositionist activities. A candidate member informed the party of the behavior of a member who appeared in the dormitory drunk and "began swearing at the party and Soviet power using unprintable and obscene words." The informer also claimed that member had entered the party for careerist reasons, and charged that because he failed to attain his goal of becoming a shop foreman, he blamed the party. At the next meeting, the accused member "repented" in the *samokritika* fashion and received a reprimand.[209] Another member lost his job for repeatedly starting brawls but he was "restored to his position thanks to the party organization and trade union." He later showed up drunk for a shop meeting and "spoke on the question of state loans in a non-Communist manner, started a big row, and also referred to the party using vulgar terms." Several days later, he appeared at work in an intoxicated state and nonparty workers remarked, "Here is your party member—he is so drunk he cannot even work." A foreman suggested that he go home, but he refused, swearing at the party and Soviet power "in every possible way." He fought with the militia and guards, attempted to wrestle away one of their weapons, and was forcibly carried out of the factory. The expulsion resolution stressed the political nature of his outbursts rather than the fisticuffs with the militia. He was expelled for non-payment of membership dues, drunkenness, rioting, and "using obscenity in his anti-Communist speech in the meeting, addressing VTsIK, the Central Committee, the Central Control Committee, and all Soviet power."[210]

In the second half of 1928, *Martenovka* starting pushing a "class struggle" line on the issues of hooliganism and discipline, albeit inverted against the workers and for the state's productivist interest. Andrea Groziosi aptly dubs this campaign Stalinism's "anti-worker workerism," in which workers were depicted in Soviet newspapers as loafers, self-seekers, thieves, drunkards, absentees, etc. The regime blamed workers for what it claimed was a "decline in labor discipline" for industry failing to complete its plan. So vicious was this unprecedented rhetorical assault against the Soviet working class that the Menshevik émigré press assumed that a capitalist class had gained a control of Soviet industry.[211]

A few weeks after the show trial of club hooligans, *Martenovka* led with a headline charging that "Drunkenness and Hooliganism Undermine the Gains of October." The article claimed that drunkenness in the shops had increased, again calling for stricter measures such as show trials.[212] By 1928, raising productivity and discipline were inextricably linked with propaganda against hooliganism on the shop floor. An article entitled "More Watchfulness in Production, Everyone for Work Discipline" called for a resolute struggle against absentees, hooligans, drinkers, and wreckers in production. "These enemies of our production are enemies of Soviet construction and the working class as a whole," the newspaper charged, admitting that even "members of the party drink and fight at the factory."[213]

The "anti-worker" campaign was a tacit admission by evolving Stalinism that the voluntary and participatory transformation of *byt* had been a failure. Henceforth state loyalists would pursue a more strident cultural transformation of society that placed the blame on workers for the regime's own failures. The "Cultural Revolution" (in practice a "Cultural Counterrevolution") subordinated all aspects of Soviet culture to the productivist needs of Soviet industry. *Martenovka* noted that

> The fox trot was banned. Now in the ballroom, in public at youth parties, the fox trot is danced under the guise of a waltz. When one watches the dancers, one sees what an aroused state they get into. It seems to me that we can expect nothing from such a waltz but depravity. That is why such waltzes should be forbidden at our parties. Parties are not for debauchery, but for the cultural rest of our youth.[214]

Workers had become less interested in politics, choosing to participate in other activities during the crisis of late NEP. While a majority of the workforce—between one thousand and sixteen hundred workers—regularly attended the twice-monthly factory general meetings after work in 1922, in 1927 only nine hundred employees attended the largest meeting of year, even though the workforce had doubled over the preceding five years.[215] Low attendance at meetings continued in the First Five-Year Plan, but three thousand workers regularly attended the factory club soccer matches.[216] Similarly, from April to the end of 1927, an astounding 48,516 workers—the vast majority of whom were youth—paid to see films in the factory club.[217]

Some workers recognized the party's double standards in its social engineering efforts. At a May 1928 general party meeting, a note to the speaker asked: "Why was Vasil'ev in the bolt shop not expelled? He is often seen drunk and he was arrested by the militia."[218] Nonparty workers were also fully aware of the enrolment of drunks in the party. A speaker at the meeting of nonparty *aktiv* in 1928 suggested giving new members six months' probation, but drinkers even longer.[219] Repair shop inebriated members included the organizer and a "completely demoralized" older member named Ukhov, who had "beat up a nonparty worker" but did not receive even a reprimand.[220] In response to why workers were not joining the party, one contributor suggested that the organization should have been more selective about those it allowed to bear arms because "party members get drunk and chase each other around with revolvers."[221]

Various attempts to curb alcoholism during NEP were ineffective. A 1928 factory circular to combat carelessness included a command to "not let intoxicated workers operate machinery."[222] Unable to combat alcoholism, factory leaders apparently tried to shift the burden onto workers' wives. On the eleventh anniversary of the October Revolution, a housewives' and women workers' commemoration pledged to "conduct a resolute struggle with alcoholism."[223] The attempt to instill among the workforce an essentially Protestant work ethic with a red veneer proved problematic because most workers did not share the state's productivist aspirations. Moreover, many workers were acutely aware of the duplicity of factory party leaders, whose behavior did not measure up to the moral standards demanded of rank-and-file workers.

The Bolsheviks believed that the political and economic transformation of Soviet society would usher in a radical alteration of workers' daily lives. Workers would be actively involved not only in changing the process of production but in their own personal transformation. By the end of NEP, however, the long-term materialist perspective to overcome the cultural inheritance of Tsarism was dropped in favor of a more coercive approach. Disputes over women's issues, Orthodox religious belief, and hooliganism did not take place in a vacuum—state loyalists in the factory abandoned earlier tolerant and egalitarian strategies on cultural issues because Stalinism mandated that all aspects of Soviet society were to be subordinated to the regime's productivist aspirations.

Yet the state offensive against the working class did not push forward on all fronts simultaneously: the *volta-face* on women's liberation prefigured the more coercive approach to antireligious work that was deferred until the First Five-Year Plan. In the early 1920s, women participated in activities that were promoted from above by the workers' state and that genuinely addressed their grievances. Working-class women judged this movement not by its rhetoric but with the same yardstick as Soviet advocates of women's liberation—by the success of the "agitation by the deed." The exclusive stress on productivity entailed a de-emphasis on issues of particular concern to female employees. Women recognized the political retreat and repeatedly complained and protested, but resistance by increasingly isolated working-women—a numerically weak minority—was ineffectual, especially because management successfully played on fears of unemployment.

More problematic for the regime's industrialization efforts was workers' continuing attachment to Orthodox religiosity, because the state's social control strategy was aimed at a majority of the workforce. The Marxist position in the early years of the revolution understood prevalent belief in the supernatural as a reflection of Russia's economic backwardness and low cultural level. Most workers, including party members, maintained religious beliefs, but did not perceive religion as inconsistent with building socialism. During late NEP, party, union, and management adopted a more rhetorically strident strategy that broke with the previous perspective of encouraging a gradual transformation over decades. Party leaders sought, but failed to win, an endorsement of work on religious holidays, setting the stage for more confrontational, arm-twisting approaches to antireligious work.

Various measures to curb rampant alcohol abuse and hooliganism were also unsuccessful, particularly as authorities viewed drinking as a question of willpower rather than as a medical or social problem. Moreover, despite Stalin's claims that state production of alcohol would decrease, the state relied on this revenue. Workers' comments in 1928 suggest that the Soviet regime had not only failed to curb problems such as hooliganism, but also that the situation had deteriorated, indicative of the much deeper social crisis. With the working class in retreat, however, the crisis fostered individual despair and alcohol abuse by many workers—including women.

The Bolshevik credo of leading by example and maintaining high moral standards was gradually reduced to mandating from positions of power. Many workers were aware of the factory leaders' duplicity, and they complained about party bosses abusing women, partaking in religious ceremonies, and running around drunk with revolvers. Despite the potentially subversive worker response, state intervention in workers' daily lives not only continued to push forward, but also accelerated. While some workers resented state policy and started to draw more politically charged conclusions against the regime, the majority of workers were withdrawing from the political realm. Cleavages between workers were reinforced, especially as unemployment escalated, and the resentment of state policy on everyday politics did not necessarily translate into anti-regime sentiments. Male employees blamed women for problems; women blamed in-migrating peasant workers; and Orthodox workers blamed Jews. The depoliticization and accompanying demoralization exacerbated exclusive tendencies among the workforce, ultimately strengthening the position of the state for pursuing its anti-working class policies.

Notes

1. Elizabeth Wood, *The Baba and the Comrade* (Bloomington, 1997), 194-195.
2. Leon Trotsky, "Culture and Socialism" in *Problems of Everyday Life* (New York, 1973).
3. Reiman, *The Birth of Stalinism*, 118.
4. Tony Cliff, *Class Struggle and Women's Liberation* (London, 1984), 139-140.
5. Wendy Goldman, *Women, the State, and Revolution: Soviet Family Policy and Social Life, 1917-1936* (Cambridge, 1993), chapter 1.
6. For example, see Wood, *Baba and the Comrade* and Choi Chatterjee, *Celebrating Women: Gender, Festival Culture, and Bolshevik Ideology, 1910-1939* (Pittsburgh, 2002).
7. Carol Hayden, "The Zhenotdel and the Bolshevik Party" in *Histoire Russe* III: 2 (1976): 157.
8. TsMAM, f. 176, op. 2, d. 107. Employment statistics.
9. *Martenovka*, 1 May 1925.
10. TsAODM, f. 429, op. 1, d. 57, l. 11. Party bureau meeting, 1 February 1927. By 1927, the mean age among 234 female production workers was almost forty, with only twenty-three women under the age of twenty-two and 106 women over forty years old.
11. TsAODM, f. 429, op. 1, d. 4, l. 49. Party meeting, 8 December 1920.
12. TsAODM, f. 429, op. 1, dd. 3, 4. Party general meetings, 1920, 1921.
13. TsMAM, f. 176, op. 2, d. 126, ll. 9-11. Metalworkers' thesis on work among women, n.d. 1922.
14. TsMAM, f. 176, op. 2, d. 171, ll. 8-9. Moscow metalworkers' plan of work for April-June 1923.
15. TsMAM d. 126, ll. 12-14. Women's organizer report on women's work in factory, 24 November 1922.
16. TsMAM, f. 176, op. 2, d. 73, l. 5. Factory announcement, 17 October 1922.
17. TsMAM, f. 176, op. 2, d. 166, l. 16. Factory committee meeting, 28 July 1923.
18. TsMAM, f. 176, op. 2, d. 123, l. 8. Women's delegate meeting, 20 November 1923.
19. TsMAM, f. 176, op. 2, d. 216, l. 5. RKK statistics for January to March 1924. Women participated in one-third of disputes affecting 2,441 workers. The figures do not break down decisions (for and against) by gender but 92.6 percent (and 2,260 affected employees) were decided in the favor of the workers.
20. TsAODM, f. 429, op. 1, d. 10, l. 50. Party bureau meeting, 24 July 1923.
21. TsAODM, f. 429, op. 1, d. 16, l. 8. Party report, December 1924.
22. TsMAM, f. 176, op. 2, d. 246, ll. 10, 30. Factory committee meeting, 11 April 1924.
23. TsMAM, f. 176, op. 2, d. 174, ll. 1-15. Zhenotdel guidelines for women's work, n.d. 1923; Communist International thesis on women's work, n.d. 1923.
24. TsMAM, f. 176, op. 2, d. 256, l. 6. Women's general meeting, 14 October 1924.
25. TsAODM, f. 429, op. 1, d. 7, l. 8. Party meeting, 1 March 1922.
26. TsAODM, f. 429, op. 1, d. 6, l. 4. Party bureau meeting, 3 March 1922.
27. TsMAM, f. 176, op. 2, d. 256, l. 22. Memorandum from factory committee chairman and party secretary, n.d. 1924.
28. TsMAM, f. 176, op. 2, d. 256, l. 3. Women and workers meeting, 8 March 1924.
29. TsMAM, f. 176, op. 2, d. 174, ll. 16-31. Delegate and general women's meetings, 1923.
30. TsMAM, f. 176, op. 2, d. 256, ll. 3-4. Women's meetings, 25 February, 14 October 1924.
31. *Martenovka*, 1 May 1925.
32. TsMAM, f. 176, op. 2, d. 256, l. 3. Women's meeting, 25 February 1924.
33. TsMAM, f. 176, op. 2, d. 256, ll. 1-30. Women's meetings, 1924.
34. TsMAM, f. 176, op. 2, d. 246, ll. 10, 30. Factory committee meeting, 4 November 1924.
35. *Rabochaia Moskva*, 10 June 1923.
36. *Rabochaia Moskva*, 8 January 1925.
37. TsAODM, f. 429, op. 1, d. 10, ll. 31, 36, 56. Party bureau meetings, 20 March, 8 May, 24 July 1923.
38. TsAODM, f. 429, op. 1, d. 15, l. 2. Party bureau meeting, 15 January 1924.
39. TsMAM, f. 176, op. 2 d. 253, ll. 2, 4. Factory committee report for spring and summer 1924.

40. TsAODM, f. 429, op. 1, d. 15, ll. 4, 40. Party bureau meetings, 5 February, 12 August 1924.

41. TsAODM, f. 429, op. 1, d. 27, l. 31. Party bureau meeting, 16 March 1925.

42. TsAODM, f. 429, op. 1, d. 27, ll. 43, 50. Party bureau meetings, 5 May, 9 June 1925.

43. TsAODM, f. 429, op. 1, d. 28, l. 33. Party general meeting, 26 August 1925.

44. TsMAM, f. 176, op. 2, d. 432, l. 33. Women's delegate meeting, 27 March 1925.

45. TsMAM, f. 176, op. 2, d. 178, l. 1 factory committee collection, n.d. 1924.

46. Goldman, *Women, the State and Revolution*, 214-246.

47. *Martenovka*, 28 December 1925.

48. TsAODM, f. 429, op. 1, d. 34, l. 86. Bolt shop party meeting, 19 August 1925.

49. *Martenovka*, 1 May 1925.

50. TsAODM, f. 429, op. 1, d. 34, l. 78. Bolt shop party meeting, 24 June 1925.

51. TsMAM, f. 176, op. 2, d. 255, l. 22. Factory Protection of Labor report, October 1924.

52. *Martenovka*, 7 November 1925.

53. TsMAM, f. 176, op. 2, d. 432, ll. 31-39. Women's delegate meetings 1925.

54. *Martenovka*, 7 November 1925.

55. Wood, *The Baba and the Comrade*, 211.

56. TsAODM, f. 429, op. 1, d. 24, l. 54. Bolt shop party meeting, 8 October 1925.

57. *Martenovka*, 25 February 1926.

58. TsAODM, f. 429, op. 1, d. 41, l. 28. General party meeting, 21 April 1926.

59. TsMAM, f. 176, op. 2, d. 545, ll. 38-39. Factory conference, 26 November 1926.

60. TsMAM, f. 176, op. 2, d. 545, l. 29. Factory conference, 1 October 1926.

61. TsMAM, f. 176, op. 2, d. 171, ll. 21-22. Factory committee report for January to June 1923.

62. TsMAM, f. 176, op. 2, d. 568, ll. 30-95. Factory committee reports 1926 and 1927.

63. *Martenovka*, 14 January 1926.

64. TsMAM, f. 176, op. 2, d. 403, ll. 1-13. Factory conference, 22 October 1927.

65. *Martenovka*, 30 March 1926.

66. *Martenovka*, 7 March 1928.

67. TsMAM, f. 176, op. 2, d. 784, l. 28. Women's delegate meeting minutes, 8 June 1928.

68. TsMAM, f. 176, op. 2, d. 545, l. 21. Factory general conference, 11 June 1926.

69. TsAODM, f. 429, op. 1, d. 80, ll. 16-17. Factory general conference, 12 May 1927; closed party meeting, 18 May 1927.

70. *Martenovka*, 7 November 1926.

71. TsAODM, f. 429, op. 1, d. 56, l. 36. Closed party general meeting, 19 October 1927.

72. TsAODM, f. 429, op. 1, d. 57, l. 11. Party bureau meeting, 1 February 1927.

73. TsAODM, f. 429, op. 1, d. 62, l. 36. Party report, September 1927.

74. *Martenovka*, 1 May 1927, 7 March 1928, 30 June 1928.

75. TsAODM, f. 429, op. 1, d. 61, ll. 17-21. Party faction of factory committee plan, June 1927.

76. TsAODM, f. 429, op. 1, d. 75, ll. 33, 42. Party bureau meetings, 24 April, 8 May 1928.

77. TsAODM, f. 429, op. 1, d. 74, l. 106. Party bureau meeting, 23 March 1928.

78. TsAODM, f. 429, op. 1, d. 73, l. 61. Maintenance shop meeting, 14 February 1927.

79. TsAODM, f. 429, op. 1, d. 70, l. 29. Repair shop party bureau meeting, 20 February 1927.

80. TsMAM, f. 176, op. 2, d. 795, ll. 22, 29-31. Rolled metal shop meeting, 2 October 1928.

81. TsAODM, f. 429, op. 1, d. 27, l. 45. Party bureau meeting, 13 May 1925.

82. RGASPI f. 17, op. 85, d. 151, l. 137. MK information summary December 1927.

83. Goldman, *Women, The State and Revolution*, 118-122.

84. *Martenovka*, 18 February 1927.

85. TsMAM, f. 176, op. 2, d. 779, ll. 30-33. Factory general meeting, 9 February 1928.

86. TsMAM, f. 176, op. 2, d. 810, ll. 51-52. Women's meeting, 13 May 1928.

87. TsMAM, f. 176, op. 2, d. 810, l. 22. Women's meeting, 7 October 1928.

88. TsMAM, f. 176, op. 2, d. 784, l. 27. Women's delegate meeting, 18 May 1928.

89. *Martenovka*, 7 January 1928.

90. TsMAM, f. 176, op. 2, d. 810, ll. 51-52. Women's meeting, 13 May 1928.

91. TsAODM, f. 429, op. 1, d. 77, l. 22. Party general meeting, 4 April 1928.

92. TsMAM, f. 176, op. 2, d. 784, l. 20. Women's delegate meeting, 10 February 1928.

93. TsAODM, f. 429, op. 1, d. 56, ll. 12-13. Party general meeting, 23 May 1927.

94. TsAODM, f. 429, op. 1, d. 77, l. 50. Party general meeting, 15 August 1928.

95. *Martenovka*, 30 June 1928.

96. *Martenovka*, 30 June 1928.

97. *Martenovka*, 7 March 1928.

98. TsMAM, f. 176, op. 2, d. 784, l. 28. Women's delegate meeting, 8 June 1928.

99. *Martenovka*, 5 July 1928.

100. TsMAM, f. 176, op. 2, d. 790, l. 6. Rolled metal shop union meeting, 6 March 1928.

101. TsMAM, f. 176, op. 2, d. 784, l. 15. Women's meeting, 8 March 1928.

102. *Martenovka*, 24 March 1928.

103. Richard Stites, *The Women's Liberation Movement in Russia: Feminism, Nihilism, and Bolshevism* (Princeton, 1978), 344.

104. John Curtiss, *The Russian Church and the Soviet State, 1917-1950* (Boston, 1953), 222, shows that in 1928 the Moscow Registry Office recorded that 57.8 percent of births had religious ceremonies.

105. Dimitry Pospielovsky, *A History of Marxist-Leninist Atheism and Soviet Antireligious Policies*, 3 vols. (London, 1987).

106. Glennys Young, *Power and the Sacred in Revolutionary Russia: Religious Activists in the Village* (University Park, PA, 1997); Daniel Peris, *Storming the Heavens: The Soviet League of the Militant Godless* (Ithaca, NY, 1998); William B. Husband, *"Godless Communists": Atheism and Society in Soviet Russia, 1917-1932* (De Kalb, Illinois, 2000).

107. Husband, *Godless Communists*, 69-71.

108. GARF, f. 7952, op. 3, d. 275, ll. 12, 53., d. 271, l. 301. P.V. Lazrenov, S.S. Leshkovtsev, S.S. Gerasimov memoirs.

109. TsIAM f. 498, op. 1, d. 241, l. 68. List of factory holidays for 1911.

110. GARF, f. 7952, op. 3, d. 275, l. 12. P.V. Lavrent'ev memoir.

111. GARF, f. 7952, op. 3, d. 215, l. 53. General factory meeting, 9 February 1918 (old calendar).

112. GARF, f. 7952, op. 3, d. 275, l. 33. S.S. Leshkovtsev memoir.

113. TsMAM, f. 176, op. 2, d. 6, ll. 16-17, GARF, f. 7952, op. 3, d. 215. General and factory committee meetings, 17, 19 December 1917(old calendar).

114. GARF, f. 7952, op. 3, d. 215, ll. 54, 83 factory committee meetings, 22 February (7 March), 5 (18) April, 1918.

115. GARF, f. 7952, op. 3, d. 213, l. 60. Factory general meeting, 8 April 1919.

116. TsMAM, f. 176, op. 2, d. 102, l. 147. Factory announcement, 30 March 1921.

117. TsMAM, f. 176, op. 2, d. 122, l. 38. Rolled metal shop meeting, 18 October 1922.

118. Curtiss, *The Russian Church*, 106-128.

119. TsGAMO, f. 19, op. 1, d. 21, l. 295. Report to Moscow Soviet, 1 April 1922.

120. GARF, f. 7952, op. 3, d. 274, ll. 45-47. G.N. Kudrov memoir. The confiscations were in 1922.

121. TsGAMO f. 19, op. 62, d. 62, l. 310. Report to Moscow Soviet 14 December 1923.

122. TsMAM, f. 176, d. 2, l. 168, ll. 13-27. Shop meetings, 12-14 December 1923.

123. TsMAM, f. 176, op. 2, d. 248, ll. 20, 27, 78. Shop meetings, April, December 1924.

124. TsAODM, f. 429, op. 1, d. 17, ll. 3-4. General party meeting, 6 February 1924.

125. Trotsky, *Problems of Everyday Life*, 33.

126. TsAODM, f. 429, op. 1, d. 16, l. 14. Party report, December 1924.

127. TsAODM, f. 429, op. 1, d. 49, l. 68. Steel foundry party bureau meeting, 17 May 1926.

128. TsAODM, f. 429, op. 1, d. 48, l. 5. Architectural shop party meeting, 30 November 1926.

129. TsAODM, f. 429, op. 1, d. 27, l. 62. Party bureau meeting, 25 July 1925.

130. TsAODM, f. 429, op. 1, d. 51, l. 64. Rolled metal shop meeting, 14 January 1926.

131. TsAODM, f. 429, op. 1, d. 40, l. 37. Factory party bureau meeting, 16 February 1926.

132. TsAODM, f. 429, op. 1, d. 48, l. 49. Bolt shop party meeting, 9 October 1926.

133. TsAODM, f. 429, op. 1, d. 34, l. 49. Bolt shop party meeting, 20 September 1925.

134. *Martenovka*, 1 May 1925.
135. TsAODM, f. 429, op. 1, d. 38, l. 26. Repair shop party bureau meeting, 28 January 1925.
136. Martenovka, 5 September 1925.
137. TsAODM, f. 429, op. 1, d. 49, l. 49. Nail shop party bureau meeting, 8 March 1926.
138. TsAODM, f. 429, op. 1, d. 48, l. 35. Bolt shop party meeting, 30 March 1926.
139. *Martenovka*, 26 March 1927.
140. TsAODM, f. 429, op. 1, d. 57, l. 79. General party meeting, 27 June 1927.
141. Martenovka, 7 January 1928.
142. Martenovka, 5 October 1928.
143. *Martenovka*, 15 May 1928.
144. *Martenovka*, 19 December 1925.
145. *Martenovka*, 14 April 1927.
146. TsAODM, f. 429, op. 1, d. 68, l. 2. Sheet metal shop party meeting, 3 March 1927.
147. Husband, *Godless Communists*, 72, 115. Births without religious ceremony dropped 3.5 percent, funerals almost 8 percent.
148. TsAODM, f. 429, op. 1, d. 77, l. 33. General party meeting, 9 May 1928.
149. RGASPI f. 17, op. 85, d. 151, ll. 77-80. MK information summary, winter 1927.
150. TsMAM, f. 176, op. 2, d. 792, l. 33. Nail shop union meeting 11 December 1928. "Jewish" holidays probably meant "revolutionary" holidays.
151. TsMAM, f. 176, op. 2, d. 784, l. 9. Maintenance shop union meeting, 7 December 1928.
152. TsMAM, f. 176, op. 2, d. 795, l. 28. Cable shop union meeting, 13 December 1928.
153. TsMAM, f. 176, op. 2, d. 578, l. 11. Factory announcement, 17 December 1928.
154. TsAODM, f. 429, op. 1, d. 84, l. 48. Bolt shop party meeting, n.d. January 1929.
155. *Rabochaia gazeta*, 14 December 1928.
156. TsAODM, f. 80, op. 1, d. 332, l. 43. District report on cultural work, early 1929.
157. TsIAM f. 498, op. 1, d. 241, l. 14. Factory announcement, 12 August 1911.
158. GARF, f. 7952, op. 3, d. 275, l. 12. P.V. Lavrent'ev memoir.
159. GARF, f. 7952, op. 3, d. 273, l. 38. F.I. Karpukhin memoir.
160. GARF, f. 7952, op. 3, d. 275, l. 235. E.I. Borovina memoir.
161. TsMAM, f. 176, op. 2, l. 6, l. 40. Factory committee meeting; 29 January 1918 (old calendar).
162. Stephen White, *Russia Goes Dry, Alcohol, State and Society* (Cambridge, 1996), 17-22.
163. *Rabochaia Moskva*, 12 December 1924.
164. TsAODM, f. 429, op. 1, d. 27, l. 96. Party bureau meeting, 13 October 1925.
165. TsAODM, f. 429, op. 1, d. 17, l. 30. General party meeting, 21 August 1924.
166. TsAODM, f. 429, op. 1, d. 27, l. 80. General party meeting, 15 September 1925.
167. TsAODM, f. 429, op. 1, d. 49, l. 112. Steel foundry shop party meeting, 4 October 1926.
168. TsAODM, f. 429, op. 1, d. 34, l. 93, d. 40, l. 37. Bolt shop party meeting, 16 September 1925; Party bureau meeting, 16 February 1926.
169. TsAODM, f. 429, op. 1, d. 51, l. 35. Rolled metal shop party bureau, 7 September 1926.
170. TsAODM, f. 429, op. 1, d. 67, ll. 36-39. Nail shop party meeting, 4 February, 2 December 1927.
171. TsAODM, f. 429, op. 1, d. 56, l. 39. General party meeting, 19 October 1927.
172. TsAODM, f. 429, op. 1, d. 80, l. 37. General party meeting, 8 September 1927.
173. TsAODM, f. 429, op. 1, d. 48, l. 94. Bolt shop report on women's work, June 1926.
174. TsAODM, f. 429, op. 1, d. 75, l. 42. Party bureau meeting, 8 May 1928.
175. TsAODM, f. 429, op. 1, d. 48, l. 87. Bolt shop cell meeting 18 December 1926.
176. *Martenovka*, 5 September; 19 December 1925; 25 February 1926.
177. TsAODM, f. 429, op. 1, d. 34, ll. 44, 54, 64. Architectural shop party meetings, 14 September; 8, 21 October 1925.
178. TsAODM, f. 429, op. 1, d. 6, l. 3. Party bureau meeting, 30 March 1922.
179. TsAODM, f. 429, op. 1, d. 7, l. 22. Party general meeting, 31 May 1922.
180. *Martenovka*, 5 September 1925.
181. *Nasha gazeta*, 7 November 1923.
182. TsMAM, f. 176, op. 2, d. 249, l. 5. Combined party and delegate meeting, 7 February 1924.

183. *Rabochaia Moskva*, 15 January 1925.

184. *Martenovka*, 21 November 1925.

185. *Martenovka*, 14 December 1926.

186. TsKhDMO f. 1, op. 5, d. 13, l. 13. Komsomol TsK discussion on hooliganism, n.d. 1926.

187. TsKhDMO f. 1, op. 23, d. 515, ll. 21-23. Komsomol TsK discussion, n.d. 1926.

188. TsAODM, f. 429, op. 1, d. 40, l. 108. Party bureau meeting, 14 September 1926.

189. RGASPI f. 17, op. 85, d. 66, ll. 80-82. MK information summary, spring 1926.

190. TsAODM, f. 429, op. 1, d. 57, l. 36. Party bureau meeting, 15 March 1927.

191. *Martenovka*, 15 September 1926.

192. TsMAM, f. 176, op. 2, d. 814, l. 29. Cultural Commission meeting, 11 March 1928.

193. TsMAM, f. 176, op. 2, d. 160, ll. 83, 1-170. Factory announcements, 1923.

194. TsMAM, f. 176, op. 2, d. 270, l. 301. Factory announcement, 2 December 1925.

195. TsMAM, f. 176, op. 2, d. 578, l. 181. Factory announcement, 10 February 1928.

196. TsGAMO f. 66, op. 22, d. 87, l. 45. Report to Moscow Soviet on the mood of workers and peasants, April 1924.

197. TsAODM, f. 429, op. 1, d. 62, l. 15. Party report, September 1927.

198. TsAODM, f. 429, op. 1, d. 38, l. 6. Repair shop party meeting, 17 August 1925.

199. TsAODM, f. 429, op. 1, d. 41, l. 30. Party general meeting, 12 May 1926.

200. *Martenovka*, 28 December 1925.

201. TsAODM, f. 429, op. 1, d. 27, l. 47. Party bureau meeting, 26 May 1925.

202. *Martenovka*, 29 January 1926.

203. *Martenovka*, 5 September 1925.

204. TsAODM, f. 429, op. 1, d. 56, l. 34. Party bureau report, October 1927.

205. *Martenovka*, 5 September 1925.

206. TsMAM, f. 176, op. 2, d. 779, ll. 30-33. Factory general meeting, 9 February 1928.

207. Brovkin, *Russia After Lenin*, 122.

208. The Platform of the Opposition, September 1927, in Leon Trotsky, *The Challenge of the Left Opposition (1926-1927)* (New York, 1980), 313, 339.

209. TsAODM, f. 429, op. 1, d. 67, ll. 55, 65. Nail shop bureau meetings, October 1927.

210. TsAODM, f. 429, op. 1, d. 73, ll. 21-22. Form-casting shop party meetings, 8, 10 October 1927.

211. Andrea Graziosi, "Stalin's Anti-worker 'Workerism,'" *International Review of Social History* 40 (1995).

212. *Martenovka*, 1 October 1926.

213. *Martenovka*, 21 September 1928.

214. *Martenovka*, 7 February 1928.

215. TsMAM, f. 176, op. 2, d. 403; d. 545; d. 692; d. 821. Factory general meetings, 1925, 1926, Factory committee report, February 1929.

216. Hoffman, *Peasant Metropolis*, 163.

217. TsMAM, f. 176, op. 2, d. 814, l.10. Factory committee report on club work, September 1928. *Martenovka*, 31 December 1926.

218. TsAODM, f. 429, op. 1, d. 77, l. 33. Party general meeting, 9 May 1928.

219. TsMAM, f. 176, op. 2, d. 810, l. 78. Nonparty aktiv meeting, 29 September 1928.

220. TsAODM, f. 429, op. 1, d. 69, l. 43. Repair shop party meeting 6 September 1927.

221. *Martenovka*, 30 June 1928.

222. TsMAM, f. 176, op. 2, d. 576, l. 13. Factory announcement 7 July 1928.

223. TsMAM, f. 176, op. 2, d. 824, l. 12. Women's meeting, n.d. November 1928.

5

CATALYSTS FOR DISSENT

Opposition Groups and Tendencies

"The bootlickers and informers in the party have taken over."
—Hammer and Sickle Opposition leaflet, May 1927

The Hammer and Sickle Factory was a hotbed of dissident activity. From 1917 until the end of NEP, virtually every opposition group and tendency attempted to win workers' support in the factory. The strength of this opposition current was rooted in the events of 1917—the unprecedented freedom and flowering of political pluralism during the revolution. As the largest metalworking factory in the Soviet capital, it was also an obvious ideological battleground for those who championed the cause of the working class. Indeed, for many workers, the revolution *was* dissent—they not only believed that they had the right to raise grievances but, as we shall see, expected Soviet representatives and institutions to respond favorably to their demands.

Frequently dissident attempts to gain support rested on articulating tangible, and sometimes quite parochial, economic demands, rather than on advancing more general ideological policies.[1] Localism extended down to the factory and even shop level, and often depended upon the skill and persistence of a single activist. In this sense, organized opposition activity was very similar to the catalytic role of revolutionaries during the Tsarist period. In the most favorable circumstances, these individuals played a far more significant role than their small numbers might suggest.

The study of such opposition groups has long fascinated scholars, and for good reason. How authorities treated organized opposition, and whether or not workers responded to dissident calls for change, says much about early Soviet society and the legitimacy of the Bolsheviks' claim to speak for a proletarian state. Source problems have, until recently, limited the investigation of dissident groups, however. Scholars of the SRs and Mensheviks have had to rely on problematic émigré sources or official Soviet press accounts, while studies on opposition within the Bolshevik Party have focused on individual leaders. Even the classic works by Carr, Cohen, Daniels, and Deutscher deal only superficially with discussion and activity at the grassroots level. The history of dissent at the local level remains relatively unexplored.[2]

Here we trace various opposition groupings in the Hammer and Sickle Factory during the eleven years after the October Revolution by examining three interrelated themes. First, to what extent were opposition groups able to connect with workers' persistent grievances and what was the depth of this support? Second, what was the state response to dissidence at the local level? Third, given that evolving Stalinism strived to be a participatory political system, how did the long-term trajectory of stifling opposition voices affect the relationship between the Communist Party and that section of Soviet society that it claimed to represent—the working class?

Miscellaneous Groups and Tendencies

A variety of dissident organizations and tendencies vied for the support of Hammer and Sickle employees. During the ultra-democratic period between the February Revolution and the Left SRs' attempted coup d'état in July of 1918, non-Bolshevik organizations disseminated their ideas and even were encouraged to do so. Thus, for example, when an anarchist asked a May general meeting to aid the newspaper *Anarkhiia*, workers voted to contribute one thousand rubles to the newspaper.[3]

In early 1918, Bukharin's "revolutionary war" strategy received wide support in the factory. With German troops occupying most of the Ukraine, the Bolsheviks split into Bukharin supporters, adherents to Lenin's peace proposal, and advocates of Trotsky's neither-war-nor-peace position. The fledgling Soviet government surrendered enormous territory to the Germans with the Brest-Litovsk treaty of March 1918. At the Fourth Congress of Soviets, the Left SRs voted against ratifying the treaty and then withdrew from Sovnarknom, ending the socialist coalition government.[4] Rather than drawing a wedge between Bolsheviks and Left SRs, however, the "separate peace" with Germany raised the ire of factory party members. The district and many other areas of Moscow were left-communist strongholds against any compromise with Germany. *Pravda* described the mood as "resolute and cheerful."[5] The Bolshevik Tumanov put forward the left-communist resolution in the factory committee: "We, the Moscow proletariat, will not accept a separate peace but an open partisan war" and even ridiculed the treaty by calling for "a separate war." The motion carried by a vote of thirteen to eleven, suggesting differences among Bolsheviks rather than a split between the LSRs and Bolsheviks. The next general meeting passed a unanimous resolution to immediately organize partisan Red Army detachments for the front, demanded the shutdown of all bourgeois newspapers, and called for an immediate search of counterrevolutionary suspects.[6]

The Workers' Opposition captured the factory party organization in early 1921.[7] The syndicalist tendency posited that producers should manage the Soviet economy through the trade unions, and openly stated their program in

Pravda. They also challenged the growing bureaucratic regime within the Bolsheviks and criticized party leaders for neglecting the economic interests of workers.[8] This appeal reflected the sentiments of party and nonparty workers that appeared repeatedly in dissident groupings in the factory: bread-and-butter agitation to improve workers' living standards and antibureaucratic rule. Unfortunately, party records provide no insight into the nature of the political discussions around the Workers' Opposition, but the absence of post-Congress resolutions denouncing the tendency contrasts markedly with the treatment of later opposition groups in the factory.[9]

The underground and extremely small Workers' Group and Workers' Truth both appear to have issued propaganda in the factory. The head of GPU, Feliks Dzerzhinskii, complained to the Politburo that many party members sympathized with the group and refused to inform on their activities.[10] A May 1923 Central Committee circular referred to agitation "in a series of large enterprises in Moscow," and during the August strike wave the two hundred-member Workers' Group vied for political leadership of the movement. Hammer and Sickle strike reports do not explicitly name the Workers' Group,[11] but given that the group was a direct offshoot of the previous Workers' Opposition and operated clandestinely, the organization likely conducted agitation in the largest metal factory in Moscow. Workers' Truth also defended the economic interests of workers and criticized the bureaucratic rule of the party apparatus from a more extreme position, arguing that by 1922 the revolution had been defeated and that a "technical intelligentsia" had usurped power.[12] In November 1922 the GPU reported that the factory committee had received copies of their journal.[13] The party secretary at the time named two Workers' Truth supporters but asserted, "The counterrevolutionary group could not establish ties with the working masses and was quickly arrested by the GPU."[14]

Right SR and Menshevik presence in the factory was weak or nonexistent. The Mensheviks spoke at Astakhov's memorial demonstration in October 1917, but the only subsequent contemporary evidence shows that the factory cell unanimously endorsed the candidacy of an ex-Menshevik in 1920.[15] Factory general meeting resolutions in the months after the October Revolution show complete unanimity against Right SRs and Mensheviks. One such motion denounced a 3 December "demonstration of white guards with the parties of the Right Socialist Revolutionaries and Mensheviks." When the Constituent Assembly prepared to convene a month later, shop delegates resolved "to rebuff to all counterrevolutionary infringements on our revolution and conquests," proclaiming support for the Soviets and "Long live the unity between Bolsheviks and Left Socialist Revolutionaries!"[16]

The Left Socialist Revolutionaries

The Left SRs supported Soviet power and collaborated with the Bolsheviks in the months after the October Revolution. A December 1917 general meeting voted to contribute one thousand rubles to the Left SR newspaper.

Apparently the Bolsheviks did not hold grudges against SRs who had wavered during the October Revolution. A late November factory committee meeting resolved in favor of "complete trust" for the former SR president of the factory committee, Lebedev, with only two abstentions.[17] The first election to the Moscow Soviet after the October Revolution returned three Bolsheviks and two SRs.[18] Significantly, Lebedev and other SR leaders spoke regularly on all issues, including reports on the political situation.[19]

This left unity was in part a response to the anti-Soviet activity from the right. The Right SRs claimed a mandate of popular support because of the elections to the Constituent Assembly, in which the disintegrating SRs received about 40 percent of the vote and the Bolsheviks about 25 percent. Lists of more radical SR candidates were presented but largely turned down, and the historian of the election, Oliver Radkey, concludes that the vote was indicative of the "broadness, depth, and power of the power of the revolution against the weakness of its foes."[20] In the few voting districts that distinguished between the Left and Right SRs, the Left SRs won overwhelmingly.[21] Post Cold-War scholarship now concedes that had the electoral process distinguished between the Right and Left SR policies, the Left SRs and Bolsheviks together would have likely won the popular election.[22] The Constituent Assembly that convened on 18 January 1918 became a rallying point for the foes of the revolution and a barometer of their weakness. The Bolsheviks ordered a single guard to shut down the meeting, and Red Guards forcibly dispersed a small pro-Constituent Assembly demonstration. Those parties that purported a popular mandate failed to pose a serious challenge to Soviet power in early 1918 because, at that time, they were unable to mobilize support. In Petrograd, as the Right SR Sokolov acknowledged, "We could not drive them against the Bolshevik movement."[23]

In general factory meetings, the Left SRs' positions were indistinguishable from the Bolsheviks' in taking a hard-line stance against perceived threats to the revolution. A February 1918 general meeting resolved to "disarm the bourgeoisie and their hangers-on" and to alleviate the food crises by "a search of all warehouses." The resolution further noted that "If there is not peace, then mobilize the entire bourgeoisie, monarchists, and priests who oppress working people and who are now helping Wilhelm crush the revolution. All of these bourgeois hangers-on will be sent into the first row of the trenches."[24]

Left SRs on the factory committee collaborated with the Bolsheviks on virtually every issue that affected workers' lives: food, housing, wages, the securing of raw materials and funding to operate the factory, hiring and firing employees, and guarding the factory.[25] Significantly, the proposed peace with Germany appears to have drawn the Bolsheviks and Left SRs closer together rather than creating a rift between the two parties, as it did on the national level. The factory SRs divided between pragmatists, who worked with the Bolsheviks to try to resolve various problems, and those SRs who favored their role as critics and voice for extreme worker radicalism. Although the Left SR Internationalist leaflet below overstates the layoff (over two thousand production employees worked in the factory in the summer),[26] a small staff reduction in the spring contributed to the factory Left SR split:

Party of LSR Internationalist
Only in Struggle Can You Win your Rights

The 28 March 1918 general Rogozhsko-Simonovskii meeting of the party of LSR Internationalists listened to the report by a party member about the speech in the general meeting of workers in the former Guzhon Factory by a member of the administration, Krasnov. From the tribune of the general meeting he defended the actions of the administration and the communist cell in regards to the workers. Krasnov argued that it is not necessary for the factory to retain more than 600 people, while the rest, 1,700 in number, because of lack of work at the factory, must go to the Labor Exchange and follow all its rules. If they refuse to go to the Labor Exchange at the end of four days, the workers would sever all ties with the factory, irrespective of their many years of work at the factory. All draft eligible workers would be immediately processed.... The party of the LSR Internationalists has always struggled and will continue to struggle for the complete freedom of labor, for the socialization of land, for socialized factories and for genuine Soviet power, freely elected by working people.... The general meeting expels Krasnov from the party and absolves itself of any responsibility for his actions. We demand immediate destruction of labor serfdom, of binding workers to work. Down with coercion! Down with turncoats! Long live freedom of labor!

28 March 1918[27]

Worker grievances escalated during the continued economic collapse. Yet even as late as 9 May 1918, cooperation between the Left SRs and Bolsheviks evidently continued. A general factory meeting elected four Bolsheviks and two LSRs to the soviets "without debate."[28] However, workers' festering grievances, combined with the intransigence of the national Left SR leadership contributed to a rapid breakdown of trust between the LSRs and the Bolsheviks. A wild factory meeting (probably in June) included LSR leaders Spiridonova and Steinberg, and Bukharin for the Bolsheviks. "The SRs criticized the Bolsheviks in every possible way" and when Bukharin spoke, "the SRs made noise, whistled, howled like wolves, and did not let him finish his speech," wrote one Bolshevik. The Bolsheviks shut down the meeting and "the next time Lebedev came to us for permission to organize a meeting, we refused."[29]

This account says much about the LSRs' ability to fan the flames of economic discontent, and may have contributed to the group's overinflated view of their influence. Left SR agitation was similar to the prerevolutionary "catalytic" role of revolutionaries rather than to the more general 1917 Bolshevik support for Soviet power. Spiridonova, an advocate of the failed Left SR coup d'état, may have misread workers' economic grievances as political support for her party. On 5 July, a day before the Left SR uprising, the factory committee rejected an LSR proposal to hold another meeting in the factory, but stated that, "if they desire, they may hold a meeting outside the factory."[30] The factory LSRs twice tried to organize meetings before the revolt but were dispersed by the Red Guards, according to one worker account.[31]

The Left SR's attempted coup d'état started on 6 July 1918 when two members, following instructions issued by their central committee, assassinated the German ambassador.[32] The next day Lenin sent a telegram that "all district soviet and workers' organizations are instructed to immediately send out as many armed detachments as possible, at least partially composed of workers, in order to catch the dispersing mutineers." He ordered units to seize the railway stations and not to release suspects until triple confirmation that they had not participated in the revolt. The Left SR fraction of the Moscow Soviet issued a statement against the rebellion but also claimed "the declarations of the central authorities about plotting and rebelling against Soviet power do not correspond to reality." They acknowledged, "Armed struggle against the soviets is not permissible" and urged their members to fight for positions in the soviets.[33]

Only a minority of Left SRs from the factory participated in the revolt. A factory Bolshevik wrote that he had worked with Left SRs in the Moscow Soviet but that the uprising had shattered the trust between the two parties. He claimed that Hammer and Sickle LSRs "actively participated in the uprising but in the factory their preparatory work was not noticed."[34] Another memoir noted only one LSR participant in the rebellion and, that "Red Guards from the factory disarmed the SRs in their club."[35] A Red Guard deployed to prevent any rebellious units from crossing the bridge over the Iauza River claimed to have stopped a group of Left SRs who protested that they were "not against the revolution, we are only against Lenin and Trotsky and their dictatorial ways."[36] With the Czech legions in open conflict with Soviet forces and allied troops in Murmansk and Vladivostok, the Bolsheviks regarded the uprising as an open declaration of war.[37] State repression against factory LSRs peaked after a member murdered Bolshevik Central Committee member Uritskii and wounded Lenin on 30 August 1918. The factory Bolshevik chairman wrote that the arrests included "many" factory committee LSRs.[38] One LSR member later wrote that after the Cheka released him it burned "all SR literature."[39]

The revolt only temporarily ended Left SR activity. Even though they had attempted a military coup and repeatedly engaged in terrorism, Soviet authorities treated the organization leniently. In November 1918, the Sixth Congress of Soviets granted amnesty to those previously arrested and LSRs who did not advocate overthrowing the Soviet regime operated semi-legally throughout the Civil War.[40] Seven months after their aborted coup d'état only an estimated two hundred LSRs were in prison, of whom thirty-four were released in June 1920.[41]

Throughout the Civil War, the Left SRs continued to fan the flames of labor discontent, although workers' political sentiments became markedly less political. In May 1919 the LSRs captured the factory committee.[42] Yet this electoral victory was hardly a ringing endorsement for their policy. The six candidates received only ten to seventy-six votes each because workers simply did not care enough to vote, and consequently the metalworkers' union nullified the election because those elected had not received a majority. The union reported that the meeting was marked by drunkenness and included a candidate who was a former member of the extreme right Union of Russian People. The election reveals workers' apolitical attitudes during the Civil War as personal survival supplanted revolutionary agendas. Speakers at the next general meeting urged workers to take the election more seriously, one of whom argued, "I agree with the suggestion made by Comrade Pavlov in his report, that the election be conducted consciously and not with hooligan-like notes as in the previous elections."[43]

The Left SR electoral success derived in part from the persistence of democracy in the factory elections. The spring 1919 factory committee election was through a secret ballot. On 30 March 1921, after the factory committee distributed election bulletins, 555 of 1,200 workers participated in the election that again was conducted by secret ballot—despite Bolshevik objections. Several SRs were elected, with Kudrov receiving 156 votes, second only to the 338 votes received by a Bolshevik who had headed a food requisitioning detachment.[44]

In May 1921, the Cheka claimed that the SR Maximalists' (a 1907 left split from the SRs) influence was "quite widespread" with five thousand members, thirty thousand sympathizers, two journals, and several newspapers. In Moscow, the Cheka reported that the LSRs, anarchists, and Mensheviks were active in several work stoppages. Although these groups agitated over economic grievances during the tumultuous first few months of 1921, "open significant counterrevolutionary agitation was not observed."[45] A recent thorough study of the early 1921 economic strike wave in Moscow has shown that although LSRs, Mensheviks, and anarchists played a role, their influence and the political aspect of the movement have been exaggerated by both Western and Soviet historians.[46] Left SR influence in the Hammer and Sickle Factory was exceptional rather than the norm in Moscow. Worker memoirs mention that the LSRs continued to hold "great sway" because "the party and trade-union *aktiv* were bled dry by the mobilization." Another worker recalled their role in the May 1921 strike, recounting that they had advocated "petty-bourgeois leveling" of wages.[47] In the spring of 1921, the factory was one of several metal factories in which a Bolshevik-dominated factory committee was replaced by SR sympathizers and the factory elected two SRs to the soviets.[48]

Left SR activity continued in 1922. On 4 January 1922 1,400 workers (of 2,500) participated in a mass soviet election meeting that started at 7:50 p.m. and ended just before midnight. Despite the recorded assertion that workers "unanimously" elected ten Bolsheviks to the city and district soviets, the length of the meeting, the high attendance, and the continued strength of the factory LSRs suggest that this was a boisterous gathering.[49]

By 1922, however, Soviet authorities had grown increasingly intolerant of the Left SRs. The trial of the SRs in the spring of 1922 was accompanied by the regime's campaign to discredit them. In February 1922, the GPU arrested forty-seven prominent SRs and announced that they faced charges of conspiring against Soviet power.[50] The party cell resolution on the campaign called for gathering support signatures from workers. On 23 May 1922, a general factory meeting resolved that "workers of the Guzhon factory consider that the party of the SRs, having killed our leaders, brought onto themselves shame and that the upcoming trial should punish them severely just as they deserve" and called for five elected shop delegates to be present in the court throughout the trial.[51]

The factory party bureau was concerned enough about LSR strength that they invited Trotsky to address a general meeting.[52] Yet when Trotsky spoke to the mass meeting of thirteen hundred on 25 May 1922, many workers expressed concern over the fate of the Left SRs. A report to the Moscow Soviet noted no "counterrevolution" agitation, but many questions about "why are those arrested being held so long?"[53] Thus, workers expected the practice of lenient treatment to prevail and LSRs continued to speak openly in factory meetings. On 19 June, the factory committee passed a resolution to mobilize for the demonstration the next day when the trial opened. Left SR committee member Kudrov argued against the motion because "the majority of the committee is nonparty but the demonstration is political. Therefore this should be the business of the factory cell."[54] The same day, a factory-wide meeting passed a resolution to mobilize for the demonstration with normal wage-rates paid to participants.[55]

Even after the trial, the LSRs continued to challenge the Bolsheviks in tainted soviet elections and still voiced their grievances in raucous factory meetings. Again in 1922, the LSR Kudrov was elected to the factory committee.[56] The Bolshevik leader Kalinin addressed a packed general meeting on 4 December 1922, which focused on the politics of the Left SRs. The meeting minutes show that one LSR member accused the Bolsheviks of not allowing them freedom of the press or the right to meet. Kalinin stated that they would not extend such rights as long as "the bourgeoisie still exists" and had not yet "submitted to proletarian rule." Another Left SR speaker claimed that the group was prepared to build a new International "in the interests of the working class." He also charged the party with having done nothing to honor the memory of the factory employee Illarion Astakhov, who was the first Moscow worker to die during the February 1917 revolution. A Bolshevik responded that the new club would be named after Astakhov. The minutes record the election of Bolshevik slates but do not record the tally.[57]

According to the Bolshevik cell secretary, Frankel, the packed general meeting started inauspiciously for the Bolsheviks because Kalinin arrived late it was "impossible to delay the meeting." The first speaker was the Left SR Steinberg. "Just when he began to speak, Comrade Kalinin arrived in an automobile. Steinberg stopped his speech and demagogically said, 'Here are your communist leaders, arriving in automobiles, late!'"[58]

Steinberg also mentioned the difficult housing situation, the shortage of provisions and work clothes, and that "workers live badly and peasants are dying of hunger. All of this," he charged, "is the fault of the Bolsheviks." Frankel admitted that Steinberg received applause but claimed that Kalinin carried the meeting, affirming that "Yes, we are the government, we drive in cars—it would be a bad government that did not do that." Then Kalinin recalled the history of the SRs during 1917, including their promises of land and peace, which only the Bolsheviks had delivered. When Steinberg tried to respond, he was whistled down and the meeting, according to Frankel, ended in a success for the Bolsheviks.[59] Other, more believable, worker accounts describe the meeting with Kalinin as "very stormy," with workers repeatedly asking questions about "immediate and concrete help."[60] Official figures claimed a resounding victory of 97.5 percent for the Bolsheviks in Rogozh-sko-Simonovskii district.[61] However, a report noted that nail and repair shops voted to amend the all-Bolshevik lists of five candidates to the city and district Soviets, substituting an SR and Worker's Opposition leader Shliapnikov for the proposed slate to the Moscow Soviet and several SRs for the district Soviet list.[62] The OGPU reported that although the factory elected five communists to the Moscow Soviet, two (of seven) shops elected SR sympathizers to the district soviet.[63] Once again, the agitation role of the LSRs is evident as they gave concrete expression and confidence to workers' bread-and-butter grievances. The Bolsheviks were so rattled that they convened a closed party meeting that addressed specific monetary assistance for the factory's workers and discussed the NEP perspective because some members disagreed with the party's economic strategy.[64]

The Left SRs continued to gain support in the factory in 1923. A 30 August 1923 factory general meeting elected a factory committee consisting of five communists, one nonparty, and one LSR. The tradition of secret ballot remained intact but "after checking the vote, noise was raised with cries of 'they swindled us!'"[65] During the December Soviet elections, both the Mensheviks and SRs distributed leaflets in several cities that called for a boycott of the elections and the OGPU reported that the Hammer and Sickle Factory was one of several enterprises in Moscow where "anti-Soviet agitation" was carried out.[66]

A 1924 party report claimed that LSRs were active in only one shop and their influence was described as insignificant.[67] Three years later, five or six SRs continued to work in the factory but did not organize underground opposition activity. Several SRs attempted to enter the party, "but when the Opposition [Trotskyists] spoke up, they again stepped back." SR speeches were described as having been of "a completely businesslike character with the exception of particular incidents." This included a speech by Kudrov against the economic policy of the overseeing trust—Mashinotrest. However, the SRs rarely spoke in meetings and "most of time they are quiet."[68]

At least three former SRs eventually joined the Communist Party but did so on an individual basis at different times. Their memoirs convey a sense of pride and sympathy toward their former organization, suggesting a less than enthusiastic endorsement of the Stalinist party—the only civic association for career advancement in the factory.[69] In 1930, the Communist Party rejected two other former SRs—one a former Moscow Soviet representative—because they gave ambiguous answers about collectivization and "the liquidation of the kulaks as a class."[70]

For six years after 1917, the Left SRs in the Hammer and Sickle Factory represented a left pole for various and sundry economic grievances. This voice of opposition was unusually strong for Moscow and helped shape the extraordinary spectacle of popular politics that reached its zenith in 1922, when between a thousand and sixteen hundred workers (60 to 75 percent of the workforce) regularly packed factory general meetings.[71] Such opposition could not be ignored, as authorities responded with a combination of economic concessions and political repression.

Yet arrests were only a minor factor in the demise of the Left SRs, many of whom continued to work in the factory and made no effort to organize underground activity, as they had in the much more repressive prerevolutionary period. Despite the Left SRs' attempted military coup d'état in 1918 and repeated terrorist activities, state security forces incarcerated only several hundred Left SRs.[72] The overwhelming majority of Left SRs who remained in the Soviet Union either entered into service for the regime or gave up politics. Thousands joined the Communist Party, such that by 1927 former SRs and Mensheviks constituted one-fourth of the active higher cadres.[73] Lacking a clear political strategy, they lost their authority and purpose as tendencies within the Communist Party usurped their role as the organized dissident voice for workers' grievances.

The 1923 Trotskyist Opposition

The Bolsheviks had cultivated a rich tradition of democracy and the restoration of intra-party democratic norms was central to the 1923 dispute. From its inception in 1903, members continuously debated a wide variety of theoretical and tactical questions.[74] Moshe Lewin describes Bolshevism in 1917 as "an authentic party of the urban masses, a legal democratic party made up of people from diverse social strata and heterogeneous ideological horizons."[75] Democratic norms continued throughout the Civil War and even when the regime was at its weakest. In early 1921, *Pravda* printed the platform of the Workers' Opposition before the Tenth Party Congress.[76] The Congress passed a resolution prohibiting organized groupings in the party; but, as recently released documents on Politburo discussions in 1923 prove, this ban was implemented as a temporary measure when Soviet power was on the verge of collapse. The 1923 discussion centered on when—not if—to restore full democracy within the party.[77]

Before October 1923, the Politburo and Central Committee disagreements that led to the formation of the Trotskyist Opposition remained beyond the purview of ordinary party members, but at the Twelfth Party Congress in April of 1923, Leon Trotsky's stature among factory activists was second only to Lenin's. The greeting from the nonparty Hammer and Sickle worker Luchkov, like many such statements at the Congress, included the slogan "Long Live Comrade Trotsky!" along with the more common "Long Live our dear Vladimir Ilyich Lenin!"[78] A year earlier, Trotsky was one of several Central Committee members who had spoken at raucous factory meetings against the LSRs.

The strike waves in the summer and fall of 1923, in which the Hammer and Sickle Factory was involved, affected many industrial centers in the Soviet Union and contributed to the formation of the Trotskyist Opposition. Feliks Dzerzhinskii, head of the GPU, asked the Politburo to demand that party members inform on others who had supported the strikes. Trotsky replied that the industrial unrest was symptomatic of a failed economic strategy that lacked coordinated planning. He also argued that the increasingly bureaucratic rule within the party had caused an extraordinary degree of discontent in the ranks. Forty-six prominent party members signed a declaration criticizing the official leadership in terms almost identical to Trotsky's, but the Central Committee refused to distribute the statement. Despite the formal ban on factions, widespread suspicion forced the leadership to allow a public discussion. Trotsky's "New Course" appeared in the pages of *Pravda* in early December and a short-lived public debate followed in the weeks before the Thirteenth Party Conference in January 1924.[79]

Officially the Trotskyist Opposition received 40 percent of the vote in Moscow, but recently released archival evidence shows widespread deliberate falsification of votes, suggesting that the oppositionists probably captured the Moscow party organization. At a 14 December 1923 Politburo session, Preobrazhenskii accused *Pravda* of being an "organ for the dissemination of untruth" because the party's main newspaper had omitted Opposition resolutions from "twenty-four or twenty-five workers' cells." At the large Shrader plant, the Opposition resolution was adopted but party leaders took "every measure" to ensure that "within two or three days a contrary resolution" was adopted.[80] At a Rogozhsko-Simonovskii district party conference, where the Hammer and Sickle Factory was located, the Opposition lost by a vote of 121 to 90.[81] Given the party secretaries' heavy-handed methods of controlling meetings, as described by Preobrazhenskii in the Politburo, these results likely underestimate the Trotskyist Opposition support in the district at the factory level.

Working-class support for the Trotskyist Opposition was formidable in the Hammer and Sickle Factory. Accounts hostile to the Trotskyists admit strong support for the Opposition. According to the factory history of the Komsomol, the youth organization's secretary, Gudkin, sided with "Trotskyism" and "youthful syndicalism."[82] Another worker memoir notes that in the steel foundry shop, three talented Trotskyists "even received the support of some of our communists." Two nights of formal discussion in the factory club included such prominent representatives as Kalinin for the Central Committee and Kosior and Preobrazhenskii for the Opposition. The meetings started after work and lasted until midnight the first night and until one in the morning the next night.[83] One member stated that "we have to acknowledge that in our factory the rebuff was not very strong as almost half the cell that was at the meeting, twenty-three of sixty voted for the Trotskyists, which is a lot for a workers' cell."[84] The Opposition may have captured the factory cell, given Preobrazhenskii's comment in the Politburo session on 14 December: "You, comrades, know the truth: wherever I speak at a meeting, a resolution on my report was adopted almost always."[85]

The active life span of the Trotskyist Opposition was only several weeks. The dissident group was active only in Moscow and received a mere three delegates to The Thirteenth Party Conference in January 1924.[86] The Conference characterized the Opposition as "a petty-bourgeois deviation from Leninism" and vowed to "politically annihilate anyone who makes an attempt on the unity of the party ranks."[87] After the Conference, however, Trotsky's status within the factory remained relatively unchanged. His role in the Civil War was acknowledged at a general meeting on the fifth anniversary of the Red Army in February: "Long live our valiant Red Army and its leader, Comrade L.D. Trotsky!"[88] Trotsky's *Problems of Everyday Life* was still sold in the factory, and an August 1924 party plenum resolved to consult "Comrade L.D. Trotsky" on a production question.[89]

In the autumn of 1924, the political controversy began anew with the appearance of *Lessons of October*, in which Trotsky defended himself against allegations that he continued to harbor Menshevik views. Under the provocative heading of "Trotskyism or Leninism?" *Pravda* and other newspapers stressed Trotsky's previous association with the Mensheviks.[90] None of these articles explained why government presses had repeatedly reissued Trotsky's 1906 seminal essay *Results and Prospects*, and Zinoviev later admitted that the party leadership had fabricated the myth of "Trotskyism."[91] The transformation of party norms in just one year was substantial. "In November and December 1923 some appearance of calm and rational argument had been maintained," with conflicting opinions expressed in the press, notes E.H. Carr. But a year later, "the sole public manifestation of the struggle was a boiling torrent of denunciation in which no adverse voice was, or could be heard."[92]

The aggressive anti-Trotsky campaign in factory cells included resolutions calling for "iron unity" in the ranks. After the Lenin Levy in the spring of 1924, the factory party membership more than doubled (to 240 members) and cells were formed in each of the six large shops.[93] Shop cells passed resolutions emphasizing the need "to end the discussion with the aim of party unity." Unfortunately, cell minutes record only the text of successful resolutions, not the actual vote tally or the transcript of the discussion. Yet even as late as November 1924, cell leaders could circumvent party mandates. In a meeting of forty people in the bolt shop, the speaker spent more time reiterating the positions of the Trotskyists than reporting on positions of the Thirteenth Congress. He summarized the Opposition's accusation that the Central Committee and the entire party apparatus were acting bureaucratically, their argument for open party democracy, and their economic strategy, including the position that it was necessary to offer cheap products to the countryside. After presenting a critical synopsis of Trotsky's *New Course* and *The Lessons of October*, the speaker then finished with a call against factional (i.e., dissenting) work and posited that the Opposition reflected "the pressure of the petty-bourgeois mood" in the party. Significantly, the cell speaker felt obligated to present the position of the Opposition and Trotsky's writings, a marked contrast from the method of denunciation in the following years.[94]

Rank-and-file support for the Trotskyist Opposition in the factory was enough to force a public debate of the issues. At least twenty-three of sixty members voted for the Trotskyist Opposition, a level of support consistent with its mass base in Moscow. Widespread working-class discontent, the deeply rooted tradition of party democracy, and the relative weakness of Stalinism at the factory level in early NEP, all contributed to an atmosphere in which dissidents could speak freely about issues of concern to many workers. The renewed campaign against Trotskyism in late 1924 became a safeguard against dissent at the local level and signaled that if party leaders had their way, such openness would not last.

The United Opposition

The years 1926 and 1927 witnessed the most acrimonious factional infighting. "At no time before or after," comments Robert Vincent Daniels, "did Opposition attacks on those in power assume so bitter a tone or go so far toward outright denunciation of the Communist leadership for betraying the ideals of the revolution." Conversely, in the course of the battle for party supremacy, the ruling Stalin-Bukharin block portrayed the Trotsky-Zinoviev-Kamenev side as "the petty-bourgeois opposition," used the GPU to break up their meetings, and tolerated anti-Semitism.[95]

The interim between the decline of the Trotskyist Opposition and the appearance of the United Opposition (or Bolshevik-Leninists) in the spring of 1926 saw a strengthening of the party machine against all manifestations of dissent. The Central Committee appointed a new MK secretary, N.A. Uglanov, with a mandate to weed out all United Opposition support.[96] The party also replaced the Rogozhsko-Simonovskii district secretary, an Opposition sympathizer, with a hard-line Central Committee supporter who, according to one account, "devoted particular attention to the factory."[97] The campaign against Trotskyism included a factory general meeting of six hundred and fifty on "Lenin, the party and a year of work without Ilyich" that contrasted prerevolutionary Bolshevism with Trotsky's association with the Mensheviks.[98] Significantly, any sign of neutrality met with a harsh rebuke. When a member failed to carry the Central Committee line in a discussion "on Trotskyism" at a guberniia conference the following factory plenum publicly denounced the representative.[99] Moreover, the former party leaders became *persona non grata* as party loyalists removed their portraits from the factory club.[100]

The immediate context for the revival of formal dissident activity in 1926 was the intra-party dispute over agrarian policy. Disagreements led to a split in the Politburo, in which Zinoviev and Kamenev stressed the necessity of more state planning and the urgency of curbing the power of wealthy peasants. These positions were remarkably similar to those advanced by the 1923 Trotskyist Opposition, and they joined with the Trotskyists to form the United Opposition in early 1926.[101]

The rise in anti-Semitism during late NEP played an important role in the party faction fight. On 4 March 1926, Trotsky complained to Bukharin that anti-Semitic agitation against the Opposition continued with impunity in factory cells and noted that Jewish party members were reluctant to report attacks because they were afraid "they would be kicked out instead of the Black Hundred gangsters." Trotsky later wrote that he had pressed Bukharin on "systematic agitation among secretaries at large Moscow enterprises." Bukharin agreed to conduct an investigation on party anti-Semitic attacks on the Opposition, but according to Trotsky, was forbidden to do so by Stalin.[102]

In early 1926, the Komsomol Central Committee passed a resolution to combat "a recent strengthening of anti-Semitism among youth" and admitted, "An anti-Semitic mood had penetrated the VLKSM [the Komsomol] ranks in a pronounced character." Komsomol leaders blamed the rise of anti-Semitism on economic difficulties, including increased unemployment, and a rise in anti-Semitic agitation by counterrevolutionaries and monarchists. By the summer of 1926, the MK information summary included a regular section on anti-Semitism that expressed concern that "recently there can be observed the growth of an anti-Semitic mood that is found reverberating among different groups of communists" and noted "comrades' attempts to explain differences based on acrimony among the nationalities." In October, Komsomol leaders acknowledged a "strong development of anti-Semitism" among Moscow workers.[103] Anti-Semitic graffiti appeared in many factories and in the Bogatyr rubber works, nonparty workers called for Stalin and Bukharin to trample the "yids." Speakers in cell meetings made openly anti-Semitic arguments. "The oppositionists—Trotsky, Zinoviev and Kamenev— are all Jews. We need to finish them off," suggested one typical rant.[104]

Party factory leaders tolerated anti-Semitism during the factional fight. A rank-and-file member argued in a meeting: "We can say quite frankly what is at the root of all the differences. We workers who are party members consider this root to be based on the nationalist tradition, while other differences are merely part of the superstructure."[105] Only one issue of *Martenovka* addressed the issue of anti-Semitism, acknowledging that anti-Semitic slogans were "written not only on the bathroom walls but also on the factory walls and read not only by workers but also by visitors" and encouraged the party and Komsomol members to initiate a campaign.[106] Had the factory party organization (numbering more than seven hundred with the Komsomol) maintained a firm position against anti-Semitism, the slogans would have been covered up immediately. Not once during 1926 or 1927 did party leaders at the factory organize a single general or party meeting, put forward one agenda item, nor give even one speech on the increase of anti-Semitism. Members were reprimanded or expelled for such offenses as alcoholism, nonpayment of dues, and hooligan behavior, but there was not one recorded reprimand or expulsion for anti-Semitism.[107]

Not until five months after the expulsion of the United Opposition, in April 1928, was the question of anti-Semitism openly addressed in a general meeting of the factory cell. A leading member admitted that the Godless "sometimes provoked anti-Semitism," argued, "Jews are people just like us," and admitted "anti-Semitic influences within the party are growing." The factory party expelled its first member for anti-Semitism the following month.[108] Having encouraged extreme nationalism in the factional struggle, party rulers later became concerned after the United Opposition expulsions that such sentiments had gained too much momentum. By August 1928, Stalin called for extreme penalties, including executions, for anti-Semitic party activity.[109] Many subsequent *Martenovka* articles on combating anti-Semitism during the First Five-Year Plan indicate that toleration of Russian nationalism was short-lived and coincided with the factional fight with the United Opposition.[110]

Reports on the mood of workers in the Rogozhsko-Simonovskii district in 1926 show that the United Opposition gained support among a different layer of workers. Significantly, party leaders considered such sympathies "backward" compared with their own anti-Semitic supporters.

> Among a considerable portion of the most backward part of the working masses there is considerable sympathy for the slogans of the Opposition. They have taken up the slogans of the Opposition: about equality, about exploitation, that the Opposition is for the poor but the Central Committee is against. There is a mood among workers for the Opposition; this mood has to be smashed.... Some places have taken up the slogans for Zinoviev about equality, about exploitation, that we do not have socialism, etc. Some say that Zinoviev stands for the poor but the Central Committee are for the rich.[111]

The summer and fall of 1926 marked the zenith of United Opposition support in the Hammer and Sickle Factory. Even before the declared formation of the United Opposition in April 1926, Ivan Zhirov, the most outspoken oppositionist, openly criticized party leaders. In a meeting of three hundred workers in March, Zhirov argued for "more democracy and leadership from below" while suggesting that the bread shortage was "the fault of the middlemen bosses and kulaks." In May he accused the MK of being "isolated from the masses."[112] The following month, he received 126 votes in a factory committee election, just fifty votes shy of electoral victory.[113]

Support for Zhirov and the United Opposition grew over the next several months. Other members started to voice criticism of the official line or qualified support for the Opposition at the shop level. For example, a sheet metal shop member stated that, though he did not endorse the Opposition, it was nevertheless true that "at the present the poor live in the worst conditions." Another complained that "our Opposition leaders gave ten years of service to the party," and that "we should fight them on the level of ideas," while a third member stated that "the Opposition was correct on certain questions and gave a push to our party to correct these issues."[114] In December 1926, *Martenovka* asserted that the Opposition had no supporters in the factory, but a skeptical worker challenged the reporter. "When the meeting discussions open," he revealed, "voices are immediately heard calling out: 'Zhirov, Zhirov, let Zhirov speak!' And for these calls he is known to every worker."[115] The next month a district party report admitted, "In the Hammer and Sickle Factory there are different discussions among nonparty workers that Zinoviev and Trotsky are correct in wanting to raise pay. This is particularly noticeable because of the renegotiating of the collective agreement."[116]

The advances and retreats by the United Opposition, however, caused confusion in their ranks, who sometimes identified themselves as Opposition supporters and other times denied connections. On one occasion, on 10

October 1926, Zhirov and Naumov worked at cross-purposes. Zhirov argued that wage increases were not keeping up with productivity, and a leading cell member retorted that Zhirov was "sympathetic to the Opposition." Naumov tried to come to Zhirov's defense, claiming, "Comrade Zhirov has no ties with the Opposition." In response to the attacks, however, Zhirov argued that on the wage issue, "the Opposition was correct and remains correct." In a meeting two months later, the United Oppositionists again retreated despite their apparent gains. Zhirov admitted that they had made mistakes and stated, "I am not an oppositionist."[117]

The tactical confusion of the United Opposition was minor, however, when weighed against the string of Soviet foreign policy catastrophes that ushered in the revival of the United Opposition in the spring of 1927. The Communist International ordered the Chinese Communist Party to remain in the nationalist Kuomintang even after the popular front strategy led to the slaughter of thousands of Communists. The Chinese Revolution raised the interest of the more politically astute workers. In February 1927 the head of the MK, N.A. Uglanov, reported on the international situation at a general factory meeting of seven hundred. Five notes requested clarification on the Chinese Revolution, including several that criticized the Communist Party compromise with Chiang Kai-shek, the nationalist military leader of the massacre of the Canton revolt. One worker asked, "What is the line of the rightist part of the Canton government, in particular Chiang, and is this not at odds with the line of the leftists?" A note to the speaker at an October meeting asked, "Tell us why in the Chinese Revolution our party does not advocate the slogan for the Soviets when Lenin directly demanded this in the Second Congress of the International?" Because the Opposition had been labeled as traitors, Christian Rakovsky's recall as the Soviet ambassador to France also caused bewilderment and confusion. Rakovsky created a diplomatic scandal when he signed a declaration calling for workers and soldiers in capitalist countries to defend the Soviet Union in the event of a war. Four notes of clarification referred to Rakovsky, one asking "If it is hoped to develop diplomatic ties with France then why did France insist on the recall of our Rakovsky?"[118]

After the Soviet diplomatic break with England in 1927, the Stalinist section of the party exaggerated the threat of war to justify intimidation against the United Opposition. General factory meetings of 650 (4 July), 300 (7 October), and 900 (4 November) all specifically addressed the international situation and the danger of war, and passed resolutions calling for iron unity. On 4 July, a speaker from the OGPU argued, "the OGPU together with the working class must resolutely rebuff attempts by our enemies to sow divisions in our ranks" and warned against "spies and provocateurs." Yet written questions to Uglanov suggest that the attempt to whip up the war hysteria for an attack on the Opposition was less than enthusiastic. "If there is a war, all of you will be in the rear, while the workers will be the first to the front," suggested one worker. Another told him "because of the growth of the bureaucracy, all the workers' enthusiasm about defending the regime has cooled." One posited, "The Opposition is a healthy occurrence. It is like steam in a kettle that needs to be vented from time to time."[119]

Although it is impossible to directly connect increasingly hostile worker notes to party representatives with Opposition propaganda, many workers' anonymous questions echoed the Opposition's politics. Thus, the following question, raised during a cell meeting, was of such concern to local party officials that it was included in the MK information summary: "Can you say whether or not there will be economic equality for everybody living in the Soviet country; and if so, when?"[120] In factory-wide union meetings as well, some workers who expressed their dissatisfaction over wages started to raise questions about the relative prosperity of Central Committee members. On 7 November 1925, *Martenovka* printed real wages in terms of 1913-1914 rubles, indicating that they had risen to 92 percent of the prewar rate.[121] However, in July 1926, after Kalinin claimed that metalworkers' real wages were 20 percent greater than the prewar rate, a worker argued that the statement was "totally untrue ... either you have not been to the market recently or you have a lot of money." In September 1926 Tomsky spoke on the British general strike and received many hostile questions about wages and working conditions, including one that asked, "Comrade Tomsky, please tell us how much you earn a year: twelve thousand rubles, or a little more or a little less? Please clarify."[122]

Rather than international issues, however, Oppositionist agitation was similar to other dissident groups as the organized sentiment for workers' economic grievances and against bureaucratic rule and privileges. Zhirov stated in a May 1927 factory party meeting: "If we listen to workers, they say that life in 1913 was better than now." He then argued that in 1913, 9 percent of the factory staff had been office workers while the figure for 1927 was nearly 12 percent.[123] Thus, the growth of the bureaucracy was not an aberration; it existed even at the factory level and affected workers' wages. In contrast to their aggressive championing of local grievances, international issues hardly figured in their day-to-day propaganda. Only a few cursory comments about the Chinese Revolution and the Anglo-Soviet Trade Union Committee appear in the United Opposition speeches. The factory oppositionists emphasized economic inequality, bureaucratic privilege, and the lack of democracy, as this Hammer and Sickle leaflet illustrates:

Comrades! Our country is in a difficult situation. The bourgeoisie has decided to strangle Soviet rule. In our party the situation is even more difficult. The bureaucratic view is that everything is fine. The bootlickers and informers in the party have taken over. That is the source for unanimity on all questions, which is contrary to Marxism at our society's level of inequality.

Everything healthy in the party has been strangled. Try to counter the speaker-bosses and you are finished. NEPmen all know more about what is going on in the TsK and MK than us, ordinary party members. They have decided to attach us to the Trust, more exactly, to remove those with the spark. Norkin, the president of the RET Trust, that guy who likes to go to parties, he will teach us how to work!

Krupskaya, Zinoviev, Trotsky and other forces are perishing and have been hounded. Why did comrade Lenin work with them openly and allow them to speak freely? Let Trotsky and Stalin or the famous theoretician Uglanov speak at our party meeting. We will see which of them is right. Now we are to vote based only on their word. Lenin taught not to trust just words.

Comrades! It is necessary to strive for freedom of speech in the party and not be afraid to speak the truth. In the district committee a certain kind of people are entrenched. They feel a great sense of well-being. In the Moscow Committee everything up through his highness the secretary should be checked out. Otherwise we will all perish from their bureaucratic, rotten lifestyle.

Comrades! We are a group of Communists who have decided to write twenty such letters. There is no other way out. We can be silent no longer.[124]

The parochial nature of the leaflet implies that the factory underground operated independently of an organized center. This was an eloquent characterization of developing Stalinism at the factory level that focused on its social function as a management tool to discipline the party and workforce. Freedom of speech had been stifled because "bootlickers and informers in the party have taken over."

Factory leaders introduced new methods of humiliation and intimidation to try to break the opposition. *Martenovka* ridiculed the dissidents as freaks and clowns.[125] In May 1927, Zhirov was able to speak at length without interruption, but the party secretary summarized the discussion by challenging party members to play a more active role. He suggested "further attempts by the Opposition to drag the party into a debate will be met with an even more determined rebuff on the part of all party members."[126] At the next meeting, factory party leaders for the first time described the dissidents' activities as criminal. One oppositionist responded, "The Opposition are in step with the party. They should not be exiled to Solovki Prison." When Zhivov attempted to speak he was met with shouts of "down!" and the meeting passed a resolution in favor of "iron unity."[127] In subsequent meetings, oppositionists were repeatedly interrupted with shouts of "Down!," "Enough!," "You lie!," and laughter. Moreover, the party factory bureau, "in accordance with current directives" about "a determined struggle with the cells of oppositionists," summoned them to appear at a party bureau session. Bureau leaders pointed out "the danger of factional work and the incorrectness of their views towards party policy" and suggested that they "openly draw a line between themselves and the Opposition."[128]

Such pressure tactics were partly successful. In August 1917, Naumov renounced his ties to the Opposition, noting in his speech before the entire factory party organization that in the context of the international situation, the dissident activity was counterrevolutionary.[129] In October 1927 Ivan Zhirov recanted his ties with the Opposition because, "after I was summoned to the cell bureau and Comrade Suslov kept after me, I realized that I was mistaken." Like many oppositionists, Zhirov caved in under enormous pressure and informed on his former comrades. To give his confession credence, he admitted, "I received Opposition documents from Chubikov."[130]

Party meetings repeatedly passed resolutions that condemned the United Opposition and called for "iron unity" in the party ranks, a tactic to flush out dissidents and ensure that members fell in line. Every resolution passed with no more than two votes against and one or two abstentions. Only once did another party member defend the Opposition. During the campaign to expel

Zinoviev from the Central Committee on the charge that he had spoken before nonparty members, a member pointed out that the party itself had distributed the tickets for the event. He further questioned, "Why expel Comrade Trotsky from the Central Committee when he did not speak anywhere?"[131]

Despite the intimidation campaign, the United Opposition launched a flurry of activity. On 3 September, the United Opposition submitted *The Platform of the Opposition* to the Politburo and although banned, the platform was secretly distributed widely among members. Much of *The Platform* appealed directly to workers by calling for wage increases, improved housing, unemployment benefits equal to an average workers' wage and an industrialization strategy that would theoretically benefit the working class.[132] Oppositionists organized hundreds of underground meetings. Trotsky attended three or four meetings a day and as many as twenty thousand people in Moscow and Leningrad participated in illegal gatherings held in workers' apartments.[133] The GPU and party loyalists infiltrated these meetings, including a party member from the Hammer and Sickle Factory sent to "expose" members. He claimed that "Trotskyists asked me to leave and I was forcibly pushed out the door and down the stairs."[134] A district report on the underground activity shows that Smilga spoke to a meeting of forty or fifty workers and that "ten people in this meeting were from the Hammer and Sickle Factory."[135] The MK recorded many apartment meetings in late October and early November. On 27 October, 150 people gathered in an apartment and "the meeting was led by Trotsky, who talked about Stalin's Thermidor politics, party suppression, and Stalinist whistling." Several nights later 125 people met in another apartment and Trotsky predicted, "We will leave from the party with blood."[136]

These illegal gatherings gave Opposition supporters confidence. At a closed meeting of 310 members on 28 October, the oppositionist Chubikov managed to read part of Lenin's Testament, despite being interrupted at least ten times by taunts and whistles. He concluded: "They are still hiding this document from us. They hid Lenin's Testament. (shouts of 'Not True') I am a real Leninist. ('Down,' noise, whistles.)" Ishchenko from the All-Union Central Trades Council argued that *Pravda* had ridiculed the Opposition for being afraid of the kulaks, but that now *Pravda* itself was calling for a forceful struggle with the rich peasants. He raised the issue of internal democracy, and amid whistling and catcalls defiantly claimed the mantle of Bolshevism for the Opposition: "If the politics of the party are not right, we will fight against it ... ('enough,' noise, whistles.) We will not bow on bent knees. We are Bolsheviks."[137]

On 18 November 1927, 429 workers, including 129 nonparty workers, attended the open expulsion meeting. Hecklers repeatedly interrupted Berezhanskii, who finished his disjointed speech on party democracy with "Well, I am done." ("You talk, you talk," laughter.) But the stenographer did not record laughter when Bakanov, the only other speaker identified as a Bolshevik-Leninist, spoke.

> Allow me to state the platform of the Bolshevik-Leninists. The speaker slandered the Opposition. In five minutes I cannot state everything but I will say that when

I received the platform that I became a Bolshevik-Leninist. It is a slander to say that the platform is based on Menshevism.... Now on the slogans for the October demonstration. Dinamo workers wanted slogans such as: 1. Carry out the Testament of Lenin. 2. Fire to the right: against the NEPmen, kulaks and bureaucrats. What in these slogans is not Leninist? The factory committee took away these slogans. They said, "This talk is against Stalin, you cannot do it." Also, workers in the Liberation of Labor Factory wanted to listen to Trotsky, they collected 450 signatures ('they were collected by trickery,' 'you lie') but the guberniia department of the union canceled it. Trotsky did not organize this; it was the masses that wanted to hear him. (noise) We are not Mensheviks—all workers will see this. Give them our platform. Against Uglanov's darkness and for Lenin's light. We will fight with our bodies and our blood. (noise) [138]

To what extent did such arguments resonate among other workers? Opposition support in several other factories illustrates the narrow gap between potential success of the dissidents carrying a vote and the slightly smaller group in the Hammer and Sickle. Although a year earlier members chanted for Zhirov, the group of five oppositionists could not win wider open support. In workplaces where their numbers were stronger, such as the Liberation of Labor and Dinamo factories, the Opposition could win victories against the leadership. Citywide resolutions attest to the fear that pervaded in the party. A summer 1926 vote to condemn the United Opposition received only twenty-two against and fifty-three abstentions in all of Moscow.[139] In May and June 1927, oppositionists spoke up in thirty-seven workers' cells in Moscow. Yet only fourteen cells in the entire city raised "no" votes or abstentions to "condemn the organizational activity of Comrade Zinoviev," and only one factory had more than a single "no" vote. In the discussion of the third plenum of the MK, fifty-three cells with 132 speakers spoke for the Opposition but only twelve cells (not the Hammer and Sickle) registered "yes" votes for Opposition resolutions.[140]

In the months leading up to the expulsion, virtually no party member echoed support for the Opposition in the general meetings. The stenographer repeatedly recorded applause for speeches to drive the oppositionists from the party and noted noise, laughing, and calls of "enough" whenever oppositionists spoke. The general resolution put forward to expel the United Opposition for "counterrevolutionary activity," which included a promise for the seven-hour day, carried with only two votes against it and one abstention. The individual expulsion resolutions likewise received overwhelming support. A list of charges against Chubikov included distributing illegal literature and attending antiparty meetings and the 7 November demonstration as an oppositionist. Similar charges were leveled against Berezhanskii, but the charges against Bakanov were based exclusively on what he had just said in the meeting. The resolution to expel him noted, "The statement in the plenum that he will fight with his blood and body against the darkness of Uglanov and for Leninist light, shows that he still participates in factional work."[141]

Anonymous notes to the speaker, Mezhlauk, indicate a sharp divergence between overwhelming electoral results and actual membership sentiment, a phenomenon explained by the orchestrated intimidation campaign and the complete collapse of democracy within the party. Significantly, all but one of the seventeen written notes show either total confusion over the proceedings, concern over the treatment of the dissidents, or hostility toward the Stalinists. Three questions requested clarification on various issues. One worker wanted to know how the seven-hour workday could be adopted without lowering wages. Another asked for clarification of Mezhlauk's invectives against the Opposition. "You say that Comrade Trotsky does not want the dictatorship of proletariat but the dictatorship of Trotsky, but why is Kamenev a strikebreaker?" A member raised the issue of the Chinese Revolution and wanted to know "what plot was discovered that was allegedly concealed by the party?" Four questions expressed general concern about the treatment of oppositionists. One worker wanted to know why the oppositionists were considered traitors: "After all," he inquired, "are they not also for the improvement of the working class?" Another asked, "Kamenev, Zinoviev and Preobrazhenskii were your comrades, why do you now pour dirt on them?" Factory members apparently were aware that leading party members had hurled debris at Trotsky during his speech when he was expelled from the Central Committee because one question asked: "Who threw the galosh at Trotsky?" Another member wanted to know if oppositionists had been arrested during the October anniversary demonstration.[142]

Seven notes indicate that members wanted a hearing for the Opposition. One asked why the MK had not published their platform. Two notes proposed immediately giving them the platform to speak; one pointed out that that there were nonparty members in the hall. "Allow them to hear the Opposition," the writer urged, and another proposed: "Give a hearing to the Opposition not from the press but here in the meeting so that we can understand a little better." Four notes addressed questions about the expulsions and the participation of the Opposition in the upcoming Party Congress. One note simply asked if they could participate in the Congress, and another suggested that expulsion would simply drive Zinoviev and Trotsky underground. Another note questioned the rationale for expelling them before the Congress, which was "in a few weeks." One worker commented on rumors in the factory about a demonstration against the expulsion of the Opposition and also asked if it was "legal to expel them before the Congress?"[143]

Two of the questions expressed general anger and disgust towards Mezhlauk. One member questioned the speakers' own credentials, recalling the hunger during the Civil War, "Comrade Mezhlauk, did you not work for the Central Provisions Administration in 1920?" Another member issued a threat to the Central Committee, claiming it had "conducted its educational campaign against the Opposition poorly" by resorting to using "rhetoric." He further argued that, "the Central Committee is used to shouting "workers, workers, etc. Your careerism will lead to the destruction of the workers. So watch out. There will come an hour when the workers will start to pound both the Opposition and the Central Committee."[144]

Various reports show that the United Opposition gained considerable support among youth in the factory and district, suggesting that the All-Union Komsomol vote (304,875 for expulsion, 1,665 against, and 2,334 abstaining) was also based on fear and intimidation rather the members' sentiments. The Komsomol reported that the Opposition did not receive a single vote in the entire Rogozhsko-Simonovskii district although there were "many notes with demands for the speaker to clarify certain points, while attempting to justify the views of the Opposition," including seventeen that "unreservedly approved the activities and work of the Opposition." Moreover, "in the cells there are groups of Komsomol members who do not speak up and do not vote for the Opposition, but outside the meetings, when talking with friends, they reason in the following way: 'How can we believe that Zinoviev and Trotsky, the best students of Lenin, want to create some kind of second bourgeois party and betray the working class?'" A note to the speaker at a Hammer and Sickle meeting posited, "Lenin in his Testament said that Stalin was a cook who would only prepare spicy dishes and we should not trust the leadership of Stalin. Is the current situation not such a spicy dish? So how can we not trust Lenin about leaving Stalin at his post of General Secretary of the party?"[145] A district party report noted an underground meeting of seventy on 25 October in which "the majority in attendance were youth. The speaker was Trotsky.... After speaking he left to go to another group."[146] MK leaders recorded the names of all Komsomol members who spoke sympathetically for the Opposition, including two in the Hammer and Sickle Factory who were not among the hard supporters later expelled.[147] A speaker at the expulsion meeting stated that Komsomol oppositionists in the district participated in the 7 November demonstration under slogans hostile to Stalin.[148] In his recantation letter, I.F. Naumov admitted "the spreading of a negative mood among the youth and workers created a lot of activity for the Opposition."[149]

A minority of nonparty workers expressed some sympathy for the Opposition, though the overwhelming majority did not care enough to attend the meeting. A report on the mood of nonparty workers towards the expulsion of Trotsky and Zinoviev recorded that five pattern shop workers openly criticized the proceedings. "It was necessary to explain to the working masses instead of the expulsions," they protested. "We do not trust the newspapers, and representatives from the Opposition needed to be given a hearing. It was incorrect to expel Trotsky. Why did they not let him into the meetings?"[150] While the more politically conscious workers were against the expulsions, only 129 nonparty workers and less than half of the combined party and Komsomol membership even bothered to attend the expulsion meeting.[151]

During the 1927 collective agreement campaign that followed the expulsions, *Martenovka* claimed that the Opposition conducted political agitation in the shops. The reports indicate that their efforts met with considerable support, though the "wide-net" campaign probably extended to many non-oppositionists who were simply against the wagecuts. On 25 November, *Martenovka* claimed oppositionists had started arguments in several shops and disturbed production.[152] Two weeks later, similar reports complained that in the repair shop "the Opposition disturbs production work. This should be stopped. In the future, for example, in reaching the collective agreement, we should safeguard undisturbed work." Another party loyalist complained that the Opposition continued to gain a hearing even among party members. "We need to strengthen discipline in the party and strengthen work in clarifying to the workers the divisive activities of the Opposition, their attempts to undermine the dictatorship of the proletariat."[153]

This dissident activity was short-lived, however, and over the next month twenty-five hundred oppositionists signed declarations renouncing their ties with the United Opposition.[154] The Hammer and Sickle recantations share many of the attributes of forced confessions found repeatedly during the rule of high Stalinism in the thirties: evidence of intimidation and ridicule, self-criticism, and informing on other party members. Naumov denied formal ties with the Opposition and claimed that his votes for their motions were merely a coincidence although he admitted committing a "tremendous mistake" in slowing down the work of the Komsomol. Zhirov confessed that he was also at fault for making "unhealthy criticisms" and vowed that in the future he would face problems before the party and the working class in a more considered way.[155] His confession included informing on another oppositionist, and reveals the pressure and humiliation of identification as an Oppositionist. "They laughed at me in the newspaper *Martenovka*," he recalled, "booted me out of the bureau, they do not give me party work" and "look at me like the devil." Zhirov ended his statement with an appeal that it not be used "in order to torment me" and pledged: "I told you the truth but if I missed something or misspoke, just ask me and I will correct it if you want and if the party needs me to. Otherwise remove members like me." Despite their prostration before the party, however, nowhere in either Naumov's or Zhirov's letters are there explicit rejections of the Opposition platform.[156]

What was the level of support for the Opposition in the Hammer and Sickle Factory? The interim between the decline of the Trotskyist Opposition and the emergence of the United Opposition is significant because the Stalinist layer of the party was successful in stigmatizing organized dissident activity and driving a wedge between hard-core oppositionists and their potential supporters. Altogether, the party expelled five United Opposition supporters, including those who had earlier recanted.[157] The evidence shows that there was widespread but passive and ephemeral support for the Opposition in 1926 in the party and among nonparty workers. The sixteen of seventeen hostile notes to the speakers indicates that in 1927 the overwhelming majority of party members supported neither side, though many members, and possibly the majority, opposed the expulsions. A year later, as we saw in chapter three, the expelled oppositionists led resistance to the collective agreement and held shop-level meetings.

The Trade Union Opposition

Within weeks after the defeat of the United Opposition at Fifteenth Party Congress in December 1927, the pro-NEP coalition of Bukharin and Stalin that had ruled the Soviet Union for three years quickly started to unravel. The sharp drop in grain collections in late 1927 led the regime to resort to "extraordinary measures" for requisitioning. Personally traveling to Siberia and the Urals in January 1928 to oversee collections, Stalin accused local leaders of incompetence and cowardice. Differences over agrarian policies were initially conducted within the framework of continuing NEP, but as Stalin and his supporters moved toward a more aggressive agricultural policy, they claimed that Bukharin and the NEP advocates constituted a "right deviation" that represented the main danger to the party. The discussions were largely confined to the upper sections of the party and, as Stephen Cohen notes, were conducted not with "candid political language but in the discreet idiom of oblique polemics" and only in mid-1929, after the conflict, were the antagonists identified in the Soviet press.[158]

By the autumn of 1928, the Stalin supporters' campaign against Bukharin extended to the trade unions that were accused of "obstructing productivity." Tomsky and the leadership of many trade unions resisted the new move for an industrial drive that they claimed would victimize the working class and transform the unions into "houses of detention." The super-industrialization program provoked widespread resistance from trade union leaders who recognized that their function, if the Stalinists got their way, would be to maximize productivity and to cease defending workers in any way. [159]

The accusations against the trade union leaders began to filter down to the factory level in October 1928. Like the 1923 Trotskyists Opposition, Moscow was again the only center of opposition activity although this time it was largely an "apparatus affair" with little involvement of the rank-and-file party membership.[160] After Stalin supporters easily gained control of the Moscow Committee, they initiated a campaign against the so-called "right wing" of the party. In a general factory meeting on 10 October at least one speaker countered the charges against the right as "mere gossip."[161] During the discussions before the Eigth All-Union Congress of Trade Unions a few weeks later, however, the battle raged in print. *Komsomol'skaia pravda* attacked the trade union apparatus for failing to "draw the masses" into the pre-Congress discussion.[162] *Trud*, at the time still controlled by the trade unionists, countered the charge.[163] The issue of self-criticism obscured the debate, but the subtext of the discussion centered on whether or not to transform the unions into productivity organs.

Delegates from the factory sided with the trade union opposition when the battle reached a climax at the December 1928 Congress. In a discussion among the Moscow fraction, a minority fought against the Kaganovich's candidacy; though only ninety-two of 560 delegates, including two from the factory, voted against him.[164] During the Congress, *Pravda* posited that an apolitical approach toward trade union work was "intolerable."[165] Kozelev from the Hammer and Sickle factory gave the most vociferous speech for the Opposition, openly challenging the *Pravda* article and criticizing *Komsomol'skaia pravda* for trying to discredit the trade-union movement. After reading part of the article he then commented, "Comrades, I think this is a slander of the trade-union movement. The Soviet Union trade-union movement does not deserve such slander from our friends, even in the manner of self-criticism." (applause.)[166] A week later, *Trud* singled out Kozelev as a dissident ringleader who had committed "a serious political mistake" for his remarks. The newspaper called him a "model bureaucrat" and demanded that he understand and accept his mistake.[167] Party leaders also accused Kozelev of calling *Komsomol'skaia pravda* "a Menshevik newspaper."[168] Kozelev's bold comments—unthinkable even a year or two later—and the Stalinist response illustrate the shift in political discourse as well as the naiveté among the Bukharin section of the party. The days of open and honest party discussion already had ended with the expulsion of the United Opposition.

The trade union leaders gained considerable support among Hammer and Sickle Factory party leaders. A combined bureau and Control Commission session on 11 January 1929 focused on Kozelev's speech, self-criticism, and the question of whether members had a right to question Politburo decisions. Several bureau members sided with the Opposition. Kozelev accused another member of lying in his report on Congress and then took up the issue of party democracy. "Can we discuss the candidature? Can we ask the Politburo to reconsider its decision? We can. Comrade Tomsky, in his own way, decided that the introduction of Comrade Kaganovich meant distrust for the party fraction..." The bureau passed a resolution condemning Kozelov's behavior at the Congress, but three of those present voted against the resolution and one abstained, indicating considerable Opposition support among factory leaders.[169]

The trade unionists were unwilling and probably unable to rally rank-and-file support to their cause. During the discussion in the bureau, Kozelev boasted, "I am on the Central Committee of the metalworkers' union."[170] But by 1928, when the Stalin section of the party moved against them, union leaders who had collaborated in the retreat over the preceding years were in no position to offer resistance. Isolated from rank-and-file workers, Stalinist loyalists easily defeated the last organized political grouping in the factory. They vowed to "purge the trade unions of trade unionism" and an extensive "cleansing," headed by L. Kaganovich, ensued at all levels of the unions.[171] While the trade union leaders and advocates of NEP put up much less of a public fight than the United Opposition, their defeat had significant ramifications. Eulogizing Peter the Great who "feverishly built mills and factories to supply the army and strengthen the country's defenses," Stalin made it clear that this new state interventionist policy first and foremost signaled an attack on the Soviet peasantry, who would have to pay a "tribute" to fund industrialization. By eliminating the trade union opposition and the last vestiges of legal defense for workers in the factories, however, the regime also prepared the groundwork for a protracted assault on Soviet labor under the new Stalinist slogan: Trade Unions—Face Toward Production.[172] In practice this meant that both the peasantry and working class would pay for the industrialization drive. Moreover, as personal loyalty to Stalin and his frequently changing policies became the prerequisite for career advancement and survival within the party apparatus, policy differences would henceforth be conducted within parameters that had more in common with medieval court intrigues than with the public debates of the earlier Soviet society.

Many opposition groups were active in the Hammer and Sickle Factory during the decade after the revolution. The SRs, the 1918 Left Communist Opposition, the Workers' Opposition, the Trotskyist Opposition, the United Opposition, the trade unionists of the Bukharin Opposition, and even the minuscule Workers' Truth and Workers' Group all gained some support in the factory. The variety of opposition support was exceptional, not because the workers' sentiments in the factory were extraordinary, but because all of these political groups competed for the loyalty of workers in the largest metal factory in Moscow. The catalytic role of opposition organizations in the 1920s was very similar to that in the prerevolutionary period: small but well-organized groups were able to provide a voice for much larger groups of workers.

The degeneration of politics at the factory level mirrored that at the higher echelons of the party. In 1922, Left SR members affiliated with a group that had tried to organize a military coup d'état, had assassinated Soviet leaders, and had bombed government offices spoke openly at factory general meetings and managed to elect two sympathizers to the district Soviet. In 1923, party sentiment and established democratic norms forced a public hearing of the ideas of the Trotskyist Opposition in print and at factory-level discussions. Authorities recognized the potentially explosive situation that opposition activity could create, and used increasingly repressive measures to counter dissident influence. If there were "irregularities" in the 1923-1924 elections, the 1927 vote was by comparison a sham and useless as an indicator of member opinion. The 1926-1927 campaign against the United Opposition was marked by fraudulent election aggregates in which members could not vote freely, the toleration of anti-Semitism, and the end of open discussion as fear and reprisals against dissidents became the party norm. Members' chants of support for Zhirov in 1926 and the notes to the speakers during the expulsion of the United Opposition in 1927 illustrate the profound discrepancy between the overwhelming Stalinist vote and the rank-and-file members' beliefs. By 1928, the first wave of mass political arrests sent several thousand expelled party members to the Gulags.

While the end of party democracy caused widespread anger and disgust among a significant section of party members and a smaller milieu of non-party workers, such sentiments were episodic. The majority of party and non-party workers had withdrawn in weariness or apathy from the political realm. As the divergence between the party and labor widened during NEP, workers became less interested in state rhetoric. Whereas over 1,000 workers regularly packed raucous factory meetings at the beginning of NEP, the general factory meetings that discussed the United Opposition drew 650, 300, 900, and 588 attendees, even though the workforce had doubled from 1922 to 1927.[173] Even the open party expulsion meeting on 18 November 1927 drew only 129 nonparty workers.[174]

This retreat from politics by the overwhelming majority of workers is crucial for understanding ascending Stalinism. Despite simmering discontent, by late NEP the relative strength of the nascent ruling class versus that of the proletariat in the class conflict favored the Stalinists. Workers' belief that they could challenge the state offensive had all but vanished. Personal survival—always a trend within the workplace—had eclipsed the politics of collective action.

Notes

1. John Hatch, "Labor and Politics in NEP Russia: Workers, Trade Unions, and the Communist party in Moscow, 1921-1926" (Ph.D. Dissertation, University of California at Irvine, 1985). Hatch also shows that sectional and regional differences characterized opposition activity in Moscow.
2. Vladimir Brovkin, *The Mensheviks After October, Socialist Opposition and the Rise of the Bolshevik Dictatorship* (Ithaca, 1987); *The Mensheviks: From the Revolution of 1917 to the Second World War*, Leopold Haimson, ed. (Chicago, 1973); Oliver Radkey, *The Sickle under the Hammer* (New York, 1963); E.H. Carr, *The Interregnum* (London, 1960); Stephen Cohen, *Bukharin and the Bolshevik Revolution: A Political Biography, 1988-1938* (New York, 1973); Robert Daniels, *The Conscience of the Revolution: Communist Opposition in Soviet Russia* (Cambridge, MA, 1961); Isaac Deutscher, *The Prophet Unarmed: Trotsky, 1921-1929* (London, 1959).
3. GARF, f. 7952, op. 3, d. 215, l. 97. Factory general meeting, 25 May 1918 (new calendar).
4. Daniels, *The Conscience of the Revolution*, 70-91.
5. Ronald Kowalski, *The Bolshevik Party in Conflict: The Left Communist Opposition of 1918* (Pittsburgh, 1991), 149.
6. GARF, f. 7952, op. 3, d. 215, ll. 55-56. Factory committee meeting and general meeting, 12 (25), 13 (26) February, 1918.
7. Hatch, "Labor and Politics in NEP Russia," 274.
8. Daniels, *The Conscience of the Revolution*, 118-153.
9. TsAODM, f. 429, op. 1, dd., 3, 4. Party meetings, 1920, 1921.
10. Deutscher, *The Prophet Unarmed*, 108.
11. TsGAMO, f. 19, op. 1, d. 62, ll. 115-129, 187-198. Reports to Moscow Soviet, 1923.
12. Daniels, *Conscience of the Revolution*, 158-161, 204, 210.
13. TsGAMO, f. 19, op. 1, d. 21, l. 14; 18 November 1922 report to Moscow Soviet.
14. GARF, f. 7952, op. 3, d. 312, l. 60. Frankel on factory during Civil War.
15. GARF, f. 7952, op. 3, d. 213, l. 294. General factory party meeting, 16 August 1920, from documents of the revolution collection.
16. GARF, f. 7952, op. 3, d. 215, ll. 11, 27. Factory committee and general meeting, 2 December 1917 and 3 January 1918 delegate meeting (dates from old calendar). The latter meeting was during the holiday break.
17. GARF, f. 7952, op. 3, d. 215, l. 11. Factory general meeting, 5 December 1917, factory committee meeting, 29 November (old calendar).
18. GARF, f. 7952, op. 3, d. 275, l. 62. S.S. Leshkovtsev memoir.
19. GARF, f. 7952, op. 3, d. 215, ll. 1-141. Factory committee and general meetings, November 1917 to July 1928.
20. Oliver H. Radkey, *Russia Goes to the Polls, The Election to the All-Russian Constituent Assembly, 1917* (Ithaca, NY, 1989), 103, 114.
21. Roy Medvedev, *The October Revolution* (New York, 1985), 111. In Petrograd the LSR vote was 16.2 percent, RSR 0.5 percent; in Kazan the LSR vote was 18.9 percent, RSR 2.1 percent; in the Baltic fleet, the LSR vote was 26.9 percent, the RSR 11.9 percent.

22. Edward Acton, "The Revolution and its Historians" in *Critical Companion to the Russian Revolution, 1914-1921*, Edward Acton, Vladimir Cherniaev, and William Rosenberg, eds. (Bloomington, 1997), 10.

23. E.H. Carr, The Bolshevik Revolution 1917-1923, 3 vols. (New York, 1985) 1:117-123.

24. GARF, f. 7952, op. 3, d. 215, l. 53. General meeting 9 February 1918 (old calendar).

25. GARF, f. 7952, op. 3, d. 215. 1-142. Factory committee and general meetings, November 1917 to July 1918.

26. TsGAMO, f. 186, op. 3, d. 3, l. 18. Factory employment statistics.

27. GARF, f. 7925, op. 3, d. 212, l. 125. LSR Internationalist leaflet, 28 March 1918.

28. GARF, f. 7952, op. 3, d. 215, l. 78. Factory general meeting, 9 May 1918 (new calendar).

29. GARF, f. 7925, op. 3, d. 275, l. 25; P.V. Lazrenov memoir.

30. GARF, f. 7952, op. 3, d. 215, l. 126. Factory committee meeting, 5 July 1918.

31. GARF, f. 7952, op. 3, d. 275, l. 115. M.G. Ob"edkov memoir.

32. Carr, *The Bolshevik Revolution*, 1: 164.

33. TsAODM, f. 3, op. 1, d. 33, ll. 1-3. Lenin telegram 7 July 1918. LSR fraction of Moscow Oblast Soviet Executive Committee statement, 20 July 1918.

34. GARF, f. 7952, op. 3, d. 275, ll. 65-66. S. S. Leshkovtsev memoir.

35. GARF, f. 7952, op. 3, d. 275, l. 115. M.G. Ob"edkov memoir.

36. GARF, f. 7952, op. 3, d. 272, l. 28. F.E. Golikov memoir.

37. Carr, *The Bolshevik Revolution*, 1:165-169.

38. GARF, f. 7952, op. 3, d. 276, l. 122. E.D. Tumanov memoir.

39. GARF, f. 7952, op. 3, d. 274, ll. 70-71. G.N. Kudrov memoir.

40. Carr, *The Bolshevik Revolution*, 1:170-179.

41. Christopher Read, *From Tsar to Soviets, The Russian People and their Revolution, 1917-1921* (New York, 1996), 207.

42. Vladimir Brovkin, *Behind the Front Line of the Civil War: Political Parties and Social Movements in Russia, 1918-1922* (Princeton, 1994), 131.

43. GARF, f. 7952, op. 3, d. 213, ll. 87-93. Factory general meetings, 24 May, 12 June 1919.

44. GARF, f. 7952, op. 3, d. 312, l. 8. History of factory during the civil war, minutes from 30 March 1921.

45. GARF, f. 393, op. 1a, d. 36, ll. 257-259. Moscow Cheka information summaries, May 1921.

46. Simon Pirani "Class Clashes with Party: Politics in Moscow between the Civil War and the New Economic Policy" in *Historical Materialism*, Vol. 11: 2, 2003.

47. GARF, f. 7952, op. 3, d. 275, l. 132, d. 276, l. 183; d. 312, l. 12. M.G. Ob"edkov memoir; Iakovlev recollection.

48. Hatch, "Labor and Politics in NEP Russia," 74, 81.

49. TsMAM, f. 176, op. 2, d. 121, l. 1. Soviet election form, 4 January 1922.

50. Carr, *The Bolshevik Revolution*, 1:181.

51. TsAODM, f. 429, op. 1, d. 7, ll. 19-20, 23. Factory general meeting 23 May 1922, party general meeting, 14 June 1922.

52. TsAODM, f. 429, op. 1, d. 6, l. 12. Factory party bureau meeting, 22 May 1922.

53. GAMO, f. 19, op. 1, d. 21, l. 262. Report to Moscow Soviet, 25 May 1922.

54. TsMAM, f. 176, op. 2, d. 120, l. 4. Factory committee meeting, 19 June 1922.

55. TsMAM, f. 176, op. 2, d. 121, l. 9. Factory general meeting, 19 June 1922.

56. TsMAM, f. 176, op. 2, d. 121, ll. 2, 3, 22. General meeting, 26 May 1922, factory committee report, 5 May 1922, general meeting, 4 December 1922.

57. TsMAM, f. 176, op. 2, d. 121, ll. 21-22. General meeting, 4 December 1922. TsGAMO, f. 19, op. 1, d. 62, Reports to Moscow Soviet, 1922.

58. GARF, f. 7952, op. 3, d. 312 ll. 57-58. Frankel recollection.

59. GARF, f. 7952, op. 3, d. 312 ll. 57-58. Frankel recollection.

60. GARF, f. 7952, op. 3, d. 275, l. 133. M.G. Ob"edkov memoir; d. 276, l. 183. P. M. Iakovlev memoir.

61. Hatch, "Labor and Politics in NEP Russia," 108.

62. TsGAMO, f .19, op. 1, d. 21 l. 43. Report to Moscow Soviet, 29 November 1922.

63. *Sovershenno Sekretno: Lubianka-Staliny o polozhenii v strane*, Sevostianov, Sakharav, et al. eds. Vol. 1: 455. The SR Maximalists united with the LSRs in September 1922 (Vol. 2: 439). This probably explains why an undated 1922 soviet election list claims that the SR Maximalists (rather than the LSRs) nominated four of their members in the factory. TsMAM, f. 176, op. 2, d. 116, l. 10.

64. GARF, f. 7952, op. 3, d. 275 l. 133. M.G. Ob"edkov memoir.

65. TsGAMO, f. 19, op. 1, d. 62, l. 210. Report to Moscow Soviet, 30 August 1923.

66. *Sovershenno Sekretno: Lubianka-Staliny o polozhenii v strane*, Sevostianov, Sakharav, et al. eds. Vol. 1, Part 2: 959. The OGPU report does not specify that it was the LSRs as those carrying out the "anti-Soviet agitation" in the Hammer and Sickle Factory though, given their history in the factory and the absence of Mensheviks, this was probably the case.

67. RGASPI, f. 17, op. 16, d. 563, l. 230. TsAODM, f. 429, op. 1, d. 16, l. 2. Factory party report January 1925.

68. TsAODM, f. 429, op. 1, d. 62, l. 40. Party report, n.d. January 1927.

69. GARF, f. 7952, op. 3, d. 273, ll.51-105, d. 274, ll. 54-91, 92-95. Memoirs of Kochergin, Kudrov, and Lebedev.

70. *Rabochaia Moskva*, 19 February 1930; *Martenovka*, 11 November 1930.

71. TsMAM, f. 176, op. 2, d. 121. General meetings, 1922.

72. The GPU annual report for 1924 notes arrests of 52 Left SR members. Nicholas Werth, "The State Against Its People" in *The Black Book of Communism* (Cambridge, MA, 1999), 135. OGPU reports to Stalin in 1925 indicate a similar number, *Sovershenno Sekretno: Lubianka-Staliny o polozhenii v strane (1922-1934 rr.)*. Editors: A.N. Sakharov, G.N. Sevostianov, V.S. Khristoforov, V.K. Vinogradov, T. Vihavainen, M. Kivinen, A. Getty, T. Martin, L. Viola, L.P. Kolodnikova. Vol. 3, part 1: 133, 191, 244, 418, Part 2: 513, 589, 663.

73. The Platform of the Opposition, September 1927, in Leon Trotsky, *The Challenge of the Left Opposition (1926-1927)*, 351.

74. Cliff, *Lenin: Building the Party*.

75. Moshe Lewin, *The Making of the Soviet System* (London, 1985), 199.

76. *Pravda*, 25 January 1921.

77. *The Struggle for Power: Russia in 1923*, Valentina Vilkova, ed. (Amherst, New York, 1996), 264-281.

78. *Dvenadtsatyi s"ezd RKP (b)* (Moscow, 1962), 497.

79. Carr, *The Interregnum*, 257-370; Deutscher, *The Prophet Unarmed*, 75-163.

80. *The Struggle for Power*, Vilkova, ed., 264-281.

81. TsAODM, f. 80, op. 1, d. 137, l. 3. Rogozhsko-Simonovskii party conference, 3 January 1924.

82. GARF, f. 7952, op. 3, d. 280, l. 31. History of Komsomol in Hammer and Sickle Factory.

83. GARF, f. 7952, op. 3, d. 266, l. 12; d. 275, l. 150. Terenin recollection, M.G. Ob'edkov memoir.

84. GARF, f. 7952, op. 3, d. 279, l. 216. Martinov recollection.

85. *The Struggle for Power*, Vilkova, ed., 274.

86. Daniels, *The Conscience of the Revolution*, 233.

87. Tony Cliff, *Trotsky: Fighting the Rising Stalinist Bureaucracy* (London, 1991), 47.

88. TsMAM, f. 176 op. 2. d. 247, l. 3. General meeting 12 February 1922.

89. TsAODM, f. 429, op. 1, d. 17, l. 39, General meeting, 6 August 1924; TsMAM, f. 176, op. 2, d. 344, l. 36. Summary of books and journals sold, 8 October 1925.

90. *Pravda*, 30 November, 9, 20 December 1924; *Rabochaia Moskva* 26 November, 2, 3 December 1924; *Molodoi Leninets*, 27, 28, 29 November, 3 December, 1924.

91. Leon Trotsky, *The Permanent Revolution* (New York, 1969); *The Stalinist School of Falsification* (New York, 1962), 89-99.

92. E.H. Carr, *Socialism in One Country, 1924-1926*, 2 vols. (London, 1959), 2:23-4.

93. *Martenovka*, 7 November, 1927.

94. TsAODM, f. 429, op. 1, d. 24, ll. 1-90. Shop cell meetings, 1924.

95. Daniels, *The Conscience of the Revolution*, 273-321.

96. Cliff, *Trotsky: Fighting the Rising Stalinist Bureaucracy*, 85.

97. GARF, f. 7952, op. 3. d. 279, l. 217. Martov recollection.

98. TsMAM, f. 176, op. 2, d. 403, l. 19. General meeting, 15 January 1925.

99. TsAODM, f. 429, op. 1, d. 28, l. 17. Factory party plenum, 11 February 1925.

100. GARF, f. 7952, op. 3, d. 275, l. 232. Parshik memoir.

101. Deutscher, *Prophet Unarmed*, 223-270.

102. Leon Trotsky, *The Challenge of the Trotskyist Opposition, 1926-1927* (New York, 1980), 44-6. Leon Trotsky, "Thermidor and Anti-Semitism," 22 February 1937, in *The New International*, May 1941.

103. TsKhDMO, f. 1, op, 23, d. 564, ll. 2-4, 35; TsK Komsomol discussion and resolution on anti-Semitism, Moscow reports to TsK Komsomol, 28 October 1926.

104. RGASPI, f. 17, op. 85, d. 66, l. 62; d. 67 ll. 27, 36-7, 60, 88. MK information summaries, May through early October 1926.

105. RGASPI, f. 17, op. 85, d. 67, l. 60. MK information summary, summer 1926.

106. *Martenovka*, 7 July 1927.

107. TsAODM, f. 429, op. 1, dd. 40, 56, 80. Hammer and Sickle Factory general Party and bureau discussions and reports, 1926-1927.

108. TsAODM, f. 429, op. 1, d. 77, ll. 19, 36. Party plenums, 4 April, 23 May 1928.

109. Reiman, *The Birth of Stalinism*, 57.

110. *Martenovka*, 29 March, 13 April 1929; 27 January, 13 April 1930; 3 January 1932.

111. RGASPI, f. 17, op. 85, d. 67, l. 23-4. MK information summary, n.d. 1926.

112. TsAODM, f. 429, op. 1, d. 41, ll. 18, 30. Factory party meetings, 3 March, 5 May 1926.

113. TsMAM, f. 176, op. 2, d. 451, ll. 20-21. Factory conference, 14 June 1926.

114. TsAODM, f. 429, op. 1, d. 50, ll. 91-92. Sheet metal shop party meeting, 21 September 1926.

115. *Martenovka*, 12 December 1926.

116. TsAODM, f. 80, op. 1 , d. 224, l. 1. Proletarskii district party report, January 1927.

117. TsAODM, f. 429, op. 1, d. 40, ll. 121-2, 162. General party meetings, 16 October, 29 December 1926.

118. TsMAM, f. 176, op. 2, d. 692, ll. 9, 15. Factory general meetings, 10 February and 7 October 1927.

119. TsMAM, f. 176, op. 2, d. 821, l. 3; d. 692, ll. 6, 15-16. General meetings, 10 February 1927.

120. RGASPI, f. 17, op. 85, d. 67, l. 16. MK information summary, n.d. 1926.

121. *Martenovka*, 7 November 1925.

122. TsMAM, f. 176, op. 2, d. 455, ll. 8, 11. Factory general meetings, 6 July and 14 September 1926.

123. TsAODM, f. 429, op. 1, d. 80, l. 21. Closed general party meeting, 18 May 1927.

124. RGASPI, f. 17, op.85, d. 237, l. 55. MK information summary, May 1927.

125. *Martenovka*, 23 December 1926; 11 November 1927.

126. TsAODM, f. 429, op. 1, d. 80, l. 21. Open party meeting, 26 May 1927.

127. TsAODM, f. 429, op. 1, d. 80, ll. 24-5. Open party meeting, 8 June 1927.

128. TsAODM, f. 429, op. 1, d. 56, l. 27; dd. 56, 80. Party bureau report, September 1927; Party meetings, 1927.

129. RGASPI, f. 17, op. 85, d. 237, l. 75. MK information summary, August 1927.

130. TsAODM, f. 429, op. 1, d. 74, l. 18. Ivan Zhirov recantation, 29 December 1927 with a note that he wrote an earlier version in October 1927.

131. TsAODM , f. 429, op. 1, d. 80, l. 28. Closed general party meeting, 29 May 1927.

132. *The Platform* was less convincing on how to pay for a program that called the regime's proposed industrial expansion of 4 to 9 percent "pessimistic." As Michal Reiman has argued, the Opposition document misjudged the accumulated wealth of better off sections of the population. *Challenge of the Left Opposition, 1926-27*, 301-394. Reiman, *The Birth of Stalinism*, 30.

133. Leon Trotsky, *My Life* (New York, 1930), 531-2.

134. GARF, f. 7952, op. 3, d. 275, l. 76. S.S. Leshkovtsev memoir.

135. TsAODM, f. 80, op. 1, d. 276, l. 12. Rogozhsko-Simonovskii party summary, 24 October 1927.

136. TsAODM, f. 3, op. 8, d. 92, ll. 44-5. MK information summary, November 1927.

137. TsAODM, f. 429, op. 1, d. 56, ll. 41-2. Closed party meeting 28 October 1927.
138. TsAODM, f. 429, op. 1, d. 56, l. 59. Open party meeting, 18 November 1927.
139. RGASPI, f. 17, op. 85, d. 67, l. 27. MK information summery, summer 1926.
140. RGASPI, f. 17, op. 85, d. 237, ll. 63, 69, 71. MK information summary, summer 1927.
141. TsAODM, f. 429, op. 1, d. 56, ll. 60-1. Party meeting, 18 November 1927.
142. TsAODM, f. 429, op. 1, d. 56, l. 62. Party meeting, 18 November 1927.
143. TsAODM, f. 429, op. 1, d. 56, l. 62. Party meeting, 18 November 1927.
144. TsAODM, f. 429, op. 1, d. 56, l. 62. Party meeting, 18 November 1927.
145. TsKhDMO, f. 1, op. 23, d. 662, ll. 99-100. Komsomol information summary, 3 December 1927.
146. TsAODM, f. 80, op. 1, d. 276, l. 12. Rogozhsko-Simonovskii party summary, 25 October 1927.
147. RGASPI, f. 17, op. 85, d. 222, l. 159. TsK information department summary of opposition activity in the Moscow Komsomol, fall 1927.
148. TsAODM, f. 429, op. 1, d. 56, l. 59. Party meeting, 18 November 1927.
149. TsAODM, f. 429 op. 1, d. 74, l. 16. I.F. Naumov recantation letter, 27 December 1927.
150. TsAODM, f. 80, op. 1, d. 276, l. 17. Rogozhsko-Simonovskii party summary, 25 October 1927.
151. TsAODM, f. 429, op. 1, d. 56, l. 57. Party meeting, 18 November 1927.
152. *Martenovka*, 25 November 1927.
153. *Martenovka*, 10 December, 1927.
154. Deutscher, *The Prophet Unarmed*, 389.'
155. TsAODM, f. 429, op. 1, d. 74, ll. 16-18. Naumov and Zhirov recantations, 27 December 1927, 2 January 1928.
156. TsAODM, f. 429, op. 1, d. 74, ll. 16-18. Naumov and Zhirov recantations, 27 December 1927, 2 January 1928.
157. RGASPI, f. 17, op. 71, d. 24, ll. 37, 42, 78. List of individuals expelled for Opposition activity, 1927.
158. Cohen, *Bukharin*, 277.
159. Cohen, *Bukharin*, 296-301.
160. Daniels, *Conscience of the Revolution*, 322-348.
161. TsMAM, f. 176, op. 2, d. 779, l. 27. Factory meeting, 10 October 1928.
162. *Komsomol'skaia pravda*, 6, 11, 14, 29 November, 9 December 1928.
163. *Trud*, 10, 13, 21 November 1928.
164. TsAODM, f. 429, op. 1, d. 92, ll. 8-9. Factory party bureau and control commission, 11 January 1929.
165. *Pravda*, 12 December, 1928.
166. *Trud*, 15 December, 1928.
167. *Trud*, 21 December, 1928.
168. *XVI Konferentsiia VKP(b), aprel' 1929 goda. Stenograficheskii otchet* (Moscow, 1962), 783.
169. TsAODM, f. 429, op. 1, d. 92, ll. 8-11. Bureau and control commission meeting, 11 January 1929.
170. TsAODM, f. 429, op. 1, d. 92, l. 10. Bureau and control commission meeting, 11 January 1929.
171. Hiroaki Kuromiya, *Stalin's Industrial Revolution: Politics and Workers, 1928-1932* (Cambridge, 1988) 27-49.
172. Cohen, *Bukharin*, 312-314.
173. TsMAM, f. 176, op. 2, d. 692. General factory meetings, 1926; d. 821, l. 3, Factory committee report, February 1929.
174. TsAODM, f. 429, op. 1, d. 56, l. 57. Party meeting, 18 November 1927.

6

THE STALINIST COUNTERREVOLUTION
Production for Production's Sake

"The Soviet government does not know how to finish off the workers."
—Workers' discussions in Proletarskii district, May 1931

The changes introduced in factory life under the First Five-Year Plan were easily as transformative as those that had been brought about during the upheaval of 1917, though in many ways they represented the antithesis of the earlier process. These changes were imposed by the state for its own distinct, productivist interests and took direct aim at those institutions of the revolution that nominally had defended workers at the end of NEP. Between 1929 and 1932, factory leaders succeeded in dramatically lowering workers' wages to pay for industrial expansion, forced political dissent underground, and compelled employees to work longer and more often. Yet precisely because the state's rapid industrialization strategy was innately detrimental to the material interests of workers, the regime failed to inculcate the workforce with its productivist values. Ultimately, the state's inability to build institutional structures for its program at the factory level compelled regime loyalists to adopt more coercive measures as substitutes for voluntary political conviction.

The changes in factory life described in this chapter would have been unfathomable, however, without a degree of labor support. Career and material incentives became significant incentives for state loyalists on the shop floor, but a small minority of workers genuinely identified with the state's goals and believed that Stalinism represented the communist ideal. The most significant attribute of loyalists in the workplace, however, was not their self-image as defenders of communism, but rather their social function and their striking isolation from the workplace majority. Stalinists resorted to shaming, browbeating, imposing fines, and authorities occasionally arresting recalcitrant or problematic workers to intimidate the overwhelming majority of those who held out from identifying with the regime's goals. Ultimately, however, the most powerful social engineering weapon in the Stalinist arse-

Notes for this section begin on page 217.

nal was the threat of hunger and the state's control over the food supply. The dire privation caused by collectivization strengthened the regime's position over a workforce that lacked the confidence to resist a comprehensive state offensive. As in the era of the Civil War, the pursuit of individualist rather than collective solutions characterized workers' behavior.

Unlike the Civil War, however, the hardships imposed on workers cannot be attributed to foreign invaders or mercenary armies: the drastic decline in living standards was instead a direct consequence of state policy. The economic debates during NEP had centered on which sections of the economy to develop and how to pay for the expansion, but by the First Five-Year Plan the Stalinist leadership had implemented a strategy of rapid industrialization that the entire peasantry and working class would pay for. As Alec Nove noted, "1933 was the culmination of the most precipitous peacetime decline in living standards known in recorded history," a regression that entailed "mass misery and hunger."[1]

The primary function of Stalinism was to make possible the accumulation of capital for expanding production at the expense of the cultural and material needs of the populace. The very centerpiece of Marx's critique of capitalism was that it demanded the conversion of the greatest possible portion of surplus value extracted from the labor of working people back into the production process. "Accumulation for the sake of accumulation, production for the sake of production: this was the formula in which classical economics expressed the historical mission of the bourgeoisie in period of its domination," he insisted.[2] In the classic application of Marx's framework to the political economy of the Soviet Union itself, Tony Cliff demonstrated that by the advent of the First Five-Year Plan all the central features of capitalism were present in a state no longer committed to socialism: the drive to accumulate capital, a ruling class that controlled the means of production for its own purposes, and the mass exploitation of the working class whose surplus-labor made industrialization possible.[3]

The NEP trajectory away from workers' collective assertion and towards individual solutions accelerated during the First Five-Year Plan. The collapse of solidarity allowed factory management to implement draconian wage reductions. For median income workers (fourth and fifth wage and skill grades), wages increased by only 2 percent at the end of 1928, and the next fiscal year the average monthly wage was lowered from 102 to 98 rubles a month.[4] From 1930 to 1931, the average daily income increased about 2.8 percent. A much larger increase in the last year of the Plan shows that, without inflation, wages had approximately doubled during the Plan.[5] Given fourfold inflation, however, workers' real income declined by half, a figure consistent with several studies on real wages during the period.[6]

Peasant Moscow

A massive influx of former peasants provided the labor resources necessary for the rapid expansion of the working class in Moscow and throughout the

Soviet Union. The industrial working class in Moscow almost tripled, from 186,500 in 1928 to 433,900 in 1932,[7] a rate of growth that surpassed the expansion of the Soviet working class, which doubled from slightly over three million to about six million.[8] Such a rural-to-urban population transfer would have been impossible without direct, coercive state intervention, which drove peasants from their holdings into the industrial centers.[9]

Pushing peasants into the cities was less problematic than getting them to identify with the state's productivist values, however. As Moshe Lewin has argued, the attempt to implement the regime's grandiose plans resulted in a prolonged "social crisis" throughout Soviet society. Particularly trouble-some for the state planners was the attempt to "telescope" rapid industrial-ization with newly arriving semiliterate peasants who had neither the skill level nor the incentive to adapt quickly to factory life. Unimpressed by low wages and barrack life, former peasants moved from job to job in search of better conditions. The societal chaos caused by unprecedented labor turnover wreaked particular havoc in industry. As Lewin has suggested, "The mighty dictatorial government found itself, as a result of its impetuous activity during those early years of accelerated industrialization, presiding over a 'quicksand' society."[10]

The Hammer and Sickle Factory workforce tripled in size during the First Five-Year Plan, from five thousand to fifteen thousand production employees.[11] The majority of new arrivals were either poor or middle-income peasants whose entry en masse into the workforce resulted in a dra-matic decline in skill level and schooling. In 1927, unskilled laborers accounted for only 45 percent of the workforce, but this figure rose annu-ally to reach 79 percent by 1930. Similarly, in 1927, 30.7 percent of new employees entering the factory had four and half or more years of schooling, but by 1930, this figure had dropped to 17 percent.[12] Official figures show that the largest increase in factory laborers was from poor peasants rather than "kulaks." By 1930, 69 percent of new workers in the factory were chil-dren of either poor or middle peasants.[13]

Peasant values clashed repeatedly with the state's productivist ethos and its agrarian policies. As late as July 1929, 60 percent of workers in one large shop still had ties to the countryside.[14] In 1930, 39 percent of nonparty workers owned land and even among party members the land ownership fig-ure was high: 32 percent of Komsomol members, and 20 percent for party members.[15] Strong rural ties influenced workers' responses to the regime's war against the peasantry. An electrical shop discussion noted that workers with ties to the countryside "are not completely healthy politically and con-sider only their own interests."[16] A February 1930 party discussion on "eliminating the kulaks as a class" noted that workers (including party mem-bers), "particularly those with ties to the village," complained about the col-lectivization drive.[17] After bread rationing was introduced, rolling mill operators were reported to "look towards the party with hostility, and they are against collectivization of the village economy."[18] Similarly, in the repair shop, "the majority is tied to the peasantry. We have party members who say: 'There they seize the grain and here they take the rest'.... We still have party members who have not handed over their surplus."[19] The prevalence of "petty-bourgeois" sentiments among metalworkers considered to be in the vanguard of the class coexisted awkwardly with the regime's strident class rhetoric.

Metalworkers were, after all, expected to be in the forefront of the "class war" against suspected kulaks, participating in factory brigades sent to the countryside to expropriate produce and assist in the collectivization drive. Several "revisionist" historians have characterized this campaign as "voluntary," with working-class participation ostensibly demonstrating popular support for Stalinism.[20] In fact, as the campaign in the Hammer and Sickle factory proves, workers participated only under the threat of arrest, and even in its early stages workers were less than enthusiastic. A detachment report from Sredne-Volzhskii Oblast in 1929 suggested serious problems. The Tartar population initially evinced a "cool" attitude toward factory workers, though members claimed that this changed after they had fixed some machines and helped the *kolkhoz* with the harvest. The report noted irregularities with "class" implications: an instructor "from the center" had imposed exorbitant grain demands not only on middle peasants (*seredniki*) but also on poor peasants, and factory observers suggested a more even-handed approach "to preserve the *smychka,* not in words, but in reality, between peasant and worker."[21]

Such misgivings among those workers expected to implement state policy in the countryside were mild compared to the open dissent that would surface in the years that followed during the collectivization drive. In December 1930, the party committee sent six "shameful deserters" to trial for deserting their *kolkhoz* posts.[22] The court apparently let them off lightly: the next spring four more workers again fled during the spring sowing, including three who had been sent to trial several months earlier.[23] In the largest metal factory in the Soviet capital, the level of 'voluntary' support for the regime's collectivization drive was such that several workers apparently favored their chances in the Stalinist court system rather than a return to their duties in the countryside.

Peasant-workers were not a passive section of the working class. During late NEP, *otkhodniki* (seasonal workers) were proportionally more likely to strike than urban industrial workers.[24] Uninitiated in the norms of Stalinist discourse, the new arrivals made statements that were often more openly seditious than those of urban laborers. Thus, in 1931, a group of Hammer and Sickle *otkhodniki* commented on the Manchurian conflict: "Enough deceiving of the Orthodox! We work year-round for nothing. If there is a war, the rear will not be reliable and the same goes for the Red Army, just like the old army when we served faithfully while holding back our resentment."[25] Similarly, the OGPU reported that one recent arrival was less than concerned about the threat of war: "I would rather have a war because I am tired of this regime. There is no meat; there is no bread; there is nothing. There are lines for everything. It is too bad I was stripped bare in the village because I would leave and go there to live."[26]

While far from passive, former peasants held values that frequently clashed with those of many older urban workers. An experienced worker complained to a Rabkrin investigator that "young workers break out of their harness; they should be harnessed back. This is because many peasant elements are not used to work discipline."[27] One experienced worker argued that "many workers have ties with the village and are more interested in their personal household. They view the factory as a source of revenue."[28] That unskilled poor peasants viewed the factory as merely a short-term source of revenue is not surprising: even the lowest wage scales represented an increase in income compared to the deprivations in the countryside.[29]

The hardships of barrack life outweighed the short-term material benefits realized from working in the factory, and worker-peasants voted with their feet by the tens of thousands. The head of the MK, L. Kaganovich, reported that the sanitary and water supply situation "today threatens us with a very large danger and I consider the question of water for Moscow the most extreme and burning issue."[30] Sanitation problems in the city's barracks in the winter of 1931-1932 led to a Moscow Soviet campaign to conduct "the struggle with infectious sickness in the city of Moscow," focusing on unsanitary conditions in city dormitories and barracks.[31] Because of the shortage of adequate housing for the Hammer and Sickle Factory, "workers say that the tempo of industrial construction does not correspond to the tempo of housing construction."[32] Additionally, whereas apartment complexes for the most privileged workers were located adjacent to the factory, many of the new barracks were located in the far eastern edge of Moscow or beyond the city limits, making it difficult and time-consuming to get to work.[33] Moreover, there was a "do-it-yourself" aspect to the housing policy. A shop meeting resolution "on the bad conditions in the dormitories" requested materials for repairing the barracks, while workers pledged to do the repairs "on days of rest and during their free hours."[34] Another worker complained that the "bad life in the barracks affects the work effort. It is damp and children shout, and this does not allow rest after heavy physical labor."[35] Attempting to relieve party leaders of any culpability for provision shortages in the barracks, *Martenovka* reported "A Thousand Workers Living in Barracks Demand Better Supplies."[36] Despite the collective agreement that promised heated barracks for the winter, workers complained about having no heat in the fall of 1932.[37]

If winters were difficult, summer's warmth offered little relief: the wooden barracks around the city were firetraps. Moscow in 1931 was a sprawling shantytown rather than a modern metropolis, with 62 percent of housing made of wood, and 86 percent of housing consisting of one- or two-story dwellings.[38] On 8 August 1932, an MK speaker responded to the "many questions about fires that took place in the last several days in Moscow." The fires damaged four barracks next to the Oil and Gas Factory, and all of the barracks in the Ball Bearing Factory adjacent to the Hammer and Sickle Factory. The speaker blamed extreme heat, dry weather, and wind, but asserted "kulak elements naturally could utilize the situation for spreading fires."[39] *Martenovka* also emphasized a supposed "class" angle to barrack fires, claiming that they "were not natural disasters" but were started "by the hand of class enemies in order to tear at our triumphant socialist construction." Wind direction probably saved the housing of thousands of workers, as the factory newspaper noted a "criminally relaxed attitude towards fire preparation," with a lack of water and fire extinguishers.[40]

Wretched barrack conditions contributed to astronomical labor turnover. Throughout Soviet industry turnover exceeded 100 percent a year from 1929 to 1933.[41] In the relatively privileged Hammer and Sickle Factory, the turnover percentage was only marginally better than the national average, peaking at 94 percent in the 1929-1930 fiscal year and dropping to about 80 percent over the next two years.[42] Some state loyalists wrote off the high turnover as a negative consequence of failing to follow Stalin's directives for industrial success. One such supporter argued, "If we correctly chose our workforce according to his directives, then they would not run away from us. Workers that we pick up from the street could care less about production."[43] But a Rabkrin inspector asserted that the "principal cause of turnover is the shortage of living space." The presence of two thousand workers without permanent living space frequently led to "incidents of spending the night in the shops."[44] Management promised new housing in early 1932, but "there are no dormitories, and no place for workers to live. They began to build them only when the workers arrived."[45] *Rabochaia gazeta* also asserted that the housing crisis caused seven hundred new arrivals to quickly depart. "Why do they stop in the factory for a week or two and then leave? Because the housing situation for workers living in the barracks is extremely foul."[46]

The tens of thousands of former peasants who entered the gates of the Hammer and Sickle Factory brought with them values and work habits antithetical to the state's productivity drive. In failing to provide them with adequate food or housing, factory management undermined its own productivist aim: many workers left after several weeks. Labor turnover severely hampered Soviet productivity, and the state responded with increasingly severe measures aimed at binding workers to their employers, all of which proved ineffectual.[47] One of the few recourses soviet workers maintained was to sell the labor-power as they—rather than the state—deemed appropriate. But as the process of accumulation became paramount in labor relations, paradoxically the Soviet proletariat diverged from the image of the "gravedigger of the ruling class" forecast by Marx and Engels. Far from promoting cohesiveness and unity among the only social force that could have collectively challenged the regime, rapid industrialization led to unprecedented labor turnover that amplified the divisions within the working class.

Shock Work and Socialist Competition

The socialist competition and shock work campaigns were the twin pillars of the state's drive to raise productivity, lower costs, and tighten labor discipline. Socialist competition entailed contractual production challenges between factories, shops, work brigades, or individuals while shock workers were those who consistently exceeded their production norms, usually by "voluntarily" working extra hours.[48] Scholarship based on limited official sources tends to

exaggerate and romanticize the participation of predominantly young workers in the movement.[49]

The state-orchestrated push from above began in April 1929. A *Martenovka*
headline stated that shock brigades embodied "the Model Communist Attitude
Towards Work" and proposed to "Strike at Self-Seeking and Undisciplined
Production. Greetings to the Avant-garde of Socialist Competition!"[50]
Another issue spelled out the purpose of the campaign in unmistakable terms:

> There must be no place in our ranks for loafers, absentee workers, malingerers and
> self-seekers.... Let's organize and conduct a competition under these slogans: for
> a resolute struggle with unexcused absences, drunkenness, slackness and self-seek-
> ing; for better quality of work; for unquestioning fulfillment of production tasks;
> for lowering the costs of production; for raising the productivity of work; for 100
> percent completion of the production program.... Long live socialist competition
> in our factory! Who will be first?[51]

Such exhortations produced few results. In the first arranged competition,
three hundred and twenty workers in the form-casting department challenged
three hundred workers in the construction shop to a "socialist competition"
for the higher production norms. Yet shock brigades collapsed because "the
young enthusiasts smashed against the cold wall of indifference by the shop's
union and party organizations.... Having barely had time to form, the
brigade fell apart under the prevailing unfavorable situation." One shock
worker claimed that although they entered work "as they would a bloody battle," the brigades fell apart after several weeks because of a shortage of effective tools. After more than two months of intensive propaganda, *Martenovka*
complained that the majority of shops were still in the planning stages, ridiculing shop leaders for having "No Time to Think about Competition."[52]

The early phase of shock work met with both active and passive shop-floor
resistance. Hopes of financial rewards helped entice the few participants.
Competitions between brigades in the rolled metal shop and similar departments in Dneprostoi and Ural factories offered "several tens of thousands of
rubles" for the winners. *Martenovka* announced 5,000-ruble bonuses for the
best workers and offered to send twenty-two workers to shock worker con-
gresses. Yet workers in the cable shop complained that if they entered socialist competition "all of us would be overstrained" and criticized the
anti-alcohol aspect of the campaign: "What do they make wine for if not to
drink?" By September, competition in the construction shop was reported to
exist "only on paper." One participant complained that other workers "try to
criticize and discredit us shock workers," and another lamented that "everywhere there is snickering and jokes about the shock brigades." *Martenovka*
asserted that "class aliens" were responsible for undermining the brigades'
efforts, but then castigated the party cells, shop union bureaus, technical
staff, and administration for their lackadaisical support for shock workers.
"Hooligan incidents" and "open sabotage" against the brigades included
physical threats against shock workers.[53] In November, "the resolution about
socialist competition between shops exists only on paper. In practice, this has

not been brought to life."[54] By December, factory party leaders acknowledged, "Workers do not enter into shock work because they are afraid it will lower pay." Moreover, "party members and candidates provide poor leadership in these campaigns."[55]

This reluctance to join the shock worker movement in 1929 is consistent with reports from around the Soviet Union, which indicate that older, skilled workers led the resistance. In the nearby AMO factory, hostility towards the shock workers was so great that the plant's party committee had to stop publicizing participants' names to protect them from attacks from other workers.[56] *Martenovka* repeatedly exaggerated the number of Hammer and Sickle workers involved in shock brigades, yet even the official figure (368 of more than 8,000 workers) near the end of 1929 illustrates the failure of the campaign and suggests that firmer measures were needed to compel participation.[57]

The movement started in earnest at the end of 1929, when the Komsomol and party leaders pushed for 100 percent membership participation in shock work. Yet even after the campaign was initiated, the party criticized the bolt shop cell, where only 20 percent of communists and 10 percent of Komsomol members participated.[58] In the eyes of state loyalists, neutrality implied resistance. In an article entitled "Who is Not With Us is Against Us," technical personnel in the steel foundry shop challenged other department specialists to declare themselves shock workers.[59] The threat of party purges supported the increasingly strident propaganda for increased productivity in late 1929 and early 1930.[60] *Martenovka* argued that one "Who Refuses to Help Competition is an Enemy of the Working Class," and focused attention on a single shop leader during the mini-purge. Asked about the development of competition in his shop, he responded, "We have worked through this question in the cell and union bureau and we explained it to the masses. But I myself do not compete."[61]

Several thousand workers declared themselves shock workers in early 1930, giving the impression that the combination of party threats and material incentives succeeded, at last, in expanding the state-orchestrated initiative. During the first three months, the number of shock workers rose from 891 to 3,452 workers. Official figures reveal the large but limited pool of workers that could be threatened and cajoled by the party machine. In April just 111 more workers joined the shock brigades.[62] Almost two months later, only another 137 had joined the movement.[63] Management distributed bonuses to particular shops, brigades, and individuals. On the whole, however, brigade and personal compensation were minimal, and often recipients were pressured to hand over their bonuses to other political causes. Career advancement, rather than immediate monetary rewards, was more significant for ambitious workers. In early January 1930, *Martenovka* stated that only the best shock workers would represent the soviets, shop committees, and factory committees.[64]

The productivity drive signaled the end of the factory committee as a democratic proletarian institution and the destruction of the last semblance of workers' control. Factory committees had outlived the Soviets and had given workers some control over the process of production throughout NEP. By early 1930, the extremely tenuous last link with 1917 in the workplace was unceremoniously severed. In early March, the editors of *Za industrial-izatsiiu* and *Trud* held meetings in the Hammer and Sickle and other factories in support of exclusively shock-worker factory committees.[65] Thirteen years (almost to the day) after the factory committee was created to defend workers' interests, it was formally transformed into its opposite: a management tool for raising productivity, working longer hours, and lowering costs. In the spring of 1930 shock workers replaced 80 percent of factory committees nationally and 51 percent in Moscow.[66]

The numerical expansion of shock work in early 1930 provided an illusion of success. In some shops "shock workers work worse than non-shock workers," including two brigades in the bolt shop that fulfilled only 45 and 63 percent of their production norms.[67] The problem was serious enough to compel *Martenovka* to rail repeatedly against the appearance of "false shock workers." By the end of March, five hundred of six hundred workers in the bolt shop supposedly participated in the campaign, but some workers "do not even know what competition is." A few weeks later, shock workers in the bolt and rolled metal shops "shamed" the entire factory because shock work existed "only on paper." The nightshift in the bolt shop included 180 communists and 130 Komsomol members but "how many of them participate in competition? Nobody knows." On May Day, the newspaper called for "unmasking" dozens of false shock workers who were accused of disrupting the industrial-financial plan by their drunkenness and absenteeism.[68] In June, an *aktiv* group investigating problems in the factory claimed that "even up to this time almost nobody knows their rights and obligations, especially the workers who recently arrived."[69]

"Shock work is not popular among workers," the NKVD was forced to acknowledge. In the nearby Dinamo factory, workers had complained that "socialist competition is exploitation," and in the Raiz factory workers suggested it was "necessary to start by feeding workers and then develop industry." In the Hammer and Sickle bolt department the Komsomol brigade reportedly collapsed altogether. In the architectural shop no shock brigades ever formed, ostensibly because of "a manifestation of self-seeking attitude by communists toward work." "Tailist" communists in the form-casting shop sided with their co-workers who refused the administration's demand to liquidate a blockage in the pouring process, while the shop's Komsomol cell was reportedly on "the brink of collapse."[70] In May, *Martenovka* reported "the death of shock tempo" in mill number two along with incidents of party members ridiculing young shock workers. A skilled worker mocked a shock worker who had loaned the state money and then needed overtime work: "You've come to earn some extra, eh? You signed up for a 1,500-ruble bond and now you have nothing to eat?"[71]

Even among the more ardent supporters of the movement, the extensive and incessant overtime led to demoralization. The few functioning brigades in the summer of 1929 worked twelve- and thirteen-hour days along with holidays, but by September they had not received their promised vacation time.[72] Almost a year later, a factory representative at an oblast union meeting reported on the disorganization in the brigades and complained, "We cannot continue in this way any longer. What kind of workers would those be who worked year round without a day off? The fellows are offended.... We are still poorly prepared. We are swimming."[73]

The next phase of the movement was launched in the second half of 1930 and continued into 1931, when rationing bonuses drew workers into the brigades in large numbers. Economic necessity rather than worker enthusiasm drove the expansion of the movement. As Donald Filtzer has argued, it was "the existence of dire scarcity that gave the shock work system its force."[74] Ration books played an integral role in the extensive expansion of shock work, as food proved superior to either propaganda or terror in furthering the state's attempts at social engineering. "What work we have done against absenteeism," boasted a Hammer and Sickle leader to the Komsomol leadership about his group's efforts to discipline workers: "If one is absent a single day without just cause, the shock worker book is taken away for three months. If one misses two days in a row then the title of shock worker and the book are taken away for six months. On the book cover we stamp 'false shock worker.'"[75] *Martenovka* warned that shock worker cards had been issued only for those who fulfilled their production norms and participated in political work. In October 1930, rolled metal shop workers complained that they had converted themselves to shock work, but had not received their bonuses as had been promised at the factory conference.[76] After repeated, frantic demands that workers fulfill the production quota for March 1931, *Martenovka* screamed that "April did Not Start with a Shock" and complained that not a single shop had completed its allocated output on the first day of the new month.[77] By June 1931, the absurdly exaggerated percentage of shock workers had dropped slightly, from 83.9 to 78.9 percent, and the party bureau blamed the decrease on "weak leadership."[78] By September 1931, eleven (of thirteen) thousand workers were supposedly involved in shock work, but Rabkrin condemned an "impersonal approach to this activity" and criticized the party, union, and management.[79]

State officials searched for scapegoats to blame for the many problems within the movement. In March 1931, *Rabochaia gazeta* accused the factory committee and Komsomol of "opportunism" in the socialist competition because over two thousand socialist competition agreements existed "only on paper," and it proposed that the leaders be brought before a revolutionary production tribunal.[80] In June 1931, district party leaders admitted that socialist competition and shock work frequently existed "only on paper" and cited the steel wire shop in the Hammer and Sickle as an example. However, the discussion also cited the "heroic" work of some communists and Komsomol members in meeting norms in the factory.[81] While the party was able to exhort members to exert themselves for short bursts at the end of extra production quarters, such methods could not be sustained.

By the summer of 1931, shock work expanded to most of the workforce, but with provision shortages the distribution of incentives suffered. In August 1931, the Komsomol Central Committee reported problems issuing extra pay for exemplary shock workers, with many factories failing to issue bonuses for three to five months. In the Hammer and Sickle Factory, management distributed only single ruble bonuses and one shop added an amendment to the collective agreement, blaming the shop administration for underproduction.[82] The next month, Rabkrin again reported that many workers in the hot shops did not receive their bonus rewards.[83]

Two years after its inception, the shock worker movement was still plagued with problems. In June 1931, *Martenovka* acknowledged the need to have "better supplies to encourage the shock tempo."[84] Two months later the OGPU reported that the shortage of meat fostered indignation among a group of workers in the rolled metal shop: "Our organizations only know how to demand that we participate in shock work and socialist competition, but they have no interest in how well the workers eat. The wife spends the whole day on line but she returns home empty-handed because there is no meat in the ZRK [Closed Workers' Cooperative]."[85] A Rabkrin inspector complained that planning brigades "are nearly non-functioning." In September of Stalinism's "third and decisive year" of the Plan, one worker informed the inspector of the widespread notion that "it is impossible to raise discipline."[86]

Supply shortages meant that privileges had to be readjusted in late 1931. "The existing opinion that shock worker books are added supply cards is fundamentally incorrect," *Martenovka* explained. A new, special card was issued for produce and goods, and this "preferential supply is for our best shock workers." The strict conditions for the new cards included a three-month fulfillment of production obligations, voluntary public work, and perfect attendance. One of the "best soldiers for socialism" proudly declared, "I always receive a card for the best shock work."[87]

Only a small minority of workers ever qualified for the economic privileges of the selective group of "best shock workers." *Martenovka* announced that these workers would no longer have to stand in line at the factory store, and that one-quarter of all goods in short supply would be set aside for them. Fifty new apartments with showers and ovens were earmarked for the best shock workers, and custom-made coats and suits were also exclusively preserved for this exemplary section of the workforce. In June 1932, 15,000 rubles were distributed to the two best shock brigades in the electrical shop, and to brigades in mill number one in the rolled metal shop.[88] Of five hundred workers in the food cooperative, only twenty-two were considered "the best shock workers," and only four party members participated in competition.[89] Similarly, in the summer of 1932, only twenty-seven Komsomol members in the first mill of the rolled metal shop received best shock worker cards but none in three other mills. *Martenovka* complained that weak shop discipline was "the fault of the Komsomol members" who needed "to pay more attention to loafers."[90] Even the few who fulfilled their quotas were unenthusiastic:

At the beginning of the month, cards were issued and they went to the ZRK and received canned goods and manufactured items, but after that they forgot about their shock worker obligations. The best shock workers enjoy enormous advantages. They receive advantages in consumer items, trips to health resorts, living quarters, rest homes, and finally, they are in the leading ranks in education. It is hard to enumerate all these rights. These rights correspond to the enormous responsibilities of shock workers in the shop.[91]

Material and career incentives substituted for political conviction among a small milieu of exemplary workers, but limited entry into the new clique produced a phenomenon of "best shock worker envy." The party expelled two "opportunist" members who repeatedly spoke up against the distribution of goods to the best shock workers and agitated in a cell meeting against the bonus pay system.[92] A factory guard apprehended a communist for stealing fish intended for the best shock workers.[93] Only 20 percent of new housing in Moscow had gas, including "the house of shock workers" for elite Hammer and Sickle workers.[94] One worker complained that "shock workers are great, but why should they be given apartments? Many of our communists live in mansions while others live in barracks full of holes. Maybe we could take a room from each of these mansions for those from the barracks without apartments."[95]

The illusion of support for shock work in the Hammer and Sickle Factory differed little from that in other factories throughout the Soviet Union. At the 1932 Komsomol Congress, speakers repeatedly applauded the enthusiasm of young workers who were in the forefront of the movement. Yet even among these select delegates, supposedly the most ardent base for Stalinism, support was suspect. Nine delegates sent a letter to *Pravda* and *Izvestiia* that ridiculed the proceedings:

> We arrived here from the factories and mills, but our families are going hungry there. Yes, hungry and going without clothes. Our amateurish politicians have brought the country extreme impoverishment. "Workers' material situation is getting better." Yes, better with dry bread and water and sometimes cabbage. You are all parasites, parasites worse than Tsarist bureaucrats and self-seekers. This is the state you have brought the worker. We are hungry and cannot work until we are given bread, meat, housing, and clothes. In our factory there is a breakdown—only 55 percent fulfillment of the plan. We say that in the next month there will not be even that much. We will not work—we cannot stand by our benches hungry and cold. We refuse to work.
>
> Nine People.[96]

The Bureaucratic Leviathan and the Illusion of Worker Support

The numerical expansion of the party was remarkable during the First Five-Year Plan as membership tripled to twenty-one hundred at the end of 1932.[97] Figures for the Komsomol are even more impressive. By July 1931, youth and Komsomol were almost synonymous, with 3,983 of 4,132 young workers holding membership.[98] These figures bestow some credibility to the notion of broad-based labor support for Stalinism.

The membership numbers are deceptive, however. The annual number of workers joining the party from 1929 to 1932 (136, 265, 1,525, and 706 respectively) shows that the rift between workers and the party continued in 1929 and 1930, but that a significant change occurred in 1931. The mass recruitment during the 1931 Soviet election campaign was later castigated because it allowed in "many alien elements."[99] During the elections, workers merely signed statements, such as "I join the party," "I join the Komsomol," and "I join the union" that led to mere "paper growth."[100] According to one memoir, the mass recruitment from 1931 to 1933 led to the purge of "a large number of alien elements."[101]

No evidence indicates that employees suddenly became impressed with the very state strategy whose most palpable result was a sharp deterioration in living standards, but the mass recruitment does illustrate a qualitative change in workers' attitudes and their accommodation to the factory regime. Employees recognized the educational and monetary advantages involved in joining the only civic organization in the factory offering career advancement. The number of workers promoted from the bench into state positions was substantial—660,000 from 1931 to 1933, or between 10 and 15 percent of the industrial working class.[102] Significantly, in an effort to build a loyal party apparatus, the party tended to promote members with no memory of party disputes during the Revolution, Civil War, or even NEP. In October 1930, the factory party secretary Gaidul' was promoted to head the *raikom* and his post in the factory was filled by 25-year-old Filatov.[103] By early 1932, half of all Moscow secretaries had been members only since 1928.[104]

Corruption, incompetence, and lethargy persisted in the factory party organization. Five general party meetings in the first half-year of the Plan drew only 290, 441, 280, 428 and 228 participants, out of between seven hundred and eight hundred members.[105] Due to "weak party leadership" in the architectural shop, "the questions of socialist competition, growth of production, and cleansing the party, were almost not touched on at all."[106] In December 1929, the factory party committee had to replace the entire leadership in the shop because of "a lack of development of self-criticism, squabbling among leaders, shoppism, self-seeking and a tailist mood."[107] In late 1929, bolt shop party leaders acknowledged that work discipline had fallen and that even party members "drink and have a bad attitude towards social responsibilities." A female party leader complained that "little attention is devoted to women's work," while another member complained of rampant alcoholism, noting that workers "bring wine into the shop." One member lamented, "comrades, we talk a lot, but we do very little."[108]

Chronic problems in the factory party organization continued in 1930. In the steel foundry shop, only two of the nine bureau members regularly attended their meetings, the shop cell displayed little discipline, and members complained: "Not to drink is impossible." Moreover, "the nonparty *aktiv* display an unhealthy attitude towards the cell. They say that in the shop self-criticism is suppressed."[109] In March, the Control Commission criticized the railway shop work because "party and professional organizations are weak."[110] In the ZRK, Komsomol members ridiculed their cell secretary: "Do not even bother asking Esin; he will not do anything."[111]

The no-holds-barred recruitment strategy of 1931, like the Lenin Levy seven years earlier, exacerbated party problems. A party leader asserted that "the main cause for not completing the production program was, along with a whole number of production blunders, the inability of party, administration, and trade union organization in the shops to mobilize the working masses."[112] By August 1931, a Rabkrin inspector described "a massive breach" of party discipline and complained that "the party organization has done nothing to strengthen discipline." Problems included nonpayment of membership dues, fighting during work, sleeping during night work, not attending party meetings, and a thoughtless attitude towards party obligations.[113]

Reports show that even with fifteen full-time organizers, the factory party organization in 1932 was in a state of disarray. By June, the party claimed 3,117 members and candidates organized into fifty-eight cells, with fifteen paid full-time organizers trying to keep the apparatus operating. A report tacitly acknowledged the paper nature of the membership when the promotion and scattering of *aktiv* in the shops left the ranks thin, a remarkable admission given that seven thousand party and Komsomol members were supposedly ready to fill the void. A member complained that "we have no clarification about work among members and candidates on questions of the day" and a disorganization of the shop *aktiv*. In addition to members not understanding the decisions of the plenum, he admitted the "occurrences of an antiparty mood."[114] One member who was singled out in May became indignant at the selectively applied double standard, and stated that he "cannot and will not accept any assignments."[115] In July, a form-casting shop member asserted, "In general we now have no political leadership in the shop" and a member in the steel foundry shop warned, "Our work now has totally halted."[116] Factory party leaders condemned the party work in August as "totally unsatisfactory," since it had allowed the allotted time for six hundred candidate members to merely lapse.[117] In the second mill of the rolled metal shop, "the cell completely collapsed." This was supposedly the fault of the leader: "Orlov is the cell secretary. He does nothing."[118] In November the party expelled five red managers for "repeated collective drinking and appearing at work in an inebriated state."[119] Notes to the new party secretary show that authorities had removed and possibly arrested a layer of factory cadres in 1932. One note asked, "Tell us Comrade Kul'kov, why do we have such awful suppression of self-criticism in the district? All the *aktiv* were removed so does that mean that all those communists were scoundrels?"[120]

Such purges became endemic to the Stalinist system, which could not overcome the structural problems of rapid industrialization with a workforce overwhelmingly resentful of state policy. Fifteen years earlier, a handful of talented Bolsheviks had been able to carry the argument against a compromise with capitalism, for striking against the Provisional Government, for armed defense of the revolution, and for Soviet power. Bolshevism was able to do so because the revolutionary strategy connected with workers' political aspirations. In 1932, a full-time staff of party functionaries could not push seven thousand party, candidate, and Komsomol members to identify with its aims. Their fundamental problem was that the movement they attempted to lead was directly antithetical to workers' interests.

Stalinist Campaigns: State Bonds

Shock work, socialist competition, and sending workers to the countryside to force peasants into collective farms were all state-initiated coercive campaigns to extract surplus for industrialization. State Bonds was another coercive campaign to accumulate capital. The pressure tactics used to extract a month's pay from almost every employee show that the loans had more in common with Mafia extortion than with revolutionary élan.

In 1928, the party initiated the first of many "loans for industrialization," in which a month's wage was exchanged for a bond note. *Martenovka* depicted departments that raced ahead in procuring the loans as planes or trains, and shops that lagged behind as tortoises or snails. Workers who refused to participate could expect to see their names on "the black board," while the best saw their names on the "red board" because "the best should be known by the entire factory, and the rest should measure themselves against them." The stick, however, played a more prominent role than the carrot and there was no room for neutrality, as party members were expected to pressure nonparticipants. "These workers do not understand that the loan increases the tempo of construction," which meant that "it is the task of every worker not only to sign up for the bond, but to also sign up less-conscious workers for a month's wage."[121]

Workers never received returns on these bonds, which were effectively an additional 8 percent wage cut. In 1929, a black market for the bonds developed and *Martenovka* accused workers of selling their holdings. Party leaders placed their notes in storage in an attempt to give confidence to the loans. One member missed the political significance of the campaign when he claimed that he had "signed up for the loan specifically in order to save up for a suit," and the factory newspaper responded, "Nothing can be expected from such turncoats—they should be relentlessly hounded out of the party."[122]

By 1929, the bond campaign became tied to larger political causes, such as the border conflict with China. Shock brigades often signed together in response to political campaigns or to denounce those who abstained, but larger contributions of several months' pay were almost always signed individually.[123] Strong-arm tactics first focused on the thousands of party members. The repair shop cell expelled a member for his refusal to contribute and failure to pay his membership dues.[124] Another member in the same shop was expelled for refusing to sign up for the loan, supposedly telling another member that "work under the Tsar paid better" and "before, the owner had a better attitude towards his worker." He asserted, "The TsK resolution does not apply to me. I signed up for what I could afford."[125] The party expelled another member in 1931 for "categorically refusing" to sign up for the loan, speaking out "against the high tempo of building socialism, and exhibiting the worst kind of right opportunism in practice." Members who had not signed up were singled out for "hiding in the bushes." Only after members were pressured into signing up were nonparty workers cajoled. *Martenovka* described several "deserters" against the loan, one of whom was against socialist competition and "all measures of the party and Soviet state." He was supposedly heard saying with clenched teeth, "You masters, fuck you. All you know is begging and asking for money."[126]

Shop percentages of contributions for 1930 demonstrate the dynamic of the movement. At the beginning of the campaign *Martenovka* printed the names of seventy-one workers who collectively contributed fifteen thousand rubles. Only a month later, after the party had brought pressure on its own members, did the quantitative reports start to appear in the newspaper. By July, 53.8 percent of workers had contributed to 64 percent of the goal. After two more weeks of incessant propaganda, 68 percent of the workforce had contributed 82 percent of the goal, but only the electrical shop attained 100 percent. In some large departments the majority of workers had yet to contribute. *Martenovka* then pressured the factory committee to send shock brigades into five lagging departments in order to harangue nonpartici-pants. Three weeks later, all but two shops had reached 100 percent. Thus, the party campaign first targeted its own members, a small minority of whom made extraordinary contributions. Only after two months of arm-twisting tactics, in which the most outspoken critics were singled out, was the goal achieved.[127]

Political redemption was offered for those who were willing to acknowledge past errors. In early 1928, a Trotskyist supporter claimed the bonds were being used "to feed the bureaucrats and pay for the Tsarist debt."[128] However, he later contributed five hundred rubles to the campaign and was pictured on the front page of the factory newspaper. In an article entitled "Rebuff the Whin-ers the Bolshevik Way," a female worker wrote, "on 13 June in the pages of *Martenovka* it was written that my speaking out played into the hands of the class enemy. I acted incorrectly and now I understand this."[129]

Shop union meetings repeatedly rammed through motions in favor of the bonds with limited resistance. The boldest dissidents spoke for the silent majority, but they also lacked the cohesion to challenge the state campaign. At the beginning of the second year of the loans, a party leader complained about "right opportunist wavering" among members on the bond issue.[130] After all shops matched or exceeded their goals in 1930, the factory news-paper ridiculed an "opportunist kulak" who had claimed that "nobody would sign up for it" and another worker who claimed that "only fools vote for the loan."[131]

Reports show continued but weakened resistance to the bond campaign in 1931. District party leaders noted "incidents of tailism" among workers, party and Komsomol members in the loan campaign in the Hammer and Sickle Factory.[132] The next day, the factory newspaper called on the union to "get busy" against a particular worker who had agitated against the loans, claiming "he is always against whatever campaign is initiated in the shop."[133]

A week later a party meeting acknowledged it had conducted weak work in realizing the state loans.[134] A previously expelled member conducted "anti-Soviet" agitation during the bond campaign by suggesting in a shop meeting that the party was "not making the country better but worse." A factory guard revealed the nature of the campaign when he complained that "you forcibly make guards subscribe to the loans."[135]

The annual bond drive displayed all the attributes of other Stalinist campaigns. Bureaucratically organized from above, the loans relied on a tiny but hardened group of state loyalists to sign up for extraordinary contributions, then proceeded to harangue other party members under the threat of expulsion, and finally to cajole nonparty workers. *Martenovka* devoted less attention to the sixth campaign in 1932 and the factory again met its goals, suggesting that the practice had conditioned workers and worn down resistance.

The Cultural Counterrevolution

In a surreal attempt to deflect attention from its assault on the working class, Stalinism revived the "class war" rhetoric of the Civil War. Special emphasis was aimed at the "Cultural Front" and much of this propaganda was targeted at specialists, bureaucrats, kulaks, and the clergy.[136] The Cultural Revolution in the workplace invoked military metaphors, such as "Into Battle for Culture!" *Martenovka* called for 50 percent of all workers to study "in full battle preparation" to provide sufficient cadres for production. The newspaper also explained that "the first duty of the best industrial shock workers is for every shock worker to be a soldier in the cultural army."[137] Moreover, the factory would not just participate in this battle:

> The Hammer and Sickle Factory is the
> Leading Detachment on the Front of the Cultural Revolution
>
> … What tasks in the cultural-political work stand before our factory? The first and main task: all cultural-political work should be subject to an even greater degree to the fulfillment of the financial industrial plan of the factory. All forms and methods—old and new—must be utilized in mobilizing workers in the completion of the industrial financial plan.[138]

Thus, the Cultural Revolution was primarily geared toward raising productivity. The cultural commission of the Lys'venski challenged the Hammer and Sickle and several other factories in early 1929 and explained how cultural work would be integrated into socialist competition. Cultural work was expected to include shop placards such as red boards for overachievers and black boards for underachievers, diagrams with obligations and percent fulfillment, production evening galas against absenteeism and waste, rewards of free film tickets for shock workers, and show trials organized for those guilty of waste in production.[139]

The cultural commission attempted to implement these activities in 1929. Red corners provided diagrams showing fulfillment of the production plan per shop; agitation brigades were sent "into battle" in fourteen departments; and an "evening for victors" was organized at the factory club.[140] Judged on its own terms—tying its success with that of socialist competition—the cultural commission's propaganda for the Cultural Revolution was a failure.

Shop-floor cultural campaigns gained little resonance among workers or Komsomol members, the supposed champions of the Cultural Revolution.[141] In September 1929, several party speakers called for show trials of Komsomol leading members because they "have a careless attitude towards the campaign against illiteracy." Moreover, because of "many disorders" in the youth-dominated club, "workers do not rest, but get irritable."[142] In October 1929, party leaders complained that Komsomol members were not participating in union work, were against the continuous workweek (five days on, then one off), and were more interested in dancing than in production issues.[143] In September 1930, *Martenovka* admitted: "nobody in our factory would deny that we have breaks in the lines of the cultural front," and described this breach as of "a chronic character." A February 1932 article argued that "Red Corners Have Turned into Sleeping Quarters." One shop leader admitted, "We do conduct work, but very rarely."[144] Even simple tasks proved too much of a nuisance, and by the end of the summer, wall newspapers had not been put up in the shops for more than a month.[145]

The antireligious campaign was no more successful than the explicitly productivist aspect of the Cultural Revolution. In early 1929, the party fraction of Godless reported that the majority of members still displayed a careless attitude toward antireligious propaganda.[146] Before Easter 1929, *Martenovka* charged: "Priests Agitate but the Godless are Silent." The newspaper noted that only fifteen Godless were active and complained that only forty rubles of the six-four thousand-ruble cultural budget were dedicated to Godless work.[147] In the construction shop discussion on religion and collectivization "we have many communists who take a beating in questions with nonparty workers."[148] Party leaders had to carry the work of the anti-Easter campaign in 1930 because "in the shop cells the Godless are not popular."[149]

Despite more strident antireligious rhetoric, many members continued to live a double life. At the end of 1930, a report noted that two-thirds of Hammer and Sickle workers' marriages took place in the church.[150] *Martenovka* remarked that a leading member of the cultural commission "is not a bad communist in production, but at home he has hung an icon with a lamp in the left corner of the room." The newspaper asked, "How can he conduct the antireligious Easter campaign?"[151]

Work schedule changes aimed at increasing productivity were perhaps the most disruptive change to workers' lives. The transition to a continuous workweek along with expanded night shifts, met with resentment and resistance. In the repair shop, the continuous workweek noted "many objections from workers," particularly among Komsomol members.[152] A report on party work during the First Five-Year Plan noted worker opposition to abolishing summer holidays and "even more considerable resistance" to the continuous workweek.[153] The chairman of the VTsSPS (Gausman) admitted the problems at a factory cultural commission meeting:

> Now the class struggle is particularly noticeable. We have data that Menshevik newspapers are spreading rumors that Soviet power is depriving workers of their holidays. Different sects are also speaking against the continuous workweek. Up to now we have not given a clear idea to workers about the nonstop production.[154]

Workers complained about the implementation of extended shift work precisely because they did have a clear idea of the implications of "continuous production." Two Komsomol members agitated against shift work because "night is for sleep, not work" and attempted to organize an illegal meeting at the factory. *Martenovka* accused the agitators of forming a "right opportunist bloc with counterrevolutionary Trotskyists."[155] Komsomol members in the form-casting shop organized similar resistance and were labeled as "Those who Act in the Interests of the Class Enemy" because they also allegedly argued against collectivization and socialist competition.[156] A cultural commission speaker admitted that after the implementation of night work, "workers have a bad attitude towards our party and government."[157] The state succeeded in forcing large numbers of workers to appear for night work, but failed to get them to adapt to the new conditions. A party leader lamented about the night shift in February 1930 that "people stand around doing nothing, saying that there is nothing to do. In the electrical shop they read newspapers. In the rolled metal shop one inebriated person walks around the furnaces in circles."[158]

Martenovka connected the continuous workweek with the campaign against religion, calling for an end to church holidays and for only the revolutionary days off. The new schedule ended the regular Saturday and Sunday break and appears to have caused widespread resentment. One worker argued that "it is Sunday that is dear to us, not some kind of Wednesday. This is just mocking religion. Of course, I'm not talking about myself. A holiday for me is when I have money in my pocket and I am relaxing." A female worker argued that "it would be bad if we do not have Sundays off because everyone is in a holiday mood.... Generally, I do not see anything good about it." Another worker complained that the shortened break meant he would not have time to return to his village.[159] During the transition to the continuous workweek, cultural commission speakers implied that sectarians were winning the cultural battle. One leader argued that "the sectarians are awake but our leadership organizations are asleep."[160] *Rabochaia gazeta* claimed that fewer Hammer and Sickle workers were absent than usual on old Christmas, and that many employees had attended antireligious evenings on the sixth and seventh of January.[161] However, *Martenovka* reported many unexcused absences during old Christmas, including fifty-three in the steel foundry shop.[162]

More strident antireligious propaganda in the spring of 1930 stressed the connection with productivity: "On Easter Days: Not One Absentee! The Struggle against Religion is the Struggle for the Five-Year Plan!" Before the holiday, "class aliens" spread rumors that the May Day celebration would be celebrated on the sixth through tenth of May to coincide with Easter.[163] Such "rumors" reflected workers' resentment, which was spelled out in clear terms in a note to a speaker at an unspecified factory in the district in early 1931:

> Comrades, thank you all very much for everything. I hope the devil takes you. Everything you say is a lie. Once a month you give rotten spoiled potatoes, but not even soap for the families. If we could have only one day like before—everything one needed used to be available. But now you only know how to rob the peasants, break down churches, and put all good people in jail. You bastards, you are all bandits.... You do not give rest to the living or the dead. I request that you read this. You only write how bad it is abroad and how good it is here. You come at night like bandits and take away father and child. You totally ruined all the peasants, broke all the churches, and lie all the time.[164]

The 1931 anti-Easter campaign was more successful. Church-influenced holidays were "particularly strong among workers with ties to the village" and *Martenovka* suggested a broad campaign that "explains the counterrevolutionary essence of religion and specifically the Easter holiday." An exemplary shock brigade, in an article entitled "Against Easter—For Shock Tempo," declared that they would not be late, would not drink, and would work at a shock tempo, and called on others to do the same. Workers were implored to "Tear the Spider-Web of Religious Lies. Let's Offer a Bolshevik Shock Tempo of Work in Answer to the Priests' Holiday. Let's Greet the Preachers' Holiday Fully Armed. Not a Single Absentee or Lateness During Easter Days." Arm-twisting and threats, rather than propaganda, ensured a successful campaign. Only sixty-nine "loafers" failed to appear for work on Easter 1931, and the newspaper called for a more stringent form of punishment than simply printing their names: "Send those who Undermine the Industrial-Financial Plan to Court."[165]

Antireligious work was no different from other aspects of a Cultural Revolution that was inextricably aimed at raising productivity. The state's victory in compelling employees to work through Easter by no means represented a triumph over religious beliefs, particularly as the factory was inundated with recent arrivals from the countryside. *Martenovka* was particularly concerned with women and the thousands of former peasants, because they "are the raw material which is especially vulnerable to the influence of preachers and sectarian proselytizers." The factory newspaper asserted that, "Filth, low culture, drunkenness, and hooliganism provide fertile soil for religion in the barracks."[166] Though state loyalists were largely successful in expelling religious practice from the factory or driving it underground, given the presence of thousands of former peasants, religious belief was likely stronger at the end of the First Five-Year Plan than it had been at its inception.

The systematic casting of suspicion upon specialists and engineers was another common subterfuge of the Cultural Revolution. The Shakhty affair in the Donbass coalfields had dramatically altered the status of engineers in the Soviet Union and was a turning point in state industrial policy. The trial of engineers for "wrecking" ushered in a state offensive against previously privileged groups in all spheres of life.[167] Yet even half a year later, specialists in the Hammer and Sickle Factory seemed oblivious to the abrupt shift in political winds, and continued to challenge party directives. In September 1928, the engineering collective passed a resolution against the proposal for the seven-hour workday.[168]

The plant's engineering corps became the scapegoats for repeated delays in the factory's reconstruction in 1929. The disagreements between management and technical personnel took on a political character because some of the factory engineers were loyal to the party's recently defeated Bukharin section of the party.[169] In May, *Trud* initiated the campaign against the engineers because "technical personnel were not interested in economic work."[170] In June, the factory party committee passed a resolution that "considers the tempo of planning the reconstruction of the factory extremely slow and does not correspond to the party directive about the development of heavy industry." Rather than reconstruction in its present location, many engineers favored relocating the factory for technical and logistic reasons.[171]

Party leaders were in no mood to negotiate, leveling bizarre, politically charged accusations against the engineers. In July, authorities characterized the argument for rebuilding the factory elsewhere as of "a wrecking character."[172] Similarly, the *raikom* considered talk of closing the factory to be based on "insufficient consideration on the part of some and outright wrecking on the part of others." Party leaders called for "a halt to all discussion about the possibility of closing the factory. Accelerate the completion of its reconstruction."[173] Various delays persisted into the fall and the party control commission placed the blame on "the massive deficiencies in the work of the technical bureau."[174]

The blaming of functionaries for the structural problems of rapid industrialization became another common staple of the Stalinist project. In February 1930, the OGPU arrested "Satel', Mattis, and others" for their "active participation in counterrevolutionary wrecking." The factory party secretary, Gaidul', posited that there was the possibility of wrecking by all of the engineering-technical workers.[175] Another party report named engineers Babadzhan and Titov, and mentioned "others."[176] *Martenovka* retroactively blamed the factory fires in 1925, 1926, and 1928 on similar "wrecking."[177]

That the factory leadership had supposedly allowed the head engineer to conduct counterrevolutionary sabotage for a decade did not go unnoticed. One party member touched on this sore point: "This person was busy wrecking for ten years but we did not see it."[178] While publicly attacking the engineers, the factory party committee admitted that the specialists' pay was lower than that in other factories: to remain competitive with other enterprises, they resolved to raise the pay of engineers by 21 percent.[179] A few weeks after arresting "wrecking" engineers, the party committee rewarded management and the surviving engineers with a resolution to build new housing for them.[180] Significantly, workers' anger played no role in the campaign against specialists, nor do they appear to have been the slightest bit interested in the proceedings. Only 145 party members attended the discussion "about the arrest of chief engineer Mattis." The meeting of "communists with ties with the village" appears to have been organized as an ominous warning for members with doubts about the party platform. "The main aim of this sabotage," according to party secretary Gaidul', "is to disrupt our production program."[181]

The most significant result of the campaign was a shattered engineering corps. In 1926, thirty-seven of fifty engineers (74 percent) were over the age of forty, including eighteen experienced engineers over the age of fifty.[182] In September 1931, Rabkrin reported that fifty-two out of one hundred engineers and technical personnel had less than two years of experience. "Many new engineers try," reported Rabkrin, but rampant production problems occurred because the new engineers had "no understanding how to work."[183]

The state-sponsored Cultural Revolution emphasized raising productivity and had little to do with culture except in a destructive sense. Workers largely ignored the state's frenzied productivist propaganda and the attack on engineers, leading to "breaks in the lines of the cultural front." The more coercive antireligious campaigns caused deep resentment because they represented an assault on workers' religious holidays and cultural values.

Dissent, Resistance, and Repression

A profound shift in public discourse and workers' resistance took place during the First Five-Year Plan.[184] Although some workers continued to speak out against state policy, Stalinist loyalists largely succeeded at stifling open dissent. Similarly, although some employees organized small-scale resistance to state policy, strike action was no longer a significant part of class conflict, and workers turned increasingly to individual rather than collective solutions to their deteriorating economic situation.

Limited data indicates that the most vulnerable and the most desperate Soviet workers—women in the textile industry—mounted the stiffest resistance to the state offensive. The number of textile strikes actually increased from sixty-six in 1929 to ninety- two in 1930, though the largest stoppage involved only six hundred workers and lasted only thirty minutes, suggesting a continuation of the late NEP trend. The largest textile strike in early 1932 involved less than six hundred workers—larger strikes in Ivanovo oblast textile mills later in 1932 and 1933 were the exception rather than the rule. Widespread discontent did not lead to a nationwide movement against state-imposed deprivations. As Elena Osokina, author of an important study on Soviet food distribution during the prewar period, argues, "For the most part, people did not deal with these problems openly, but rather adapted survival strategies to fit the conditions."[185]

Complaints about the food shortages dominated workers' grievances. In February 1929, the party ridiculed a member in the railway shop who asked, "What kind of Soviet power is this—fuck all of you—if my wife has to stand in line for six hours for a loaf of bread?"[186] During early NEP, the party had supported workers' grievances over food supplies, but in August 1930, *Martenovka* ran a series of articles about "counterrevolutionary provocation" involving complaints about shortages.[187] Factory cooperative supplies were chronically short. In October 1930, the factory was promised 350 tons of potatoes, but received only 215.[188] *Martenovka* and the cooperative bureau blamed speculators for the shortages, organized raids in and around the factory, and sent "more than twenty-five wreckers" to trial.[189] In an attempt to alleviate the shortages, the factory ZRK became the first closed Moscow cooperative, limiting access to workers and their families.[190] In August 1931, workers had to wait in line for four or five hours for vegetables.[191] In order to win "the struggle with lines," the factory stores opened at 7 a.m. and closed at 11 p.m.[192] The ZRK party fraction vowed to organize a "competition" between sections to liquidate lines, but a few days later, the party condemned the ZRK for the weak food supply.[193] The next month, the OGPU still reported cooperative lines for milk, bread, meat, and sausages.[194] Archival sources show that authorities throughout the Soviet Union were inundated with thousands of appeals that protested against the long hours spent standing in line, the difficulties involved in purchasing food, and the abysmal quality of the food served in workers' cafeterias.[195]

Supply and sanitation problems also plagued the factory cafeterias. An April 1931 party report found that all seven cafeterias and six buffets (with the exception of management's) were in an unsanitary state. Only cold lunches were available, except in the management cafeteria.[196] In August, the factory was short five hundred lunches a day and workers "expressed open and hidden dissatisfaction. Lately lunch portions are going down" and "the quality is deteriorating so that even on meat days, ground meat is half mixed with cereal."[197]

Party leaders blamed lower-level functionaries for the food crisis. In March 1931, the Politburo wrote that it "considers it shameful for the Moscow organization that every month no less than ten thousand *puds* of workers' and office workers' bread is falling into the hands of speculators, thanks to the deficiencies of the trade and distribution apparatus in Moscow."[198] Yet it was the Stalinist policy of industrialization at any cost, rather than speculators or foreign aggression, that created the food shortages. In July 1931, the Politburo resolved to export an added six million *puds* of grain from the new harvest by 2 August.[199] Even from a productivist perspective the policy was counterproductive once nourishment was reduced beyond a minimum threshold. As one worker in the rolled metal shop complained: "Our work is difficult. Such work requires good food, but we are kept on salt fish, which cannot satisfy. It is impossible to fulfill the financial production plan when you can barely drag yourself around."[200]

The MK claimed that the food situation in the factory had improved slightly in the second half of 1931. In the third quarter, Hammer and Sickle workers supposedly received 621 calories for lunch, with 150 grams of meat, 150 grams of fish, 15 grams of fat, and 48 grams of cereal, and this was later raised to a total of 790 calories, incremented to 200, 200, 20, and 60 grams respectively.[201] Yet during this same period the OGPU reported a cockroach infestation and a utensil shortage that forced workers to eat with their hands.[202] By the end of 1931 the OGPU also reported "a sharp deterioration" of food and worker dissatisfaction, noting that thirty workers absolutely refused to take lunch because it was so bad.[203]

Workers' complaints about the food shortages continued in 1932. One worker told a Rabkrin inspector that "the supply is frequently interrupted and workers often do not get bread." Another worker noted that this contributed to the instability of the workforce: "We have deficiencies in workers' supplies and recently this has also strongly influenced the workforce turnover."[204] The factory was not equipped to feed the almost fifteen thousand workers employed. In May, party leaders demanded that the ZRK take urgent measures to alleviate the "catastrophic" vegetable supply.[205] In June, the party committee asserted that the sharp deterioration in the quality of lunches contributed to the factory operating at a loss. "Extreme dissatisfaction" with the supply situation was connected with an increase in unexcused absentees, drinking, and theft, rendering it difficult to "mobilize workers and office staff for the completion of the plan in quantity and quality."[206] By August the food supply had again worsened.[207] A note to a speaker in September asked, "Why is the produce industry developing so badly that everyone only gets two *funts* of bread?"[208] A December report to Nikita Khrushchev stated that management was given more control over supplies for workers.[209]

Factory leaders were less lenient with grievances that had more explicit political overtones. More than a year after the mass expulsions, Trotskyists continued to win party support in the factory. In February 1929, Kozlov and Churchin argued in a repair shop meeting that life for the workers was getting worse every year, with less help for the unemployed, with women driven to prostitution, and with men resorting to thievery. A *Martenovka* headline claimed that "The Trotskyists Attempt to Disturb the Party and Working Class in the Construction of Socialism," and shops passed resolutions denouncing the Trotskyists.[210] In February, the party bureau announced preparations for cleansing the cells of overtly "counterrevolutionary Trotskyists" in conjunction with the campaign to exile Trotsky from the Soviet Union.[211] The persistence of "a Trotskyist mood in the shop" led party leaders to charge the cell secretary with not giving oppositionists "a strong enough rebuff."[212]

In the spring of 1929, the party expelled three members for Trotskyist sympathies.[213] An anonymous note in a Rogozhsko-Simonovskii district party conference related that "Trotskyists write in their leaflets that workers from many factories were sent to jail for speaking in meetings" and asked, "Is this true?"[214] Widespread political arrests in 1929 suggest that it was true.[215]

Repression meant that Trotskyism in Moscow persisted only as a symbol of resistance rather than as an organized activist current with a presence in the factories. In late 1930, the party expelled a member in the Hammer and Sickle Factory for leading the resistance to night shift work. The "kulak agitator" Belkin asserted unabashedly in a meeting that "Trotsky and his associates are honest revolutionaries."[216] MK leader L. Kaganovich admitted in early 1932 that in Moscow there were still "elements that clearly sympathize with Trotskyism."[217] Workers at the huge Glukhova textile mill carried portraits of Lenin and Trotsky at their May Day 1932 celebration.[218] Ten days later, the OGPU reported that leaflets distributed at the same factory in the

Nogin district called on workers to follow the example of Ivanovo-Vozhne-skii, Tver', and Kiev by striking against hunger, and concluded with the words "Long Live Comrade Trotsky!"[219]

Denunciations of various oppositionists led to confusion, and occasionally party leaders' disingenuous assertions brought unintended credibility to Trotskyists and Bukharinists. Thus in July 1931 the party secretary announced at a factory conference that an average fourteen-kopeck raise (in reality a wage reduction, given rampant inflation) supposedly rebuffed "the Trotskyists and right opportunists' slander that the party is not bettering the material condition of the workers." During the party cleansing in early 1930, leaders castigated a party shop union bureau member who had provided a technically accurate, but politically incorrect, response to the question of the current role of the union: "to lower the wage-rate."[220] In September 1929 a member pointed out in a shop cell meeting that since "now you do not know who is the right tendency and who is the left. That is why there is fear of speaking up at meetings."[221] Almost three years later, another party mem-ber reiterated this theme: "In old times life was better. We do not understand what is right, what is left. In general they are good people."[222]

Wild charges against dissenters helped Stalinism gain firm control over all meetings by early 1929. Even as late as 1928, workers made open threats to factory management in delegates' meetings, but a few months later, only state loyalists spoke. Only 7 out of 178 spoke at a delegates' meeting in January 1929—meetings that rank-and-file militants had controlled a few years earlier. A few weeks later at a factory conference, just 11 workers spoke from the floor.[223] Stifling open dissent certainly did not mean support for regime policy as workers continued to hand party leaders hostile anonymous questions. A speaker from the Moscow Soviet was asked, "Why are there lines for produce?" Another worker asked, "How much does it cost to operate the Soviet state apparatus and how much did it cost to operate the Tsarist state apparatus?"[224]

Management brandished an array of disciplinary measures aimed at raising productivity. Fines against workers were aimed at clamping down on poor attendance. Disciplinary fines and propaganda focused on absenteeism, which constituted more than half (1,733 of 3,168) of the breaches of disci-pline in the second year of the Plan. Next in priority were offenses for dam-aging equipment (458), refusing work assignments (335), and showing up late or leaving early (272).[225] In the second year of the Plan less than 1 per-cent (0.84 percent) of the workforce was absent without just cause, and only slightly more in October 1930 (0.86). After former peasants entered the fac-tory en masse, the number of absentees rose precipitously. One shop meet-ing noted "a colossal number of unexcused absences" and resolved to implement the November 1932 TsIK decree to fire workers who did not show up and to confiscate their apartments.[226]

Revolutionary Production Tribunals, a short-lived phenomenon of late 1930, were another attempt to instill work discipline. Fellow workers judged breaches of discipline such as unexcused absences, worker transience, and dis-ruption of production. Three to five shock workers, "the most advanced soldiers for the Five-Year Plan," oversaw the sessions, and had the right to discipline offenders by publishing their names in the factory newspaper; transferring them to other work, shift, or wage-categories; or firing and expelling them from the union.[227] Reports on the few tribunals show that they fired and lowered the wage-category of several workers for "careless attitude towards work" and for allowing a furnace to stand idle. The factory newspaper accused the rolled metal shop leadership of displaying "right opportunism in practice" because it failed to hold tribunals to curb absenteeism. A few weeks later *Martenovka* applauded the work of the tribunals in the repair shop and form-casting shops for punishing workers who were absent during Christmas.[228]

The entry of thousands of former peasants into the workforce and the corresponding drop in labor discipline rendered systematic production trials an impossible undertaking. Some of the disciplinary practices continued, such as lowering wage categories, but were enforced by management. In May 1932, two party members were expelled for leading a minor revolt against wage and skill grade reductions for poor quality:

> After the communist Frolov's demagogic suggestion during the *subbotnik* at the factory *sovkhoz* (Reutovo), workers and administration were separated into different brigades. After the *subbotnik* there was a drinking bout. The majority of the cell bureau members, the shop committee fraction, and shop administration actively participated.... After the drinking bout, Frolov put forward the slogan "Beat the administration!" and began beating the foreman Strekalov. Frolov shouted, "Here is your 35 percent! Here are your 2.50 rubles!" This was the amount by which Frolov's wages were reduced for poor quality of work.[229]

Another coercive and short-lived attempt to raise discipline was "the Stalinist Raid." In December 1931, *Martenovka* urged "Hammer and Sickle Workers, Tomorrow Join the Stalinist Raid!" The next day, *Pravda* and *Martenovka* shock brigades entered different shops at eight in the morning and expected the *aktiv* to help verify Stalin's six conditions for productivity success, but the factory newspaper admitted that there were many "deserters." In the wire-pulling shop only twenty-five appeared, in the cable shop thirty, in the electrical shop ten, and in the repair shop just five. Yet, after repeated cajoling, the factory newspaper claimed two thousand workers participated and that two days later, their ranks had increased to five thousand.[230]

Many workers resorted to theft in order to survive. In May 1930, the metalworkers' union reported that the entire drivers' section had participated in theft.[231] From August 1931 to 5 November, management recorded 138 thefts totaling 4,138 rubles. One worker was sentenced to three years and another to four years for stealing clothes and selling them in the market. *Martenovka* complained that despite repeated warnings, employees continued to steal metals and other items from the factory.[232]

Although strikes were no longer the dominant method of resistance in the class conflict, workers repeatedly engaged in small-scale actions and party members continued to push the boundaries of party discipline. In April 1929, three party members led a petition of workers in the wire-pulling department against the new rates specified in collective agreement. Workers organized an impromptu meeting to discuss what action to take. "Egorov knew that workers wanted to organize a meeting about the per item rates but he did not warn anyone about it and refused outright to work at the new rate. His is the first name on the petition about the conflict."[233] The party reprimanded Egorov, who was denied full party membership, while Pimenov acknowledged that he had been "tailist."[234] The third member, Slavin, was later brought before the control commission for "hounding the administration," agitating against extra work to ameliorate damages caused by an accident in the shop, and "spreading rumors about the arrest of Babazhan and Minevrin."[235] That two workers were apparently arrested helps to explain why no strikes occurred during the First Five-Year Plan. The rules of industrial action had changed considerably since the short-lived strikes a year earlier, though the party was still relatively lenient with party members willing to admit their "mistakes" in public.

The relatively privileged position of metalworkers in the Soviet capital probably contributed to the cessation of strike activity. As rationing spread throughout Moscow in the fall of 1929, workers received better rations than white-collar workers, including twice as much meat. Soviet leaders were keenly aware of the implications of potential workers' rebellions in Moscow and Leningrad, and instituted prophylactic measures to prevent them. During the deteriorating crisis of 1932, Moscow received extraordinary supplies, followed closely by Leningrad. Within relatively better off Moscow, heavy industry workers were particularly privileged, with ration cards stamped twice a month. As Elena Osokina notes, "the Politburo oversaw the provisioning of Moscow and Leningrad and lowered the norms of industrial workers in the capital cities only as a last resort, after cutting the rations for all other groups of the population." This is not to suggest that metalworkers received large rations—by 1933 workers in the capital received only thirty-five to forty grams of meat a day—insufficient for heavy manual labor. But even with meager rations, workers in the capital had real advantages over workers elsewhere.[236] To engage in strikes entailed the obvious risk of losing such privileges.

Metalworkers had other relative advantages. Rapid industrial expansion led to what Kenneth Straus has described as an "inverted" labor market, one characterized by chronic labor shortages rather than unemployment. This shortage opened up unprecedented opportunities for previously underrepresented sections of the working class—including women, younger workers, and former peasants. From only 356 workers in 1929 (6 percent), the 1,951 women constituted almost a quarter of the workforce in 1933, though they continued to be employed in less skilled positions. By 1932, 70 percent of workers recruited to the factory plan came from peasant backgrounds and by 1933 almost half (46 percent) of the workforce was under the age of twenty-three. Though the overwhelming majority of new peasant arrivals quickly fled the factory, thousands of the new recruits entered the factory's various schools and training programs. By 1931, 1,738 workers were studying to increase their skill level, 2,658 teenagers were enrolled in factory vocational schools, and over 613 workers were studying to become engineers and technicians.[237] For those exceptional workers willing to play by the rules of the game and tolerate barrack life, horrific work conditions, and low wages, such training offered a career path to a skilled position in the prestigious metal industry.

The labor shortage afforded workers a degree of leverage in various disputes. In the summer of 1930, groups of workers demanded that if "the factory committee does not give us cigarettes, then give us our final payment." *Martenovka* called for other workers to "rebuff the self-seeking mood," and retorted, "Some of the comrades do not even smoke." In April 1931, the factory newspaper again criticized the "self-seeking mood" of several workers in the form-casting shop for demanding credit for three hours of overtime work. Fifty workers in the ZRK signed a petition demanding wage leveling in August 1931. *Martenovka* charged the department leader with "right opportunistic practices" because he had admitted, "We have economic leveling, depersonalization, and turnover, and we can do nothing about it."[238] The Trotskyist *Biulleten' Oppozitsii* reported another dispute about overtime in the summer of 1932. Because of the shortage of skilled labor, some workers, especially communists, often worked ten to twelve hours a day, but during the provision crisis of August 1932, 250 workers refused extra overtime.[239]

Challenging party superiors could end one's political career. In September 1931, the party removed a shop bureau member after he had argued in a cell meeting that "we will not fulfill the industrial financial plan." *Martenovka* suggested that he accept his mistake, which was indicative of a "right opportunist mood in our ranks."[240] The same month, a repair shop leader complained of lack of support from the factory leadership. The entire repair shop cell had to appear before the factory bureau and the accused was forced to save his political career by admitting his mistake:

> In his speech in a repair shop open meeting of the cell, Strel'chik, the cell secretary, accused the leadership of the party of opportunism. The bureau considers that comrade Strel'chik committed a deep political mistake and breach of party discipline by appealing to the nonparty masses against the leadership with an unwarranted accusation in an open meeting. The bureau of party committee considers the claim by Strel'chik about the lack of help from the party committee to be totally incorrect and unsubstantiated. The bureau demands that Strel'chik immediately admit his political mistake.[241]

During the clampdown on dissent, *Martenovka* focused its attention on the more outspoken critics. Whereas two years earlier the factory newspaper had countered rumors about workers being fired for speaking against state policy, by 1930 such open agitation was no longer tolerated. Nestorov defiantly stated, "I will not let Komsomol members rule me." Party members petitioned to have him removed for "counterrevolutionary" agitation and slander, and for disrupting the "Bolshevik tempo" of work. Daily he protested that although he was formerly a Bolshevik, "I see now that with Soviet power everything is for the workers' only on paper.... So do not wait all the way to the end of the Five-Year Plan. You need to take care of your-self first; the state is rich so it will take care of itself. Why do we need com-petition? What is the Five-Year Plan loan for?"[242] Five months later Nestorov had still not relented: "Why so much work for such poor pay? Let them raise it, then we will really work." *Martenovka* accused Nestorov of being a "class alien" who spoke "differently from our workers' language." Yet this was pre-cisely the proletarian language that had been forged during the revolution-ary era, a discourse that Stalinism no longer tolerated. The newspaper suggested that shop organizations "need to pay more attention to Nestorov and carefully watch how he works."[243]

Even with increased presence from state agents, some workers continued to voice defiance. In December 1930, the Komsomol gave a "Sharp Rebuff to the Kulak's Sidekick Volkov" because he had spoken against the *kolkhoz* movement in a meeting. He was warned to acknowledge his mistake, "but he stubbornly insisted on his conclusions and tried to support them with better arguments." In response, the factory newspaper suggested that the Komso-mol cell "should busy itself with Volkov's political education."[244] In May 1931, the OGPU reported workers' discussions in the district about how "the Soviet government does not know how to finish off the workers." They complained that after lowering the wage rate, increasing production norms, and raising the prices of all goods, "workers have been left with no room to breathe." Maleev, from the form-casting shop stated, "Mikoyan said in one meeting that real workers' pay would go up because of the lower prices in the cooperative. But what do we really see? Just the opposite."[245]

By 1931, the OGPU was strong enough to record the names of individu-als who made utterances against the system. In the rolled metal shop, Stepan and Kiselev complained that "Our newspapers lie about how bad life is abroad. Workers there go to work in clean clothes, but here we go to work in worn out shoes. Workers live better under capitalism." In the steel foundry Kartsev asserted: "They promise a lot, but do not give anything. The Central Committee resolutions are only promises."[246] A wire-pulling shop member noted many utterances "against the regime and the party," which one worker had described as "good-for-nothings."[247] The threat of war and insurrection met with indifference and even sedition among some workers. The party accused a young electrician of having a "clearly counterrevolutionary atti-tude" because he stated, "this regime is not ours. It is the regime of invaders. If there were an insurrection, nobody would defend it."[248]

Workers noticed the increased presence of state operatives in their ranks. In the nearby AMO Factory, an engineer explained, "Everyone understands that in every department and shop its secret agents work, and that all con-versations are known. Otherwise they would not know a damn thing."[249] At a district party meeting, the Hammer and Sickle Factory representative spoke about an individual member who had "slandered the party line, which reflects the capitalist elements in the party."[250] A *Martenovka rabkor*, inves-tigating problems in the summer of 1932, approached a group of workers during lunch. "I stood near these comrades and waited to see if they were going to talk. There was no conversation."[251]

Stalinist loyalists were largely successful at shutting down open dissent. Cell secretaries were expected to curb open opposition to party directives and any tolerance was a sign of political opportunism. The steel foundry cell displayed a "conciliatory attitude" towards anti-Soviet moods because a member made a speech against the *kolkhoz* movement. A "drastic change" was needed in the cell because "a slowdown and unwillingness to lead the struggle against class alien elements is a manifestation of right opportunism in practice."[252]

Official falsification of information, combined with the suppression of dissent, increased the proliferation of underground rumors among workers. Rather than believing that their deteriorating situation would continue to decline, many workers believed cataclysmic events were on the horizon. In May 1931, the OGPU stated that some workers in the district talked about how life had become "unbearable." Since workers believed that "it has become impossible to live," they drew the conclusion that "the crash of the Five-Year Plan is gradually coming." Other workers in the district claimed that "the communists have accomplished what they wanted" and that though there were goods, "workers have no means to pay for them." This meant that workers "have to be satisfied with bread, but even that will end soon." Another woman was alleged to have spread rumors in the Hammer and Sickle Factory food cooperative that "many factories are already on strike, but you are still working."[253] The OGPU recorded the assessment of one worker in the district who claimed, "I have many party acquaintances who openly say that the end is near, that the party is completely split. Such leaders as Bukharin and Rykov see that everything is turning out badly, that people were just being tortured for thirteen years. What is there left for us to do? We just observe what is happening at the top."[254]

It was wishful thinking to believe that some other force would come to the aid of a battered working class whose collective will to fight had been destroyed. By September 1932, the factory newspaper had already begun the campaign for the next step: "We are Moving to the Front of the Second Five-Year Plan!"[255] A note to the speaker at a factory meeting asked: "Will there be three Five-Year Plans? The first one is not even done and the second has already started."[256] Other anonymous notes to speakers, along with ubiquitous antiparty graffiti, illustrate the profound popular resentment against the state by the end of the First Five-Year Plan. An enraged Kaganovich wanted to know how it was possible that openly anti-Soviet slogans proliferated on school walls, including "Down with Soviet power" and the letters in a "Sickle and Hammer" sign transformed to read "Death and Hunger."[257] Hostile anonymous notes to factory party leaders continued the next year. One note warned the party committee secretary, "if you do not change it will be bad for you." The factory director Stepanov reported to the OGPU that he repeatedly received similar notes threatening to kill him.[258]

Factory leaders successfully drove open dissent underground during the First Five-Year Plan and eliminated organized resistance. The state strategy for crushing dissent focused on the more outspoken critics of its policies, labeling any form of dissent in the same terms as it had the Opposition.

Some younger workers and peasants, less accustomed to the Stalinist rules of discourse, expressed open hostility to the regime's policies, and anonymous notes to speakers show that these brazen workers spoke for a wider milieu. The state was also successful at preventing strikes, although some workers continued to organize smaller actions, particularly when labor shortages gave them leverage.

In one sense, party leaders and their loyal shop floor advocates could be satisfied with their accomplishments during the First Five-Year Plan. They oversaw a process in which wages were driven down by more than fifty percent; in which the average workweek was extended by at least an extra twenty hours per month; and in which a month's wages were handed back to the state in the form of a "loan." And they managed to accomplish all of this while sharply curtailing open dissent against the Stalinist system, let alone provoking overt rebellion. Under their direction, the unions—which at least nominally had retained their integrity as institutions of basic working-class defense as late as the end of NEP—had been transformed into adjuncts in management's drive for increased productivity. Similarly, the party, which had previously represented, in some sense, the vanguard of the Soviet workers' movement, was also transformed into an effective instrument for overseeing the extraction of surplus value for production's sake.

While repression was a factor in this process—particularly in the marginalization of political oppositionists and in the persecution of engineers, lowerlevel functionaries, and speculators—terror was not Stalinism's primary, or even most efficient, tool for disciplining the workforce. Nor was state propaganda particularly effective on its own: it was unproductive at best and at times counterproductive, because workers were astute enough to discern the profound discrepancy between official rhetoric and their deteriorating standard of living. Evidence in the Hammer and Sickle Factory suggests that rather than propaganda or terror, Stalinism relied more heavily upon the weapon of hunger—on its control over food distribution—and on its success in enlisting a loyal minority to police the shop floor on behalf of the state.

Yet Stalinism was much better at destroying than at building up social institutions. Neither propaganda nor coercive social engineering strategies could overcome the deep structural problems accompanying rapid industrialization or the inherent contradictions involved in pushing materiallydeprived employees to work longer hours for less pay. Scapegoating, self-incrimination, and chronic, intermittent purges were symptoms of the regime's weakness, not its strength. Harsher measures were implemented as substitutes for voluntary conviction, but even Revolutionary Production Tribunals, Stalinist Raids, management fines, and the strategic use of food as a weapon of coercion did not transform workers into docile productive units.

Rather than being passive recipients for Stalinism's rhetoric, many workers saw through the regime's self-serving and inverted "class war" propaganda. They recognized that state policy was forcing them to pay for rapid industrialization, even if the regime did not know how to "finish off" the working class. Occasional public utterances and the indignation expressed in the private notes handed to speakers at factory meetings show that in some ways workers had not yet completely submitted to those who ruled over them, but also attest to the lack of collective confidence with which they confronted their new rulers. The turn to strategies of individual survival became the norm for a divided workforce that had been drained of its vitality and cohesion.

Unlike the temporary workers' retreats earlier in the century, by 1932 the relationship between rulers and ruled had become firmly entrenched and there would be no return to workers' militancy. The dull drone of uninterrupted productivity drives and the seemingly endless demands for more sacrifice and austerity were not ephemeral phenomena, but now comprised the basic features of the Stalinist system. The revolutionary era, during which workers had repeatedly and confidently asserted their collective power, had now come to a decisive end.

Notes

1. Alec Nove, *An Economic History of the U.S.S.R.* (New York, 1989), 199.
2. Karl Marx, *Capital* (London, 1976) 1: 742.
3. Tony Cliff, *State Capitalism in Russia* (London, 1974). What drove the process of accumulation in the USSR, Cliff argued, was not competition between private capitalists engaged in commodity production, but a nation-state seeking to compete militarily in the world arena. In Joseph Stalin's famous 1931 attack on the critics of rapid industrialization, he wrote, "One feature of the history of old Russia was the continual beatings she suffered because of her backwardness." To avoid, future military defeats, he warned, "We are fifty or a hundred years behind the advanced countries. We must make good this distance in ten years. Either we do it, or we shall go under." Joseph Stalin, *Collected Works* (Moscow, 1951) 13: 40-41.
4. *Martenovka*, 6 February 1929; GARF f. 7952, op. 3, d. 198, l. 1. Production and wags funds, 1928-1929 and 1929-1930.
5. *Martenovka*, 6 December 1928, 24 July 1931, 5 March 1932.
6. See Filtzer, *Soviet Workers and Stalinist Industrialization*, 91, for a summary of scholarly estimates on real wages during the First Five-Year Plan.
7. Hoffman, *Peasant Metropolis*, 222.
8. Filtzer, *Soviet Workers and Stalinist Industrialization*, 45. Including building and transport laborers, the working class expanded from about 4.6 to over 10 million workers.
9. R. W. Davies, *The Industrialization of Soviet Russia: The Socialist Offensive, The Collectivization of Soviet Agriculture, 1929-30* (London, 1980); Moshe Lewin, *Russian Peasants and Soviet Power: a Study of Collectivization* (London, 1968); Lynne Viola, *Peasant Rebels under Stalin* (Oxford, 1996).
10. Moshe Lewin, *The Making of the Soviet System* (New York, 1985), 221-257.
11. *Martenovka*, 3 January 1929, 2 January 1933.
12. GARF, f. 7952, op. 3, d. 214, ll. 1-6. Factory statistics, 1931.
13. *Za industrializatsiiu*, 12 January 1932.
14. TsAODM, f. 429, op. 1, d. 106, l. 51. Wire pulling shop party bureau report, 3 July 1929.
15. GARF, f. 7952, op. 3, d. 214, ll. 1-6. Factory statistics, 1931.
16. TsAODM, f. 429, op. 1, d. 107, l. 98. Electrical shop party meeting, 4 April 1929.
17. TsAODM, f. 429, op. 1, d. 109, l. 11. Party committee meeting, 11 February 1930.

18. TsAODM, f. 429, op. 1, d. 103, l. 31. Rolled metal shop party bureau meeting, 24 April 1929.
19. TsAODM, f. 429, op. 1, d. 104, ll. 87-88. Repair shop party meeting, 16 November 1929.
20. Lynne Viola, *The Best Sons of the Fatherland* (New York, 1987). In *Workers, Society, and the Soviet State,* 302, William Chase asserts "That many urban workers supported a solution to rural question is clear from their active involvement in the movement of the 25,000ers" and claims 70,000 "volunteered."
21. TsMAM, f. 176, op. 2, d. 819, ll. 8-9. Report by Hammer and Sickle workers brigade, 1929.
22. TsAODM, f. 429, op. 1, d. 109, l. 230. Party bureau meeting, 16 December 1930.
23. TsAODM, f. 429, op. 1, d. 113, l. 41. Party bureau and shop secretaries meeting, 13 March 1931.
24. RGASPI, f. 17, op. 85, d. 311, l. 7. TsK information department summary on strikes during NEP. In 1926, 44,240 *otkhodniki* participated in 264 strikes (of 826 nationally) and the next year 29,069 *otkhodniki* participated in 334 (of 905) strikes.
25. TsAODM, f. 80, op. 1, d. 398, l. 172. OGPU district report, n.d. November 1931.
26. TsAODM, f. 80, op. 1, d. 398, l. 75. OGPU district report, 27 August 1931.
27. TsMAM, f. 1289, op. 1, d. 326, l. 11. Rabkrin report, 9 September 1931.
28. TsMAM, f. 176, op. 2, d. 830, l. 12. Production suggestions, 1929.
29. Nove, *An Economic History of the U.S.S.R.,* 199.
30. RGASPI, f. 81, op. 3, d. 20, ll. 70-85. MK report by L. Kaganovich, 1931.
31. RGASPI, f. 17, op. 20, d. 291, l. 133. Secretariat MK meeting, 2 December 1931.
32. GARF f. 5469, op. 15, d. 57, ll. 42-43. Metalworkers' summary on reelection to Soviets, 1 January 1931.
33. Straus, *Factory and Community in Stalin's Russia,* 216.
34. TsMAM, f. 176, op. 2, d. 835, l. 10. Construction of new shops meeting, 20 May 1932.
35. TsMAM, f. 176, op. 2, d. 834, ll. 56-57. Reconstruction brigade meeting, 29 March 1932.
36. *Martenovka,* 26 September 1932.
37. *Trud,* 10 September 1931.
38. RGASPI, f. 81, op. 3, d. 20, l. 70. MK report by L. Kaganovich, n.d. 1931.
39. TsAODM, f. 4, op. 2,. d. 6, ll. 95, 96. MGK meeting, 8 August 1932.
40. *Martenovka,* 10 August 1932.
41. Filtzer, *Soviet Workers and Stalinist Industrialization,* 52.
42. Kornokovskii, *Zavod 'Serp i Molot,'* 230.
43. TsMAM, f. 176, op. 2, d. 834, l. 9. Construction of new shops meeting, 20 July 1932.
44. TsMAM, f. 1289, op. 1, d. 326, l. 26. Rabkrin report, 9 September 1931.
45. TsMAM, f. 176, op. 2, d. 834, l. 10. Construction of new shops meeting, 20 July 1932.
46. *Rabochaia gazeta,* 2 September 1931.
47. Filtzer, *Soviet Workers and Stalinist Industrialization,* 112-115, 236-246.
48. Filtzer, *Soviet Workers and Stalinist Industrialization,* 70.
49. In *Stalin's Industrial Revolution,* 316, Hiroaki Kuromiya argues that Stalinism's "class war ideology of the industrialization drive created a basis for the survival of the regime."
50. *Martenovka,* 20 April 1929.
51. *Martenovka,* 9 April 1929.
52. *Martenovka,* 30 April, 20 May, 6, 8 June, 7 November 1929.
53. *Martenovka,* 8 January 1930, 30 April, 18 June, 21 September, 25 November 1929.
54. TsMAM, f. 176, op. 2, d. 813, l. 44; Cultural Commission meeting, n.d. November 1929.
55. TsAODM, f. 429, op. 1, d. 100, l. 34. Bolt shop party meeting, n.d. December 1929.
56. Kuromiya, *Stalin's Industrial Revolution,* 128-135.
57. *Martenovka,* 25 November 1929.
58. TsAODM, f. 429, op. 1, d. 94, l. 71. Party plenum, 21 December 1929.
59. *Martenovka,* 17 February 1930.
60. Kuromiya, *Stalin's Industrial Revolution,* 236, notes the late 1929 party and union resolution to purge the factories of "class aliens" because of the resistance to shock work.

Evidence in the Hammer and Sickle Factory suggests that the threat of the party purge played a role in forcing party members to join the movement.

61. *Martenovka,* 21 January 1930.
62. GARF 5469, op. 14, d. 193, ll. 243, 323. Metalworkers' information summaries, 21 May, 20 July 1930.
63. *Martenovka,* 25 June 1930.
64. *Martenovka,* 8 January, 20 May, 2, 25 June 1930.
65. *Rabochaia Moskva,* 4 March 1930.
66. Kuromiya, *Stalin's Industrial Revolution,* 196.
67. *Rabochaia gazeta,* 27 February 1930.
68. *Martenovka,* 21, 28 March, 9 April, 1 May 1930.
69. *Trud,* 4 June 1930.
70. GARF f. 374, op. 27, d. 1962, ll. 36-97. NKVD summary, early 1930.
71. *Martenovka,* 20 May 1930.
72. *Martenovka,* 21 September 1929.
73. GARF f. 5469, op. 14, d. 60, ll. 30-31. Moscow Oblast Metalworkers' meeting, 19 August 1930.
74. Filtzer in *Soviet Workers and Stalinist Industrialization,* 96.
75. TsKhDMO, f. 1, op. 3, d. 85, l. 63. Komsomol Central Committee discussion, 15 August 1931.
76. *Martenovka,* 3 September 1931, 4 October 1930.
77. *Martenovka,* March; 3 April 1931.
78. TsAODM, f. 429 op. 1, d. 113, ll. 111-112. Party plenum and party *aktiv* meeting, 23 June 1931.
79. TsMAM, f. 1289, op. 1, d. 326, ll. 51-52. Rabkrin report, 9 September 1931.
80. *Rabochaia gazeta,* 15 March 1931.
81. TsAODM, f. 80, op. 1, d. 386, ll. 13, 14. Rogozhsko-Simonovskii bureau meeting, 5 June 1931.
82. TsKhDMO, f. 1, op. 3, d. 85, ll. 49, 56, 57. Bureau of TsK Komsomol discussion, 22 August 1931.
83. TsMAM, f. 1289, op. 1, d. 326, ll. 52-53. Rabkrin report, 9 September 1931.
84. *Martenovka,* 30 June 1931.
85. TsAODM, f. 80, op. 1, d. 398, l. 75. OGPU district summary, 27 August 1931.
86. TsMAM, f. 1289, op. 1, d. 326, ll. 85-86. Rabkrin report 9 September 1931.
87. *Martenovka,* 30 November 1931, 12 October 1932.
88. *Martenovka,* 26 December 1931, 15 March, 2 June, 6 August 1932.
89. TsAODM, f. 429, op. 1, d. 117, l. 18. Party committee and shop secretaries plenum, 4 June 1932.
90. *Martenovka,* 20 September 1932.
91. *Martenovka,* 14 September 1932.
92. *Martenovka,* 8 January 1932.
93. TsAODM, f, 429, op. 1, d. 116, l. 63. Factory control commission meeting, August 1932.
94. RGASPI, f. 81, op. 3, d. 20, l. 85. MK report by L. Kaganovich, n.d. 1931.
95. TsAODM, f. 3, op. 49, d. 15, l. 115. MK information summary, 19 September 1932.
96. TsKhDMO, f. 1, op. 23, d. 1008, l. 37. Letter sent to *Pravda* and *Izvestia,* dated 8 June 1932.
97. TsAODM, f. 429, op. 1, d. 129, l. 7. Party secretary report on work during First Five-Year Plan, 27 February 1933.
98. *Martenovka,* 24 July 1931.
99. TsAODM, f. 429, op. 1, d. 129, l. 77. Party secretary report on work during First Five-Year Plan, 27 February 1933.
100. GARF f. 7952, op. 3, d. 267, ll. 11-12. Filatov recollection of factory work during First Five-Year Plan.
101. GARF, f. 7952, op. 3, d. 279, l. 221. Martov recollection.
102. Filtzer, *Soviet Workers and Stalinist Industrialization,* 48.
103. *Martenovka,* 12 October 1930.

104. RGASPI, f. 81, op. 3, l. d. 147, l. 111. L. Kaganovich speech, 23 January 1932.
105. TsMAM, f. 176, op. 2, d. 819, l. 51. Report on work in club, April 1929.
106. TsAODM, f. 429, op. 1, d. 93, l. 69. Party committee meeting, 21 June 1929.
107. TsAODM, f. 429, op. 1, d. 100, ll. 20-21. Architecture shop cell meeting, 4 December 1929.
108. TsAODM, f. 429, op. 1, d. 100, l. 33. Bolt shop meeting, n.d. December 1929 (undated).
109. *Martenovka*, 11 February 1930.
110. TsAODM, f. 429, op. 1, d. 110, l. 5. Factory control commission meeting; 25 March 1930.
111. *Martenovka*, 13 August 1931.
112. TsAODM, f. 429 op. 1, d. 113, l. 98. Party committee and party *aktiv* meeting, 13 May 1931.
113. TsMAM, f. 1289, op. 1, d. 326, l. 76. Rabkrin report, 9 September 1931.
114. TsAODM, f. 4, op. 2, d. 26, ll. 31-66. MKG discussion on Hammer and Sickle Factory organization, 7 June 1932.
115. TsAODM, f. 429, op. 1, d. 116, l. 12. Party committee meeting, 31 May 1932.
116. *Martenovka*, 14 July 1932.
117. TsAODM, f. 429, op. 1, d. 116, l. 68. Party bureau meeting, 31 August 1932.
118. TsAODM, f. 3, op. 49, d. 15, l. 113. MK information summary, September 1932.
119. TsAODM, f. 429, op. 1, d. 116, l. 121. Party committee meeting, 29 November 1932.
120. TsAODM, f. 3, op. 49, d. 37, l., 78. MK summary on closed party meeting, 13 December 1933.
121. *Martenovka*, 11, 20 June 1931.
122. *Martenovka*, 17 July, 31 August 1929.
123. *Martenovka*, 7 September 1929.
124. TsAODM, f. 429, op. 1, d. 104, l. 31. Repair shop party meeting, 5 August 1929.
125. TsAODM, f. 429, op. 1, d. 104, ll. 76-77. Repair shop party meeting, 2 October 1929.
126. *Martenovka*, 8, 21 June, 7 September 1929.
127. *Martenovka*, 22 June; 22, 25 July; 1, 5, 8, 23 August 1930.
128. TsAODM, f. 429, op. 1, d. 129, l. 8. Party secretary report on work during First Five-Year Plan, 27 February 1933.
129. *Martenovka*, 7 February, 12, 19 June 1931.
130. TsAODM, f. 429, op. 1, d. 94, l. 24. Party committee meeting, 27 September 1929.
131. *Martenovka*, 28 July, 1 August 1930.
132. TsAODM, f. 80, op. 1, d. 386, l. 23. Rogozhsko-Simonovskii party bureau meeting, 24 June 1931.
133. *Martenovka*, 25 June 1931.
134. TsAODM, f. 429, op. 1, d. 113, l.30. Party committee and *aktiv* minutes, 3 July 1931.
135. *Martenovka*, 10 July 1931.
136. Sheila Fitzpatrick in 'Cultural Revolution as Class War' in *Cultural Revolution in Russia, 1928-1931.*
137. *Martenovka*, 5 September 1930, 10 March 1931.
138. *Martenovka*, 14 April 1931.
139. TsMAM, f. 176, op. 2, d. 823, ll. 16-18. Challenge from Lys'venski factories' cultural commissions to Hammer and Sickle and other factories, early 1929.
140. TsMAM, f. 176, op. 2, d. 823, ll. 19-20; Cultural commission, 10 June 1929.
141. Fitzpatrick in 'Cultural Revolution as Class War,' 25, asserts a positive response to Stalinist rhetoric, particularly among Komsomol members whom she describes as "enthusiasts of Cultural Revolution."
142. TsMAM, f. 176, op. 2, d. 819, l. 42. Cultural commission meetings, 24 September, n.d. November 1929.
143. TsAODM, f. 429, op. 1, d. 104, ll. 1-2. Repair shop party meeting, 17 October 1929.
144. *Martenovka*, 27 September 1930, 13 February, 20 July 1932.
145. TsAODM, f. 3, op. 49, d. 15, l. 111. MK information summary, 19 September 1932.
146. TsAODM, f. 429, op. 1, d. 92, ll. 89-90. Party bureau meeting, 26 March 1929.
147. *Martenovka*, 30 April 1929.

148. TsAODM, f. 429, op. 1, d. 104, l. 58. Construction shop party meeting, 3 July 1929.

149. *Martenovka,* 17 April 1930.

150. Husband, *Godless Communists,* 115.

151. *Martenovka,* 30 April 1929.

152. TsAODM, f. 429, op. 1, d. 104, ll. 1-2, 31. Repair shop party meetings, 5 August, 17 October 1929.

153. TsAODM, f. 429, op. 1, d. 129, l. 32. Party secretary report on work during First Five-Year Plan, 27 February 1933.

154. TsMAM, f. 176, op. 2, d. 819, l. 31; Cultural Commission meeting 14 September 1929.

155. *Martenovka,* 3 November 1930.

156. *Martenovka,* 4, 10, 13, 25 November 1930.

157. TsMAM, f. 176, op. 2, d. 819, l. 44. Cultural commission meeting, n.d. November 1929.

158. TsAODM. f. 429, op. 1, d. 111, l. 9. Party meeting of foremen and communist administrators, 22 February 1930.

159. *Martenovka,* 29 September 1929.

160. TsMAM, f. 176, op. 2, d. 819, l. 31. Cultural Commission meeting, 14 September 1929.

161. *Rabochaia gazeta,* 19 February 1930.

162. *Martenovka,* 20 February 1929.

163. *Martenovka,* 12, 17 April 1930.

164. TsAODM, f. 80, op. 1, d. 398, l. 37. OGPU district report on elections to Soviets, unspecified factory, 4 February 1931.

165. *Martenovka,* 1, 7, 10, 13 April 1931.

166. *Martenovka,* 15 November 1931, 1 May 1932.

167. Kuromiya, *Stalin's Industrial Revolution,* 15.

168. TsMAM, f. 176, op. 2, d. 783, l. 114. Engineering collective meeting, 21 September 1928.

169. Straus, *Factory and Community in Stalin's Russia,* 46.

170. *Trud,* 10 May 1929.

171. TsAODM, f. 3, op. 11, d. 763, l. 4. MK information on reconstruction of the Hammer and Sickle Factory, March-November 1929. Party committee resolution, 8 June 1929.

172. TsAODM, f. 3, op. 11, d. 763, ll. 12-14. GIPROMEZ letter, 23 July 1929.

173. TsAODM, f. 3, op. 11, d. 763, l. 27. MK information on reconstruction of the Hammer and Sickle Factory, July 1929.

174. TsAODM, f. 429, op. 1, d. 94, l. 62. Control commission meeting, 30 November 1930.

175. TsAODM, f. 429, op. 1, d. 109, l. 51. Party secretary report on counterrevolutionary activity of the chief engineer Mattis, 3 February 1930.

176. TsAODM, f. 429, op. 1, d. 129, l. 22. Party secretary report on work during First Five-Year Plan, 27 February 1933.

177. *Martenovka,* 4 March 1930.

178. TsAODM, f. 429, op. 1, d. 111, l. 7. Meeting of communist foremen and managers, 22 February 1930.

179. TsAODM, f. 429, op. 1, d. 94, l. 8. Party committee meeting, 16 August 1929.

180. TsAODM, f. 429, op. 1, d. 109, l. 59. Party committee resolution, 12 March 1930.

181. TsAODM, f. 429, op. 1, d. 111, l. 7. Meeting of communist foremen and managers, 19 February 1930.

182. TsMAM, f. 176, op. 2, d. 462, l. 68. Engineering collective meeting, n.d. May 1926.

183. TsMAM, f. 1289, op. 1, d. 326, ll. 11-16. Rabkrin report, 9 September 1931.

184. This profound change in public "discourse" has gone completely unnoticed by advocates of the linguistic (or postmodern) academic fad. For example, see Hoffman's *Peasant Metropolis* and Payne's *Stalin's Railroad.*

185. Elena Osokina, *Our Daily Bread: Socialist Distribution and the Art of Survival in Stalin's Russia, 1927-1941* (Armonk, New York, 1999), 53, 92-93.

186. *Martenovka,* 28 February 1929.

187. *Martenovka,* 1, 8, 11, 14, August , 1930.

188. TsAODM, f. 429, op. 1, d. 109, l. 160. Party committee meeting; 8 October 1930.

189. *Martenovka,* 1 October 1930.

190. *Rabochaia gazeta*, 16 February 1931.
191. TsAODM, f. 4, op. 1, d. 5, l. 147. MGK discussion, 31 August 1931.
192. *Rabochaia gazeta*, 30 August 1931.
193. TsAODM, f. 429, op. 1, d. 114, l. 8.; d. 113, l. 167. Party ZRK fraction meeting, 28 August 1931. Party bureau meeting, 31 August 1931.
194. TsAODM, f. 80, op. 1, d. 398, ll. 110, 113. OGPU district reports September 1931.
195. Lewis Siegelbaum and Andrei Sokolov, *Stalinism as a Way of Life* (New Haven, 2000), 39.
196. TsAODM, f. 429, op. 1, d. 113, l. 74. Party committee, 23 April 1931.
197. TsAODM, f. 80, op. 1, d. 398, l. 91. OGPU district summary, 1 September 1931.
198. RGASPI, f. 17, op. 3, d. 817, l. 3. Politburo meeting, 25 March 1931.
199. RGASPI, f. 17, op. 162, d. 10, l. 106. Politburo meeting, 5 July 1931.
200. TsAODM, f. 80, op. 1, d. 398, l. 75. OGPU district report, 27 August 1931.
201. RGASPI, f. 81, op. 3, d. 148, ll. 111, 105. Kaganovich report on Moscow food supply, January 1932.
202. TsAODM, f. 80, op. 1, d. 398, l. 171. OGPU district report late November 1931. RGASPI, f. 17, op. 20, d. 349, l. 46. District Party bureau committee meeting, 2 December 1931.
203. TsAODM, f. 80, op. 1, d. 398, l. 189. OGPU district report, 8 December 1931.
204. TsMAM, f. 176, op. 2, d. 834, ll. 31, 39. Construction of new shops meetings, 21 May, 20 July 1932.
205. TsAODM, f. 429, op. 1, d. 117, ll. 11-12. Party committee and cell secretaries meeting, 16 May 1932.
206. TsAODM, f. 429, op. 1, d. 117, l. 18. Party committee and cell secretaries meeting, 4 June 1932.
207. *Martenovka*, 6 August 1932.
208 TsAODM, f. 3, op. 49, d. 16, l. 3. MK information summary, 7 September 1932.
209. TsAODM, f. 3, op. 49, d. 23, 159. MK report to Khrushchev 20-25 December 1932.
210. *Martenovka*, 28 February 1929.
211. TsAODM, f. 429, op. 1, d. 92, ll. 65-66. Party plenum, 27 February 1929.
212. TsAODM, f. 429, op. 1, d. 92, ll. 92-93, Party plenum, 13 March 1929. Repair shop leaders defended their secretary against the accusations. TsAODM, f. 429, op. 1, d. 104, ll. 54-55. Repair shop party closed plenum, 27 March 1929.
213. *Martenovka*, 13 April 1929.
214. TsAODM, f. 80, op. 1, d. 332, l. 2. Note to speaker at a district party conference, early 1929.
215. Getty and Naumov, *The Road to Terror*, 588. The number of Secret Police arrests for "counterrevolutionary crimes" approximately doubled from 1928 to 1929 and the number of arrests for "anti-Soviet agitation" went from 0 to 51,396.
216. *Martenovka*, 3, 11 November 1930.
217. RGASPI, f. 81, op. 3, d. 148, l. 133. L. Kaganovich report, January 1932.
218. Aleksandra Chumakova's memoirs in *Samizdat: Voices of the Soviet Opposition*, George Saunders, ed. (New York, 1974), 191.
219. TsAODM, f. 3, op. 49, d. 15, l. 141. OGPU information summary, September 1932.
220. *Martenovka*, 24 July 1931, 21 January 1930.
221. TsAODM, f. 429, op. 1, d. 106, l. 67. Wire pulling shop party meeting, 4 September 1929.
222. TsAODM, f. 429, op. 1, d. 116, l. 139. Party bureau minutes, 8 April 1932.
223. TsMAM, f. 176, op. 2, d. 821, ll. 30, 31. Information on re-election to Soviets. Delegates' meeting, 15 January, general conference, 9 February 1929.
224. TsAODM, f. 429, op. 1, d. 100, l. 30. Architectural shop cell meeting, 14 February 1929.
225. GARF, f. 7952, op. 3, d. 198, l. 10; d. 202, l. 18. Factory statistics.
226. TsMAM, f. 176, op. 2, d. 835, l. 2. Construction of new shops meeting, 26 November 1932.
227. *Martenovka*, 25 September 1930.
228. *Martenovka*, 29 September, 8 October, 11 November 1930, 13, 19 January 1931.
229. TsAODM, f. 429, op. 1, d. 116, ll. 7-8. Party bureau meeting, 25 May 1932.

230. *Martenovka,* 20, 22, 23, 24 December 1931.
231. GARF 5469, op. 14, d. 193, ll. 230-231. Metalworkers' information summary, 7 May 1930.
232. *Martenovka,* 2 February, 16 August 1932.
233. TsAODM, f. 429, op. 1, d. 106, l. 23. Wire pulling shop cell meeting, 9 April 1929.
234. TsAODM, f. 429, op. 1, d. 106, l. 23. Wire pulling shop cell meeting, 9 April 1929.
235. TsAODM, f. 429, op. 1, d. 94, ll. 47-48. Control commission meeting, 5 November 1929.
236. Osokina, *Our Daily Bread,* 39, 62-63, 77, 91.
237. Straus, *Factory and Community in Stalin's Russia,* 65, 74, 77, 117-125.
238. *Martenovka,* 23 August 1930, 10 April 1931, 14 August 1931.
239. *Biulleten' Oppozitsii,* September 1932.
240. *Martenovka,* 27 September 1931.
241. TsAODM, f. 429, op. 1, d. 113, ll. 85-86. Party bureau combined with bureau of repair shop meeting 14 September 1931.
242. *Martenovka,* 19 November 1930.
243. *Martenovka,* 12 April 1931.
244. *Martenovka,* 21 December 1930.
245. TsAODM, f. 80, op. 1, d. 398, ll. 47-48. OGPU district report on political mood of workers, 16 May 1931.
246. TsAODM, f. 80, op. 1, d. 398, l. 73. OGPU district report, 26 August 1931.
247. TsAODM, f. 3, op. 49, d. 15, l. 111. MK report, 19 September 1932.
248. TsAODM, f. 429, op. 1, d. 116, l. 139. Party bureau minutes, 8 April 1932.
249. TsAODM, f. 80, op. 1, d. 398, l. 172. OGPU district report late November 1931.
250. TsAODM, f. 80, op. 1, d. 425, l. 27. Filatov report to Proletarskii district party, February 1932.
251. *Martenovka,* 14 July 1932.
252. *Martenovka,* 3 March 1932.
253. TsAODM, f. 80, op. 1, d. 398, l. 47-48. OGPU district report on political mood of workers 16 May 1931.
254. TsAODM, f. 80, op. 1, d. 398, l. 172; OGPU district report late November 1931. The report did not specify the factory.
255. *Martenovka,* 23 September 1932.
256. TsAODM, f. 3, op. 49, d. 16, l. 7. MK summary, 7 October 1932.
257. TsAODM, f. 4, op. 2, d. 3. Plenum MGK, 13 May 1932.
258. TsAODM, f. 3, op. 49, d. 37, l., 78. Closed party meeting 13 December 1933.

CONCLUSION

Revolution versus Counterrevolution

The Cold War shaped the framing of the history of the Russian Revolution in the latter half of the twentieth century. The protagonists put forward interpretations that actually shared much common ground. Both schools promoted the notion that Stalinism was a natural and inevitable outcome of 1917, both schools identified socialism with Stalinism, and both schools viewed the working class as a social force easily manipulated by the state. Both schools also utilized the privilege of non-archival access to make "speculative" arguments to explain the demise of working-class militancy. While historians of European and United States labor have painstakingly attempted to reconstruct and explain the many advances and retreats of workers' movements, Soviet labor history continues to lag far behind because of the ideological baggage of the Cold War. To be sure, fifteen years after the archives of the former Soviet Union opened their doors, not a single archival-driven study has been produced to support either of the Cold War interpretations. Yet many of the central tenets of the two state-sponsored interpretations are still invoked to explain the rise and rule of Stalinism—early Soviet repression and worker identification with Stalinism.

Workers in the Hammer and Sickle Factory were neither terrorized by the early Soviet state nor impressed with Stalinism's agenda and propaganda. Events in the largest metal factory in Moscow closely mirrored the contours of the Russian and Soviet working-class militancy, and provide insights into the dynamic of the movement. Class conflict and workers' changing perception of their own power are central to explaining why the most unruly proletariat of the century came to tolerate the ascendancy of a political and economic system that ultimately proved antagonistic to their interests. Certainly, *all* contemporary protagonists of the class conflict in the revolutionary era—socialists, the Okhrana, management associations, Tsarist government officials, the Provisional Government, the early Soviet government, dissident groups, and the Stalinist regime—recognized the potential power of the working class.

Notes for this section can be found on page 229.

Workers' experience in the factories was the decisive factor in shaping their perception of themselves, other employees, their employer, and their society. To be sure, events outside the workplace also influenced their view of the world, yet time after time in each of the rising waves of revolt, workers began to emphasize their common interests against their employer. When they went on the offensive, the numerous and overlapping divisions within the work-force tended to be weakened and workers often displayed a strong sense of class solidarity with workers in other factories. Conversely, when workers retreated from unified action, latent divisions within the workforce resur-faced, allowing management to regain the upper hand, force through con-cessions, isolate strikes, and victimize leaders.

The temporal delimiters to the volatile shifts in Moscow Metalworks workers' confidence are clear. Demoralized and passive after the 1905 Revo-lution, the labor movement was reborn in the wake of popular indignation in aftermath of the Lena Goldfields massacre as workers repeatedly struck for both economic and political reasons. Revolutionaries played a "catalytic role" in the movement that grew in intensity during two waves of unrest separated by a significant retreat at the beginning of the war. Divisions between young and old workers, male and female workers, and between shops were strength-ened as management easily defeated the first wartime strike. Continued war losses, declining real wages, and the shattered hopes for political reforms after the proroguing of the Duma, all weakened the nationalist and conserv-ative sentiments that briefly dominated in the factories. Workers started to overcome the sectional interests within the workforce by championing the grievances of young and female workers. Their awareness of the growing chasm between the interests of labor and capital drove the movement for-ward. Repeated rounds of Okhrana arrests—much more widespread and sys-tematic than the few arrests of strikers during NEP—proved futile in the face of a resurgent and well-organized workers' movement. Indeed, as the work-ers' movement quickly learned the lessons of class conflict, repression only fostered better organization to avoid victimization.

The gradual evolution of workers' confidence and solidarity accelerated after the February Revolution. By direct action, workers immediately insti-tuted the eight-hour day, fired managers, created a factory committee to represent themselves, and raised diverse demands over wages, women's issues, the rights of the factory committee, and control of production. In the Marxist sense of a working class conscious of its collective strength, 1917 marked the zenith of proletarian power in the twentieth century. As political questions came to the fore in the late summer, the differences between the socialist programs were clarified in practice. By August, Russia had moved to the edge of civil war, as the ruling classes gave concrete expression for their utter contempt for the revolutionary aspirations of the lower classes by sup-porting Kornilov's attempted military coup. Workers also recognized that the revolution could only end by the forceful rule by one class over the other. The Bolsheviks won the political arguments for the 12 August general strike against the Provisional Government, for arming workers to defend the revo-lution, and for all political power to be transferred to the soviets.

The 1917 Revolution and the Civil War determined who would rule Russian society. Within the factory, however, the first year of the revolution was marked by proletarian collective action, whereas a desperate and apolitical individualism pervaded factory life during the Civil War. Workers' behavior during this period shows that rather than being terrorized, they were almost completely unfazed by a state that had virtually ceased to exist. The social, political, and economic breakdown, and the isolation of the revolution not only created a rift between workers and state, but also shaped the social conditions that allowed Stalinism to evolve.

Evidence from the Hammer and Sickle Factory shows that despite the hardships of factory life in the aftermath of seven years of war, the fissure between the battered Soviet state and the working class was actually narrowed during early NEP. Workers repeatedly turned to their representatives on the factory committee and other union institutions to raise their grievances. They also participated in mass meetings, they repeatedly went on strike as shop-specific stoppages spilled over into other departments, and they realistically expected support from the party and union. By 1924, the state and class negotiated a temporary truce in which union contracts and arbitration bodies substituted for direct action to meet employee concerns. Hundreds of workers joined the party because they identified with its socialist goals. Similarly, the majority of female production employees participated in women's activities because they expected and received a favorable response to their concerns.

This temporary truce between the state and working class derailed the resurgent working-class militancy of early NEP. The early Soviet participatory institutions differed markedly from those of both the Tsarist and Stalinist eras. It was workers' trust and involvement in workplace institutions that gave the factory regime an essential degree of legitimacy.

The Stalinist project of national economic development, combined with the deep social crisis of late NEP, eroded this accord. Workers continued to raise grievances and complaints, but the threat of unemployment and a lack of confidence in their own collective power placed them on the defensive. As shop-level meeting minutes show, overlapping sectional differences within the workforce were strengthened by the late NEP crisis. Divisions between male and female workers, between newly arriving former peasants and urban workers, between older and younger workers, and between shops were all reinforced. In many ways, the late NEP working class retreat displayed attributes that were the *norm* in Europe and the United States when labor was on the defensive: employers used the cudgel of unemployment to wrest concessions from the unions; union leaders backtracked and tried to secure whatever small victories possible; disgruntled workers voiced increasing displeasure, started to blame other workers as solidarity weakened, and yet remained loyal to their union that offered them a degree of protection. The difference, of course, was that the Soviet state was both the employer and leader of the unions and had come to power based on a victorious workers' revolution. The contradictory role of unions could not possibly have lasted when the state offensive against the working class escalated.

Repression was not a factor in the demise of workers' militancy from 1925 to 1927. Authorities did not arrest a single striking worker at the Hammer and Sickle Factory, nor did they even expel an Oppositionist from the party for leading one stoppage. The Cold War mythology of state agents arresting large numbers of striking workers and sending them to the Gulags does not correspond to what is now known about Soviet industrial relations. Significantly, several late NEP strikes show that the letter of collective agreements, rather than repression, was decisive in resolving disputes.

Yet the strikes were also limited to a small number of workers in individual shops and illustrate how far solidarity and workers' confidence had slipped in just several years. In early NEP, striking workers elected representatives to avoid victimization, controlled delegate meetings, attended boisterous mass meetings, and repeatedly won pay increases. By 1928, state loyalists firmly controlled all meetings, avoided open discussion of collective agreements, fired strike leaders, and repeatedly cut wages. Archival sources also prove widespread working class discontent against a regime that had lost much of authority to rule and was beset with profound fissures in its own ranks. That Stalinism managed to survive 1928 has obscured the narrow gap between seething working-class anger and open revolt.

By the end of NEP, the factory committee and other union bodies had lost much of their authority. The party was even more discredited. Instead of workers entering the party en masse, the overwhelming majority of workers refused to join because they recognized the demise of party democracy, and the profound contradiction between state propaganda and policy. The party crackdown against dissent was connected to the intensification of the labor process and the reduction of workers' living standards, but during NEP did not extend to nonparty workers. Party leaders reverted to padding membership figures by lowering the standards for the few who wanted to join and by refusing members' requests to leave. Significantly, however, workers continued to place hopes of reform within existing factory institutions. Given that these institutions had previously responded sympathetically to their concerns, such expectations for reform were quite rational.

The Stalinist production drive during the First Five-Year Plan halved wages and destroyed the extremely weak remnants of workers' control. The factory committee that had been created during the revolution to defend workers was transformed into an institution to lengthen work hours, increase productivity, and drive down wages. The less frequent labor actions entailed a fundamental shift away from strike action as individual rather than collective solutions dominated workers' behavior. Unlike the temporary lull in years of reaction from 1908 to 1911, however, the new downturn in worker activism would be more permanent: the proletarian movement that lasted for almost a third of the century in four distinct waves of militancy had reached the end of the revolutionary epoch. Unable to gain voluntary support for its program through inverted class rhetoric, management coercion rested on social pressure by a milieu of hardened state loyalists to bully other workers and utilized its control over food as its most effective weapon to discipline the workforce. Rather than the logical culmination of 1917, the victory of Stalinism represented a veritable counterrevolution in which the drive for accumulation triumphed over human need.

Severing the extremely tenuous connection with the revolution, however, simultaneously undermined the Stalinist project itself. The state sought—but did not receive—a popular mandate for its policies. The structural problems of rapid industrialization could not be solved because peasant-workers did not adapt easily to industrial life and because the very nature of the project was antithetical to workers' interests. Although a small minority of upwardly mobile workers identified with Stalinism, the overwhelming majority of workers were denied the benefits of career advancement, "best shock brigades," and other productivist enticements. Workers who had paid for the industrialization drive resented the state for repeatedly cutting their wages, forcing them into working longer hours, and depriving them of their religious holidays. By 1931, workers in the capital's Proletarskii district talked about how the regime did not know how to "finish off the workers." Far from being an all-powerful machine pulverizing Soviet society, even party loyalists expressed disillusionment and believed profound changes were imminent. However, a sense that some external force from above would lead this change illustrates that workers' confidence in their collective power was a distant memory.

We now know that the parameters of proletarian resistance to Stalinism ranged from open revolt in Ivanovo,[1] to simmering, but fractured, discontent in the Hammer and Sickle Factory. While metalworkers' grievances and hatred towards their new bosses escalated, their relatively privileged position in the highest-priority industry and the enormous risks involved in strike action militated against the kind of unity that would have been necessary to any credible challenge to the regime.

One of the most prominent historians of the Russian Revolution, Orlando Figes, views the entire revolutionary era as a great tragedy and laments, "The ghosts of the Russian Revolution have not been put to rest."[2] The voices of these "ghosts" in the factories can finally be heard. Workers participated in the socialist experiment and developed their own conception of an egalitarian, classless society that was completely at odds with both private capitalism and ascending Stalinism. Yet the dominant scholarly perspective of connecting the dots from 1917 to brutal Stalinist repression was not an invention of the Cold War, nor of the academy alone. Victor Serge, perhaps the Russian Revolution's most uncompromising intellectual, challenged this assertion over sixty years ago:

> It is often said that "the germ of all Stalinism was in Bolshevism at its inception." Well, I have no objection. Only, Bolshevism also contained many other germs—a mass of other germs—and those who lived through the enthusiasm of the first years of the first victorious revolution ought not to forget it. To judge the living man by the death germs which the autopsy reveals in a corpse—and which he may have carried in him since his birth—is this very sensible?[3]

The Russian working class was neither victim nor pawn, easily manipulated from above, but a social force that drove Tsarism and capitalism from power and had the potential to do so to Stalinism. The defeat of the working class was not predetermined, but instead was decided in the working-class movements of Europe and the mills and factories of the Soviet Union itself. Karl Marx and Frederick Engels were correct—even more so in regard to periods of mass social upheaval. The history of the Russian Revolution is the history of class struggle.

Notes

1. Jeffrey Rossman, "Worker Resistance Under Stalin: Class and Gender in the Ivanovo Industrial Region, 1928-1932" (Ph.D. Dissertation, University of California at Berkeley, 1997).
2. Orlando Figes, *A People's Tragedy*, 824.
3. Victor Serge, *Memoirs of a Revolutionary* (London, 1967), xvi-xvii.

INDEX